THE WORLD OF EMOTIONS

Clinical Studies of Affects
and Their Expression

THE WORLD OF EMOTIONS

Clinical Studies of Affects
and Their Expression

With Commentaries by

Charles W. Socarides, M.D., Editor

International Universities Press, Inc.

New York

Library of Congress Cataloging in Publication Data
Main entry under title:
The World of Emotions

    Bibliography: p.
    Includes index.
    1. Emotions—Addresses, essays, lectures.
2. Affect (Psychology)—Addresses, essays, lectures.
3. Psychoanalysis—Addresses, essays, lectures.
I. Socarides, Charles W. [DNLM: 1. Emotions—
Collected works. 2. Psychoanalysis—Collected works.
3. Affective disturbances—Collected works.
BF531 C357]
BF531.C37   152.4   77-12735
ISBN 0-8236-6867-3

The editor expresses his gratitude to the following persons and publishers for their kind permission to use the works contained in this book:

Carl P. Adatto, James Alexander, Jacob A. Arlow, Enid Balint, Marianne Bergler and the Edmund and Marianne Bergler Psychiatric Foundation, Martin S. Bergmann, Wilfred R. Bion, Helene Deutsch, Sandor S. Feldman, Ralph R. Greenson, Ernest A. Haggard, Kenneth S. Isaacs, Jack Kleiner, Marianne Kris, Sidney Levin, Ping-nie Pao, Peter T. Rado, Robert L. Sadoff, Melitta Schmideberg, Joseph W. Slap, Otto E. Sperling, Roy M. Whitman, Louis Zetzel, *Diseases of the Nervous System*, *International Journal of Psycho-Analysis*, International Universities Press, *Journal of the American Psychoanalytic Association*, *Psychiatric Quarterly*, *Psychoanalytic Quarterly*. "On Disillusionment: The Desire to Remain Disappointed," by Charles W. Socarides is reprinted from the *British Journal of Medical Psychology* by permission of Cambridge University Press; "On the Affect of Horror," by James Alexander, and "On Nostalgia," by Jack Kleiner, are reprinted by permission of the *Journal of the Philadelphia Association for Psychoanalysis*.

Manufactured in the United States of America

For Alexandra Anne

Contents

ACKNOWLEDGMENTS

I owe a special debt of gratitude to Irene Azarian for her belief in the importance of this volume and her support and encouragement throughout its preparation; to Natalie Altman for her unrivaled editorial skills and remarkable ability to know an author's intentions at times better than the author himself; and to Gladys Levinson for her valuable suggestions in the preliminary phases of this project.

Above all, my thanks, gratitude, and love go to my wife, Barbara Bonner Socarides, who shared with me over a four-year period the multiple affects, the tribulations, as well as the joys and delights associated with the compilation, writing, and editing of this book.

FOREWORD

In a very real sense, affects are at the core of the psycho-analytic situation. The analyst is continuously occupied with determining the depth and scope of the patient's emotions, to appraise them accurately, and relate them to problems and conflicts which invoke them or from which they have become detached. It is his task to point out repeatedly the patient's affective relationship to him, no matter how displaced or repressed. To have experienced a sufficiently broad range of affects himself is essential for the analyst if he is to exercise the all-important empathy with his patients so essential to accomplishing genuine structural changes.

Furthermore, and especially since the advent of ego psychology, it is essential to trace the development of affects from as far back in the life of the patient as possible. In order to develop effective insight, the patient must repeatedly experience the fusion of affect with the cognitive awareness that arises from interpretations. In the process of working through, no true resolution of conflicts is possible without such fusions. To accomplish this is a formidable task, one with which the analyst must be affectively comfortable, or else his own emotional limitations may seriously blemish the ultimate outcome of treatment. Those who undergo training in this most demanding of disciplines must be made aware of their own affective range and must transcend most of the internal barriers to their own emotional experiences. In the training of psychotherapists, the most effective teachers are those capable of bringing to their students an understanding of the nature of affective experience.

For this task, Dr. Socarides is superbly fitted. To his highly sensitive and wise choice of psychoanalytic articles on affects, he has added singularly illuminating comments which make for exciting reading. It would be difficult to fault his selection or to add to his elucidations. While primarily intended for teaching, this book will be of interest to even seasoned analysts. The rereading of such landmark papers, of clinical descriptions of numerous affects, stimulates renewed thinking on a subject of basic importance.

Nathaniel Ross, M.D.

EDITOR'S INTRODUCTION

The relation of man to himself, to others, to things, and to the world around him can be identified, defined, and understood in terms of his affective life. It is through our awareness of our predominant emotion at any given time that we interpret our whole state of being. Whether we feel happy or sad, up or down, hopeful or despairing, responsive or withdrawn, determines in great part what we do and how we do it: eagerly, reluctantly, confidently, uncertainly, graciously, rudely, compassionately, contemptuously. Our emotions are what mobilize us for action and sustain that action regardless of its direction or purpose.

Emotions, though, are mysterious in their ways, hard to define, even harder to understand. Byron recognized their paradoxical nature. Says Don Juan, "And if I laugh at any mortal thing,/'Tis that I may not weep."

Emotions can conceal underlying motives; they can reveal the truth; they can serve as a defense; they can promote aggression. The absence of an appropriate emotion can surprise us; why don't we grieve when we undergo a loss we would have expected to find excruciatingly painful? Why do we fail to be amused by a joke others find hilarious? Why does one person experience envy and another feel smug under similar circumstances? Why do people cry at a happy ending? Where are the borders between faith, trust, and gullibility?

1

What initially sparked my growing interest in compiling this anthology was writing my own paper "On Vengeance: The Desire to 'Get Even'" (1966). A search of the psychoanalytic literature revealed that, except for a paper by Karen Horney (1948) on vindictiveness—related to but not identical with vengeance—there was no detailed study of this important subject. To my increasing delight, however, I began to perceive that over an 80-year period the psychoanalytic literature had become dotted with many brilliant and illuminating papers on the various affects of man. Articles on depression, bitterness, arrogance, boredom, enthusiasm, envy, gratitude, jealousy, and querulousness were of great relevance to the formulation of the psychodynamics of vengeance, helping me to clarify my concepts and casting light on various facets of the problem, and led to my paper "On Disillusionment: The Desire to Remain Disappointed" (1971).

There have been many valuable studies of the emotions throughout the history of psychoanalysis, starting with Freud's earliest writings. There is, however, no comprehensive collection, no "catalogue" of these many important psychoanalytic studies of the affects. This volume brings together for the first time these many contributions in a format designed for study and enjoyment. The extensive search and research through the literature required for this compilation has provided me with the opportunity of reading and often discovering for the first time articles spanning the 80 years of psychoanalytic writings. It has given me the pleasure of rediscovering the richness of the contributions made by psychoanalytic colleagues past and present, some of them frequently referred to, but others, despite their value, often neglected in the literature today. A major task was the exclusion for reasons of space of many valuable articles. The magnificent papers of Freud (1917,

1919, 1926, 1927a) and Abraham (1912, 1924a) have been omitted because of the reader's presumed familiarity with them and because of their wide availability elsewhere.

Over the years of teaching and clinical practice, I have been struck by the extent to which such words as "arrogance," "envy," "boredom," "smugness," "gloating," and "enthusiasm" are regarded as self-explanatory or in a sense taken for granted. When one of my students describes a patient's attitude or behavior as sarcastic, bitter, or arrogant, he often uses such terms as if they truly depict the patient's motivational state. But these words are descriptive, and, although quite correct, overlook the rich unconscious psychodynamic material underlying every affective state.

Our aim in defining an affect precisely is to divide it into its component parts and the combination of emotions that go into its formation. It should be carefully differentiated from other affects that may appear similar to it. For example, a disillusioned patient differs from a disappointed one or a depressed one; and the difference, dynamically, is crucial. Cynicism should be separated from bitterness or despair. Refinement in definition leads one to search for the genetic development of the specific affect and provides vital information about the level of functioning of the patient in general.

My aim is to present those papers which focus largely on the clinical manifestations of specific affects. It is beyond the scope of this book to present a systematized overview of the many theoretical contributions to our understanding of affects or to propose pathways to a new and comprehensive theory of affects. Rather, it is my hope that these articles will stimulate us in further penetrating the mysteries of emotions so that in time they can be understood in terms that rival our progressive understanding of the psychodynamic forces leading to conflict.

From the beginning, difficulties in defining "affect," "emotion," and "feeling" have inhibited our efforts (Brierley, 1937; Rapaport, 1942, 1953; Panel, 1968; Jacobson, 1971; Pulver, 1971; Panel, 1974). In my commentaries to the articles that follow, I use the word affect in its broadest sense, synonymous with emotion and feeling, to designate the whole complex set of psychological and physiological manifestations. Such a definition includes the affective motor phenomena and behavior patterns as well as the phenomena for which the term "affect equivalents" has been customarily employed (Jacobson, 1971).

In describing an emotional reaction, one is struck by the observation that an affective phenomenon can be approached in a wide variety of ways. For example, an affect can be classified in crude qualitative terms under the headings of subjective pleasure or pain; descriptively, under the predominant ideational system associated with it in consciousness; by reference to the instinct or component instinct from which it is derived; by considering whether it is fixed or labile, whether it is primary or secondary, whether it reflects a tension or discharge phenomenon; and whether it is simple or compound (mixed and/or fused) (Glover, 1939, p. 300).

Pioneer concepts of classification were suggested by Brierley (1937), Landauer (1938), and Glover (1939). More recent contributions have been made by Rapaport (1953), Engel (1962), Panel (1968), and Jacobson (1971). Jacobson's classification represents our furthest advance in making affect theory consistent with other features of psychoanalytic theory.

Freud (1915a) commented that were it not for the fact that instincts attach themselves to ideas and manifest themselves as affective states, we would know nothing about them. However, simple affective abreactions (instinctual re-education, in a sense) are no longer the principal aims of psychoanalytic therapy. Recall and insight without affective experience do not usually yield therapeutic advance. Affects serve as guides in treatment, and without them insight is ineffective.

Patients have difficulty in three areas relating to affects: in feeling them, in recognizing them, and in expressing them (Panel, 1974). In certain diagnostic categories, typical problems in affectivity may often be found. Schizoid patients, for example, usually complain of an inability to feel their emotions, while in the obsessional there is a split between the idea and the feeling. In the latter, the energy invested in ideas appears quite small, while the thinking process itself is intensely libidinized (Panel, 1968). Hysterics engage in self-dramatization rather than recognizing what they are expressing. In other patients, the complaint of being unable to recognize their principal feelings may derive from their acute awareness of an "emotional tangle," creating in them a sense of confusion, "a tendency to rank affects in a very personal hierarchy, some affects being preferred to others and being used in a stereotyped way" (Panel, 1974). Patients with narcissistic character disorders demonstrate a failure to communicate affect, which represents a defense against an object tie, beneath which lie important omnipotent fantasies of self-sufficiency and denial of the need for an object. Through no longer desiring the object, the anxiety that would result from instinctual wishes can thereby be avoided.

Essential to the goal of psychoanalytic therapy is the analysis of the content, origin, and functional role of any affect. Of equal importance is the understanding of disturbances in affects and affect defenses. Indeed, every known mental mechanism may be employed against affects. The most primitive defense is complete blocking of an affect. Affects may be delayed, displaced, or postponed. The quality of an affect itself may be changed. The denial of the meaning of an affect may result in reaction formations against the affect, leading to counterphobic attitudes; derivatives of averted affects may make their appearance "at the wrong time, can be directed toward the wrong object, or can show the wrong quality" (Fenichel, 1941). Affects may be projected. There is a continuum from the compulsives, who isolate the affect from content, to those who feel no affect whatever.

The analysis of affect defenses makes the patient accessible to the experience of affect. Frequently the degree or quality (intensity) of an affect may be disturbed in the sense that it is heightened (Winterstein and Bergler, 1935).* The obverse condition may be present when an affect ordinarily expected in response to a particular situation is completely absent (Deutsch, 1937).* Deutsch's (1942)* "as-if personalities" are devoid of particular affects and attempt to create them. Other individuals who demonstrate incapacities to bear affects such as anxiety have been described by Zetzel (1949),* who, in what may be termed a companion paper (1965), demonstrated the increased capacity of certain patients to bear particular affects such as depression. Specific problems are seen in those who show varying degrees in the capacity to experience affects such as love (Bergmann, 1971).* Certain individuals may experience paradoxical affects, such as aggression from anxiety or sexual excitement from fear. In a classic paper, Sperling (1948)* described the spacing and crowding of emotions in order for patients to deal more adequately with them.

The papers that follow are illustrative of the multiple clinical aspects of affective life and the myriad forms of their expression. The challenge posed in fathoming their secrets proves equal in measure to the scientific reward, for: "In the

---

* This paper is reprinted in this volume.

living subject, and particularly in man, affects, affects first and last, serve to explicate behavior and psychological happenings" (Spitz, 1965, p. 85).

THE PROBLEM OF MELANCHOLIA

Sandor Rado

(1927)

Our increasing understanding of the affect of depression can be represented in historical sequence by the work of five major psychoanalytic writers: Abraham, Freud, Rado, Lewin, and Jacobson.

Abraham was the first to focus psychoanalytic attention on depression and melancholia. As early as 1911 he discovered that melancholia represents a reaction to the loss of love. Six years later Freud published his monumental "Mourning and Melancholia" (1917). The year after Freud's "The Ego and the Id" (1923), which implemented Abraham's suggestions, Abraham published a second and more comprehensive work on melancholia, "A Short Study of the Development of the Libido Viewed in the Light of Mental Disorders" (1924a). This intense period of concentrated study of depression reached a temporary culmination in Rado's "The Problem of Melancholia" (1927b).

This area of study was further illuminated by the highly original and creative clinical research of Bertram Lewin in The Psychoanalysis of Elation *(1950). Utilizing concepts of the oral triad, the Isakower phenomenon, and the dream screen, Lewin advanced our understanding of both depression and elation. Edith Jacobson (1964, 1971) has contributed to attempts at a unified and comprehensive theory of depres-*

Editor's note: It is apparent in this article that Rado uses the term melancholia as a synonym for severe depressive reactions, either psychotic or of a psychosislike nature.

9

sion, in terms of ego psychology and with an emphasis on preoedipal development.

In his lectures to psychoanalytic students, Rado was fond of stating that in depression we meet our most outstanding and dramatic therapeutic successes or come face to face with our most dismal failures. Building from Freud's and Abraham's previous work, Rado made penetrating and incisive contributions to the origin and meaning of the depressive symptom. In this article he portrays the characteristics of the ego of persons predisposed to depressive states, differentiates neurotic from psychotic depression, and places heavy emphasis on the hitherto neglected yet vital aspect of depression, namely, the unconscious adaptational function of the expiatory process in all depressions. He introduces for the first time a psychoanalytic term—alimentary orgasm, to signify the experience of elation, the triumph over depression, which can be likened to the experience of satiation at the mother's breast.

Although the dynamics described in Rado's paper apply to psychotic depressions, the insights they provide into those depressions commonly referred to as neurotic are of inestimable value, for similar dynamic processes are involved.

The insight which psychoanalysis has gained into the clinical picture of melancholia is the result of the investigations of Freud and Abraham. Abraham was the first to turn his attention to this subject. As early as 1911 he asserted that melancholia represents a reaction (comparable to that of grief) to the loss of love (the object) (Abraham, 1912). Some years later Freud (1917), having in the interval begun his researches into the nature of narcissism, took the decisive step which led to the analytical elucidation of the subject of melancholia. He recognized that in melancholia the object which has been renounced is set up again within the ego and that thus in his self-reproaches the patient is continuing his aggressive tendencies against that object. The first conditioning factor in this process he showed to be the regression from an object relation to a narcissistic substitute for it, and next, the predominance of ambivalence, which replaces love by hate and oral incorporation. In a later work, Freud (1923) supplemented this hypothesis by the observation that the cruelty of the superego in melancholia results from the defusion of instincts which accompanies the act of identification. In 1923 Abraham published a second and comprehensive work on melancholia. By a number of excellent individual observations he was able to confirm Freud's conclusions in all points and he added several important clinical discoveries. He emphasized the melancholiac's incapacity for love—an incapacity springing from his ambivalence—, indicated the large part played in the mental productions of such patients by cannibalistic and oral instinctual impulses, and revealed in the history of their childhood a "primal depression" from which they had suffered at the height of their Oedipus development as a reaction to the double disappointment of their love for mother and father.

We now understand the mechanism of melancholia in so far as Freud has dissected it into its separate parts and Abraham has traced the forces at work in it to elementary impulses of the component instincts. But the plan according to which these separate mental acts are combined to form the whole structure of melancholia, its origin, and its specific meaning are still wholly obscure.

The most striking feature in the picture displayed by the symptoms of depressive conditions is the fall in self-esteem and self-satisfaction. The depressive neurotic for the most part attempts to conceal this disturbance; in melancholia it finds clamorous expression in the patients' delusional self-accusations and self-aspersions, which we call "the delusion of moral inferiority." On the other hand, there are in the behavior of melancholiacs many phenomena which are in complete contradiction to the patient's general self-abasement. Freud (1917) described this remarkable inconsistency in such patients. He adds the explanation that these latter reactions are still being roused by the mental attitude of rebellion, which has only later been converted into the contrition of the melancholiac. As observation shows, the acute phase of melancholia (or depressive conditions) is regularly preceded by such a period of arrogant and embittered rebellion. But this phase generally passes quickly, and its symptoms are then merged into the subsequent melancholic phase. In the transitory symptoms which occur during analytic treatment we have an impressive picture of this process. Let us now endeavor to throw some light on this rebellious phase from the patient's previous history and a consideration of the type of persons who are subject to it.

We will begin by describing the characteristics which may be recognized in the ego of persons predisposed to depressive states. We find in them, above all, an intensely strong craving for narcissistic gratification and a very considerable narcissistic intolerance. We observe that even to trivial offenses and disappointments they immediately react with a fall in their self-esteem. Their ego then experiences an urgent craving to relieve in some way or other the resulting narcissistic tension. Their ego may be completely absorbed by this and be paralyzed for all further activities. A stronger individual, on the other hand, will scarcely react at all to such frustrations, will endure without harm trivial variations in the degree of his self-esteem, and will accommodate himself to the inevitable delay in its restoration. Those predisposed to depression are, moreover, wholly reliant and dependent on other people for maintaining their self-esteem;

they have not attained to the level of independence where self-esteem has its foundation in the subject's own achievements and critical judgment. They have a sense of security and comfort only when they feel themselves loved, esteemed, supported, and encouraged. Even when they display an approximately normal activity in the gratification of their instincts and succed in realizing their aims and ideals, their self-esteem largely depends on whether they do or do not meet with approbation and recognition. They are like those children who, when their early narcissism is shattered, recover their self-respect only in complete dependence on their love objects.

Thus the favorite method employed by persons of this type of increasing their self-respect is that of attracting to themselves narcissistic gratification from *without*. Their libidinal disposition is easy to comprehend; the instinctual energies which they direct toward objects retain strong narcissistic elements, and therefore passive narcissistic aims prevail in their object relations. Freud (1917) postulated that the melancholiac's object choice conforms to the narcissistic type; this characteristic may be regarded as a special instance of my general statement.

Besides dependence on the love object we find in persons prone to depressive states a number of secondary characteristics which must be present in order to make up this typical disposition. Such persons are never weary of courting the favor of the objects of their libido and seeking for evidences of love from them; they sometimes expend an astonishing skill and subtlety in this pursuit. This applies not only to the objects of their purely sexual feelings; they behave in exactly the same way in relations in which their sexual instinct is inhibited in its aim and sublimated. They are wont to have a considerable number of such relations, for they are most happy when living in an atmosphere permeated with libido. But as soon as they are sure of the affection or devotion of another person and have entered into a fairly secure relation with him or her, their behavior undergoes a complete change. They accept the devoted love of the beloved person with a sublime nonchalance, as a matter of course, and become more and more domineering and autocratic, displaying an increasingly unbridled egoism, until their attitude becomes one of full-blown tyranny. They cling to their objects like leeches and feed upon them, as though it were their intention to devour them altogether. But all this takes place without their self-critical faculty being aware of it; as a rule they are just as unaware of the wooing character of their attitude as of its subsequent reversal or of the tenacity with which their sadism fastens on their love objects. Taking this attitude into consideration we can hardly wonder that they react with embittered vehemence to aggression on the part of others or to the threat of withdrawal of love, and that they feel the final loss of the object of their tormenting love to be the greatest injustice in the world.

Such, approximately, is the process leading to the indignant rebellion which precedes the turning of the subject's aggressive tendencies against himself in melancholia. Let us for the moment leave out of consideration the introjection of the object, to which process Freud has traced the reversal of mood in this disease, and let us try to see how melancholia can be accounted for on the same psychological premises as have explained the patient's passing into the phase of rebellion. It will then be obvious that his contrition can only be a reaction to the failure of his rebellion—a fresh weapon (the last one) to which his ego has recourse in order to carry out its purpose. That which it could not accomplish by rebellion it now tries to achieve by remorseful self-punishment and expiation. The ego does penance, begs for forgiveness, and endeavors in this way to win back the love object. I once (Rado, 1927a) described melancholia as a great despairing cry for love, and I believe that our present context justifies us in so conceiving of it.

But, you will object, this cannot be so, for the melancholiac has surely withdrawn his interest from the object; it exists for him no longer. How can he be striving to be reconciled to this object and to recapture its affection? You are right; but the melancholiac has transferred the scene of his struggle for the love of his object to a different stage. He has withdrawn in narcissistic fashion to the inner world of his own mind and now, instead of procuring the pardon and love of his object, he tries to secure those of his superego. We know that his relation to the object was marked by the predominance of the narcissistic desire to be loved, and it is quite easy for this aspiration to be carried over to his relation with his own superego. It is as if the ego of the melancholiac were to say to his superego: "I will take all the guilt upon myself and submit myself to any punishment; I will even, by ceasing to care for my bodily welfare, offer myself as an expiatory sacrifice, if you will only interest yourself in me and be kind to me." Thus it seems that in melancholia there is an attempt to decide the conflict with the object on a field other than the real one: there is a narcissistic flight from the object relation to that with the superego and, by this regressive step, the ego is removed from reality.

From this behavior of the melancholiac we may venture to divine the processes which once took place within him at the time when the formation of his superego was in progress. He was a child of a narcissistic disposition, whose self-esteem depended entirely on his parents' love. What an improvement in his mental situation when he began actively to reproduce their requirements in his own mind! He was then able to say to them: "There is no need for you to correct me any more, for I tell myself what you expect of me and, what is more, I will do it." But there were also times when he was naughty and his parents were very angry. Then he understood that he had only to pay the penalty and to ask for forgiveness, in order to be reconciled to them. The next time he offended, it occurred to him that he might do penance of his own accord and punish himself in order quickly to win his parents' forgiveness. Incidents of this sort are related to us in our patients' analyses, and children are known actually to carry out this idea. We can easily imagine that, later, this process takes place in the child without his knowing it. He begins *unconsciously* to reproduce within his mind the punishments anticipated from his parents and, in doing so, he unconsciously *hopes to win love.* Some unmerited narcissistic injury, e.g., an estrangement from his parents through no fault of his own, is probably the original motive for such an unconscious attempt at reparation. In some such way we may reconstruct the process by which the person who subsequently succumbs to melancholia (and certainly he is not alone in this respect) produces the mechanism of self-punishment.

But as soon as the active reproduction of parental punishment ceases to have reference in the conscious mind to the parents themselves and is carried out unconsciously, the intention is no longer that the subject should be reconciled to them but to the superego, which is their internal mental representative. Instead of the early process of putting matters right in actual fact with the parents, we have the purely psychical process by which he puts them right with his superego, as happens later in melancholia. But in relation to external reality this inner process remains entirely ineffective. With the unconscious reproduction of parental punishments the oral-narcissistic process of introjection (the formation of the superego) has overstepped the limits of its social usefulness: self-punishment is a part of the infantile relation to the object, a survival which controverts reality and takes an inward direction. In its dread of losing love, the infantile ego has clearly gone too far; its narcissistic craving remains unsatisfied, even when it submits itself to the destructive effects of self-punishment. In so far, then, as the ego in melancholia gives itself up to this mechanism, it has broken off its relations with reality and jeopardized its existence in vain.

We have seen how self-punishment takes place in the hope of absolution and has its origin in the longing for love. Now I am sure you will share my critical suspicion that the close connection between *guilt, atonement, and forgiveness*, so deeply rooted in our mental life, cannot possibly owe its enormous importance simply to the experiences of the growing child in the course of his training. It is certainly a momentous step when the child begins to grasp the idea of guilt and to experience the peculiar quality of the sense of guilt. But it seems as though he were already prepared for this experience, so as to understand straightaway the next conception: that of punishment and expiation and, above all, that of final forgiveness. Our study of melancholia enables us actually to see into the history of this mental structure—a history reaching back to the primal dawn of the mind—and to lay bare the ultimate foundations of experience upon which it is built. Here I may refer to a conclusion which I have already suggested elsewhere (Rado, 1927a). Briefly, it is this: that, when the child passes from the period of suckling, he carries with him, indelibly stamped on his mind, a sequence of experiences which *later* he works over so as to form the connection: guilt-atonement-forgiveness. You can observe in the nursery how the infant, if its craving for nourishment awakens in the absence of the mother, flies into an impotent rage, kicks and screams, and then, exhausted by this reaction to its helplessness, falls wholly a prey to the torments of hunger. But you know also that this cruel experience is finally followed with *unfailing certainty* by the reappearance of the mother, and that in drinking at her breast the child experiences that oral-narcissistic bliss which Freud (1916-1917) is certainly right in describing as the prototype, never again attained to, of all subsequent gratification. The whole process constitutes a single sequence of experiences, countless times repeated, of whose responsibility in determining future development we surely need no further proofs. From the paroxysm of rage in the hungry infant proceed all the later forms of *aggressive reaction* to frustration (e.g., devouring, biting, striking, destroying, etc.) and it is on these that the ego, in the period of latency, concentrates its whole sense of guilt. The hypercathexis of the impulses of aggression with manifest feelings of guilt is the consequence of a normal advance in development, which the material produced in our analyses enables us to follow without effort, while the knowledge arrived at by Freud makes it easily intelligible. At the height of the phallic phase the infantile ego (intimidated by the dread of castration— loss of love) has to renounce its dangerous Oedipus wishes and to secure itself against their recurrence. To do this it forms out of the primary function of self-observation a powerful institution (the superego) and develops the capacity for becoming aware of the criticisms of this institution in the form of a dread of conscience (the sense of guilt). The newly acquired reaction of conscience deals a death blow to the Oedipus complex, but the impulses embodied in that complex undergo different fates. The genital impulse succumbs to repression; its motor elements are inhibited and the group of ideas (incest fantasies, masturbation) which were cathected by it vanish from consciousness and leave no trace behind them. The aggressive impulse, on the other hand, cannot be warded off in so effectual a manner. Its driving force is, it is true, paralyzed by the setting up of a powerful anticathexis, but the ideas cathected by it are retained in consciousness. Evidently the ego is incapable of erecting a barrier against the manifestations of aggression as it does against those of gross sensuality. The former are constantly presented to it by the unavoidable impressions of daily life and not least by the aggressive measures adopted by those who train the child. Education must therefore content itself with *condemning* his acts of aggression in the most severe terms and causing him to attach to them the ideas of guilt and sin. The close relation between genitality and repression on the one hand and aggression and defense through reaction on the other—a relation to which Freud (1926) has drawn attention—thus has its roots in the child's practical situation. Subsequently, the repressed guilt connected with genitality (i.e., the guilt which is incapable of entering consciousness) hides itself behind the guilt of aggression, which persists undisguised in the conscious mind; and thus the sadistic impulse (which, genetically, goes back to the infant's out-break of rage) also becomes the manifest carrier of the whole feeling of incest guilt, this being displaced from its genital source. The torments of hunger are the mental precursors of later "punishments" and, by way of the discipline of punishment, they come to be the primal mechanism of self-punishment, which in melancholia assumes such a fatal significance. At the bottom of the melancholiac's profound dread of impoverishment there is really simply the dread of starvation (that is, of impoverishment in physical possessions), with which the vitality of such part of his ego as remains normal reacts to the expiatory acts which threaten the life of the patient. But drinking at the mother's breast remains the radiant image of unremitting, forgiving love. It is certainly no mere chance that the Madonna nursing the

Child has become the emblem of a mighty religion and thereby the emblem of a whole epoch of our Western civilization. I think that if we trace the chain of ideas, *guilt-atonement-forgiveness*, back to the sequence of experiences of early infancy: *rage, hunger, drinking at the mother's breast*, we have the explanation of the problem why the hope of absolution and love is perhaps the most powerful conception which we meet with in the higher strata of the mental life of mankind.

According to this argument, the deepest fixation point in the melancholic (depressive) disposition is to be found in the situation of threatened loss of love—more precisely, in the hunger situation of the infant. We shall learn more about it if we examine more closely that experience of oral-narcissistic bliss which is vouchsafed to him in his extremity. I have elsewhere (Rado, 1926) tried to demonstrate that pleasurable stimulation of the mouth zone does not constitute the whole of the oral-libidinal gratification but should rather be regarded as its more conspicuous antecedent. I thought there was reason to refer the climax of this enjoyment to the subsequent, invisible part of the process, which I termed "the alimentary orgasm" and which I have assumed to be the precursor, along the road of evolution, of the later genital orgasm. We now see that the alimentary orgasm of the infant at the mother's breast is a phenomenon with important consequences, whose influence radiates out into the whole of his later life. It satisfies the egoistic cravings of the little human being for nourishment, security, and warmth, fulfills the longings of his budding object instincts and, by the blending of all these factors, it induces in him a kind of narcissistic transport which is inseparably connected with them. It is perhaps more correct to say that this tremendous experience of gratification contains, as yet inextricably combined, all the components which subsequent development will differentiate and carry forward to different fates. But it comes to the same thing: we cannot fail to recognize that the infant's dawning ego acquires in this narcissistic gratification that mental quality which it will later experience as "self-satisfaction." This feeling is, in its origin, the reaction of the dawning ego to the experience which is biologically the most important to it, namely, that of alimentary orgasm. Later on the principal incentives for stimulating self-esteem will be the ego's developments in the direction of power and all the forms of activity by which it obtains gratification—we can actually distinguish within self-esteem a progress from the oral to a sadistic-anal and thence to a genital level (corresponding to the varying technique of acquisition)—but the peculiar quality of the experience persists as a specifically differentiated memory-symbol of that early ego reaction which was conditioned by the alimentary orgasm.

If we take into consideration the fact that the quality of feeling which is experienced as self-esteem can, by the addition of fresh factors, advance in successive stages to the pitch of exaltation, triumph, ecstasy, and intoxication, we may feel that the chain of connected ideas is brought to a satisfactory end. I discovered already some time ago through another channel that states of intoxication in adults are derived from the experience of blissful repletion in the process of nutrition. Now it is precisely for melancholia that the genetic sequence here worked out—*alimentary orgasm - self-satisfaction - intoxication*—is of importance. As we have heard, the melancholiac tries to restore his seriously diminished self-esteem by means of love. His behavior strikes us as morbid, because it is related not to the object but to his own superego. But it leads to a result which is entirely logical though nonetheless pathological. I refer to mania, in which condition, as Freud (1921) has recognized, the ego is once more merged with the superego in unity. We may add that this process is the faithful intrapsychic repetition of the experience of that fusing with the mother that takes place during drinking at her breast. The earliest (oral) technique for the renewal of self-satisfaction is revived on the psychic plane and results—as is psychologically perfectly correct—in the transports of mania. The manic condition succeeds the phase of self-punishment with the same regularity with which formerly, in the biological process, the bliss of satiety succeeded to hunger. We know, further, that the ego has yet another pathological method to which it can resort in order to bolster up its tottering self-esteem. This method also takes the alimentary orgasm as its prototype: it consists of a flight into the pharmacotoxic states to which the victims of drug addiction have recourse.

The ego, finding that its rebellion against the loss of its object is futile, changes its psychological technique, confesses that it is guilty, and passes into a state of remorseful contrition. Here the question arises, exactly why and of what does the ego feel itself guilty? In depressive neurotics we need to get through a great deal of work in order to answer this question with any certainty. With the melancholiac, however, who in this respect is so frank with us, we have only to listen attentively and then we easily arrive at the inner meaning of his self-reproaches. He feels guilty because by his aggressive attitude he has himself to blame for the loss of the object, and in this we certainly cannot contradict him. We observe, too, that this confession of guilt by the ego is modeled on infantile prototypes and its expression is strongly reinforced from infantile sources. Nevertheless, precisely the most striking characteristics of the melancholiac's atonement would still be incomprehensible were it not that we know that this behavior is contributed to very largely from another quarter.

There is indeed another psychic process at work, parallel with the melancholic atonement. It has its origin in the sadistic trend of hostility to the object, which has already shown its force in the ambivalent character of the love relation, which later supplied the fuel for rebellious reactions, and which brought the ego over to the other view, namely, that the object alone was to blame for the quarrel, having provoked the rigor of the ego by its caprice, unreliability, and spite. Freud's discovery, which I mentioned at the beginning of this paper, revealed to us the surprising fact that in melancholia this overmastering aggressive tendency of the id proves stronger than the ego. When the latter has failed ignominiously to carry through the claims of its hostile impulses toward the object (i.e., when the phase of rebellion collapses) and thereupon adopts an attitude of masochistic remorse toward the superego, the aggressive tendency of the id goes over to the side of the superego and forces the ego itself, weakened by its expiatory attitude, into the position of the object. Thereafter the superego visits upon the ego all the fury which the ego would otherwise have been capable of visiting upon the object. In the past the ego sallied forth into the world in order to find gratification for its narcissistic craving for love, but the demands of its sadism brought it to grief; now, turning away from reality, it seeks for narcissistic gratification within the mind itself, but, here again, it cannot escape the overpowering force of the aggressive instinct. The self-punishments assume forms very different from that of the expiation which may have hovered before the imagination of the ego, and are carried to a degree far in excess of it. In its remorse the ego turned, full of confidence, to a benevolent being, whose punishments would be but light; now it has to bear the consequences of its infantile trustfulness and weakness. Since, in its perplexity, it cannot rid itself of the hope of the forgiveness which shall save it, it submits to the role of object, takes upon itself the whole guilt of the object, and suffers without resistance the cruelties of the superego. Its own self is now almost annihilated—only its various dreads (expressed in distorted forms) betray that the core of the ego still exists. Such total capitulation on the part of the ego to the sadism of the id would be incomprehensible if it were not that we realize that it falls a victim to the indestructible infantile illusion that only by yielding and making atonement can it be delivered from its *narcissistic* distress.

The repentant ego desires to win the forgiveness of the offended object and, as an atonement, submits to being punished by the superego instead of by the object. In the undreamed-of harshness of the superego the old tendency of hostility to the object is expending its fury on the ego, which is thrust into the place of the hated object. Thus, the result of this synthetic process is a very extensive loss of the relation to reality and complete subjection of the ego to the unrestrained tyranny of the sadistic superego.

The individual who is later to succumb to melancholia retains all his life, in consequence of the exaggerated ambivalence of his instinctual disposition, very considerable residues of his infantile, supplicating mode of thinking. When he gives play alternately to his ambivalent impulses and thus succeeds in completely withdrawing his consciousness from the light or dark side of the object, as the occasion requires, he is behaving in a manner hardly different from that of the child. It is only clinical observation of this phenomenon, so entirely characteristic of neurotic ambivalence, which enables us by reasoning a posteriori to throw light upon the corresponding process in the development of the child. When, with the outbreak of melancholia, the strong current of regressive processes begins to flow, the subject's idea of his latest love object, which has hitherto corresponded to reality, must also give way in the end to the archaic demands made on the function of thought by his ambivalence, which has now broken free of all restraint. The "good object," whose love the ego desires, is introjected and incorporated in the superego. There it is endowed with the prescriptive right (formerly so vehemently disputed in relation to the real object) to be angry with the ego—indeed, very angry. The "bad object" has been split off from the object as a whole, to act, as it were, as "whipping boy." It is incorporated in the ego and becomes the victim of the sadistic tendency now emanating from the superego. Thus, the logical inconsistency is entirely cleared up.

This conclusion now enables us to discover in its fullest implications the hidden meaning of the mechanism of melancholia. The worst fault by which the "bad object" has incurred guilt, according to the reproach of the ego, is its ambivalence, by which it has "provoked" the ego's hostility. Now if the "bad object" which resides within the ego is chastised and finally destroyed, all that remains is the object purged of its "bad" element, i.e., the "good object"; moreover, the hostility of the ego (of the id) is satisfied and has spent itself. Nothing now stands in the way of the purified ego's uniting itself with the object, which is also purged of offense, in reciprocal love! When the subject swings over to mania this, the goal of the melancholic process, is fully attained. The "bad object"—as Abraham (1924a) recognized —is expelled from the ego by an anal act, and this is synonymous with its being killed. The ego, freed of its own aggressive tendencies and its hated enemy, heaves a sigh of relief and with every sign of blissful transport unites itself with the "good object," which has been raised to the position of the superego.

Thus we come to realize that the process of melancholia represents an attempt at reparation (cure) on a grand scale, carried out with an iron psychological consistency. It is designed to revive the ego's self-regard, which has been annihilated by the loss of love, to restore the interrupted love relation, to be as it were a prophylactic measure against the ego's ever suffering such severe injury again and, with this end in view, to do away with the causes of mischief, namely, the ambivalence of the ego and that of the object. As to attaining any *real* effect by this line of action, the crucial point is that it does not take place on the right plane, in relation to the object world, but is carried out, subject to a narcissistic regression, entirely between the separate institutions in the patient's mind. It cannot restore to the ego the lost object; the final reconciliation with the object (after this has been replaced by the superego) is accomplished not as a real process in the outside world but as a change of the situation (cathexis) in the psychic organization. From this purely psychic act, however, there ensues an important *real* result: the restoration of the subject's self-esteem—indeed, its leap into the exaltation of mania. The difference is clear to us: the melancholic process, set going by a grievous shattering of the subject's narcissism, can by means of a purely psychic shifting of cathexis attain to its *narcissistic* goal (the restoration of self-esteem), even though reality be thereby ignored. Once passed into the state of mania, the ego immediately finds its way back into the object world. With all its energy released by the sudden change in cathexis it rushes upon reality and there expends its violence. What determines the behavior of the manic patient is the oral derivation of the psychogenic transport; it is a striking fact that in mania the adult with his manifold potentialities of action and reaction reproduces the uninhibited instinctual manifestations which we observe in the euphoria of the satiated suckling. That the quality of the reactions of a period of life in which the superego did not as yet exist should be the pattern upon which is modeled the manic state (the basis of which is a temporary withdrawal of the superego) is exactly what we should expect.

I should like to devote a few remarks to the problem of *neurotic* depression. Observation shows that the depressive process, in so far as it has caught in its grip the ego of the person suffering from a transference neurosis, is carried out in exact accordance with the mechanism of true melancholia. That is to say, neurotic depression also has as its basis a narcissistic turning away from reality, the external object being replaced by psychic institutions and an endeavor being made to solve the conflicts on the intrapsychic plane instead of in the outside world, and by means of a regressively activated oral technique. But there is this difference: these processes almost wholly consume the ego of the melancholic and destroy those functions in him which relate to reality, while in a transference neurosis they are as it were merely superimposed upon an ego which is, indeed, neurotic but is more or less intact. In the depressed neurotic the object and, with it, the relation to reality, are preserved: it is only that the patient's hold on them is loosened and the weak ego has begun to give up the struggle with the world—a struggle which it feels to be unbearable—, to turn inward in a narcissistic fashion, and to take refuge in the oral-narcissistic reparation mechanism. Thus, neurotic depression is a kind of partial melancholia of the (neurotic) ego; the further the depressive process extends within that ego at the cost of its relations to the object and to reality, the more does the condition of narcissistic neurosis approximate melancholia. Accordingly, in an acute access of depression we should expect the issue to turn on whether in the ego's narcissistic machinery, the oral mechanisms gain the upper hand or whether the sadistic-anal (and genital) mechanisms, whose hold on the object world is firmer, are strong enough to safeguard the ego from the plunge into melancholia.

THE PSYCHOLOGY OF SCREAMING

M. Nina Searl

(1933)

During the 1920's and 1930's, Searl of London was one of the first psychoanalysts to engage in systematic observational studies of infants and children. Relatively unknown in America, she can rightly be acknowledged as one of the pioneers and originators of this method of psychoanalytic investigation. A felicitous result of her work, which was mainly devoted to the study of emergent sexuality in infants and children, was this unique paper on screaming.

Screams are essentially aggressive attacks in situations that preclude other forms of effective attack and/or flight. The scream may be the vocal accompaniment to a child's —or an adult's—attack of rage.

When screaming fails to achieve any satisfaction, autoplastic changes take place. Thus, a habitually or chronically screaming infant or child experiences consequences and vicissitudes evident in his unconscious and conscious mental life as an adult. Searl cites clinical examples from observing a three-year-old and a five-year-old child.

The function of the cry or scream is to attain what the child desires through omnipotent wish fulfillment (Ferenczi, 1916). If the cry or scream is not followed by a removal of disturbing, painful elements, or by the relief of tension by the parent, the child loses connection with this primary quality of love, and the cry becomes solely a scream of rage with which to attack the "bad parent." In such instances, "the discharge element is then of great importance. It is a violently aggressive effort, to get the 'pain' out of the infant or child and into the bad parent."

In instances of prolonged screaming in which the infant has been unable to accomplish anything by his screaming, he is scarcely more than "an embodied scream ... in which almost all of object relations are abandoned...." Searl suggests that this situation may well provide a basis in experience for the belief in the omnipotence of infantile death wishes rather than in one's own powerlessness. She asserts that the violent screaming fit may play a significant role in forming the earliest divisions of "self against the self" (later to be termed "splitting") and may be of etiological signif- icance in respiratory conditions, sore throat, stuttering, stammering, bronchial asthma, and severe speech inhi- bitions.

What are the later vicissitudes that screaming infants and children become heirs to? An infant "screamer" may in adult life be extremely silent or, at the other end of the spectrum, may "have never ceased to scream." The latter very often speak of their enjoyment of and pleasure in screaming farces, howling successes, and shrieks of laughter. On the other hand, later symptoms of weakness and exhaus- tion may well have as early precursors exhaustion experi- ences from prolonged screaming in infancy and childhood. A feeling of complete emptiness pervades some patients' lives due to the first temporary frustrations of all wish fulfillment incidental to the failure of their screaming attempts. From the hate that is implied in screaming there may well develop a highly sexualized love life in some patients, a demon- stratively affectionate attitude whose purpose is to deny the terrors of being left alone and of preventing recurring solitariness.

Searl has not only provided a significant glimpse of the traumatic nature of acute fits of screaming in infancy, but also has indicated how the individual manner of dealing with this phenomenon determines the later path of character formation and even of psychic conflict.

Aside from situations of overwhelming terror in a reality situation or screams of rage due to deep frustration, screaming in our adult patients is most commonly found in the nightmare. The manifest emotion permits a few general conclusions about the nature of the latent thoughts, but this is inconclusive unless the latent thoughts are uncovered and analyzed.

My main theme is the infant's scream of intense rage. The whole field of the psychology of screaming is too vast a subject. I am concerned with those violent screaming fits which not only signalize, but in themselves constitute, the infant's most painful situations. I personally find I am only now beginning to understand them. No psychoanalytic writings have carried me very far in their specific problem apart from that of anxiety in general, though Melanie Klein's work is full of their derivative fantasies. Screaming fits must contain the core of the problem of infantile anxiety, and on the importance of that there is no need to insist.

I suggest, first, that such screams are essentially aggressive attacks in situations in which, as in infancy, other forms of effective attack or flight are precluded; second, that where they fail to achieve any satisfaction, even of the rage itself, i.e., where they fail alloplastically, they work autoplastically; and third, that it is worth while to trace out some of the metamorphoses or vicissitudes of the scream, which is certainly one of the earliest instinctual activities.

I suggest that not only do actual baffled screams of rage provide the germ of anxiety as a danger signal, Freud's view of the trauma of birth, but also that the division of the psyche against itself in later screams (which I hope to demonstrate) provides the endopsychic basis of all conflict. Ambivalence itself can exist without conflict in early infancy, in the sense that the infant can cry lustily one moment, red with rage, and suck happily the next, the moment the desired object appears. There seems no, or very little, *organization* toward an object. But there are also times when screaming interferes with the satisfaction of even the hungry child. These situations, I think, form the primitive basis of true ambivalence, as of the superego and of all psychic conflict.

We have further learned from Freud that flight is of no avail against an instinct unless it has been projected into the external world. But physical flight also is impossible to an infant. How, on any basis of ontogenetic experience, can it play any part in infantile mentality? The infant can turn away his head, can expel from his mouth, can refuse to open it, can make movements of attack with hands and feet, though ineffectually. But his one powerful weapon in any situation of discomfort or danger, internal or external, is a scream. If it does not bring him the succor he needs, he uses it to keep at bay whomever or whatever is unwelcome in actual presence, to discharge his own undesirable tensions, to attack at a distance those hated unseen powers who do not come to the relief of his instinctual needs. The most primitive of human reactions to danger is not flight but screaming.

This is an example taken from the later stages of the analysis of a five-year-old boy in the midst of his struggle with his earliest aggressive impulses connected with feeding. Terry does not answer a question I put to him, and immediately shows me what he, were he I, would do with such a child as himself. He takes a celluloid frog which always tells of his phallic desire to maintain a love relation (the frog "who would a-wooing go"), shows me its closed mouth ("It won't open, it won't open," he says), takes the scissors and, crouching in the same position as the frog, digs the scissors into the frog's mouth. Quickly rising, for it is not safe to be the frog, he hurts his back sharply on the corner of his open drawer. He is again the frog, even in his effort to escape the role, and Terry's mouth is forced open by a howl, his body collapses on me. But as I hold him and he continues to shriek, he stiffens against my hands and is temporarily inaccessible to all interpretation. For another quick division of roles has taken place; he must not be both the superego (alias the strict parent) and the suffering frog; if he has to be the frog-child, I must be the bad parent, and he arches his back in an effort to escape both me and the pain, identified cause and effect, and closes his ears against me. Momentarily it feels to him a phallic contest of sound—his screams must penetrate my ears more effectively than my words his ears. This incident was connected with the first unwelcome spoon-feeding during his early months of breast feeding, and represented his own account of it.

Bennie, three years old, had a very violent attack of screaming on coming back into the treatment room after spilling water in the lavatory. I was not quick enough to prevent the acute fit of anxiety by interpretation. He was temporarily inaccessible to any interpretation and tried to run out of the room away from me. He told me later that he thought there was a man in the room going to shoot him. His scream was certainly intended to shoot *me*. He tried in this way to show himself stronger than the supposed man.

These examples lead from the successful scream, ending in love and satisfaction, apparently unproductive of conflict, to the scream which does not accomplish even its secondary object, that of putting the enemy to flight or killing him. None take us to the extremes of baffled rage. No even approximately successful early analysis will provide us with examples. However, few of us are unfamiliar with them extra-analytically. But first let us pause on the note of contrast, already provided in Ferenczi's (1916) well-known work on the stages of infantile omnipotence. A successful scream does put the infant, boy or girl, here identically equipped, in a position equal or even superior to that of the father or other rivals with regard to the mother or her substitute. It penetrates through closed doors to unmeasured distances, and is indeed the magic phallus in the first place, only later by force of comparison, when no longer at his disposal. It does obtain what the child desires, and from this aspect is a successful extension of the seeking and finding mouth. This unsuccessful cry which yet leads to a state of tolerable satisfaction brings independence and self-confidence. But the unsuccessful cry which is succeeded by no removal of disturbing or painful elements, no relief of tension, loses its primary quality of love, longing, search, hope for the good parent, and becomes a scream of rage with which to attack the bad parent. The discharge element is then of great importance. It is a violently aggressive effort to get the "pain" out of the infant or child and *into* the bad parent. An adult patient, struggling with acute mental and some physical discomfort, which in a little child would unquestionably have provoked noisy crying, suddenly and angrily said, "I want to take all my pains and throw them at you." The first effort seeks to overcome "pain" by love. The second uses hate, but retains an object who may still give some form of relief. The ambivalent struggle still exists. When this again accomplishes nothing, there succeeds a third state in which one can say the infant is scarcely more than an embodied scream, in which almost all object relation is abandoned, the struggle of ambivalence is ended by the complete occlusion of love and desire for relief. The eyes are tightly closed—the infant is shut away in a world of his own—a world of horror, we cannot doubt. If he shows any awareness of the outer world of people, he screams the louder and seems to endeavor to shut himself the further away from it. His body is rigid, often with an arching of the back away from supporting hands. The face turns scarlet, purple, "black." There being no comfort left, the effort seems to be to drive everything out of the body via head and mouth. This effort failing, there is sometimes a reversal. The child, as if further enraged at this powerless rage itself, holds his breath and there is temporary silence; the climax of rage which is yet an anticlimax. All this time the child is completely inaccessible to all calming, comforting influences, and refuses the breast even where the original drive was that of hunger. Sometimes only a sharp smack, pain overcoming pain, seems effective in these crises to force back to the child's consciousness the fact of the existence both of his own body and of the bad parent of whom he has so effectively disposed. The most distressing feature for the infant is his powerlessness in such a state. But I think there is a very important addition to be made to such a statement. It is true with regard to real life; it is untrue with regard to psychic death. For the child in a blind rage *has*, as far as his own feelings are concerned, killed all that is good in his world, obliterated every trace of a good helpful parent. It is a situation which provides a basis in experience for belief in the *omnipotence* of infantile death wishes, rather than in their powerlessness.

What is the usual end of such screaming fits? The body ego in its self-preservative function asserts itself, not against an external but against an internal foe; it is powerful by means of its weakness—the weakness of exhaustion. The screaming gradually ceases with many a sob and a temporary return to show that the storm has not dispersed. It seems to me important to note that the infant has not stopped screaming as a result of any real satisfaction. He has stopped only because his own body has refused to let him go on any longer; and this in the course of the strongest exertion of his own power he has ever known. It is the most profound division in the psyche. The body ego, that very kernel of the ego, has reasserted itself at the expense of the id. The infant may many times before have wanted to do what he could not accomplish. But since any considerable disappointment or failure to deal with instinctual tensions always issues into crying, we can be sure that the violent screaming fit ended only by exhaustion marks the most acute of early divisions of the self against the self. There seems to be sometimes a stronger identification of the self with the restraining body, productive, I think, of the inhibited type of child; and sometimes a stronger identification with the scream. The important point at the moment is a further identification of the restraining body with all those other restraining bodies— of the parents and their substitutes—which have already often prevented and will again still more often prevent the infant from doing what he seeks to do. And this identifi- cation of a part of the self with restraining authority is connected with the most violently aggressive trends con- ceivable, and with an experience of the most acute dis- comfort and lack of satisfaction.

The conclusions to be emphasized are:

1. There is a division of the psyche in which one part, the body ego, takes on the function of restraint of aggression in the most painful circumstances when external authority is of no avail.

2. The infant does actually experience the fact that his most aggressive attack upon his world is equally an attack upon himself, and an acutely unpleasant one. His screams, intended to attack the bad parent, do really rasp his own throat, nearly suffocate him, and then exhaust him. I can

conceive of no situation in actual experience more fitted to form the basis of the most sadistic type of superego and of profound belief in the law of talion punishment.

It seems of importance whether the return to cognizance of the external world takes place in isolation, in an actually unfriendly or frightened atmosphere, or with friendliness which can counteract the feeling that the world of love and happiness has really been annihilated. For one can hardly overestimate the child's terror of his own most violent screams. I have seen a little boy, who was very severely inhibited in speech, running all round the room in an effort to escape or find refuge from his own shrieks, which yet were very far from being actually those of unmixed spontaneous rage. Mary Chadwick (1927) tells of a six-year-old boy, also with a very extensive speech inhibition, who covered his ears lest he should hear his own cough. This connected with screaming fits, from which he had been left to recover in isolation.

I will briefly indicate some of the later vicissitudes of screaming. The screaming fit, ended in actuality by fear and without satisfaction, is still dynamic in the psyche. In this it is of course no different from other traumatic situations; Freud long ago made us familiar with the fact of fixations to such experiences. I suppose no one will question that the extremity of baffled rage and helplessness which I have described does indeed form an early traumatic situation.

1. *Active into passive.* This is identical with the change from sadism into masochism. Keeping to situations rather than to trends, it means being screamed at instead of screaming. Anxieties of both children and adults at the crying of babies are familiar enough. It is the boomerang return of their own never (psychically) completely silenced scream. Compare the two instances just given of children terrified of their own shrieks or coughs. The more disguised forms are

perhaps less familiar. All later expressions of anger, in particular angry words, which in hysterical women of a very uncontrolled type can indeed issue into direct screaming, curses, even creaking furniture, can mean to child or adult the danger of this same boomerang return of their own scream, imbued with the same intensity of hate, the same death-wish content, the same absence of counteracting factors. The analyst's silence may mean not only "dead," but also "too furious to speak"—the holding of the breath.

There is another interesting change in conversion symptoms from active into passive which is, I think, of importance; although I hesitate whether to place it under this heading, under a separate one of "imitative magic," or under "repression," these different factors all playing their part. I have already mentioned the actual physical hurt which the child experiences from his own scream, and the closeness of identification with the hated object that this implies; since what is intended to hurt the foe hurts the aggressor. I have reason to think that where this original close identification with a hated object persists, where the aggression of the scream becomes apparently entirely changed into physical suffering, according to the preponderance of the particular sensation involved, rasping, bursting, suffocating, etc., we have a most potent factor in the various throat and breath affections.

Eben, the very inhibited boy of seven whom I have already mentioned, incapable of normal speech or learning, treated so far for twenty-six weeks, had had three or four attacks of asthma before he came to me. One of these was so severe that oxygen was administered. Except the first, which was rather asthmatic bronchitis, these attacks of asthma occurred on a separation from one or both parents. This boy's anxiety and his fixations to the first months of his life are so excessive that he frequently spends the greater part of

the treatment hour lying on the couch, generally mastur-
bating. Four times he has for a few seconds breathed very
asthmatically, apparently purposely, as a threat: "This is
what I would do if . . . " Each time it has had the same connection of separation from one of his parents. Each time it
has ceased on interpretation of its connection with early
screaming situations. He has lived in London for the last nine
months, away from his father with the exception of holidays
and his father's occasional visits to town; and he left for
home recently with his father and without his mother. He
has had only one attack of asthma in this period. This was
accompanied by sickness and kept him away from analysis
for three days. It followed the second occasion on which,
with some weeks' interval, he had ventured to turn on the
water tap and let some water overflow. The first time he had
an attack of nettle rash. His impressively uttered two words
on his return, "hot water," showed he had understood the
nettle rash to be a punishment with burning hot water for his
naughty activity with cold water. The asthma sequel was less
completely masochistic, contained more of defiance, and on
his return he managed not only to resume his water play, but
also again to make some overflow—this time without any
deterrent illness, but with much inhibiting anxiety. The
partially releasing interpretation with regard to the asthma
was of a struggle in his throat with the angry words of an
angry mother, scolding him for being a bad dirty boy. It was
only later from his own material—his loud shrieks in the
room and efforts to run away from them, as well as from
other analyses—that I was able to give the further interpretation of the struggle with the scream itself, of what he
wanted to do with it to his mother, of what he then supposed
she wanted to do with her angry words to him. The result
was a further release.

Terry, a little boy of five, was expecting to end his not

fully completed analysis with me in a fortnight. He developed sudden acute ear trouble, and had abscesses opened in both ears. He was away in the country for some weeks, very well and happy, and then returned to the scene of his trouble and to four weeks more analysis. The second day, largely as a result of very insufficient clothing in unexpectedly cold weather, he developed a bad throat with a temperature of 102. The doctor diagnosed a "raging tonsillitis." His mother agreed that he should be brought to me wrapped in blankets in a taxi. I had, since his previous illness, become aware of the significance of screaming—"piercing shrieks"—both for ear and throat trouble. Previous analytic work, in connection with his ambivalent attitude to me both on leaving and returning, had shown this to be a transference repetition of early attitudes to his mother after he had had long screaming fits alone in the dark. Therefore the whole of this hour's analysis turned on the importance of these screaming hates both for ears and throat. The next day he came to his analysis by bus and walking, temperature down, as well as usual, except for a slight cold which soon cleared up.

The symptom of exhaustion needs further investigation in its connection with the exhaustion experienced after long screaming—the first temporary death of all wish life, the feeling of complete emptiness. This, I think, is again understood by the child as a punishment for (or a direct result of) his own intensely aggressive wishes toward the body of the defaulting parent. It is perhaps well to emphasize that when we meet these symptoms in our patients they already have a long history which must be unraveled, and that I do not in any way deny the presence of factors with which we are more familiar: displacement to erotogenic zones, etc. I think, however, that the historically earliest and pathogenically most important is that of the most furious type of screaming, and it is to this neglected situation that I wish to direct attention in this paper.

2. *Reversal of content.* This is evident in the genesis of the scream of rage itself. Love, or the desire for that which the child loves, changes into rage and hate. But there is very clear evidence that a second reversal sometimes takes place. There is an effort, often extraordinarily successful, to change hate into love, and particularly into highly sexualized love. This is the familiar path of reaction formation, and, like all reaction formations, can occur only where there is a solid basis of the reactive tendency, beneath that reacted against, on which to build. For example, it is the intensity of desire and love activating the scream in the first place which makes possible the later effort to overcome with love the subsequent scream of intense rage and hate.

Terry had several times been left alone at night, and had had some very acute screaming fits. He made an extraordinarily complete reaction to them in a demonstratively affectionate attitude, though not in any obviously abnormal or unpleasant way. When he came to me at three years old he was a strikingly intelligent, "normal" child, with only occasional aggressive outbursts. It required an extensive analysis before the anxiety of the situations of screaming rage and their aggressive hatred could be freed, and the solid basis of love of his mother released. One could hardly have suspected the extent to which this little boy's unusual grasp on reality and his highly genitalized love attitude had had to serve the purpose of denying his terrors when left alone and of preventing recurring solitariness. The hatred of his own body which refused to do what he wanted—continue screaming until his screams accomplished something tangible, bring his mother to him, or take him to her—the terror of his mother's body which he wanted to attack, indeed felt that he had attacked and exhausted, apparently changed into love of his own body (we have here an important source of narcissism), and of hers. His demonstrative affection needed to supply him with constant proofs that he had not indeed harmed his mother's body, and that she did not wish to retaliate on him. I do not here refer in detail to his relation to his father. He tried to overcome hatred and rivalry in the Oedipus situation in the same way. Very important aspects of the whole Oedipus situation were (1) its intensification through this attempt to deal with the early aggression by possession of the mother's body, and therefore by rivalry with her, with the father, and with other children; (2) the consequent anxiety and attempts at complete repression because the hatred and feeling of impotence aroused in this competition meant the danger of a recurrence of that very screaming rage it was intended to overcome. That is, the rise and fall of the Oedipus situation both, in their most difficult aspects, arose from the same cause. Intensity of phallic desire as well as of castration anxiety were both conditioned by the repressed memories of screaming rage.

3. *Repression.* I must here touch only the fringe of this vast subject, appearing already under the two previous headings. Its ramifications spread all through life.

A very important and interesting result of the abandonment of screaming is its return in other forms. So-called loss of bowel and bladder control, already attained, almost invariably supervenes with every possible quantitative variation. It has long been known that feces and urine become weapons of aggressive hatred. As with the first screams, I think they are first used to compel the attention of the mother or her substitute, an intermediate stage between love-gift and hate-weapon.

4. *Inhibition.* Where screaming has long persisted, its complete disappearance is of serious portent, and is only accomplished by a very extensive system of inhibition.

The main aim of this paper has been not only to show the traumatic nature of acute fits of screaming in infancy, but to indicate ways in which the individual manner of dealing with it may determine the later path of psychic conflict.

It seems that the human psyche never wholly abandons any situation of "pain"; never wholly moves forward until "pain" has been changed into pleasure, until satisfaction of one type or another has been attained; is never entirely subject to pain, fear, or threats. Some measure of satisfaction of the whole of the psyche alone sets free the psyche, as a whole, to move away from its infantile fixation points.

ANXIETY WITHOUT AFFECT

Gregory Zilboorg

(1933)

*In this early paper Zilboorg describes a familiar clinical
situation for which psychoanalysis has not as yet provided a
complete and full understanding: namely, the patient produces intellectual material dealing with anxiety situations,
experiences the physiological accompaniments of anxiety,
and yet there is no affective expression of anxiety. What is
presented to the analyst are the "smooth surfaces of
emotions . . . the affectless intellectual musings and the
monotony of an intellectual rut." The ego continually rejects
the content of the anxiety, but how is this achieved?*

*Zilboorg postulates that the patient "steps out" of the
picture, engages in passive, protracted, regressive defensive
maneuvers, engages in a simulation of a true motor expression of affect, splits affects into component parts, may not
experience the appropriate intensity of feeling due to the
shallowness of his affects, and may experience his "inner
world" as an "outer world," thereby not perceiving the affect
as his own.*

*From the vantage point of our present knowledge of
some of these patients, many of them may be termed "as if"
characters (Deutsch, 1942).*

*Ross's (1967) paper on "The 'As If' Concept" represents
our furthest point of theoretical and clinical understanding
of these individuals. He reported that the "as if" phenom-*

enon is represented developmentally at the two- to three-year level of imitativeness and therefore does not represent true or secondary identification. There is a preponderance of narcissism, and the object choices, if they can be called that, are of a narcissistic type. The singularly poor affect may indeed reflect a severe retardation of ego maturation especially with respect to object relations, and the relative affectlessness is predefensive in nature, although it may be a part of later defensive structures. Absence of affect may represent "the persistence of the operation of the primitive stimulus barrier against overwhelming instinctual pressures" (Ross, 1967, p. 81).

Anxiety, normal or neurotic, once it comes to full expression, is always intimately connected with, or accompanied by, a self-conscious feeling tone which is in some way related to a sense of fear and which apparently represents or is the affect of anxiety. Anxiety is an unpleasant state of indefinite expectation which is related to no specific object; only when it becomes related to, i.e., when it "acquires" an object, does it become fear. Clinically, however, i.e., as far as the subjective perception of the affective tone is concerned, it is well-nigh impossible to distinguish anxiety from fear. Patients, when under the spell of anxiety, frequently state that they are afraid, or feel frightened, even though they may be unable to tell what they are afraid of or why they are frightened; on such occasions they thus attempt to describe their feelings, rather than the relationships of these to things or events. On the other hand, when both ideational content and the anxiety remain repressed, the modes by means of which the individual defends himself against the breaking through of either assume protean forms, of which the most successful are certain types of acting out. We hardly need to mention the variety of conversion phenomena which so successfully ward off both ideational content and affect. If, however, the ideational content does break through the barriers of psychological isolation, an affective outbreak in its direct or regressive form becomes inevitable, so that feeling tone, ideational content, and motor component all come to expression together. To give point to this statement, one may cite the extreme case of a schizophrenic who for a long time remained in a state of perplexed depression and apprehensive withdrawal before he broke into an uncontrollable rage; for many days he became vehemently preoccupied with madly throwing his own feces against the windowpanes or the walls of his room. Armed with a handful of his excreta, he demanded that he be permitted to go to have intercourse with his mother: "My father did it— why can't I do it? I was there once and I want to get into her again!" There seemed to be no end of his hatred. The affective accompaniment of this rather denuded feature of his Oedipus complex was quite in keeping with the ideational content and could be brought to expression after anxiety had been properly disposed of. One is reminded, in this connection, of Ferenczi's apt statement that anxiety is the common currency against which any affect is exchanged when the ideational content enters the field of awareness without undergoing the insulating influence of isolation. We must expect some definite affective reaction; if it is anxiety we happen to deal with, we shall naturally expect the affective components of anxiety to come to the fore. We may now recapitulate the above statement somewhat schematically, as follows: an anxiety reaction consists, grossly speaking, of three components: ideational content, feeling tone (affect), and motor reaction; ideational content may appear isolated, with feeling tone and motor expression repressed; we can observe this in some forms of obsessions. Feeling tone may come into the foreground, while the ideational content remains repressed, but the motor accompaniment on such occasions will also be present; as an example of this, one may cite any attack of an anxiety neurotic; during such an attack he is aware of his anxiety (affect) and shows it by his pallor, tremulousness, rapid heart action, and respiratory rate, etc., i.e., the motor component. Finally, the motor component may come into evidence with both ideational content and affect remaining repressed; we can observe this in cases of neurotic lacrimation of hand sweating or mild myoclonic or ticlike phenomena behind which are concealed both forbidden thoughts and anxious feelings. As has been said, all three components may break through simultaneously. One mathematically possible combination appears unthinkable, i.e., the breaking through of both ideational content and motor expression without the affect involved; for once one knows the thought which gives rise to fear, has this thought in mind and actually trembles, it is impossible to imagine that under such circumstances one would not also be aware of fear.

While following this rather obvious and generally accepted trend of thought, I had to pause and puzzle over a singular reaction displayed by a patient, a medical student of twenty-five, who in the course of his analysis tenaciously resisted facing his anxiety and who finally chose a mode of response which seemed to deviate considerably from what one might have expected in the usual course of events.

The patient had been in analysis for about fourteen months at the time the incident which is about to be related occurred. The only son in the family, he had a married sister who was two or three years older than he, and one unmarried sister, two or three years younger; both parents were living. He came to be analyzed because he felt undecided as to his career; he was not interested in many things in general or anything in particular, and was not certain as to what he actually wanted to do. His father had planned that his son should ultimately enter his business, but the patient was definitely disinclined to follow this plan; as a matter of fact, this was the only thing in the patient's life about which he was definite, although he was unable to explain definitely why. He was a good student at college, from which he graduated with distinction, his major interest being physics and mathematics. He possessed a keen mind, quite logical and clear, as one would expect in a person with physico-mathematical interests, and possibly talent. His father was well-to-do, and the patient was receiving from him a yearly allowance which afforded the possibility of comfortable and independent living; he lived at the parental home, however. His relation to his parents and sisters was objectively as vague as his choice of career; he liked them, he was tolerant about their failings and pleasantly lukewarm to their merits. There was an air of tepid intellectual serenity about his attitude toward them and other people. Yet he had one or two intimate friends to whom he was quite loyal, even though he preserved toward them as toward everybody else an attitude of tolerant intellectual disapproval mixed with benevolent irony. The uncrystallized and profoundly passive orientation of his personality found its naturaι expression in his sexual life; he masturbated from an early age, presumably without conscious fantasies and without any conscious sense of guilt. At the age of twenty, he established for a time a manifest homosexual relationship with an intimate friend. According to the patient's own description, it was a pleasant relationship that "must have made" an impression on him, since he decided (without being in any way upset) to break it off, and since he began soon afterwards to consider being analyzed. As one listened to the story of this his first love affair, one definitely gained the impression that it was devoid of romance and thrills. Fellatio was pleasant, the friend's penis in his mouth tasted like a large piece of fat—this was the patient's own summary of his sexual reaction. At about the same time he considered having intercourse with a girl. He was abroad at that time; the girl was a foreigner. She refused at first, then agreed, but at the last moment nothing happened. This last moment is psychologically quite instructive. They were alone in a room. He brought her to the point of agreeing. As she lay on the bed, the patient perceived the urge to move his bowels; he thought it would be better if he first emptied his bowels. So he repaired to the toilet and upon his return discovered that the affair was off as far as both parties were concerned—all this was told to the analyst in a tone of even matter-of-factness.

This is about all that was learned about the patient in the course of fourteen months of analytic work. His moods fluctuated imperceptibly, if at all. Occasionally he would say that he was or had been sad, but it would be more a statement of fact than an expression of feeling. He had dreams, but would either remember only the fact that he had a dream or recall one or two dream fragments to which he would give no free associations. These fragments usually dealt with more or less frank hints that his attitude towards the analyst was a passive homosexual one, and that he would wish the analyst to have anal intercourse with him. Attempts to interpret these dreams in the face of scanty associative material would elicit a mild reaction of assent: "Yes, it must be some sort of homosexual attitude." It was apparent that the chronic standstill of the patient's affective life in and outside the analytic hours must have been due to an extremely pathological passivity, combined with a severe reaction formation in regard to his extraordinary anxiety and possibly to some as yet undiscovered unconscious gratification which he must have been obtaining in or outside the analysis in order to keep himself in his tenacious state of pathological psychic equilibrium. Yet he wanted to be analyzed; he rejected repeatedly any suggestion to interrupt temporarily or to stop the analysis altogether. He would come regularly and punctually and fill his analytic hour with reports of medical lectures which he had just heard, or of the recent political news. In short, he gave the analyst a series of unsystematic but rather complete courses in anatomy, physiology, pharmacology, politics, economics, social science, physics, etc. Occasionally he would betray a serene intellectual concern about free associations and would argue approximately as follows: he was helpless before the problem of free associations; for since discussion of politics and of the anatomy of the brachial plexus are per se, or otherwise, of no import to analysis, he would have to guide his thoughts into proper analytical channels, whatever it might mean. But such guidance would require a voluntary effort and then the associations would stop being free. He confessed he was unable to "understand" the method.

His father suffered from a vascular disease and from time to time had attacks of pain. It was at the time of one of these attacks, the severest that the father had had up to this time, and one which kept him bedridden for many weeks, that the patient was faced with a problem connected with a love affair. It was not actually a real love affair; like everything else in the patient's life, it was more in the nature of a passively accepted arrangement. The girl played the role of the aggressor, and he spent his summer holiday with her in the country away from the parental home. It was his first consummated heterosexual love relationship. As the time came to return to the city, he was faced with the wish of which he was only half aware: to keep the girl. He did not want to marry her and would not want to break with her. She held out for marriage, and would agree to a temporary continuation of the liaison if he left his home and lived with her. The patient at that time admitted that he experienced a "sort of conflict," and he felt rather sad. As always in the past, things seemed to arrange themselves without his having to do too much; he thus drifted into taking a small apartment where he would live with the girl "most of the time." In the meantime his father's condition grew worse and the advisability of an amputation was considered. All through this period the patient's general demeanor failed to change to any appreciable degree. Only occasionally one would be able to sense rather than actually observe that the patient was somewhat perturbed and possibly worried. He would admit to being concerned and feeling sad, but he continued to talk in the same general way on the same general topics. At times, one would be on the verge of becoming convinced that nothing could ever make any sizable dent in the smooth surface of his emotions. Thus he did not say anything until a week or so after he had had intercourse with the girl, and even then he limited himself to a casual response to a direct question. When it was pointed out to him that it was strange to find him so placid and unimpressed by his first sexual victory over a girl, he readily agreed that it was strange. He did not deliberately conceal the fact; it just did not happen to occur to him. He was quite active sexually and showed no disturbance of potency.

At any rate, at the time when his father was passing through one of the acutest periods of his illness, the patient came one day and, in his usual quiet and placid manner, related the following:

He had just attended a lecture in clinical neurology. There was a demonstration of a patient with a thalamic lesion. The man was making funny noises; one could not tell whether he was laughing or crying and he—our analytic patient—had at the moment a "peculiar reaction": he felt a sort of a tightness in his scrotum and the "pilomotor muscles" (the patient's own words) in the region of his pubes and on his head "sort of raised the hair." This said, the patient proceeded to speak on the anatomy of the thalamus—in his usual manner. At this point he was asked to tell something more about his "pilomotor reaction"—did he have any special thoughts at that time? No, not any that he could remember. Yes, now when he comes to think of it, he did have some thoughts. At that instant, the patient's voice dropped, his face became pale and his breathing became accentuated. Yes, the thought of a bicycle came to him. He went no further; after a very brief pause his usual smiling expression reappeared. He was then asked what the instructor did to elicit the reaction to the thalamic lesion. This he could not at first remember; but a moment or two later he recalled that the instructor stroked the man's thigh. Instantaneously the pallor on our patient's face reappeared. He stated that he felt again the "pilomotor reaction" and thought of a bicycle, no, of a tricycle. He began to breathe very heavily, his head began to move as if spasmodically; he said his heart was beating very fast, he could not breathe, he saw himself with a gash on his leg and father approaching him with a knife. He also saw himself with a deep bleeding gash on his forehead and father coming toward him with a steel knife. The incident lasted about two minutes; then the patient quieted down with a "Queer!" uttered in a low tone of voice, and almost instantaneously he regained his usual serene self. Throughout the episode he spoke in a semi-muttering voice, but his words were said distinctly, although the flow of speech was quite uneven on account of his labored breathing. Immediately after, he began to relate in his usual manner how his younger sister had dinner with a friend the night before, what she said about her friend, etc. In other words, he behaved as if nothing untoward had

happened. He was then asked whether anything ever actually happened in his life in connection with a bicycle or
tricycle, or a wound, or a steel knife, and, if so, when. He
did "seem to remember something." At this point he had
another attack identical with the one just described. As he
regained his composure, he was asked to describe what he
felt during the attack. This he was not quite able to do. Was
it fear? No. Was he anxious? No, he could not say he was.
How would he describe what he felt? Well, he felt his heart
beating fast, he "had to" breathe rapidly, his muscles were
sort of tremulous, and "that was about all." He stated this in
his quiet and simple unemotional manner.

With an air of half-amused curiosity, he related in the
next hour that, following the previous hour, as he left my
office he felt "queer," and as he sat down at the wheel of his
automobile he exclaimed loudly: "That's that!"—so loudly
that passers-by turned around to look at him; he then drove
off with a start, almost running into another car. That
evening he recalled (not during the analytic session) that
when he was six or eight he did injure his forehead in some
way and his father did bring a steel knife to press against his
head to prevent the formation of a bump. There was also
something about his sister, he said, and a bicycle, but that
was all he could remember. All this was told without any
apparent feeling, but as was learned later, upon leaving the
analyst that day, suddenly, while in the street, he felt that he
was really frightened without knowing why, and he ran
quickly for a few steps as if running away from some danger.

From that time on the analysis fell back into the
monotony of its intellectual rut. It was impossible to elicit
anything of consequence for about three weeks, when one
day he came and stated that he had had several dreams.

He dreamt that he was in a taxicab a short distance from
his home. The meter was running very fast. It was not a "15

and 5" meter but x and x for each half mile (the sum representing his fee for an analytic session; this he did not notice at first). Finally the taxi stopped. The meter showed n dollars and 10 cents. He objected to paying. It was really a ridiculously large sum. He was not angry, because he knew he was not going to pay; moreover, the policeman who was right there took the patient's side.

The n dollars, he volunteered, represented the fee for his analytic hours, and the 10 cents the price of the bus fare he paid the day before to come to my office; his car was left in a garage for some repairs and he had to come by bus.

Another dream followed immediately: he was running away from some man; there were now two and then three people. When there were two, one of them was the patient himself as a little boy of six or seven. When there were three, one of them was the patient watching the chase of the little boy who was a stranger to him; the man looked "perhaps somewhat" like the analyst. There was a red light which seemed familiar, but he was unable to say any more about it than that. He was running very fast and was *really very frightened*; he finally ran into a bed, the man now was an ogre catching up with him, rushing toward him and finally leaning over him, apparently ready to harm him mortally. He was *terribly frightened*, and just at that moment he saw the ogre transformed: it was his father, with "nice soft lips," smiling; his skin was smooth, freshly shaven and powdered. He woke up.

This dream was told with the patient's usual equanimity, but with a flicker of interest unusual for him.

The bed was a double bed like the one in his parents' bedroom when he was little, or—was there a double bed?— he wondered. That light was familiar. The ogre leaning over him made him think of the crow that clipped the lip of Leonardo. He was unable to contribute any more in that hour, but he did mention the next day that he used to get frightened in the night when about six years old and go for protection to the parental bedroom; also, he asked his mother about that light and she said that there actually had been such a light in their house; it was in the hall leading to the bedroom.

Following this the patient reverted to his usual affectless intellectual musing throughout the analytic sessions. On one occasion, he said, he again experienced during a lecture the same "reaction" as when the "thalamic patient" was demonstrated, and at once he again recalled his head injury and his father with the steel knife, but it all lasted only a minute. Again he was asked whether he felt fear or any other emotion at that time, and he answered: "No, as before, it was purely physiological: my pulse rate increased and I began to breathe rapidly."

However, since this reaction was first displayed one could notice a change in the patient's demeanor—a change which came on very gradually, even imperceptibly; the patient became somewhat pensive, as it were; during the analytic hour he wondered a little why he did, or thought, or felt certain things.

We shall leave out of consideration the patient's many specific problems, which were so poignantly sketched by his behavior and dreams, since these, interesting as they are, are outside the scope of this paper. His castration fear, his homosexuality, his profound mother attachment, which was so deeply repressed—all played a paramount role in the major part of his analytic reaction, and as far as this psychological material and its constellations are concerned, our patient differed in no respect from a number of other familiar cases. What seems in this patient quite different from the usual clinical picture is his emotional reaction. Let us examine his affective responses a little more closely: once, in the street, he experienced a sense of fear which was strong enough to make him run; in other words, the content of his anxiety, be it in its frank or distorted form, was totally repressed, but it was close enough to the surface to set into play both affect and its motor accompaniment, and he was aware of both. In the dream in which he was being chased, he was also aware of his affect and its motor accompaniment, and this time the content of his anxiety appeared in a more or less distorted form: in the form of being chased and of a danger of being eaten up by an ogre (passive homosexual wishes), of feminizing his father (concealed incestuous wishes, castration of father, etc.), and of seeking refuge in what was apparently the parental bed (evidently an emotional reverberation of the primal scene). However, despite these hints that the dream gives to the patient's ego, he was unable when awake to muster up enough of affective continuity to live out and gain emotional insight into his problem. He revealed to a limited, but none the less convincing, extent how he succeeded in escaping with his affect: thus he related that only now and then was the man chasing the patient who at the moment was a little boy; most of the time, however, the patient himself remained an onlooker watching the chase of a little boy who was a stranger to him. In other words, in this dream his ego rejected the content of the anxiety successfully enough to display only affect and motor response. That he did this is clear; how he was able to do it is rather obscure. If we recall now his dream of the taxi driver, we shall again see how elastic the patient's method of escaping anxiety is. When he was running away from the ogre he would, as soon as the tension became too great, step out of the picture, as it were, and watch the whole scene as an outsider. Or else, when his hostility began to make itself known, he projected his castration hatred onto the taxi driver and threw himself under the protective wing of his homosexual wishes (policeman—law—father). But when castration anxiety (affect woven into ideational content) became too active, so that it broke into consciousness in the form of a screen memory, too transparent to be neglected by the ego, his motor system was the first to yield and by some tour de force he again succeeded in escaping: he felt no fear. At the risk of appearing repetitious, we shall state again: despite the simultaneous appearance in consciousness of the content of anxiety and the motor discharge of the *phenomenon of anxiety*, no subjective *feeling tone* could be observed or elicited. One is led at once to think of an incidental clinical lesson which this episode teaches, namely: the affect is at times so elusive that to avoid its coming out into the open the patient simulates, as it were, *its true motor expression* which, he hopes, as frequently happens in such cases, will be mistaken for real feeling. One is naturally tempted to construct some formula for this singular splitting up of certain affective reactions, but at first glance one fails to find an explanation for it, and hence one seems limited to the mere statement of this clinical fact. Then one thinks of the pleasure-pain principle and comes to the obvious conclusion that evidently this particular mode of splitting up of the affect into its components serves best to avoid psychic pain. This being the case the following questions arise: (1) if this is so, why do we not find this phenomenon more frequently, since this method appears much more simple and psychoeconomically more efficient than the ordinary method of compulsion-neurotic isolation or even that of conversion hysteria, and (2) in what respect does this method of avoiding the affect of anxiety differ from that of a conversion hysteria, since *la belle indifference des hysteriques* might also be achieved by means of respiratory, cardiovascular, and muscular conversion symptoms?

The very formulation of these questions leads us into

the field of clinical phenomenology and we cannot escape the impression that, simple as this method appears, it is really quite complex, for it suggests a warding off of anxiety despite the presence of the ideational content, and reducing it to its physiological skeleton; such a reaction appears to imply that the ideational content (in our case castration anxiety) is also isolated as in a compulsion neurosis, but it is isolated in a particular way, in that it becomes foreign to the ego despite its presence in consciousness, and it is reduced to the role of a simple internal stimulus which releases a purely physiological reaction. Evidently such a phenomenon becomes possible only when the whole mass of ideas and their representations, which are usually charged with a great deal of affect, are reduced to nothing more than a catalytic role in the production of the physiological response. In other words, to us the imagery of the bicycle and the wound on the head or leg may very well appear to be (as it fundamentally is) castration imagery, while to the patient it appeared as nothing more than an indefinite, even amorphous, "something" that automatically sets into play a set of very primitive cardiovascular and respiratory reactions *without content*.

If we limit ourselves for a moment to the purely phenomenological side of our patient's reaction, we cannot help being impressed with the so-called shallowness of the affect which he displayed and which is reminiscent of that shown by a goodly number of catatonics. It is not unusual to see early catatonics display sudden tensions, rapid breathing, and increase in cardiac rate, their eyes at the time remaining closed or staring at a fixed distant point. The attack over, such patients frequently quiet down, revert to their seemingly placid dullness, and occasionally even smile in a half-responsive, half-abstracted manner. Many such patients, in common with early depressive schizophrenias and very early so-called benign stupors, a short time before the stupor sets in appear perplexed, apprehensive, and tense. These states of depressive perplexity gradually go over into transitory attacks of anxiety reactions, of which only the physiological accompaniment can be observed, and then very gradually they enter a peaceful stupor. In this respect they differ radically from those who enter acute catatonic excitements or acute stupors, for the latter display frank and unmistakable anxiety states just before the onset of the catatonic attack proper. However, those who enter a stupor via a perplexity state, or a state of timidity and tension, reveal very little, if any, of their ideational content. It is only after their recovery from the stupor that a retrospective study of the main trends can be made—the imagery and affect which they had to face on the road from the early stages of the psychosis to the stupor.

We are quite justified in assuming that somewhere midway between the projection of one's total inner life into the outer world and this new outer (inner) world there is a moment when the individual perceives this inner world as an outer one and, rid as he is of his ego, he reacts to its demands, which are now coming from without, with an increase of tension. This is probably the meaning of the catatonic's peculiar physiological anxiety, during which the affect implied in the content of his ideation disappears, because this very ideation is no longer perceived as one's own—the cathexis has been withdrawn from it. This assumption, if it is correct, may possibly throw some light on the mysterious disappearance of the affect, i.e., of the feeling tone proper. The affect does not actually disappear; it is merely withdrawn from the ego and, the latter itself being disposed of, the sense of danger too disappears. In other words, the feeling tone of anxiety being essentially fear acting as a defensive measure for the ego, this fear itself becomes biologically unnecessary in the absence of the ego.

Our patient's impulsive running in the street, his irrational exclamation—"That's that"—followed by an impulsive start of his car, as if he were quite ready to run into someone or be run into, transgresses the average limits of purely neurotic behavior. He seemed to give cause to believe that he had reached a turning point in his analysis, sensing or even courting the possibility of developing a psychotic outcome. Such a possibility opened itself before him only after he had succeeded, for a moment at least, in regressing to the most primitive form of anxiety, i.e., its physiological prototype, even in the face of frank imagery of ideation and memories connected with castration. How— that is, by means of what mechanism—he achieved it, I am not prepared to say, but it is quite probable that we are dealing here with a potential catatonia, and it is not unlikely that his way of handling his anxiety is most typical of catatonia. If the hypothesis outlined above is in any respect correct, it would appear that a complete understanding of this phenomenon in many neurotics and so-called normals could be gained only by a detailed study of frankly catatonic material. We have been accustomed heretofore to draw upon neuroses for a deeper understanding of some psychoses. It becomes more apparent that the reverse procedure also becomes important, and that certain of our queries will have to be answered mostly by a detailed study of psychotic material.

THE PSYCHOLOGY OF PATHOS

ALFRED WINTERSTEIN AND EDMUND BERGLER

(1935)

Pathos is a quality in speech, writing, music, or artistic representation that excites a feeling of pity or sadness. This particular characteristic or modality with which certain individuals imbue their behavior, actions, and speech, however, makes one feel that one is in the presence of a strong, emotionally laden situation. This quality of intensification and elaboration of affective experiences imparts an unmistakable imprint to emotional expression.

The word "pathos" is originally from the Greek, meaning suffering or feeling. It has undergone numerous important changes in meaning over the centuries. As early as the sixteenth century it meant a pathetic (sad or pitiful) expression or utterance. In the following century it was used to signify the power of stirring tender or melancholy emotions. In addition, it has been associated over the centuries with the idea of something "inflated, vague, shallow, or rather spurious." In this early psychoanalytic paper the term is used "to signify a state of suffering, of being carried away by emotion . . . any vehement affect underlying this mode of expression."

Winterstein and Bergler's article on pathos remained the only article on this emotional quality for over 40 years, until the appearance of Alexander's excellent paper in 1973. While noting the merit of Winterstein and Bergler's contribution,

Alexander comments that the German word "pathos" has a somewhat different meaning from the English equivalent. To Alexander, it is "an affect of adult life, at least in its fully developed form" (p. 122). In his opinion, in order to exist at all, pathos requires a certain amount of tranquility and seriousness, and one's ability to feel pathos tends to preserve the capacity for tenderness. "It elevates the quality of object relationships . . . produces gentleness in depth . . . is not a reaction formation . . . but is the fused product of sublimation in the libidinal sphere and of neutralization in the sphere of the aggressive drive energies . . ." (p. 124). It also serves to ward off more painful affects and affective states, according to Alexander. In my clinical experience I have commonly encountered pathos as part of the affective release during severe regressive states in psychoanalytic therapy.

In the following contribution to our psychoanalytic knowledge of the affects, the authors point out that the genesis of the quality of pathos does not occur until or near the onset of puberty. Pathos, "even the genuine uninhibited pathos of a man whose sense of justice has been wounded, owes the vehemence of its expression, and perhaps all possibility of its expression, to the repressed unconscious layer of hate which belongs to the pubertal period." In later life, the pathetic reaction serves the purpose of mastering the sense of guilt within both hate impulses and incestuous wishes, or more correctly, according to the authors, the helplessness that springs from the latter. The return of the repressed hatred is expressed as pathos.

In pathos there is an endopsychic reversal of roles by means of projection; the ego assumes the role of the superego and reduces the object of its aggression to the status of an ego.

There are two aspects to pathos: a masochistic *aspect and a* pathetic *one, the former being the martyr type and the latter the accuser type. In the struggle between egoistic interests and superego ideals, the conflict is dealt with masochistically, the ego deriving, in addition, a secondary gain from its "good behavior." Thus, an ego-syntonic emotion from higher levels is exalted, but its pathetic expression betrays its connection with the deeper layer of the repressed Oedipus complex.*

In their article the authors refer to Bergler's extensive work, "The Psychology of the Cynic" (1933) which, in a general sense, appears to be a contrasting form of behavior. This valuable monograph on cynicism has been recently translated (1975) into English by Hella Freud Bernays.

The word "pathos" ordinarily signifies lofty expression in speech of a passionate emotion. But inasmuch as emotion and its expression in words overlap one another, the word pathos, signifying the state of suffering, of being carried away by emotion, is used to describe any vehement affect underlying this mode of expression, and in particular a mood of solemnity and exaltation. Pathos is not unknown, either, in music, architecture, painting, and plastic art. The idea of it is readily associated with the notion of something inflated, vague, shallow, and rather spurious; the type of person with little command of expression mostly regards the pathetic individual as half a lunatic, half a comedian.

We do not apply the term "pathos" to describe the behavior of children. True pathos only really develops with the onset of puberty; when pathos marks a child's conversation, it leaves us with the impression of an imitation, of something "secondhand." This is in agreement with what clinical observations concerning the genesis of pathos reveal.

It is not rare to find children already reacting to reproaches which, whether justified or not, are felt as a narcissistic wound, by adopting the same tone and automatically repeating them ("turning the tables": "It is you, not I": projection onto others). After the superego has been set up as the internalized representative of the parents, its reproaches evoke the same pathetic reaction in response; for the super-ego likewise converses with the ego in pathetic tones. One may say that the ordinary language in which the superego converses with the ego is in the main pathetic.

It is necessary to note the fact, in itself a surprising one, that every reproach, no matter how nonsensical, evokes in the average man as a defense a reaction of pathos in some form: say, of abuse, leveled at the "enemy," or of indigna-tion at him. This state of affairs, in which reproaches, justified and unjustified, arouse a pathetic reaction, remains exactly the same whether the defense takes direct visible form or is masked by indifference; whether it is loudly voiced, occurs as a thought, or remains a purely unconscious process. This indignation is logically so much the more difficult to understand, since every man's continued experi-ence of the aggression of his fellows against himself must have led to its disappearance—if only by a process of hardening.

The explanation of the fact that, as we constantly see, attacks provoke an *inner* reaction of pathos ("the skunk!"; "the dirty crook!"; etc.) even in the most insensitive indi-viduals, is to be found in the *endopsychic* situation. The superego, in its chronic state of readiness to cast reproaches, makes full use of every opportunity for reproaching the anxiety-ridden ego. One of the ego's methods of defense consists in the projection of these reproaches onto the object, the innocent-guilty complainant. Accordingly, the pathetic type treats his object as aggressively as his superego does his ego. The advantage of this displacement onto an object consists in establishing the fiction that one's indignation is justified, and in converting an internal conflict into one which is external, projected, and so more easily resolved. Thus everyone reacts pathetically to the attacks of the external world, but this results from the economic opportunities available in this way for endopsychic discharge, and is not due to the presence of real grounds for indignation.

The origin of the pathetic voice of the superego in that of the teacher is confirmed by a beautiful example given by Melanie Klein (1932) in her book *The Psychoanalysis of Children* (p. 49). Peter, a boy of four and a half, who practiced mutual masturbation with his brother, during one of his hours put two pencils on a sponge and said: "This is the boat that Fritz (his younger brother) and I got in." He then put on a deep voice—as he often did when his superego came into action—and shouted at the two pencils: "You're not to go about together all the time and do disgusting things." This scolding on the part of his superego at his brother and himself was also, as Melanie Klein adds, aimed at his parents, whose equally forbidden activities he had secretly observed, and who must surely have originally leveled remonstrances of the kind at him (mechanism of projection).

During the period of puberty, when the ego has to bear the full brunt of the superego's reproaches on account of its Oedipus wishes, its greater strength now enables it to deal with the conflict by resorting to aggression, rebelling against the oppressor and assailing him with words ("It is you who are guilty"), which, owing to the increased volume of hate, now have the character of true pathos, and are no longer merely a childlike imitation of it. Verbal aggression as a means of disposing of the superego conflict (pathetic re-action) serves also in later life the purpose of mastering the sense of guilt rooted in hate impulses and incestuous wishes, or more correctly, the helplessness which springs from it. It does so in the form of a return of the repressed hatred as pathos; genital guilt has become wholly inaccessible to consciousness. What occurs in pathos is, so to say, an *endopsychic reversal of roles by means of projection.* A reproach emanating from the superego or taken over by it from the external world is dealt with in such a way that the ego assumes the part of the superego and reduces the object of its aggression to the status of an ego. As Jones (1929a) has explained in his paper on "Fear, Guilt and Hate," this process is made possible by creating a fantasy of the other person being in the wrong, or by maneuvering reality so as to bring this about. Accordingly, even the genuine uninhibited pathos of a man whose sense of justice has been wounded owes the vehemence of its expression, and perhaps all possibility of expression, to the repressed unconscious layer of hate which belongs to the pubertal period.

But besides the *aggressive* solution of the superego conflict, which in the last resort is employed to relieve the burden arising from the sense of guilt, there is also a *masochistic* one, distinguished by the pathos of surrender, the pathos of the martyr. We could speak of an "accuser" type of pathos and a "martyr" type. The utterances of those whose devotion to the powers above them is such that they are ready to lay down life itself also reveal a strong and genuine pathos. Self-dedication to God, country, or party, to a group or union, all allegiance to a compelling idea, is the projection of the ego's submission to the superego. In these cases, as has been said, the conflict is dealt with masochistically, and the ego derives in addition a secondary gain from its "good behavior." Even here, the ego-syntonic emotion from the higher levels, which urges to exalted and pathetic expression, betrays its connection with the deeper layer of repressed Oedipus complex, and this time with the inverted, negative form. The joyful surrender to a mightier power, to a Higher Will, derives its energy from the tender feminine relation of the boy toward his father (mother identification). Perhaps Nietzsche, who speaks of the "pathos of distance," the distance between subject and object (ultimately between child and father), wished so to give expression to this masochistic aspect of pathos.

Besides the *genuine* pathos which carries conviction, there is also a theatrical, spurious variety, a kind of affected and overstrained adolescent pathos. Here it is not always so much the emotion itself as its apparent intensity, urging toward expression in pathos, which is responsible for the observer's impression of something spurious. This heightened intensity will then be serving an urgent need to "make oneself felt," an attempt to compensate for a sense of impotence actually deeply felt.

Occasionally we encounter a diametrically opposed type, whom we could well designate as "antipathetic." Pathos has a uniformly distressing effect on him. Here we have to do with individuals who ward off an original tendency to pathetic reaction; they have repressed it, then, evidently on account of their anxiety of their sadistic superego. This anxiety (in the last resort castration anxiety) has the result that both variants of pathos, the "accuser" type and the "martyr" type, cease to be available as mechanisms of defense against the superego, so that other methods have to be found. One frequently adopted is the "mechanism of cynicism." As was pointed out by one of the authors (Bergler, 1933), the cynic is faced with the same problem of dealing with a superego conflict. The cynic is subjected to the constant pressure of his ambivalence and—grotesque as it may sound—to the equally constant pressure of his punishing superego, whose prohibitions relate to this very ambivalence, so that the unconscious compulsion to confess becomes the mainspring of action. The ego of the cynic frees itself from this conflict by "turning the tables," by showing to the rest of the world (the despised "other fellows") that this forbidden ambivalence is to be found in them too. Implicit in all cynicism is the challenge to the listener: "Confess that in your heart you think exactly the same as the cynic who rouses your indignation." Here, the "other fellows" are conceived as a part of one's own superego. At the same time, this demonstration of the ambivalence in others is a means of forestalling the attack that is expected as a punishment from the external world, the latter being perceived by the individual as part of his own superego. It is indeed a peculiar war on two fronts which the individual carries on against his superego, which appears in a double shape: as the internal unconscious conscience and as the external world. The cynic's onslaught appears to be aimed at this external world aspect of the superego; but in reality he is defending himself against his severe internal superego, which is beyond the reach of his consciousness and is only perceived as a sense of guilt. The rabidity of the cynic does not proceed simply from aggression; it is equally the expression of his desperate struggle to ward off his "inner foe," the endopsychic superego, and he sees to it that the contest is carried out on "foreign soil." The cynic treats the external world with the same severity as his superego treats his ego; and at the same time he is attacking his own superego in the external world.

It would seem that the tendency which we often find in people to pathetic expression is a reaction formation springing from a powerful, but suppressed, pleasure in uttering obscene words (also from anal and urethral erotism). We can understand that the communicating link is provided by curses, imprecations, and blasphemies, as constituting ways of effecting discharge of affect by means of words, for the words here in question are drawn from the opposite poles which lead from all that is most sacred and sublime to all that is most proscribed and accursed. Once more we are left with an obeisance to the superego—"good behavior" of a precautionary and compensatory kind.

While the pathetic sees tragedy everywhere, the humorist refuses to take reality seriously. In pathos, the ego deals with a reproach emanating from the superego by means of an endopsychic reversal of roles on projective lines: the ego is cast for the aggressive role of superego and forces the object to take the part of ego. In humor, according to Freud, the superego receives a hypercathexis and speaks to the intimidated ego in kindly words, discounting with a smile the dangers which threaten it. In pathos, the resolution of the conflict between ego and superego proceeds from the ego; in humor, the first step toward reconciliation is taken by the superego. Humor denies the claims of the external world, which menace the individual's narcissism, and as a manifestation of regression it approaches more nearly to the *primary* narcissistic stage; the pathos of the "accuser" type presupposes the differentiation of a strengthened ego from the external world. Here the narcissism is secondary. The case seems to be different for the masochistic pathos of the "martyr" type, in which secondary narcissism joyfully abdicates in favor of the original narcissistic all-oneness. In this instance, the little ego is absorbed into a higher unity, and the regressive process is more profound than in the humorous attitude.

We also speak of pathos in connection with other forms of art. Pathos is a case of intensified expression, and, indeed, intensification or exaggeration is postulated as a general requirement of artistic expression by many people. So far as relates to pathos in the plastic arts, nowhere does it pour forth in such abundance as from the sublime Renaissance sculptures of Michaelangelo, full to overflowing with life—we sense the passionate, heavily charged, turbulent emotion, a sustained fortissimo of expression; but occasionally, too, as in the creations of baroque art, an exaggerated fullness of life, a theatrical pathos; a tendency toward extremes of pathos in the use of color and gesture characterizes Expressionism, which, as its very name reveals, aims at the *expression* of states of mind. The father of this modern art movement is that great and remarkable painter of the late Middle Ages, Matthias Grünewald, many of whose pictures produce an affect of pathos to the point of distortion.

Our investigations have brought us to the conclusion that pathos constitutes a technique of defense employed by the ego in its endopsychic struggle with the superego. The "accuser" and "martyr" types of pathetic both deal with a conflict between ego and superego, but along different lines: the former chooses projection and aggression, and the latter submission and masochistic self-surrender. But it seems that pathos is *not merely* the passive *reaction* of the ego to an attack proceeding from the superego. It also includes *aggression* on the part of the ego as a measure of precaution against the superego. It is not rare for the superego, by reason of the ego's interpolation of the "mechanism of pathos," to find itself deprived of one of its most useful weapons of attack against the ego. That, moreover, is why the pathetic "beating one's breast" in which the ordinary citizen indulges is such an excellent means of self-deception.

ABSENCE OF GRIEF

HELENE DEUTSCH

(1937)

Helene Deutsch, first analyzed by Freud and then by Abraham, and a founder of the Vienna Psychoanalytic Institute in 1925, has written on a wide diversity of theoretical and clinical subjects. Two years after her migration to Boston from Vienna in 1935, she published this short, important, clinical paper, which was dedicated to a recently mourned and beloved friend.

Her paper deals with the affect of grief and the defenses against this affect; thus, its succinct title does not adequately reflect its scope.

That an affect may be completely repressed is an everyday clinical observation. But what is often overlooked are the causative connections between symptoms in adulthood and events involving loss occurring in childhood, in which grief and mourning have been repressed. In many such instances there may be an apparently "mature" acceptance of a loss. What Deutsch makes unmistakably clear is that in some manner and at some time the affect of grief must be expressed.

There are three possible reactions to loss. The first is to experience grief, that is, to engage in a reactive expression of feeling. The second is to repress it, resulting in an omission of an affect. The third possibility is that grief may be expressed in a disguised unconscious form at a much later time, e.g., the development of hypochondriacal complaints, obsessional behavior, apparently unmotivated weeping, etc.

73

Thus grief may be hidden from awareness through the use of various psychic mechanisms such as projection of emotions onto others, displacement, acting out of a sense of guilt, and even in criminal behavior. Illustrative of the latter, Dostoevsky's character Raskolnikov in Crime and Punishment *may be correctly viewed as the "pale criminal"—guilty before the crime is committed and driven to it by an unconscious need for punishment secondary to unresolved guilt feelings arising from childhood loss and aggression.*

Clearly Deutsch's paper, as well as several others in this volume (see Zilboorg, Zetzel, Sperling, Deutsch) demonstrates that the study of the absence of affects or disturbances of affects themselves is of equal importance with understanding the full expression of emotions.

Mourning as a process is a concept introduced by Freud (1917), who considers it a normal function of bereaved individuals, by which the libido invested in the lost love object is gradually withdrawn and redirected toward living people and problems.

It is well recognized that the work of mourning does not always follow a normal course. It may be excessively intense, even violent, or the process may be unduly prolonged to the point of chronicity when the clinical picture suggests melancholia.

If the work of mourning is excessive or delayed, one might expect to find that the binding force of the positive ties to the lost object had been very great. My experience corroborates Freud's finding that the degree of persisting ambivalence is a more important factor than the intensity of the positive ties. In other words, the more rigorous the earlier attempts to overcome inimical impulses toward the now lost object, the greater will be the difficulties encountered in the retreat from that ultimately achieved position.

Psychoanalytic findings indicate that guilt feelings toward the lost object, as well as ambivalence, may disturb the normal course of mourning. In such cases, the reaction to death is greatly intensified, assuming a brooding, neurotically compulsive, even melancholic character. Indeed, the reaction may be so extreme as to culminate in suicide.

Psychoanalyic observation of neurotic patients frequently reveals a state of severe anxiety replacing the normal process of mourning. This is interpreted as a regressive process and constitutes another variation of the normal course of mourning.

It is not my purpose to dwell at length upon any of the above-mentioned reactions. Instead, I wish to present observations from cases in which the reaction to the loss of a beloved object is the antithesis of these—a complete absence of the manifestations of mourning. My convictions are: first, that the death of a beloved person must produce reactive expression of feeling in the normal course of events; second, that omission of such reactive responses is to be considered just as much a variation from the normal as excess in time or intensity; and third, that unmanifested grief will be found expressed to the full in some way or other.

Before proceeding to my cases, I wish to recall the phenomenon of indifference which children so frequently display following the death of a loved person. Two explanations have been given for this so-called heartless behavior: intellectual inability to grasp the reality of death, and inadequate formation of object relationship. I believe that neither of these explanations has exclusive validity. Should an intellectual concept of death be lacking, the fact of separation must still provoke some type of reaction. It is also true that although the capacity for an ultimate type of object relationship does not exist, some stage of object relationship has been achieved. My hypothesis is that the ego of the child is not sufficiently developed to bear the strain of the work of mourning and that it therefore utilizes some mechanism of narcissistic self-protection to circumvent the process.

This mechanism, whose nature we are unable to define more clearly, may be a derivative of the early infantile anxiety which we know as the small child's reaction to separation from the protecting and loving person. The children of whom we are to speak, however, were already of a sufficiently advanced age when the loss occurred that suffering and grief were to be expected in place of anxiety. If grief should threaten the integrity of the ego, or, in other words, if the ego should be too weak to undertake the elaborate function of mourning, two courses are possible: first, that of infantile regression expressed as anxiety, and second, the mobilization of defense forces intended to protect the ego from anxiety and other psychic dangers. The most extreme expression of this defense mechanism is the omission of affect. It is of great interest that observers of children note that the ego is rent asunder in those children who do not employ the usual defenses, and who mourn as an adult does. Under certain circumstances an analogous reaction occurs in adults, and the ego has recourse to similar defense mechanisms. The observations serve to show that under certain conditions forces of defense must be set in operation to protect a vitally threatened ego, when the painful load exceeds a threshold limit. Whether these defense mechanisms are called into operation depends upon the opposition of two forces: the relative strengths of the on-rushing affects, and of the ego in meeting the storm. If the intensity of the affects is too great, or if the ego is relatively weak, the aid of defensive and rejecting mechanisms is invoked. In the first instance, quantitative considerations are of greater importance; in the second, special circumstances render the ego incapable of working through the mourning process. This might be the case, for example, should the ego at the time of the loss be subjected to intense cathexis on some other account. For instance, the ego might be in a state of exhaustion by virtue of some painful occurrence just preceding the loss or, conversely, be engrossed in some narcissistically satisfying situation. In brief, if the free energies of the ego have been reduced by previous withdrawals for other interests, the residual energy is unable to cope with the exigent demands of mourning.

We speak then of a relative weakness of the adult ego induced through experiences, as compared with the child's ego which is weak by virtue of the stage of its development. We assume, therefore, that a particular constellation within the ego is responsible for the absence of a grief reaction; on the one hand the relative inadequacy of the free and unoccupied portion of the ego, and on the other hand a protective mechanism proceeding from the narcissistic cathexis of the ego.

But all considerations of the nature of the forces which prevent affect are hypothetical and lead into the dark realms of speculation. The questions—whether the psychic apparatus can really remain permanently free from expressions of suffering, and what is the further fate of the omitted grief— may be better answered by direct clinical methods.

Among my patients there have been several who had previously experienced a great loss and who exhibited this default of affect. I should like to present their stories briefly.

CASE 1

The first case is that of a young man of nineteen. Until the death of his mother, when he was five years old, this patient had been a very much petted youngster, with an affectionate and undisturbed attachment to his mother and with no special neurotic difficulties. When she died, he showed no grief whatsoever. Within the family this apparently "heartless" behavior was never forgotten. After his mother's death he went to live with his grandmother, where he continued to be a thriving, healthy child.

His analysis revealed no special conflicts in his early childhood which could explain his affective behavior. He could remember from his early years having been angry with his mother for leaving him, but this anger did not exceed the normal ambivalent reaction common to children under similar circumstances. The young man brought no other material which could throw light on the unemotional behavior of his childhood. His later life, however, revealed certain features which indicated the fate of the rejected affect. Two characteristics of his behavior were particularly striking: he complained of depression which had first appeared without apparent cause during puberty and which had recurred with no comprehensible motivation, and he was struck by the fact that he could break off friendships, and love relationships, with amazing ease, without feeling any regret or pain. He was, moreover, aware of no emotional disturbance so long as the relationships lasted.

These facts rendered comprehensible the fate of the repressed affect in childhood. Lack of emotion repeatedly recurred in analogous situations, and the rejected affect was held in reserve for subsequent appearances as "unmotivated depressions." The service performed by the postulated defense mechanism was purely in the interest of the helpless little ego, and contented itself with a displacement in time and a dynamic distribution of the mourning.

CASE 2

A thirty-year-old man came into analysis for the treatment of severe neurotic organic symptoms of purely hysterical character and, in addition, a compulsive weeping which occurred from time to time without adequate provocation. He was already grown up when his very dearly loved mother died. When the news of her death reached him, in a distant university city, he departed at once for the funeral but found himself incapable of any emotion whatsoever, either on the journey or at the funeral. He was possessed by a tormenting indifference despite all his efforts to bring forth some feeling. He forced himself to recall the most treasured memories of his mother, of her goodness and devotion, but was quite unable to provoke the suffering he wanted to feel. Subsequently he could not free himself from the tormenting self-reproach of not having mourned, and often reviewed the memory of his beloved mother in the hope that he might weep.

The mother's death came at a time in the patient's life when he was suffering from severe neurotic difficulties: inadequate potency, difficulties in studying, and insufficient activity in all situations. The analysis revealed that he was having severe inner conflicts in relation to his mother. His strong infantile attachment to her had led to an identification with her which had provided the motive for his passive attitude in life. The remarkable reaction to his mother's death was conditioned by several factors. In his childhood there had been a period of intense hate for the mother which was revived in puberty. His conscious excessive affection for his mother, his dependence upon her and his identification with her in a feminine attitude, were the neurotic outcome of this relationship.

In this case, it was particularly clear that the real death had mobilized the most infantile reaction, "She has left me," with all its accompanying anger. The hate impulses which had arisen in a similar situation of disappointment in his childhood were revived and, instead of an inner awareness of grief, there resulted a feeling of coldness and indifference due to the interference of the aggressive impulse.

But the fate of the omitted grief is the question of chief interest for us in the analytic history of this patient. His feeling of guilt toward his mother, which betrayed itself even in conscious self-reproaches, found abundant gratification in severe organic symptoms through which the patient, in his identification with his mother, repeated her illness year after year. The compulsive weeping was the subsequent expression of the affect which had been isolated from the concept— "the death of mother."

The identification with the mother which was such a preponderant factor in the libidinal economy of our patient was perhaps the most important motive for the refusal of the ego to grieve, because the process of mourning was in great danger of passing over into a state of melancholia which might effect a completion of the identity with the dead mother through suicide. When the analysis succeeded in bringing the patient into the situation of omitted affect, the danger of suicide became very actual. So we see that in this neurotic individual there developed, in addition to the existing pathological emotional conflict, a process of defense serving as protection to the severely threatened ego.

CASE 3

A man in his early thirties without apparent neurotic difficulties came into analysis for nontherapeutic reasons. He showed complete blocking of affect without the slightest insight. In his limitless narcissism he viewed his lack of emotion as "extraordinary control." He had no love relationships, no friendships, no real interests of any sort. To all kinds of experiences he showed the same dull and apathetic reaction. There was no endeavor and no disappointment. For the fact that he had so little success in life he always found well-functioning mechanisms of comfort from which, paradoxically enough, he always derived narcissistic satisfaction. There were no reactions of grief at the loss of individuals near to him, no unfriendly feelings, and no aggressive impulses.

This patient's mother had died when he was five years old. He reacted to her death without any feeling. In his later life, he had repressed not only the memory of his mother but also of everything else preceding her death.

From the meager childhood material brought out in the slow, difficult, analytic work, one could discover only negative and aggressive attitudes toward his mother, especially during the forgotten period, which were obviously related to the birth of a younger brother. The only reaction of longing for his dead mother betrayed itself in a fantasy, which persisted through several years of his childhood. In the fantasy he left his bedroom door open in the hope that a large dog would come to him, be very kind to him, and fulfill all his wishes. Associated with this fantasy was a vivid childhood memory of a bitch which had left her puppies alone and helpless because she had died shortly after their birth.

Apart from this one revealing fantasy there was no trace of longing or mourning for his mother. The ego's efforts of rejection had succeeded too well and had involved the entire emotional life. The economic advantage of the defense had had a disadvantageous effect. With the tendency to block out unendurable emotions, the baby was, so to speak, thrown out with the bath water, for positive happy experiences as well were sacrificed in the complete paralysis. This condition for the permanent suppression of *one* group of affects was the death of the *entire* emotional life.

CASE 4

This was a middle-aged woman without symptoms but with a curious disturbance in her emotional life. She was

capable of the most affectionate friendships and love relationships, but only in situations where they could not be
realized. She had the potentiality for positive and negative
feelings, but only under conditions which subjected her and
her love objects to disappointment. For no apparent reason
the patient wept bitterly at the beginning of every analytic
hour. The weeping, not obsessional in character, was quite
without content. In actual situations which should produce
sadness, she showed strikingly "controlled" emotionless
behavior. Under analytic observation the mechanism of her
emotional reactions gradually became clear. A direct
emotional reaction was impossible. Everything was experienced in a complicated way by means of displacements,
identifications, and projections in the manner of the "primary processes" described by Freud (1900) in *The Interpretation of Dreams.* For example: the patient was highly
educated and had a definite psychological gift. She was very
much interested in the psychic life of others, made a study of
it, and used to bring detailed reports of her observations. On
investigation one discovered that what she had observed in
the experience of another individual did not really pertain to
him but represented a projection of her own unconscious
fantasies and reactions. The true connection was not recognized for want of a conscious emotional reaction.

She found vicarious emotional expression through
identification, especially with sad experiences of others. The
patient was capable of suffering a severe depression because
something unpleasant happened to somebody else. She
reacted with the most intense sorrow and sympathy, particularly in cases of illness and death affecting her circle of
friends. In this form of experience we could trace the displacement of her own rejected affects.

I am inclined to regard this type of emotional disturbance as schizoid, and have the impression that it is a not

infrequent type of reaction, which in its milder form usually passes unnoticed.

In the analysis of our patient one could discover how the displaced emotional discharges were related to early unresolved experiences. The original grievous experience was not a death but a loss in the divorce of her parents.

It gradually became clear that she had actually sought out the situations in which she had an opportunity to share the unhappiness of others, and that she even felt a certain envy because the misfortune had happened to another and not to herself. In such instances one is inclined to think only of masochistic tendencies as responsible. Certainly the gratification of masochism must play a role.

Observation of this patient, however, directed my attention in another direction. I believe that every unresolved grief is given expression in some form of other. For the present I limit the application of this *striving for realization* to mourning, and am convinced that the unresolved process of mourning as described by Freud (1917) must in some way be expressed in full. This striving to live out the emotional may be so strong as to have an effect analogous to the mechanism which we see in criminal behavior from feelings of guilt (Freud, 1923), where a crime is committed to satisfy unconscious guilt feelings, which preceded the crime instead of following it. Analogous is the situation in which suppressed affect following a loss seeks realization subsequently. We must assume that the urge to realization succeeds under the impetus of an unconscious source of affect energy, exactly as in the case of the criminal who is at the mercy of his guilt feelings. I suspect that many life stories which seem to be due to a masochistic attitude are simply the result of such strivings for the realization of unresolved affects. Our last-mentioned patient was a particularly clear example of this assumption.

The process of mourning as reaction to the real loss of a loved person *must be carried to completion.* As long as the early libidinal or aggressive attachments persist, the painful affect continues to flourish, and vice versa, the attachments are unresolved as long as the affective process of mourning has not been accomplished.

Whatever the motive for the exclusion of the affect—its unendurability because of the ego's weakness, as in children, its submission to other claims on the ego, especially through narcissistic cathexis, as in my first case, or its absence because of a previously existing conflict with the lost object; whatever the form of its expression—in clearly pathological or in disguised form, displaced, transformed, hysteriform, obsessional, or schizoid—in each instance the quantity of the painful reaction intended for the neglected direct mourning must be mastered.

I have already postulated a regulator, the nature of which is not clear to me. I have thought that an inner awareness of inability to master emotion, that is, the awareness by the ego of its inadequacy, was the motive power for the rejection of the emotion or, as the case may be, for its displacement.

In any case, the expediency of the flight from the suffering of grief is but a temporary gain, because, as we have seen, the necessity to mourn persists in the psychic apparatus. The law of the conservation of energy seems to have its parallel in psychic events. Every individual has at his disposal a certain quantity of emotional energy. The way in which emotional impulses are assimilated and discharged differs in each individual and plays its part in the formation of the personality.

Probably the inner rejection of painful experience is always active, especially in childhood. One might assume that the very general tendency to "unmotivated" depressions is the subsequent expression of emotional reactions which were once withheld and have since remained in latent readiness for discharge.

LAUGHTER AS AN EXPRESSIVE PROCESS: CONTRIBUTIONS TO THE PSYCHO-ANALYSIS OF EXPRESSIVE BEHAVIOR

Ernst Kris

(1940)

In this scholarly paper one can readily perceive the kernels of some of Kris's later creative work, which occupied three decades of clinical research. His aim was to examine the contribution psychoanalysis can make to the understanding of expressive processes, in this case laughter. He defined expression itself as "the speech of human countenance."

Kris, attempting to answer the question "When does one laugh?", addressed himself to two central issues: laughter as a social act and the control of laughter. Laughter breaks out when a sum of psychic energy "which had been employed for the cathexis of certain psychic trends suddenly becomes unusable." Telling a joke affects the listener as an invitation to common aggression and common regression. "Laughter indicates in a double sense mutual understanding and mutual guilt."

Kris points out that sometimes our ego is in opposition to laughter, and we try to control it by making a "serious face." Such suppression produces an artificial expression, a special kind of rigidity. We also subjugate the desire to laugh by producing a smile.

Kris describes some typical disturbances of laughing and smiling. Among these is a particularly artificial and empty smile which one sees in dancers and acrobats. This smile is a mask, a substitutive act, recognizable as such because it forces aside another expression, that of exertion. When we attempt to be sympathetic over someone's affliction and our face becomes awkward and embarrassed, there is a "derailment of the pathognomy." This is due to the failure to interdict contradictory impulses, the intended impulse and the one that breaks through.

Kris describes a patient who is afflicted with psychogenic compulsive laughter. The unconscious meaning of this symptom was the feeling of superiority. But in addition, it was a defense against anxiety. "I need not be afraid. It is laughable. I laugh so I am not afraid for he who laughs is powerful, strong, and superior." Furthermore, it can be a deeper defense against anxiety: "Look at me and see how I laugh. A fool like me who is always laughing is a very harmless person." In this connection one of my patients, an acrobat and gymnast, ascribed his survival in a Nazi concentration camp to his playing the fool, performing calisthenics atop high and dangerous places, to the laughter and merriment of his captors.

I can confirm the truth of Kris's statement "how narrow the dividing line is which separates the expressions of opposite affects," such as laughter and grief. I have frequently had occasion to observe the facial reaction of those responding to the tragic news of a loved one's death. The initial reaction was almost indistinguishable from imminent laughter, but almost immediately a more appropriate expression took its place.

FORMULATION OF THE PROBLEM

It is possible to distinguish two formulations of the problem in regard to the psychology of laughter. One examines the occasion and cause of laughter and the underlying question runs: "*When* does one laugh?"; the other examines laughter as a physical process and the underlying question is: "*How* does one laugh?" The first question has as its focus the psychology of the comic, and the second the facts of physiology and anatomy. Laughter as a physical process, and more precisely as an *expressive* process, will form the starting point of this paper, but a choice must be made out of the problems in this field and some things must be omitted which would otherwise stand in the foreground. For our aim is to examine, by means of this example, what contribution psychoanalytic considerations can make to the understanding of expressive processes; it is clear that the scope of those considerations is only a limited one and cannot cover the whole subject.

The expression of the human countenance and its play of feature have a mysterious power. They play a decisive role in the contact between man and man, always confronting us with the riddle: what is the relation between man's appearance and his personality? In every field of psychological research, approaches to this question have been sought. Psychoanalysis too has contributed to such attempts: the countenance of a predominantly anal or oral person has been described by a successful use of intuition (Abraham, 1921). But we do not intend to pursue such attempts here; what we shall deal with is not the characterological side of expressive behavior, but expressive activity itself and the course it takes.

When seeking orientation with regard to the expressive behavior of another person, one uses two kinds of data: his unintentional reactions to stimuli and the signals he makes to his fellow men, because only a part of his expressive behavior is directed toward the other person, whereas the whole of it is perceived by the latter and serves the purposes of social contact. Expression as a means of contact is called "the speech of the human countenance." We venture on such a comparison not in order to demarcate the line between the verbal and the pathognomic giving of information, but because this comparison offers a useful approach for a survey of the problems which pathognomy presents to science and the scope of our limited subject can be defined with its help. We distinguish at the outset between *linguistic* questions and those concerning the *history of speech*. We may ascribe to the latter the researches of Darwin, who tried to discover how pathognomy had developed in the course of human evolution as a medium of communication, a question concerning the prehistory of expressive behavior. But even since its establishment the speech of the human countenance has certainly not been without its history. It became differentiated according to age, social position, race, and period, in the same way as speech through human gesture, of which it is regarded as the most universal part. Compared with these questions of prehistory and history, those of the linguistic branch of research would seem somewhat more modest. One can direct one's research to the vocabulary of pathognomic speech, to the *types* of pathognomic expression, and, in the case of laughter, to types and subtypes of laughter; the answering of these questions falls into a descriptive or classifying field of work. A further investigation can be made of the *grammar* of pathognomy, where the question is one of the method of formation of each separate pathognomic act, and in the case of laughter, the method by which it arises as a bodily, and, in particular, as a pathognomic process, which concerns the anatomy and physiology of pathognomy. Finally, one can investigate the *syntax* into which the vocabulary and grammar of pathognomy are fitted. This question, which relates to the central regulation of the pathognomic processes, will be in the foreground of our discussions, while others can only be incidentally touched upon.

My aim is to give an exposition of the operation of the ego in the phenomenon of expression and this will be exemplified by references to the process of laughter.

The Ego and Laughter

LAUGHTER AS A SOCIAL ACT

Let us consider first a concrete situation, by analyzing which we shall try to proceed step by step to a more general understanding. Some people are in a room together and in one part of it laughing begins; it spreads and becomes a social act. We then look for an explanation of the phenomenon; we shall try to give it step by step, without avoiding detours, and yet without being able to complete it in one important point.

Laughter breaks out, according to Freud's theories, which have been confirmed again and again, when a sum of psychic energy which has been employed for the cathexis of certain psychic trends suddenly becomes unusable. What use can we make of this theory for our problem?

Let us start with a special case, that of some kind of occasion which provokes a common outburst of laughter among some people whom we are watching—the telling of a joke perhaps. This is a familiar example which we know from Freud's description: the communication of an experience or the mutual experience of the comic through the telling of a joke affects the listener like an invitation to common aggression and common regression. One part of the psychic energy which is freed—if we consider an aggressive joke, for instance—comes from the saving of an expenditure of energy for repression, the other part, the pleasure gain, comes from a common regression and common utilization of infantile modes of thought. The pleasure gain from regression shows us that the adult requires a certain cathexis, i.e., expenditure of energy, to curb in himself the way of working of the primary process, which breaks through in the infantile modes of thought contained in the comic of adults. And so laughter indicates in a double sense mutual understanding and mutual guilt.

To apply this to our example: the united action which takes place within the human group, the group formation in laughing, is to be understood as a joint way of reacting. This seems to be in accordance with the fact that when someone joins a laughing group, as a stranger to it, he becomes acutely conscious of being an outsider. He cannot join in the laughter when the others laugh; for them anything is good enough to laugh at, everything adds to their mirth; to him, the things that amuse them seem senseless and stupid; he has not made the intellectual regression with them, and it will be some time before he can adjust himself and then, in laughing, become part of the laughing group.

But how does it happen that an alliance is formed between those who laugh—that laughter becomes a group situation? Can we hope to find an answer that will satisfy us by means of this illustration of telling jokes? An argument against this is provided by simple observation: in a group situation one may join in the laugh without quite knowing what the laughter is about, in fact without even knowing anything about it at all. At this point laughter is not necessarily a reaction to a common stimulus. The laughter of the group no longer requires a "butt" to laugh at, it can itself represent both content and sealing of the pact. The motive for laughing will sink into the background in this way, as the mass tie becomes sufficiently strengthened, at the same time that the controlling and inhibiting function of the individual becomes restricted. Every weakening of the ego can hasten this condition, a slight intoxication being the most certain method.

At this point let us consider once more our illustration, the telling of a joke. Here too the aim is the creating of a group, the establishing of a community, schematically a "group of two." But the weaker the identification secured by the group situation, so much the cleverer must the device be and so much the better the joke; conversely, these standards are lowered if the collectivity is firmly established, until laughter, apparently without cause, or easily provoked, leaps from one person to another. But what is the source of the freed psychic energy in this case, and how shall we understand laughter in this case to be discharge of pleasure?

For an explanation we must focus our attention on the fact that laughter is a *bodily* process, which may be distinguished by two characteristics: by the coming into prominence of a rhythmic movement, primarily depending on an interference with outward breathing brought about by the intercostal muscles, and by an accompanying excitation of the whole body, which is clearest in an attack of laughing: one is convulsed with laughter.

Instead of any description, I will introduce here a quotation from the best psychological tradition. Cicero (*De Oratore*, IV, 441) declares: *"Ore, vultu denique ipse toto corpore ridetur."* Laughter begins with the mouth, gradually spreads over the whole face, and finally indeed over the whole body—i.e., a pathognomic act is changed into or, more exactly, changed back into a motor one. Here also it is a matter of regression, the reduction or renouncing of functions which the ego otherwise carries out. These conditions also—no matter whether of reduction or renunciation—are to be understood as regression to an earlier level of behavior, if we think along the lines of the ontogenesis of human motor activity. The motor activity of infants has rhythmical muscular actions as its principle character, and these become coordinated in the course of cortical development. The acquiring of bodily control culminates, from four to six years of age, in a phase of development distinguished by the grace with which individual movements are carried out, and it has been described as the period of luxury of movement in children. One can observe something analogous in the expressive behavior of childhood. At first there are strong but undifferentiated reactions to pleasure and unpleasure; differentiation takes place by a gradual acquisition of newer forms of communication and by a toning down of the older ones. Let us visualize the face of an infant at the moment when it begins to be contorted: we do not know whether he is going to laugh or cry. (Anticipating what comes later, I may add that it is possible for an adult also at the peak of an emotional experience to say that he does not know whether he feels impelled to laugh or to cry.) It is only the continuous development of the pathognomy of the child which leads gradually to an ability to supplement involuntary reactions to stimulus by signals to the environment, which show differentiated mental processes. Considering the two lines of development together, we may say that a generalized periodic and undifferentiated process of expression is developed in the service of the reality principle in two directions not previously differentiated, toward *purposive* movements and *expressive* movements. Their distinction only emphasizes the statement that all purposive movements are expressive as well; a person's walk, the way in which he performs a purposive movement, can tell us something about his nature, what sort of a person he is. The converse does not hold: not all expression is purposive.

The musculature was originally used in the service of the pleasure principle for the relief of the mental apparatus from situations of stimulation, by discharging uncoordinated stimuli in movement and by sending innervations to the interior of the body, which set going pathognomy and general movement. Only when the reality principle was introduced did the uncoordinated movements become "purposive actions," or—and this is my insertion—appropriate signals, i.e., they were used for an effective mastering of the outer world and—by the same token—for making contact with the environment.

The language of the body is replaced by the language of words. Thereby a state of affairs arises which is of fundamental importance for the development of minor acts: the acquisition of speech was the event which determined the fate of one branch of general movement, namely, movements of expression; that branch is the more archaic means of expression, and its plasticity is lessened through verbal language. Experimental research confirms this. In the case of children of normal intelligence the capacity to use expressive movements for purposes of making themselves understood gradually diminishes, and for early latency it is true to say that the higher the level of intelligence, the less the capacity to use the body as an apparatus for expression.

The phrase "language of words instead of language of the body" nevertheless requires some modification. Bodily processes of expression are not completely replaced; certain forms of expression—gestures and the whole field of pathognomic expressions—remain. The amount of what remains varies according to social position and the level of culture, but for the normal person expression *toto corpore* is eliminated. This elimination, which among civilized peoples certainly does not take place only under the pressure of education, appears to correspond to an evolutionary curve in phylogenesis: it is evident that expressive movements shown by "less civilized" peoples are more lively and various than our own. But even primitive society recognizes limitations, as well as conditions under which special freedom is permitted to expressive movement: these considerations are part determinants of orgy and dance as ritual customs.

To complete our review let us turn our attention to the animal species. An animal lacks the capacity to point things out; in short, an animal has no index finger, its whole body being its apparatus for expression. This anthropological approach marks out a field which includes the development from autoplastic to alloplastic behavior and allows us to recognize pathognomy as the legitimate residue of what was once a more universal method of behavior. The more archaic methods of expression, however, have not lost their power of attraction; we recognize them in various phenomena of human behavior and may ask under what conditions civilized man is inclined to turn again to the archaic type of expression, namely *toto corpore*.

A survey of these conditions is not difficult: if we disregard cases of pathological damage to the central nervous system, it is always a matter of alteration in the extent of the ego's power, of the limitation of one or more of its functions on the part of or in favor of the id. The clearest cases are those in which the ego is overwhelmed by instinctual claims or affects. The role of the instinct can be seen at once: in states of sensuous excitement everything presses forward with a different rhythm. And, as Edward Glover (1924) has pointed out, the motor apparatus functions in many ways that remind us of the movements of an infant. Something analogous is true of facial expressions: what would be regarded as normal in the speech of the countenance is overstepped in states of physical excitement. One speaks of an expression of animal greed. What is still more evident—though it can only be noted aphoristically here—is that no fixed pattern of expression has been evolved for orgasm. The id has no expressive behavior. A state of violent emotion has similar characteristics: in a furious temper the human countenance can become a grimace, at times of the keenest despair there is a breaking through of rhythmical movements in attacks of uncontrollable sobbing and crying. Something similar happens in the act of laughing, and it enables us to see how narrow the dividing line is which separates the expressions of opposite affects. But we are now concerned with the differences and not the likenesses. The rhythmic shaking of the body in laughter is marked by the positive and not the negative sign. It is pleasurable, it serves to discharge mental energy in the service of the pleasure principle. In laughter too the whole body becomes, to a varying degree, an apparatus for expression; archaic pleasure in movement is reactivated and is socially permissible.

Let us return once more to our starting point. Group laughter, as shown in infectious laughter, is to be understood as regression in common. It requires no occasion; what is tolerated in this case need not be some special way of thinking, or aggressive thoughts, but the behavior itself, namely laughter. But according to this theory some part at least of the energy set free for laughing comes from a diminution of expenditure, which would otherwise be used to safeguard our adult behavior, making it appear that we are "in complete control" of our motor and expressive behavior.

THE CONTROL OF LAUGHTER

That laughter holds a unique position is made very plain by the fact that we can seek out laughter. We are inclined to give in to it and long for the relief it brings. "I should like to laugh today!" we say, and we often succeed. Looked at from this point of view, laughter belongs to the extensive group "enjoyments," the tame descendants of primitive orgies, which are characterized by the same relief and the same voluntary sinking below the wearisome high level of adult everyday behavior. But that is not the only conceivable case and perhaps not even the most frequent.

We may also start laughing without meaning to; it can also happen *in opposition to* the ego and it can attack us quite suddenly. We become weak with laughing; he who laughs is defenseless. When laughter overcomes us and disarms us, we speak of an attack of laughing; it has been repeatedly compared to an epileptic attack. An attack of laughter is often very difficult to stop; it is much easier to prevent it starting, to control it before it develops. This is best done, as everyone knows, by diligently turning our attention to something else: the ego function of attention is called up to check a threatened process which would otherwise be uncontrollable. This method of procedure is universally valid for the function of attention. It is characteristic of this function that it lays claim to the whole of us; any other activity interferes with it; we hold our breath when we pay attention. On the basis of this theory, which one may accept, of a close relation between many automatic actions of the body and ego functions, let us return once more to the suppression of laughter by a voluntary diversion.

But how does this switching-over work in the case of laughter? Two extensive groups of substitute actions are observable in the pathognomic apparatus. It is possible to make a serious face instead of laughing; the laughter is suppressed, but a somewhat artificial expression persists. This artificiality can be described as a special kind of rigidity. The approach to motility is shut off and is anxiously kept shut; all play of the facial muscles is stopped in order to prevent them being seized by laughter. The other way out is more remarkable: if one can call the first a complete turning away of the ego, the second strikes one as a victorious fight, in which the desire to laugh is subjugated and becomes reduced to a smile. A movement producing sound and spreading to all parts of the body is reduced to a play of the muscles around the mouth. This is the way out which polite manners recommend. In the West it goes back to Plato and Seneca, but it has been constantly in force outside the bounds of Mediterranean civilization; the most famous instance of this is well expressed in the 144th letter of the Earl of Chesterfield to his son, in which he says: ". . . and I could heartily wish, that you may often be seen to smile but never heard to laugh while you live." But what was taught as a model of behavior for the English gentleman in the eighteenth century has a general currency, though with a varying intensity: for us too smiling is "higher" than laughing; we regard it as the humanization of laughter. But however indisputable this theory seems to me, it still requires some comment, because if we test our theory that the smile is a restricted and more civilized form of laughing by applying it to the development of the individual, to the "ontogenetic model," it does not fit. The smile of the child is older than his laugh and not the product of later development.

The smile has just as many riddles as the laugh. Just as we do not intend to touch on all the questions relating to laughter, so we have just as little hope, or even less, of contributing anything new to the "riddle of the smile." By a few remarks only shall we attempt to establish its connection with our subject.

The smile retains the privileged place of the first-born in pathognomic functioning. One can say that it appears everywhere as a substitute expression, to bring about a moderation of any pathognomic situation which was of a contorting kind: anger that has been repressed, fright that has been assimilated, crying that has been overcome, can turn into a smile. If we also think of the smile in all these cases as an earlier form of laughing we may be inclined to attribute to it a function of discharge. We could put forward some such view as the following: that in all these cases the smile expresses a relief of tension, a discharge of very small amounts by the ego. It would be very difficult, however, to verify such a connection by observation. For the use of the smile as a substitute act of the pathognomic apparatus extends still further: the "keep smiling" custom of the West, the unvarying smile of the Oriental which is imposed by social custom and ritual, the stiff compulsive smile of many people who are to a greater or lesser degree mentally disturbed and smile in order to hide an affect, chiefly anxiety—all these show the smile being used as a mask, in a series extending from the normal to the symptomatic.

SOME TYPICAL DISTURBANCES OF PATHOGNOMIC ACTIVITY

So far we have represented in a very onesided way the contribution which the ego makes to expressive behavior, in that we have ascribed to it, first and foremost, the inhibition of primitive pleasure in movement. It is now time to proceed to a wider examination of the subject.

To begin with, there is a statement from Freud (1915d) to the effect that the ego's control over motility is so firmly rooted that it regularly withstands the onslaught of neurosis and only breaks down in psychosis. This statement can obviously be valid only within certain limits; even if the ego's control over motility breaks down only in a psychosis, limitations of this control certainly exist within the spheres of both normality and neurosis. I should now like to discuss a few examples illustrative of such limitations in the control of the pathognomic apparatus. They will be arranged in a scale extending from the normal to psychotic behavior.

We start with the fact that two fundamental functions of the ego are liable to disturbance. The first concerns the integration of the separate pathognomic impulses—it is bound up with those tendencies of the ego which strive toward synthesis; the second is related to the temporal sequence of the pathognomic procedure.

Let us consider the first kind of disturbance. The examples used to exemplify it relate mostly to laughing or smiling.

1. Often the integration of an individual pathognomic impulse cannot take place because the ego "hinders" it; the inhibition may be intentional. The suppression of an expression, the stifling of physical pain, and in fact all those cases in which we mean to hide what goes on in us belong to this group. It is clear how near we are here to the border of the pathological; it is obviously already crossed when "not to reveal oneself" becomes an instinctual aim. But in pathological cases also the process in relation to the pathognomic apparatus itself can be described in a simply way: we will make use for the purpose of an example chosen for its transparency.

One frequently observes that dancers and acrobats have a particularly artificial and empty smile; it is directed toward the audience and is supposed to heighten the effect of their performance by giving the impression that it is effortless. Here also the smile is a mask, i.e., a pathognomic substitutive act, which is recognizable as it forces aside another expression. This is an attractive example because we are able to say why this smile is not a convincing one. Examination of the pathognomic position shows that we get the impression of an artificial, empty smile because there is a false innervation either of a branch of the zygomatic muscle—which is manifested by the position of the lips—or, more frequently, of the orbicular muscle, which is contracted instead of relaxed. It is easy to understand how just this grammatical mistake arises—this refers to the introductory observations which I made in reference to a grammar of pathognomic speech. The contraction of the orbicular muscle is known to be a reaction to exertion, which one may surely ascribe to the dancer who has to perform a difficult step correctly, or to the athlete attempting some physical feat. The artificiality of the smile is thus caused by the fact that *only the mouth* smiles, that the smile is not echoed in other parts of the face. In short, it is a case of failure of integration of differently directed pathognomic impulses. One can describe the disturbance from two points of view. Either an expression of something artificial arises because the appropriate pathognomic expression—it would be one of exertion—has to be withheld, or the expression of a smile has failed because all the different facial muscles do not vibrate together correctly, all the pathognomic impulses in the direction of smiling have not been integrated.

2. The example I shall now use is one mentioned incidentally by Freud (1909). It concerns the laugh or smile of a condoling person and represents an actual derailment of the pathognomic act, a parapathognomy. We enter a room with a sympathetic face, we are filled with compassion or fellow feeling and are about to press the hand of the afflicted person in order to show our sympathy, when a smile intrudes itself on our features which we are not able to deal with pathognomically and which gives our face an awkward and embarrassed expression, or else we feel that we want to laugh and fear we may do so; compulsive laughter does actually occur in pathological cases.

We all know what is generally accepted as the explanation of this phenomenon: a repressed, condemned—and usually aggressive—thought has presented itself, has disturbed the pathognomic activity and has turned it into parapathognomy. The topography and dynamics of the process are easily discernible: it is a matter of *pathognomic parapraxis*. There has been a failure to integrate contradictory impulses, the intended impulse and the one which breaks through. This is as far as we can go in the description of the process, since any attempt to pursue it further into its pathological ramifications would lead us away from our subject. We may, however, state briefly that we have touched here upon one of the origins of the grimace, because the way in which anger produces facial distortion is not fundamentally different from that of a parapraxis. If in one case it is a matter of the sudden upheaval of a suppressed impulse, in the other it is a storm of affect, the control of which is unsuccessful: the result can be the same in both cases—distortion resulting in a grimace. Failure to integrate emotional expressions may be brought about not only by instinct and affect, not only by aggression, anger, and doubt —by the passions, that is to say—but also by a disturbance in the ego itself, such as fatigue occurring in certain states of exhaustion; the victorious athlete occasionally makes a grimace of this kind.

3. We have so far considered examples of inhibition of function and unsuccessful purposive acts within the field of expressive phenomena, without crossing the borders of pathology; what now follows refers to an extremely large group of phenomena which can be roughly described as neurotic disturbances. For this purpose, phenomena are grouped together which range from simple hysterical conversion symptoms—such as frequent blushing, increased perspiration of the face—to such things as tic.

An example may be introduced, the case of a young man suffering in a mild degree from psychogenic compulsive laughter. I will enumerate the determinants and the meanings of his laughter in the order in which they occurred in the psychoanalytic sessions. One of the very early meanings which lay very near consciousness was superiority; it always appeared in his ordinary life when he felt in fantasy that an opponent was defeated or could be defeated, and in the transference when he had seen through the analyst: "You are not omnipotent, you are a man like me, I can defeat you." Already in this setting one cannot fail to see a close relation between laughter and anxiety as well as a mastery of it. This function of laughter rests upon the formula: "I need not be afraid; it is 'laughable' "—and, in the language of denial: "I laugh, so I am not afraid, for he who laughs is powerful, strong, and superior."

In a deeper layer, laughter has a still closer and more direct relation to defense against anxiety: "Look at me and see how I laugh; a fool like me who is always laughing is a very harmless person"—and by this means he thinks he is able to evade the responsibility which he so much dreads in connection with his aggressive wishes.

Just as in this sense laughter serves the purpose of autoplastic representation—debasement to the level of the laughable buffoon—so in the next layer to it there is an even clearer indication of an autoplastic and double meaning in the opened mouth in the act of laughing: the showing of the teeth in the laugh serves an aggressive purpose in that it is meant to be an aggressive grimace, still full of that secret significance which attaches to all the masks used by primitive peoples. At the same time the mouth opened for laughing is in the service of homosexual and feminine instinctual tendencies, and is used to seduce the dreaded and ridiculed object in a feminine way.

This example was inserted here to make clear how extraordinarily rich in possible meanings the process of laughter is. All possible overdeterminations of clinical material—in which, however, though we have not explicitly mentioned it, they are not all of equal importance—are represented independently in the field of normality; it is obvious that all these and many other meanings belong to laughter and can be expressed and conveyed by it. It is easier to prove this theory in relation to the role which laughter plays in cult and myth than by observation itself: it represents aggression and seduction simultaneously, is associated with birth or rebirth and procreation, is the sign of godlike strength and so of godlike privilege, but is also the sign of the rebellion of the human race, and one feels continually forced to the conclusion that ultimately defense against anxiety, mastery of anxiety, and pleasure gain are compressed together in the one act.

The young man, from whose analysis we selected a part, finds it very difficult to control his laughter. An attempt to suppress it produces a fixity of expression or a slight distortion of the features. The integration of the pathognomic impulses continually miscarries; a piece of the pathognomic apparatus is sexualized. The laughter itself functions as an assault which is passively experienced; the attempt to get control of the laughter—by means of a plausible occasion, by voluntarily laughing it off—serves the purpose of a defense against the passive experience. The symptom has become libidinized and has the full value of a satisfaction. Here also the language of the body has replaced the language of words, autoplastic movement has ousted every other method of elaboration.

One might suppose that one could understand many pathognomic disturbances of schizophrenics by the application of Freud's theory of attempts at restitution. The loosened contact with the outer world has to be reinstated, a certain apathy in the pathognomic processes has to be overcome. This attempt miscarries; a natural behavior is not achieved, but instead artificial ways and mannerisms appear, which produce a pathognomic effect. How this struggle can shift from one expressive pattern to another I endeavored to show some years ago in relation to the self-portraits of a sculptor who was insane, and certain other analogous phenomena may be set beside them.

One further reflection. If we review the whole field of phenomena in which laughter occurs as an expression of mental activity, we find that one and the same physiological and muscular process can range from scorn to humor, and from pleasure to sadness. How is this possible? How can such a thing come about?

I am of the opinion that it is the central function of the ego which controls our pathognomic apparatus and supervises the shaping of expression. We hear a laugh in the next room and listen to it at first with uneasy surprise, but soon we get our bearings and feel at ease about it. It was the gay laugh of a happy person, or the ironical laughter of someone who has been offended. In this case too the temporal course of the process is not the least important factor in our recognition.

The shaping which the physiological act of laughter undergoes through the agency of the human ego is a clear and impressive example of the fact that everything which we recognize to be a process of giving form and shape to psychical material is to be regarded as an ego function.

Let us return once more, in view of this theory, to the analogy we used when seeking to present the problems to be dealt with in a scientific examination of expressive behavior. The speech of the countenance is limitless and capable of great variety of expression; vocabulary, grammar, and syntax are astonishingly copious, and this richness is all the more impressive precisely because pathognomy is remarkably poor in what would correspond to verbal roots, to *etyma*, in speech. Let us not bind ourselves to a comparison with speech which threatens here only to hinder our understanding; let us try to account for the fact that all the various manifestations of the expressive function are closely related at the start. In the illustrations which are to be found in old textbooks on facial expression, one notices how easily and through how slight an alteration in the illustration the whole of the expression changes. Here also it is only a step from laughing to crying. Or again, if photographs are covered so that only a part of the face, mouth and lips, or eyes and forehead, show, we can complete each one in our mind into very different expressive situations. Only when we see the complete face as a whole and with its temporal changes do we get the expression. This view of things seems banal and self-evident if one is relating it to one's own perception, since no one has ever doubted that the expression of the human countenance is a question of Gestalt in the sense used by Gestalt psychology. But I do not plead for this point of view here as a contribution to the understanding of pathognomy but for its creation, not as an attribute of our perception but as an achievement on the part of the body, by whose agency this entity is brought into being. In regard to disturbances of expression, in cases, for instance, in which what is usually automatic about the function becomes conscious, everyone can experience in himself, can feel in his own motor actions, how integration and temporal regulation may fail. It is, however, only these functions that ensure the richness and fullness of the speech of the human countenance.

And laughter too, which lies on the border between expressive and purposive motor behavior, only acquires its meaning as an expressive action through undergoing this formative process in its nature and the course it takes. Only because of the wide scope of its significance does it become human and in the Aristotelian sense peculiar to man.

SOME FORMS OF EMOTIONAL DISTURBANCE AND THEIR RELATIONSHIP TO SCHIZOPHRENIA

HELENE DEUTSCH

(1942)

In the mid-1930's Helene Deutsch made a highly original and valuable contribution to the study of affects. The condition she described later came to be known as the "as if" personality, which is not an affect per se, but clearly a disturbance in the production of normal affects. Her conclusions concerning the meaning of this phenomenon have been verified over the years by a number of other investigators describing similar states in their patients (Panel, 1966; Ross, 1967).

"Every attempt to understand feeling and manner of life of this type of person forces the observer to the inescapable impression that this individual's whole relationship to life has something about it which is lacking in genuineness and yet outwardly runs along 'as if' it were complete." The person seems normal, and there is nothing to suggest any kind of disorder. Behavior is not unusual, and intellectual abilities seem unimpaired. Yet there is something intangibly wrong. What is lacking is an affective relation to the environment, although relationships are seemingly intense and bear all the earmarks of friendship, love, and sympathy.

Careful clinical examination reveals that these individuals are devoid of any trace of warmth and "all inner experience is completely excluded." They are, in fact, impersonators of life. They do not suffer from the repression of their affective life but from a "real loss of object cathexis."

But how do such individuals manage to function in life and interpersonally? Deutsch concluded that they have a complete, passive attitude to the environment with a highly plastic readiness to pick up signals from the outer world and to mold themselves and their behavior accordingly. Burdened by a lack of real warmth and an emptiness and dullness to the emotional atmosphere around them, they attempt to establish their validity and existence through identification. They do not complain of lack of affect, for they are never conscious of it.

Deutsch concluded that these individuals may have been drilled in love, honor, and obedience without ever actually feeling these emotions directly. She rightly concludes that one may be dealing with latent or borderline schizophrenic individuals, but expresses doubt about whether these patients could be termed truly psychotic.

Over the years it has become apparent that Deutsch's suspicion of an underlying psychosis in some of these individuals is all too true. In-depth studies show that an underlying borderline organization can be discerned in a great number.

The type of sexual object choice in "as if" personalities is often a narcissistic one. A. Reich (1953) provides a striking clinical example of such a woman who established transitory and pseudoinfatuations with men. These represented a more primitive, narcissistic fusion with devalued and poorly differentiated objects. This reflected a severe degree of pathology and lack of differentiation of the ego ideal together with an insufficiently developed superego and an extreme degree of aggression against the objects upon whom the ego ideal is constructed.

Beyond the serious disorder of the patient's affliction are the serious emotional disturbances that are likely to occur in the hapless, unwitting "victims" of these patients—the spouses, lovers, children. For the "as if" personality, often endowed with a high, unimpaired intelligence, distorts the meaning of reality and corrupts affective life through intellectualizations and rationalizations, all the while wearing the mask of sanity.

Lastly, the prognosis for recovery in these patients may be largely dependent on the ability of the therapy to revive or reawaken the blighted seeds of pleasure, pride, and self-esteem, for it is pleasure perceived, anticipated, and enjoyed that becomes the glue cementing together insight, change, and performance modification.

Psychoanalytic observations of a few types of emotional disturbances are presented in this paper, and a series of cases reported in which the individual's emotional relationship to the outside world and to his own ego appears impoverished or absent. Such disturbances of the emotional life take various forms. For example, there are the individuals who are not aware of their lack of normal affective bonds and responses, but whose emotional disturbance is either perceived only by those around them or is first detected in analytic treatment; and there are those who complain of their emotional defect and are keenly distressed by the disturbance in their inner experiences. Among the latter, the disturbance may be transitory and fleeting; it may recur from time to time but only in connection with certain specific situations and experiences; or it may persist and form a continuous, distressing symptom. In addition, the emotional disturbance may be perceived as existing in the personality or it may be projected onto the outside world. In the one case the patient says, "I am changed. I feel nothing. Everything seems unreal to me." In the other, he complains that the world seems strange, objects shadowy, human beings and events theatrical and unreal. Those forms of the disturbance in which the individual himself is conscious of his defect and complains of it belong to the picture of "depersonalization." This disturbance has been described by many authors. In the analytic literature the reader is especially referred to the studies of Oberndorf (1934, 1935), Schilder (1939), and Bergler and Eidelberg (1935).

Most of the psychoanalytic observations in this paper deal with conditions bearing a close relationship to depersonalization but differing from it in that they were not perceived as disturbances by the patient himself. To this special type of personality I have given the name "as if." I must emphasize that this name has nothing to do with Vaihinger's system of "fictions" and the philosophy of "As If." My only reason for using so unoriginal a label for the type of person I wish to present is that every attempt to understand the way of feeling and manner of life of this type forces on the observer the inescapable impression that the individual's whole relationship to life has something about it which is lacking in genuineness and yet outwardly runs along "as if" it were complete. Even the layman sooner or later inquires, after meeting such an "as if" patient: "what *is* wrong with him, or her? Outwardly the person seems normal. There is nothing to suggest any kind of disorder, behavior is not unusual, intellectual abilities appear unimpaired, emotional expressions are well ordered and appropriate. But despite all this, something intangible and indefinable obtrudes between the person and his fellows and invariably gives rise to the question, "What is wrong?"

A clever and experienced man, a patient of mine, met

another of my patients, a girl of the "as if" type, at a social gathering. He spent part of his next analytic hour telling me how stimulating, amusing, attractive, and interesting she was, but ended his eulogy with, "But something is wrong with her." He could not explain what he meant.

When I submitted the paintings of the same girl to an authority for his criticism and evaluation, I was told that the drawings showed much skill and talent, but there was also something disturbing in them which this man attributed to an inner restraint, an inhibition which he thought could surely be removed. Toward the end of the patient's not too successful analysis, she entered this critic's school for further instruction in painting and, after a time, I received a report in which her teacher spoke in glowing terms of her talent. Several months later I received a less enthusiastic report. Yes, the girl was talented, her teacher had been impressed by the speed with which she had adopted his technique and manner of artistic perception, but he had frankly to admit, there was an intangible something about her which he had never before encountered, and he ended with the usual question, "What is wrong?" He added that the girl had gone to another teacher, who used a quite different teaching approach, and that she had oriented herself to the new theory and technique with striking ease and speed.

The first impression these people make is of complete normality. They are intellectually intact, gifted, and bring great understanding to intellectual and emotional problems; but when they pursue their not infrequent impulses to creative work they construct, in form, a good piece of work but it is always a spasmodic, if skilled, repetition of a proto- type without the slightest trace of originality. On closer observation, the same thing is seen in their affective re- lationships to the environment. These relationships are usually intense, and bear all the earmarks of friendship, love, sympathy, and understanding; but even the layman soon perceives something strange and raises the question he cannot answer. To the analyst it is soon clear that all these relationships are devoid of any trace of warmth, that all the expressions of emotion are formal, that inner experience is completely excluded. It is like the performance of an actor who is technically well trained but who lacks the necessary spark to make his impersonations true to life.

Thus the essential characteristic of the person I wish to describe is that outwardly he conducts his life as if he possessed a complete and sensitive emotional capacity. To him there is no difference between his empty forms and what others actually experience. Without going deeper into the matter, I wish at this point to state that this condition is not identical with the coldness of repressed individuals in whom there is usually a highly differentiated emotional life hidden behind a wall, the loss of affect being either manifest or cloaked by overcompensations. In the one there is flight from reality or a defense against the realization of forbidden instinctual drives; in the other, a seeking of external reality in an effort to avoid an anxiety-laden fantasy. Psychoanalysis discloses that in the "as if" individual it is no longer an act of repression but a real loss of object cathexis. The apparently normal relationship to the world corresponds to a child's imitativeness and is the expression of identification with the environment, a mimicry which results in an ostensibly good adaptation to the world of reality despite the absence of object cathexis.

Further consequences of such a relation to life are a completely passive attitude to the environment with a highly plastic readiness to pick up signals from the outer world and to mold oneself and one's behavior accordingly. The identification with what other people are thinking and feeling is the expression of this passive plasticity and renders the person capable of the greatest fidelity and the basest perfidy. Any object will do as a bridge for identification. At first the love, friendship, and attachment of an "as if" person have something very rewarding for the partner. If it is a woman, she seems to be the quintessence of feminine devotion, an impression which is particularly imparted by her passivity and readiness for identification. Soon, however, the lack of real warmth brings such an emptiness and dullness to the emotional atmosphere that the man as a rule precipitously breaks off the relationship. In spite of the adhesiveness which the "as if" person brings to every relationship, when he is thus abandoned he displays either a rush of affective reactions which are "as if" and thus spurious, or a frank absence of affectivity. At the very first opportunity the former object is exchanged for a new one and the process is repeated.

The same emptiness and the same lack of individuality which are so evident in the emotional life appear also in the moral structure. Completely without character, wholly unprincipled, in the literal meaning of the term, the morals of the "as if" individuals, their ideals, their convictions, are simply reflections of another person, good or bad. Attaching themselves with great ease to social, ethical, and religious groups, they seek, by adhering to a group, to give content and reality to their inner emptiness and establish the validity of their existence by identification. Overenthusiastic adherence to one philosophy can be quickly and completely replaced by another contradictory one without the slightest trace of inward transformation—simply as a result of some accidental regrouping of the circle of acquaintances or the like.

A second characteristic of such patients is their suggestibility, quite understandable from what has already been said. Like the capacity for identification, this suggestibility, too, is unlike that of the hysteric for whom object cathexis is a necessary condition; in the "as if" individual the suggestibility must be ascribed to passivity and automatonlike identification. Many initial criminal acts, attributed to an erotic bondage, are due instead to a passive readiness to be influenced.

Another characteristic of the "as if" personality is that aggressive tendencies are almost completely masked by passivity, lending an air of negative goodness, of mild amiability which, however, is readily convertible to evil.

One of these patients, a woman, and the only child of one of the oldest noble families in Europe, had been brought up in an unusual atmosphere. With the excuse of official duties, and quite in accordance with tradition, the parents delegated the care and training of their child to strangers. On certain specified days of the week she was brought before her parents for "control." At these meetings there was a formal check of her educational achievements, and the new program and other directions were given her preceptors. Then after a cool, ceremonious dismissal, the child was returned to her quarters. She received no warmth and no tenderness from her parents, nor did punishment come directly from them. This virtual separation from her parents had come soon after her birth. Perhaps the most inauspicious component of her parents' conduct, which granted the child only a very niggardly bit of warmth, was the fact—and this was reinforced by the whole program of her education—that their sheer *existence* was strongly emphasized, and the patient was drilled in love, honor, and obedience toward them without ever feeling these emotions directly and realistically.

In this atmosphere, so lacking in feeling on the part of the parents, the development of a satisfactory emotional life could scarcely be expected in the child. One would expect, however, that other persons in the environment would take the place of the parents. Her situation would then have been that of a child brought up in a foster home. In such children we find that the emotional ties to their own parents are transferred to the parent substitutes in relationship to whom the Oedipus develops with greater difficulty, perhaps, but with no significant modifications.

This patient, in accordance with ceremonial tradition, always had three nurses, each of whom wanted to stand first in the eyes of the parents and each of whom continually sought the favor of the child. They were, moreover, frequently changed. Throughout her whole childhood there was no one person who loved her and who could have served as a significant love object for her. *

As soon as she was able to conceptualize, the patient immersed herself intensively in fantasies about the parents. She attributed to them divine powers through which she was provided with things unattainable to ordinary mortals. Everything she absorbed from stories and legends she elaborated into the myth about her parents. No longing for love was ever expressed in these fantasies: they all had the aim of providing a narcissistic gain. Every meeting with the real parents separated them further from the heroes of her imagination. In this manner there was formed in the child a parental myth, a fantasmic shadow of an Oedipus situation which remained an empty form so far as real persons and emotions were concerned. Not only did reality which denied her parent relationships lead to narcissistic regression into fantasy, but this process gained further impetus from the absence of any substitute object-libidinal relationships. The frequent change of nurses and governesses and the fact that these persons were themselves subjected to strict discipline, acted on orders, and used all available measures to make the child conform to the demands of reality, measures in which a pseudotenderness was consciously used as a means to attain didactic ends, precluded this possibility. The child was trained very early to cleanliness and strict table manners, and the violent outbreaks of anger and rage to which she was subject in early childhood were successfully brought under control, giving way to an absolutely pliant obedience. Much of this disciplinary control was attained by appeal to the parents so that everything the child did which was obedient and proper she referred to the wish or command of the mythical father and mother.

When she entered a convent school at the age of eight, she was completely fixed in the "as if" state in which she entered analysis. Superficially, there was no difference between her life and that of the average convent pupil. She had the customary attachment to a nun in imitation of her group of girls. She had the most tender friendships, which were wholly without significance to her. She went devoutly through the forms of religion without the slightest trace of belief, and underwent seduction into masturbation with quasi feelings of guilt—simply to be like her comrades.

In time, the myth of the parents faded and disappeared without new fantasies to take its place. It disappeared as her parents became clearer to her as real persons and she devalued them. Narcissistic fantasies gave way to real experiences in which, however, she could participate only through identification.

Analysis disclosed that the success of her early training in suppressing instinctual drives was only apparent. It has something of the "trained act" in it and, like the performance of the circus animal, was bound to the presence of a ringmaster. If denial of an instinct was demanded, the patient complied, but when an otherwise-inclined object gave permission for the satisfaction of a drive, she could respond quite without inhibition, though with little gratification. The only result of the training was that the drive never came into conflict with the external world. In this respect she behaved like a child in that stage of development in which its instinctual drives are curbed only by immediate external authority. Thus it happened that, for a time, the patient fell into bad company, in unbelievable contrast to her home environment and early training. She got drunk in low dives, participated in all kinds of sexual perversions, and felt just as comfortable in this underworld as in the pietistic sect, the artistic group, or the political movement in which she was later successively a participant.

She never had occasion to complain of lack of affect, for she was never conscious of it. The patient's relationship to her parents was strong enough to enable her to make them heroes of her fantasy, but for the creation of a warm dynamic Oedipus constellation capable of shaping a healthy future psychic life in both a positive and a negative sense the necessary conditions were obviously lacking. It is not enough that the parents are simply there and provide food for fantasy. The child must *really* be seduced to a certain extent by the libidinal activity of the parents in order to develop a normal emotional life, must experience the warmth of a mother's body as well as all those unconscious seductive acts of the loving mother as she cares for its bodily needs. It must play with the father and have sufficient intimacy with him to sense the father's masculinity in order that instinctual impulses enter the stream of the Oedipus constellation.

The patient's myth bore some similarity to the fantasy which Freud called the "family romance" in which, however, the libidinal relation to the parents, though repressed, is very powerful. By repudiating the real parents, it is possible partly to avoid strong emotional conflicts from forbidden wishes, feelings of guilt, etc. The real objects have been repressed, but in analysis they can be uncovered with their full libidinal cathexis.

But for our patient there was never a living, warm emotional relationship to the parents or to anyone else. Whether after weak attempts at object cathexis the child returned to narcissism by a process of regression or never succeeded in establishing a real object relation as the result of being unloved is, for all practical purposes, irrelevant.

The same deficiency which interfered with the development of the emotional life was also operative in the formation of the superego. The shadowy structure of the Oedipus complex was gradually given up without ever having come to an integrated and unified superego formation. One gains the impression that the prerequisites for such a development also lie in strong oedipal object cathexis.

It is not to be denied that at a very early age some inner prohibitions are present which are the precursors of the superego and are intimately dependent on external objects. Identification with the parents in the resolution of the Oedipus complex brings about the integration of these elements. Where this is absent, as it was in our patient, the the identifications remain vacillating and transitory. The representatives which go to make up the conscience remain in the external world, and instead of the development of inner morals there appears a persistent identification with external objects. In childhood, educational influences exerted an inhibitory effect on the instinctual life, particularly on the aggressions. In later life, in the absence of an adequate superego, she shifts the responsibility for her behavior to objects in the external world with whom she identifies herself. The passivity of this patient as the expression of her submission to the will of another seems to be the final transformation of her aggressive tendencies.

As the result of this weak superego structure, there is

little contact between the ego and the superego, and the scene of all conflicts remains external, like the child for whom everything can proceed without friction if it but obey. Both the persistent identification and the passive submission are expressions of the patient's complete adaptation to the current environment, and impart the shadowy quality to the patient's personality. The value of this link to reality is questionable because the identification always takes place with only a part of the environment. If this part of the environment comes into conflict with the rest, naturally the patient is involved. Thus it can come about that the individual can be seduced into asocial or criminal acts by a change in his identifications, and it may well be that some of the asocial are recruited from the group of "as if" personalities who are adapted to reality in this restricted way.

Analysis of this patient revealed a genuine infantalism, that is, an arrest at a definite stage in the development of the emotional life and character formation. In addition to particularly unfavorable environmental influences, it should be noted that the patient came from a very old family overrun with psychotics and invalid psychopaths.

Another woman patient had a father who had a mental illness and a mother who was neurotic. She remembered her father only as "a man with a black beard," and she tried to explain as something very fascinating and wonderful his absences as he was moved to and from a sanatarium and an isolated room at home, always under nursing care. Thus she built a myth around her father, replacing him in fantasy by a mysterious man, whom she later called an "Indian" and with whom she had all sorts of experiences, each of which served to make her a superhuman being. The prototype for the Indian was the father's male nurse, whom the little girl saw mysteriously disappearing into her father's room. The education and upbringing of the child were relegated to nurses, but despite this she succeeded in establishing a strongly libidinal attachment to the very abnormal mother. Her later relationships had elements of object-libidinal attitudes, sometimes warmer, especially in homosexual directions, but never sufficiently to change their "as if" quality. The failure to develop an adequate object cathexis was, in this patient, related to the birth of her brother, toward whom she developed an unusually aggressive envy. Comparisons of genitalia led the little girl to scrutinize her body for hours on end in a mirror. Later, this narcissistic activity was gradually sublimated. At first she tried to model parts of her body in clay in order to facilitate her mirror studies. In the course of years she developed great skill in modeling and was for a brief time under the tutelage of a sculptress. Unconsciously, it was the fantasy of repeatedly displaying her body to the world. In later years she created only large, very voluptuous, matronly female figures. These proved to be weak attempts to recreate the mother she had lost in childhood to her brother. Ultimately she abandoned sculpture for music simply because she believed her teacher failed to appreciate her sufficiently.

Most conspicuous in her childhood was a monkeylike imitation of her brother with whom she was for years completely identified, not in fantasy but by acting out. Disastrously for both, the brother quite early betrayed unmistakable signs of a psychosis which culminated in a catatonic excitement. The sister imitated all her brother's bizarre activities and lived with him in a world of fantasy. Only her partial object-libidinal cathexis and a displacement of the process from the brother and identification with more normal objects saved her from being institutionalized. I was inclined at first to regard her condition as the result of an identification with her psychotic brother; only later did I recognize that the etiology of her condition lay deeper.

I believe this patient is similar to the first, despite the differences in their development. In the second, it seems that a disappointment shattered the strong relationship with the mother, that the mysterious absence of the father made it impossible for the little girl to find in him a substitute when her relationship to her mother was shaken, and that further relationships to objects remained at the stage of identifications. By such identification she averted her intense hatred of her brother and transformed her aggression toward him into an obedient passivity in which she submissively identified herself with him. She developed no other object relationships. Her superego suffered the same fate as that of the first patient. The myth of the father and the very early devaluation of the mother prevented integration of her superego and left her dependent on persons in the external world.

A third patient, a pretty, temperamental woman of 35 with many intellectual and artistic talents, came to analysis because she was "tired" after a long series of adventures. It soon became clear that, as the result of a certain combination of circumstances, her interest in psychoanalysis was actually an interest in the analyst, especially in her profession. While she frequently spoke of her tremendous interest in child psychology and in Freud's theory and read widely on these subjects, her understanding of them was extraordinarily superficial and her interest entirely unreal. More careful observation disclosed that this was true not only for all her intellectual interests but for everything she did or had ever done. It was surprising to recognize in this woman, who was so indefatigably active, a condition so closely related to the pseudo affectivity of the "as if" patient. All her experiences too were based on identifications, though her identifications were not so straightforward as were those of the other type of patient which is, one might say, more monogamous and adheres to but one person or one group at a time, while this patient had so many concurrent identifications—or symbolic representations of identifications—that her conduct appeared erratic. She was, in fact, considered "crazy" by those who knew her. Her friends, however, had no notion that her apparently rich life concealed a severe lack of affect. She had come to me because of a wish to change her character, that is, to create more peace and harmony in her life by identifying herself with a "particularly solid" professional personality.

After six months the analysis appeared to be unusually successful. The patient learned to understand many things about herself and lost her eccentricities. She determined to become an analyst and when this was denied her, she collapsed. She was completely lacking in affect and complained, "I am so empty! My God, I am so empty! I have no feelings." It transpired that prior to analysis she had got into serious financial difficulties by breaking off various friendships and love relationships and had realized that she would soon have to work. It was with this intention that she came to analysis. Her plan was to become an analyst by identification with her analyst. When this proved impossible, this seemingly very able and active woman changed into a completely passive person. From time to time she had extraordinarily violent fits of childish weeping or outbursts of rage, flung herself on the floor and kicked and screamed. Gradually, she developed a progressive lack of affect. She became completely negativistic and met all interpretations with, "I don't understand what you mean by that."

At two points in this patient's development she had suffered severe trauma. Her father was an alcoholic, and the patient often witnessed his brutal mistreatment of the mother. She sided vehemently with the latter, and when she was only seven had fantasies in which she rescued her mother from her misery and built a little white cottage for her. She saved every penny and worked hard in school to attain this aim, only to discover that her mother was not merely a passive victim of her husband but took pleasure in being brutalized. The consequent devaluation of her mother not only deprived her of her only object of love but also arrested the development of a feminine ego ideal of an independent, adequate personality. She spent the rest of her life trying to make up for this lack by creating a whole series of identifications, in the same way as the "as if" patients.

Deprived of tenderness and affection in her childhood, her instincts remained crudely primitive. She vacillated between giving these instincts free rein and holding them in check. She acted out prostitution fantasies, indulged in a variety of sexual perversions, often giving the impression of hypomania. She emerged from these debauches by identification with some conventional person and achieved by this means a kind of sublimation, the form dependent on the particular object. This resulted in a frequent shifting of her occupation and interests. So long as it was possible for her either to retain such a relationship or to allow herself the gratification of very primitive drives, she was not aware of her lack of affect.

The following cases of emotional disturbance bear close similarity to the "as if" group but differ in certain respects.

A seventeen-year-old boy of unusual intellectual ability came for analysis because of manifest homosexuality and a conscious lack of feeling. This lack of emotion included his homosexual objects, about whom he created all sorts of perverse fantasies. He was obsessionally scrupulous, modest, exact, and reliable. He was passively oral and anal in his homosexuality. The analysis was extremely rich in material but progressed in an emotional vacuum. While the transference was frequently represented in his dreams and fantasies, it never became a conscious, emotional experience.

One day I gave him a ticket to a series of lectures in which I was taking part. He went to my lecture and had severe anxiety on the stairs leading to the lecture hall. By thus mobilizing his anxiety in the transference, the analysis began to progress.

An only child from a highly cultured environment, with a father who was strict and ambitious and a mother who dedicated her life to this handsome and talented son, he nevertheless suffered the fate of affective deficiency. The fact that he grew up in an atmosphere in which he never needed to seek for love, that he was overwhelmed with tenderness without having to make any effort to obtain it, paralyzed his own active strivings for tenderness. He remained bound to primitive instinctual impulses, and because there were few infantile anxieties which were not warded off with scrupulous care, there was no motive in him to build up defense mechanisms.

He underwent the trauma of the depreciation of his ego ideal when he discovered that his admired father was uncultivated and limited. This realization threatened to depreciate his own value, for he was like his father, bore his name, and heard his resemblance to him repeatedly stressed by his mother. Through rigidity and strictness in ethical and intellectual demands, he strove to become better than the self which was identified with the father. In contrast to the previous patients, he did not identify himself with a series of objects. Instead of having emotional relationships with people, he was split into two identifications: one with his beloved mother and the other with his father. The first was feminine and sexualized; the second was overcompensatory, rigid, and narcissistic.

Unlike the "as if" patients, he complained of lack of feeling. He completely lacked the tender emotions which would have given warmth to his emotional life. He had no relation to any woman, and his friendships with men were either purely intellectual or crudely sexual. The feelings he had were of a character he would not let himself express. These were very primitive aggressions, the wildest, most infantile sexual drives, which were rejected with the declaration, "I feel nothing at all." In one way he told the truth; he was really lacking in any permissible feelings, that is, in the tender, sublimated emotions.

The tendency to identification is characteristic also of this type of affective disturbance. Even though this patient did not completely sink his personality in a series of identifications, the strongest section of his ego, his intellect, lacked originality. Everything he wrote and said in scientific matters showed great formal talent but when he tried to produce something original it usually turned out to be a repetition of ideas which he had once grasped with particular clarity. The tendency to multiple identifications occurred on the intellectual level.

Another patient of this group, a 30-year-old married woman who came from a family in which there were many psychotics, complained about lack of emotion. In spite of good intelligence and perfect reality testing, she led a sham existence and she was always just what was suggested to her by the environment. It became clear that she could experience nothing except a completely passive readiness to split into an endless number of identifications. This condition had set in acutely after an operation in her childhood for which she had been given no psychological preparation. On recovery from the anesthesia she asked if she were really herself, and then developed a state of depersonalization which lasted a year and turned into passive suggestibility which concealed a crippling anxiety.

Common to all these cases is a deep disturbance of the process of sublimation which results both in a failure to synthesize the various infantile identifications into a single, integrated personality, and in an imperfect, one-sided, purely intellectual sublimation of the instinctual strivings. While critical judgment and the intellectual powers may be excellent, the emotional and moral part of the personality is lacking.

The etiology of such conditions is related first to a devaluation of the object serving as a model for the development of the child's personality. This devaluation may have a firm foundation in reality or be traceable, for example, to shock at discovery of parental coitus at a period of development when the child is engaged in its last struggles against masturbation and needs support in its efforts toward sublimation. Or, as in the case of the boy described above, the successful sublimation may be interfered with by a sexualization of the relationship to an object who should serve the child as a model for its ego ideal, in this instance, a grossly sexual identification with his mother.

Another cause of this kind of emotional disturbance is insufficient stimulus for the sublimation of the emotions, as the result of being given either too little tenderness or too much. Infantile anxiety may suffer a similar fate. Too harsh or too indulgent treatment may contribute to failure in the economic formation of defense mechanisms resulting in remarkable passivity of the ego. It will be recalled that, in the case of the boy reported, an attack of anxiety not only mobilized the transference but also opened the way to his recovery.

The question must be raised as to how the tendency of "as if" personalities to identification with current love objects differs from the same tendency in hysteria. The great difference between the latter and the "as if" disturbance lies in the fact that the objects with which the hysterics identify themselves are the objects of powerful libidinal cathexes.

Hysterical repression of affect brings freedom from anxiety and so represents a way out of the conflict. In "as if" patients, an early deficiency in the development of affect reduces the inner conflict, the effect of which is an impoverishment of the total personality which does not occur in hysteria.

The patients described here might make one suspect that we are dealing with something like the blocking of affect seen especially in narcissistic individuals who have developed loss of feeling through repression. The great fundamental difference, however, is that the "as if" personality tries to simulate affective experience, whereas the individual with a blocking of affect does not. In the analysis of the latter it can always be shown that the once developed object relationships and aggressive feelings have undergone repression and are not at the disposal of the conscious personality. The repressed, affectively toned segment of the personality is gradually uncovered during the analysis, and it is sometimes possible to make the buried part of the emotional life available to the ego.

For example, one patient had completely repressed the memory of his mother, who died when he was four, and with whom, it was clear, the greater part of his emotions had been involved. Under the influence of a very weak but nonetheless effective transference, isolated memories gradually emerged. At first these had a negative character and denied all tenderness. During analysis this patient showed also another form of emotional disturbance, namely, depersonalization. Before analysis his self-satisfaction had been unshaken. He defended himself against the transference with all his power. In the analytic hours, when clear signs of a transference in statu nascendi were perceptible, the patient would complain of sudden feelings of strangeness. It was clear that in him the depersonalization corresponded to the perception of a change in cathexis. It remained a question whether this was due to a new libidinal stream emerging from repression, or to a suppression of feelings connected with transference. The inner conflict in such an instance of repression of affect has little similarity to that of an "as if" patient. The analogy rests only on the affective impoverishment in both.

The narcissism and the poverty of object relationships so characteristic for an "as if" person bring to consideration the relationship of this defect to a psychosis. The fact that reality testing is fully maintained removes this condition from our conception of psychosis.

Narcissistic identification as a preliminary stage to object cathexis, and introjection of the object after its loss, are among the most important discoveries of Freud and Abraham. The psychological structure of melancholia offers us the classical example of this process. In melancholia, the object of identification has been psychologically internalized, and a tyrannical superego carries on the conflict with the incorporated object in complete independence of the external world. In "as if" patients, the objects are kept external and all conflicts are acted out in relation to them. Conflict with the superego is thus avoided because in every gesture and in every act the "as if" ego subordinates itself through identification to the wishes and commands of an authority which has never been introjected.

From the beginning, both the personal impression given by the patients themselves and the psychotic disposition in the family, especially in the first two analytically observed cases, make one suspect a schizophrenic process. The tracing of the severe psychic disturbance directly back to the developments of early childhood seems to me completely justified, and whether this speaks against the diagnosis of a schizophrenic process must, for the time being, be left undecided. My observations of schizophrenic patients have given me the impression that the schizophrenic process goes through an "as if" phase before it builds up the delusional form. A 22-year-old schizophrenic girl came to me after a catatonic attack, oriented for time and place but full of delusional ideas. Until the onset of the confusional state she had led an existence almost indistinguishable from "as if" patients. Her bond to objects with whom she identified herself, and who were always outstanding women, was extremely intense. As a result of rapid shifting of these relationships, she changed her place of residence, her studies, and her interests in an almost manic fashion. Her last identification had led her from the home of a well-established American family to a communistic cell in Berlin. A sudden desertion by her object led her from Berlin to Paris where she was manifestly paranoid and gradually developed a severe confusion. Treatment restored her to her original state, but despite warnings, her family decided to break off the analysis. The girl was not able to summon enough affect to protest. One day she bought a dog and told me that now everything would be all right; she would imitate the dog and then she would know how she should act. Identification was retained but was no longer limited to human objects; it included animals, inanimate objects, concepts, and symbols, and it was this lack of selectivity which gave the process its delusional character. It was the loss of the capacity for identification with human objects which made possible the erection of a new, delusional world.

Another schizophrenic patient for years had had a recurrent dream in which in great pain and torment she sought her mother but could not find her because she was always faced with an endless crowd of women, each of whom looked like her mother, and she could not tell the right one. This dream reminded me of the stereotyped, recurrent mother figures in the sculpture of the second "as if" patient.

Freud (1923) speaks of "multiple personality" as the result of a process in which numerous identifications lead to a disruption of the ego. This may result in manifest psychopathology, or the conflicts between the different identifications can assume a form which need not necessarily be designated as pathological. Freud refers to a purely inner process of ego formation, and this does not apply to the "as if" identifications with objects in the outer world. However, the same psychological process in the "as if" personality will also on one occasion have a more "normal" resolution and on another a pathological outcome which may be more or less severe.

Anna Freud (1936) points out that the type of pseudo affectivity observed in "as if" patients is often found in puberty. I believe that the depreciation of the primary objects (also typical of puberty) who served as models for the ego ideal, plays an important role in both. Anna Freud describes this type of behavior in puberty as incurring the suspicion of psychosis. I believe that the reflections which I have presented here will also serve for puberty. At one time the process will lie within the bounds of the "normal" and at another it bears the seeds of a pathological condition. The type justifies the designation "schizoid," whether or not schizophrenia later develops.

Whether the emotional disturbances described in this paper imply a "schizophrenic disposition" or constitute rudimentary symptoms of schizophrenia is not clear to me. These patients represent variants in the series of abnormal distorted personalities. They do not belong among the commonly accepted forms of neurosis, and they are too well adjusted to reality to be called psychotic. While psychoanalysis seldom succeeds, the practical results of treatment can be very far-reaching, particularly if a strong identification with the analyst can be utilized as an active and constructive influence. In so far as they are accessible to analysis, one may be able to learn much in the field of ego psychology, especially with regard to disturbances of affect and, perhaps, make contributions to the problem of the "schizoid" which is still so obscure.

In the great delusional formations of the psychoses we see primitive and archaic drives returning from the depths of the unconscious in a dramatic manner. Regression takes place because the ego has failed. We speak of this as a "weakness of the ego" and assume that the reasons for this failure are psychological, constitutional, or organic. Psychoanalysis can investigate the first of these, especially in prepsychotic conditions to which these cases belong.

PSYCHOPATHOLOGY OF INGRATITUDE

Edmund Bergler

(1945)

Gratitude derives from the Latin and French, and means a state of being thankful for and appreciative of efforts received. Those in a state of chronic ingratitude often exhibit indignation, disillusionment, and pessimism with mankind. Citing Freud's early work (1915a) and Ferenczi's (1916) on developments in the stages of reality, Bergler states that the problem of ingratitude undoubtedly originates in the child's early development or faulty development of his sense of reality.

The child, filled with primordial omnipotence, in time delegates part of it to parental figures, but he may forever remain with the conscious and/or unconscious conviction of all-power and all-might within himself. This results often in his believing that through his own will he can command good or bad fortune or events that befall him. Some children get off to a "bad start" and never relinquish this feeling. Bergler proposes three reasons for the ingratitude of men toward each other in the face of beneficent acts.

Although ingratitude is not ordinarily thought of as an affect but as a character trait, especially if chronic, close clinical examination reveals it to have all the essential features of an affective state. It is an acute or sustained emotional response toward a source of benefit and pleasure to which one reacts with aggression. The intention of the latter is to disappoint, displease, and express lack of appreciation, and, if possible, to punish and diminish the source of beneficence. Ingratitude inspires emotional thinking aimed to justify the aggressive reaction.

One is reminded that ingratitude can release even more powerful and devastating affective reactions. This is nowhere more evident than in King Lear's outrage and tragic despair:

> *Ingratitude, thou marble-hearted fiend,*
> *More hideous, when thou show'st thee in a child,*
> *Than the sea monster* [I, iv, 283]
> *[and later in the same scene:]*
> *How sharper than a serpent's tooth it is*
> *To have a thankless child* [I, iv, 312]

A constant source of indignation stems from human ingratitude, and every complainer has a stock of favorite examples of it. The conclusions about human nature which are generally drawn from these examples are either moralistic, pessimistic, or resigned. Strangely enough, few people ask themselves whether gratitude does not surpass human capacity and what the psychological reasons for gratitude or the lack of it are.

Gratitude as a moral requirement presupposes that human beings react logically, the reasoning being, "I did you a good turn; you have to act accordingly." What is overlooked is that gratitude has an affective case in history. Let us look at its genetic record.

The very young child does not feel gratitude for food, loving care, attention, and gifts, since he misjudges reality in the most amazing way. His yardstick is his own megalomania. Freud and Ferenczi have advanced the idea that the child learns only gradually to distinguish between his own body and the outer world. Consequently he regards everything "good" coming from the outer world not as such, but as a gift he gives himself; only the "bad" refusal comes from the outside, according to this fantasy.

Gratitude has, therefore, a bad start. But the adult "forgets" only too conveniently his own early youth. Would he remember, he would see the picture differently. He would recall that he took everything "good" for granted, that he considered every denial, as necessary as it might be and even for his own good, a terrible injustice.

Every educator knows that gratitude and decency in general must be taught to the child. Gratitude as an inborn drive is clinically not observable. What is seen clinically, however, is a difference in the success of the effort to teach expression of gratitude.

We expect, from a cultured, decent human being, gratitude toward his benefactor. The fact that "grateful" people do exist proves that pedagogy is not as hopeless a task as some pessimists assume. Parents do build up the feeling of gratitude in the child by making it a moral dictum. Since the child identifies with his parents, he can, if he is one of those not too neurotic persons sometimes euphemistically called "normal," restrict his original feeling that everything done for him is to be taken for granted and even show gratitude. In other words, the ability to show gratitude is an artifact built up after overcoming early misconceptions. It is a part of the adaptation to reality.

The majority of people are neurotic to some degree. Freud once mentioned his feeling of fright at the realization that he had the whole of humanity as a patient. This does not mean that everyone has a full-fledged neurosis. It means, however, that everyone has neurotic tendencies. If these tendencies increase quantitatively, we speak of them as neurosis.

One of the necessary weapons of education is restriction. If the child interprets this restriction as malice—and the more neurotic the child the more likely he is to do so—he acquires a feeling similar to that which a patriotic Frenchman had toward the Nazi invaders of his homeland: that everything is permissible against the aggressor. If one objects that the example is absurd, since there is no possible comparison between loving parents and barbaric brutes, the answer is that unconscious misjudgment of reality is one of the basic neurotic symptoms and signs. One cannot argue with a neurosis on logical grounds, especially since the child projects his own aggression onto his parents. The witch of fairy tales, who eats children, is a product of this conception.

Another objection might be raised at this point. One might say that, even if the situation in early childhood were as described, it would seem that the child would grow up and correct his misjudgment. True, the neurotic child grows up. His unconscious, however, does not. Neurosis is basically an anachronism; the repressed part of the personality governs. His Majesty the Baby in the neurotic individual is the leader, not his logic, that is, his conscious. No neurotic is unconsciously as old as his birth certificate indicates; in unconscious development he has remained between the ages of one and three.

All educational restrictions concerned with libidinal and aggressive wishes lead the child to feel frustrated, with resultant feelings of hate. Basically he has two ways out of the dilemma: identification with his educator or unconscious continuation in a disguised form of the old "slave revolt" at the price of suffering. Choice of the former way results in normality; of the latter, in neurosis of different types depending on the genetic level of the fixation or regression.

Another objection might now be raised. If we grant that the child in the grownup prevents gratitude, how can we account for the direct acts of aggression and "meanness" with which some persons repay their benefactors? Clinical experience proves that it is really dangerous to be "nice" to some people; they immediately repay such treatment with some mean trick, whereas previously they showed only indifference. The explanation of this enigma is that the benefactor, by his kind deed, enters the magic circle of the patient's neurotic repetition compulsion. The neurotic then uses him unconsciously as a hitching post for repetition of injustices allegedly experienced, and seeks revenge on him. The fact that the accidental benefactor is not identical with the early "disappointers" and has himself caused no disappointment does not matter; unconsciously he is identified with the early "disappointers," and all hatred, real or compensatory, is heaped on him. He is the innocent victim of the repetition repertoire of his neurotic beneficiary.

Two other factors must be taken into account to explain the inner aggression of some neurotic individuals toward their benefactors. First is the limitlessness of the child's desire for love and exclusive attention. The moment the benefactor is thrown into the neurotic circle of the beneficiary's past, his deed of kindness is measured unconsciously, not according to real facts, but to imaginary ones. His good turn is compared inwardly to the alleged lack of love, attention, and kindness about which the beneficiary inwardly grieves. This debt is projected upon the benefactor, with the result that his deed becomes an infinitesimal part-payment of an old debt. Thus the neurotic, by means of this queer form of unconscious mathematics, changes a kind act into a negligible installment on an unpaid billion-dollar obligation.

The second factor to be considered is the quantitatively different amount of unconscious self-damaging tendencies from which every neurotic suffers as an indispensable condition of his neurosis. Psychic masochists have a queer approach to reality. They are submissive toward the stronger person but very aggressive toward the weaker. The moment the benefactor does a good deed, he is inwardly classified as "weak," and consequently treated by the neurotic with all the aggression at his disposal. Therefore, not gratitude but aggression appears on the surface. Samuel Johnson stated: "Gratitude is a species of justice." True, but he forgot to mention that unconscious justice is regulated not by reason but by irrational feelings.

Moreover, some people are incapable of "taking" a graceful action, and provoke in return until their benefactor becomes disgusted with them. Numerous anecdotes have reference to this. For instance, there is the story that in a small community an elderly ne'er-do-well was invited once a week to dinner by a wealthy man. Although the ne'er-do-well had excelled previously only in exorbitant eating, one day he brought with him an uninvited young man. After dinner his host asked him, "Who is the young man?" "Oh," was the answer, "that is my son-in-law, and I promised him food and a home in his marriage for the first years." If we interpret this story, we see that the beneficiary does not want, unconsciously, the gift bestowed on him, but rather provokes being thrown out, so that he may have a new source of complaints—overlooking, of course, his own unconscious provocation.

Some beneficiaries have convenient methods of discarding their specific benefactors—by misjudging their motives. ("He did it for publicity," or "He did it to make me feel humiliated," etc.) Or they even believe that the benefactor should be grateful to them for giving him the opportunity to "straighten out his accounts with God" by doing a good deed.

The unconscious reasons for doing a good turn are not discussed here. They are not less complicated than those of ingratitude.

Some people advance the idea that gratitude is so seldom encountered because people don't want to be reminded of their own beginnings, when they needed help. This deduction is faulty. People forget their previous dependence and their bill of gratitude because they live unconsciously on the basis of the autarchic fantasy. This unconscious fantasy negates everything worthwhile as coming from the outside; once more, we are confronted with childlike megalomania.

Instinctive knowledge of human reactions has led some philosophers to warn against expecting gratitude. To quote a few: Charron: "He who receives a good turn should never forget it; he who does one should never remember it." And Rousseau: "Gratitude is a duty which ought to be paid, but none we have right to expect." La Rochefoucauld even warned against believing in gratitude when it is shown: "The gratitude of most men is but a secret desire to receive greater benefits." His observation is often correct, although the psychological reasons are more involved than he suspected. For instance, we sometimes see a display of gratitude on an irrational basis. "Simple" people are sometimes grateful because they feel that a kind act of a person whom they consider socially above them brings them psychologically into the orbit of the higher social stratum. Via identification, they pay tribute in their gratitude—to themselves. Sometimes exactly the opposite attitude is encountered. Every kind action of a benefactor on a socially higher level is made worthless by the beneficiary's inner thought of the injustice he experiences in not being on the same economic or social level.

A special type of ingratitude is cashed in by people with new ideas—the scientist, the inventor, the poet, the prophetic homopoliticus of a high level. Biography and observation alike prove that almost every "great man" who is ahead of his time is ridiculed; he is fortunate indeed if he is not completely ostracized during his lifetime. Gratitude comes to him only posthumously. "The public," remarked Henrik Ibsen ironically, "doesn't require any new ideas. The public is best served by the good, old-fashioned ideas it already has" (*An Enemy of the People*). Many statements of scientists, humorists, and educators bear out this observation. Sir William Osler complained: "In science the credit goes to the man who convinces the world, not to the man to whom the idea first occurs." Don Marquis remarked bitterly: "If you make people think they're thinking, they'll love you. If you really make them think, they'll hate you." Thomas Raynesford Lounsbury said ironically, "We must view with profound respect the infinite capacity of the human mind to resist the introduction of useful knowledge."

Taking stock of the complexity of the problems involved in ingratitude, we come to the conclusion that we don't further understanding of this human reaction by complaining and moralizing about "the still small voice of gratitude." Only by unearthing the unconscious reasons for even "simple" human reactions can we come one step further toward unraveling their mystery. The more "normal" or "typical" such reactions are, the less we know about them.

ON QUERULANCE

Melitta Schmideberg

(1946)

This article is not only an illuminating account of the affect of querulousness, but also provides those who are not familiar with the psychoanalytic literature on delinquency with a glimpse into the richness of Dr. Schmideberg's clinical observations in her many years of dealing with antisocial individuals, juvenile offenders, and others in trouble with the law or society. She offers insights into the mechanisms responsible for the formation of the sense of justice in the child, and conclusions on the methods of child upbringing which lead to antisocial behavior.

The querulous individual is "unable to forgive or forget. Time makes no difference." The wrong he has suffered can never be remedied. While displaying a complete lack of insight and scant consideration for the feelings and rights of others, he deems himself extremely sensitive and understanding. He is almost entirely unaware of the intensely aggressive attitude that finds expression in his complaints. Provoking argument, he is deaf to argument. Obsessed by grievances, he does not wish to listen to "explanations."

Editor's note: With apologies to Dr. Schmideberg, I must note an error in the author's use of the word "querulance" as a noun describing the state of being querulous. The correct word, according to the *Oxford Universal Dictionary* (1955), is "querulousness." Accordingly, the correct adjective is "querulous" and the adverb is "querulously."

143

Simultaneously, a refusal to engage in a discussion of his complaints only invites an increase in his querulousness.

This chronic contentiousness is most commonly found in borderline cases, those with seriously disturbed object relations. It is, furthermore, one of the most difficult obstacles to overcome in establishing a therapeutic bond between patient and analyst. Even the smallest incident may be interpreted as a slight, arousing a barrage of contentious verbalizations against anyone, including and especially the analyst.

The emotional equation operating in these patients is: unconscious sadism leads to unconscious guilt, which in turn is replaced by querulousness. It is a defensive dramatization of the statement: "I am not guilty; I am only complaining." Furthermore, if an individual can then prove the legitimacy of a grievance, the unconscious sadism and aggression can become overt, and he can then engage in openly aggressive and even antisocial behavior. The dramatic appearance of manifest aggressive behavior swiftly puts an end to querulousness and is added proof of the meaning of its unconscious psychodynamic function.

A patient in the throes of a full-scale querulous attack bears many striking resemblances, at least superficially, to a nondelusional paranoiac. Many of these patients seem close to paranoia at times. Querulousness can in fact be referred to as one of the "paranoid affective states," along with bitterness and vengeance.

The clinical syndrome of querulance is a familiar one. The patient reiterates his complaints endlessly in a stereotyped manner and with intense feeling. This grievance constitutes a major, if not the main, interest in his life. He is unable to forget or forgive. Time makes no difference: a grievance thirty years old is as fresh as one which arose only yesterday. He feels that the wrong he has suffered can never be remedied. The pathological lack of insight is characteristic, and while he himself is extremely sensitive, he usually shows scant consideration fo the feelings and rights of others. He is mostly unaware of the intensely aggressive attitude which finds expression in his complaints, or else considers it more than justified by the wrongs he has sustained. He is deaf to any argument, although he often provokes argument, and refusal to reason with him only increases his querulance. He expends much time and emotion in proving his case (often having recourse to litigation), and it must be admitted that he frequently has perfectly valid arguments, but either his reaction is altogether excessive or else he is unable to see anything but his own point of view. It is perfectly true that it is unfair that a customer who comes in later should be served first, but no ordinary person would nurse a grievance for days or weeks because of such an "injustice."

Only by listening conscientiously to the arguments of my querulent patients did I realize how good-natured and peaceful the ordinary person is. He does not even forgive; he just forgets. The problem of the querulent patient is largely his inability to forget. Another problem is his inability to see the other person's point of view. The following is a characteristic incident. The importation into England of two hundred cigarettes from the Isle of Man is allowed duty-free. When a patient, who imported a few more than this authorized maximum, had to pay duty on the lot, she displayed a violently querulent reaction: how could the customs officer be so petty as to object to a few cigarettes? It was impossible to make her realize that she imported not merely a few cigarettes but more than two hundred. She discounted the two hundred because they were within her rights. Similarly, she always had to demand more than was conceded to her, and when eventually she met with a refusal she was deeply hurt and reacted contentiously, forgetting all the other person had done or suffered for her. This type of patient usually loses all his friends, which in turn stimulates further his sense of grievance.

Contentiousness is most commonly found in borderline cases with seriously disturbed object relationships, and is one of the most difficult symptoms to cure. Although at first sight the significance of the patient's sense of grievance seems easy to understand analytically, its structure is overdetermined and, owing to its defensive function, of great dynamic importance—a fact which explains the difficulty of curing it. The handling of the patient demands great tact. He is obsessed by his grievance and does not want to listen to anything else. He is not interested in the interpretations, which he stigmatizes as evasions; he wants to get the analyst to take sides, and his querulent reaction increases if the analyst declines to discuss the issue "objectively." A slight stimulus is sufficient to rouse all his contentious feelings against the analyst. Two of my patients wanted to start proceedings against their former analysts. Such patients generally have a number of standing grievances, going back over many years, but they are always ready to adopt fresh ones. A patient started a "new life" every few years with high hopes; as soon as she commenced this new life her old life with all its grievances faded into insignificance. As soon as her high hopes for a new life became disappointed—as they invariably did—she acquired new and deep-seated grievances.

A patient concentrated all her feelings on one event which had occurred more than ten years before. By reason of her failure in an intelligence test (she was schizophrenic and somewhat defective), she had been refused admission into a certain class in school. Whenever she thought of this she fell into a rage, behaved violently, cried, screamed, bit the pillow, and could think for many days of nothing else. Once she wrote such a querulent letter to the teacher—with whom she had had no contact for over ten years—that this woman answered by advising her to undertake treatment. The patient is still unconsciously attached to this teacher; as long as the attachment persists, the grievance persists too. The low level of intelligence causing her to be rejected signified her lack of a penis, which prevented her from being loved by her mother. Being hindered in her intellectual development meant for her being prevented from developing into a man. She was compelled to regard the treatment meted out to her as a grave injustice; otherwise she would have had to acknowledge her low level of intelligence, and thus suffer an unbearable narcissistic wound. Her querulent phases subsided at times (partly because she escaped into a pleasant fantasy far removed from reality), and it was interesting to see on what occasions they sprang into existence again: for example, after she had taken her cat to be castrated. To avoid the unconscious guilt at having had the cat castrated, she had to exaggerate her own grievances; to avoid being reproached, she reproached others.

This defensive function of querulance is most important. A patient told me that her parents used to keep count, so to speak, of every kind action and expected her to be eternally grateful. The only way this unbearable burden could be lightened was by keeping count of her grievances against her parents. She collected grievances as others collect stamps, but as she felt guilty over the pleasure which she derived from every new and cherished grievance she overcompensated by becoming querulent.

A patient was full of grievances and reproaches against his former analyst and played with the idea of taking her to court in order to recover the fees. There was reason to assume that he had been seduced as a child by his nurse and he feared that she might betray him or give him up to the police. The analyst was a substitute for this nurse, and his wish to take proceedings against her was prompted by the desire to prevent her from giving him away.

A prostitute, who came for analysis, and her friend were put on probation for stealing. The patient found this situation particularly unbearable, and induced the friend to transgress the conditions of probation with the result that the latter was sent to prison. The violence of her querulance on both occasions surpasses imagination. For many months there was no limit to the reproaches she heaped upon everybody who had been responsible for getting her put on probation (i.e., had helped her to this end), saying how much more she would have preferred to go to prison. When her friend was sent to prison she launched equally violent reproaches against everybody for not being able to prevent this happening. Her querulent attitude was her reaction to the shock of being caught stealing (in her fantasies of omnipotence she had been convinced that this could never happen) and a defense against the frightening reality. In blaming everybody—her solicitor, her friends, the doctors, and myself—and charging them with the responsibility, she behaved as if prison and probation existed solely through our fault; she tried to deny her own guilt and the existence of the police and of the legal system. The sentence on her friend proved the seriousness of the matter and revived earlier experiences, but the main point is that she was anxious to prove that it was everybody's fault but her own, which it was exclusively.

After being put on probation, this patient became frightened of the police and avoided prostitution for some time. When she resumed it, she developed a tendency to call in the police in order to have her client ejected. She was prone to suspect him of stealing (partly because of her fear that he might hurt her, partly in order to show that he was no better than she). This behavior was designed to prove to herself that she had no fear of the police; that far from avoiding them, she actually summoned them to her aid.

The same extremely querulent patient (she was frequently involved in litigation) was in arms at the amount of her electricity bill and anxious to prove that the company's charge was an unjust one. It became clear that she felt guilty for having spent so much on heating, an indulgence of which her father would have severely disapproved; accordingly she had to show that the blame fell on the company and by means of legal proceedings to reproach and punish the company as her father would have done to her.

When a neon light was placed on the roof of her house she became wildly querulent for weeks, and went so far as to damage the electric wires under the planks of her staircase— a punishable offense. She contended that the neon light interfered with her sleep through its reflected light and vibrations—she suffered severely from insomnia—and that the electric wires which she had gone to great trouble to unearth might endanger not only her but her friend. In the analysis she had a fantasy that she could safely commit murder by inducing a person to touch the live wires in ignorance of their existence. While in her fantasy she hoped for impunity through pretending ignorance of the danger, her querulance served to draw everybody's attention to this imagined danger.

I need not point out the symbolism of the dangerous electric wires in her house, or the sexual anxieties and introjection fears expressed in her pathological sensitiveness to light, noise, and vibrations. But the main factor in this example of querulent behavior was the suppressed wish that her friend should die.

In another instance, the patient threatened to take out a summons against her landlord for not having sent her a receipt. It turned out she was afraid that he might charge her again, and when I told her that she could safeguard herself by giving checks, she let the matter rest. At another house she felt that she had a legitimate grievance against her landlady, so she stole various things and wantonly destroyed the electric fittings (another expression of her castration complex). In this case she avoided a querulent reaction by expressing her resentment in antisocial conduct. Against yet another landlord she took legal proceedings because he addressed the receipts to her and not, as she had asked, to her friend. She had become homosexual during the course of the analysis, and she insisted that her friend with whom she lived should be regarded and acknowledged as her husband. Her parents were very much against this friend and refused to have anything to do with her. In her innumerable complaints that a homosexual girl is not treated as a man, she had shifted her grievances derived from the castration complex to her friend. Her legal dispute with the landlord over his omission to give receipts in her friend's name was also motivated by her ambivalent attitude toward this friend. She wanted to make the friend feel a financial dependence on her with the same bitter sense of humiliation she had herself felt when she had been dependent upon her parents. She overcompensated for this overbearing attitude by quarreling with everyone who did not treat her friend as well as she demanded.

Every time she got a bill she was deeply frightened. She unconsciously thought of the bills she ran up as insatiable demands (oral-sadistic attacks as a punishment for her oral greed displaced from eating to shopping) as well as proof of her wicked extravagance. The only small return for the pain of having to pay bills was the receipt to which she attached a quite unusual significance. Her parents used to impress on her how grateful she ought to be for all the money which they so grudgingly spent on her. She paid her bills equally reluctantly, and demanded a receipt in the proper form as her parents had demanded thanks in the proper form. Her attitude to money, apart from the anal reactions which were expressed in it and were very important, revealed a wish to return to babyhood, to the time when she still knew nothing of money. Many people have a mildly querulous attitude toward paying bills, which often takes the form of suspicion that they have been overcharged; it is partly to be explained by the narcissistic injury implied by the fact that one is no longer cared for for one's sake but for money.

For two or three years a schizoid patient spent the first half of every session in pointing out that I had been a few minutes late, or commenting on the remarkable fact that I was not late, or complaining that the analysis did not help him. In so doing he wasted time and thus forestalled any possible reproaches on my part. He treated me like a naughty child who arrived late, and did not learn well (did not analyze well), and could be kept up to the mark only by nagging. In this he was following the example of his parents and teachers but exaggerating their unpleasant manners. This exaggeration was a mocking caricature of them, but feeling guilty about mocking them he had to take his own exaggerations seriously. The projection of these exaggerations to others caused anxiety; the identification with them made him querulous.

In another aspect, the analytic situation was felt by this patient as a repetition of the experience of being beaten by his father. As a child his reaction of hate and vexation toward his father for beating him was quite out of proportion, and largely a denial and overcompensation for the unconscious homosexual masochistic gratification. A quer-

ulent attitude and pathological jealousy, which often contains a querulent element, are largely due to fear of masochism and an overcompensation for this. The patient reacted
excessively to any minor injury, as he was afraid of his
tendency to submit to anything. In several patients querulent
attitudes were observed to form a reaction to a brief phase of
masochistic adaptation, but in all other cases the masochistic
tendencies were very important.

A patient became morbidly querulent because his
naturalization took somewhat longer than that of a friend.
This delay stimulated all his persecutory anxieties and his
fears that things might be found out and held against him, of
being unwanted, etc. But he was also vexed at receiving less
consideration than his friend and, as it seems childish to him
to admit this, he tended to exaggerate the injury to his
narcissism into paranoid anxieties about which his friends
were more ready to reassure him. In some cases it is felt as a
kind of *lèse-majesté* to be kept waiting, neglected, wronged,
etc., and a certain narcissistic compensation is derived from
imagining that these hurts are not due to chance, but inflicted with hostile intention (justifying one's own hostility).
The attempt to deny narcissistic injuries by raising them to
the level of hostile intentions usually stimulates and in-
tensifies the basic paranoid anxieties. In other cases the
grievance allays paranoid fears, and it is a characteristic trait
in some individuals of this type that they repeatedly contrive
means of justifying grievances. The feared superego punishment is projected in paranoid anxieties, while the grievance
represents the (unjust) punishment already received. The
unjust punishment diminishes guilt and sanctions further
aggression. By turning his paranoid apprehensions into
actual happenings the patient hopes to master them, to find
allies and protectors, and to establish his innocence. Often
he succeeds in libidinizing the situation and then derives

much masochistic-libidinal satisfaction from feeling himself a martyr. Sometimes the paranoid fears are not all bound in the contentious attitude but are expressed openly and independently. Thus in one patient three systems could be observed (apart from obsessional, hysterical, and depressive symptoms): (a) being wronged by parents and parent substitutes; (b) a morbid sense of grievance against a person representing himself; (c) paranoid fears of the police or the authorities and fear of being taken to court.

Querulent behavior is an antisocial activity within the law and, the patient hopes, one encouraged by the law. In the case of the prostitute who reacted to similar situations with either querulent or antisocial behavior, the intense aggression underlying the former was restrained and concentrated on a single aim; but when she felt particularly unfairly treated, restraint was thrown overboard and she indulged in openly antisocial conduct.

The contentious type is usually unaware of any conscious satisfaction from his aggressive tendencies; the antisocial patient is usually not conscious of his feelings of grievance and need for justice. The paranoiac projects his persecutory object, the manic patient his persecuted object to the outside world, while in depression both remain internalized. I have the impression that certain antisocial acts of aggression represent a mixture of manic and paranoid mechanisms in so far as both the persecuted and the persecuting objects are externalized. I believe that this is also true of morbid contentiousness. This sometimes resembles manic reactions, as when the patient talks ceaselessly for twenty-four hours. The instinctual eruption is, however, more controlled and restrained than that of the manic patient. All my contentiously-minded patients suffered from serious depressions. The phenomenological difference between contentious and manic reactions is largely that the sense of grievance which the manic patient denies in his elation, the querulent type particularizes and overemphasizes. Another difference is the presence in the latter of obsessional traits which represent the restraining and canalizing factors. The mechanisms of denial, isolation, undoing, displacement, and condensation are typical of the querulent patient. In his inability to compromise, to forget or overlook trifles, his lack of humor and of any sense of proportion, and the vehemence with which he wants to impose his rigid standards, he resembles the obsessional neurotic. He wishes to establish a world which does not admit of the slightest deviation from his standards of justice, just as an obsessional neurotic must have things scrupulously clean, exact, or symmetrical.

The querulent patient exalts himself by taking over the role of authority, or of God, in his attempts to set the world to rights. Several of my querulent patients had half-conscious fantasies of saving the world, or future generations. These dictated patients' choices of professions as economist or psychotherapist, and in another case the decision to become a communist. The querulent phase usually started either as a reaction to injured narcissism, being rudely disturbed in some preconscious fantasy of grandeur, or to everyday frustrations which were felt as a kind of lèse-majesté. It is unpleasant to have to pay rent or to be kept waiting, but the worst of it is that these bring home the fact that one is not the Queen of England. Frustrations are painful to everybody, but in narcissistic people they are always accompanied by the shattering of dreams of grandeur, and it is this that gives rise to the contentious attitude.

Marked as the narcissistic attitude of all these patients was, it was always a secondary and compensatory narcissism, a reaction to a sense of insecurity, guilt, anxiety, and the loss of an object relation. All were seriously disturbed in their object relations. None of them had satisfactory personal contacts, although in several cases there was a deep devotion to a person or cause that was highly exalted and idealized, and which invariably turned out to be a narcissistic projection of themselves.

I was impressed by the excessive and unreal character of the idealizations in all my querulent patients. These far surpassed anything I have ever observed in other cases. A part of the idealization is genuine, containing much of naïve trustfulness, and memories of happy moments in infancy isolated from all that is hurting and disappointing. But the greater part of it is an overcompensation. The child exalts the parents in order to protect them against its own hostile criticism and soiling contact. Extreme idealization is largely based on isolation, which is a reaction formation against genital or anal contact regarded as soiling or contaminating. The more painful or humiliating it has been made for the child to be in the wrong, the greater will be its satisfaction in finding grounds for criticizing its parents. Often the knowledge that parents are in the wrong gives rise to the fear (or hope) that God will punish them. But if the triumph releases more aggression than the child can control, it will only feel guilty and upset, and try to avoid recognizing that its parents are ever in the wrong by idealizing them excessively and denying reality. Excessive idealizations also serve to overcome intense reactions of disgust and pity and paranoid anxieties by means of equally intense libidinization. A patient idealized in an altogether excessive and unreal way a girl who was found to represent his most dreaded father substitutes. The idealization of justice is another example of an attempt to deal with paranoid fears by libidinization. The prostitute said that not only could she not tolerate any sign of weakness on my part, but even found it painful to realize that I was human. As a child her ideal of perfection was to bear children who had no bowels. A young child, still unable to live up to its ideals of perfection (cleanliness), displaces them to adults whom it admires enormously for never dirtying themselves and, as it often imagines, never defecating at all. On this ideal of cleanliness are based all later conceptions of mental perfection, e.g., justice; and this explains why patients react so often to disillusionments with overwhelming feelings of disgust. The patient who is unable to love himself because he falls short of his superego demands, projects his narcissistic ideal of perfection to his parents, or at a later stage to certain highly idealized persons. A disturbance of these idealizations comes as a narcissistic shock. A patient told me that he must always have love centers and hate centers; he concentrated all his love on one person and all his hate on another. It was essential for him to maintain a sharp separation between his feelings of love and hatred. Extreme idealization presupposes a far-reaching suppression of criticism and hostility, and may thus lead to pathological aggression in other directions, and account for querulent or antisocial behavior. Excessive idealizations (the parents do not defecate) based on a denial of reality are bound to lead to conflict when reality can no longer be ignored. Consequently an upbringing which sets too much store on idealizations is a bad preparation for life in a world which is far from being an ideal one. Because extreme idealizations are based so much on overcompensation, a disappointment is likely to change devotion into hostility. The object of the querulent patient's hatred is often a person who was at some time idealized but then disappointed him. Both the patients who contemplated taking their former analyst to court and who nagged me ceaselessly had originally gone to absurd extremes in their idealization of analysis. A morbidly querulent attitude is the patient's reaction to the narcissistic hurt of being disappointed in his ideals (intensified by paranoid anxieties, reactions of disgust, etc.), and expresses his refusal to accept the injustice of this world. By this attitude, which is a copy or caricature of his parents' educational methods, of their scolding, nagging, beating, and punishing, he hopes to compel society or certain individuals in it to conform to his ideals.

Paradoxically enough, excessive idealizations may not only give rise to querulance, but may also be responsible for criminality. The prostitute had extreme ideals of cleanliness, justice, and correct behavior. Not being able to live up to these ideals, she went to the opposite extreme and became a prostitute and a thief. Normal people would have found some compromise between their ideals and their instinctual life. For her this was impossible, not only because of the gulf between the two, but also because compromise and contact with anything profane was in her eyes tantamount to giving up or soiling her ideals. In becoming a prostitute she not only gratified her instincts but also acted out masochistically her humiliation, projecting her ideals of perfection onto her mother. It was most important to her that these ideals of perfection should be preserved in others, and it was impressive to see how great was her emotion when, believing that the magistrate had acted unfairly, she told me that her father had always brought her up to believe in British justice. When she was told that her extremely provocative behavior toward the probation officer was inviting serious trouble, she reproached me for being and wanting her to be a hypocrite. This was all the more paradoxical as she had cheated, lied, and broken the law on numerous occasions without any qualms.

Contentious types and criminals overestimate the law. It is astonishing how much knowledge of the law they possess compared with the average individual. The litigious spirit clings fast to the law and tries to enforce it, the criminal breaks it, a few "good citizens" are afraid of it, but the majority is not particularly aware of it. They treat it like an old parent, recognize its beneficial aspects, tolerate its short-comings, humor it, show it some respect—a little with tongue in cheek—and do not take it all too seriously. Because the contentious type takes law and justice too seriously, and is lacking in a sense of humor, he is severe both on himself and on others. One tends to feel skeptical when such people declare that they only care for right and justice, because of their absurd behavior and intense aggression. Analysts are often inclined to study only the deeper unconscious, i.e., symbolic meaning of the defensive or rationalizing functions of such an attitude, and omit to consider such declarations at their face value. The child believes that justice is the prerogative of adults. A querulent patient never forgave her mother for saying "One does not argue with children." Another remembers with great bitterness that she was blamed when she stole, but when somebody stole from her, instead of taking her part, her father blamed her for leaving her things about.

A child may be punished for something which was passed over yesterday and is joked about tomorrow; it is blamed for things its parents do without qualms. Adults usually have some neat explanation at hand to cover up their inconsistent and unjust behavior against which children are helpless. Whenever trouble arises, the child is likely to be held responsible, and there are very few adults who would ever admit to a child that they had been in the wrong. Justice between parents and children does not exist because there is no equality, and those in authority are judges in their own cause. The nursery is like a fascist state; a great parade is made of justice, but it depends on the good will of the authorities whether they dispense justice or punish whoever dares to complain.

The fact that men may prefer death to a life without freedom and justice shows how bitterly they must have resented the lack of these in their childhood. Seeing that most children put up with the situation fairly well, the factors which make injustice either tolerable or intolerable require examination. It is a great achievement for a small child to adapt itself to standards of justice and social codes. The harder it has found this task, the more intense will be its reaction to any departure from these standards. If it cost a child a great deal to learn to wait its turn, it will be especially resentful if a late arrival receives prior attention. "Justice" is a compromise between parent and child, an agreement that the parent will not hurt ("punish") the child unless it "deserves" it. The more a child dreads its parents, the more will it cling to "justice" as an obsessional compromise and defense against paranoid fears. A child brought up without kindness and forbearance cannot renounce justice. God, justice, and morality are authorities above the parents to which the child appeals for protection. Adaptation to the environment presupposes much forbearance on the part of the child, but it cannot be expected to display this virtue when the parents themselves are self-righteous, severe, and intolerant, or devoid of a sense of humor. Justice is an obsessional compromise between parent and child, between society and the individual, between superego and id, between vengeance and crime. The obsessional traits in our legal system and forms of procedure—the firm adherence to the letter of the law, the absurd attempts conscientiously and correctly to assess the punishment according to the wrong done—are noteworthy, and are due to the fact that the law is a compromise between and a defense against primitive sadism and equally primitive pregenital anxieties. The detachment essential to the performance of justice is a reaction formation against primitive hate and rage. The contentious personality stands in such great need of justice to enable him to keep his sadism in check, while he still hopes for the injustice that would justify its breaking through. The little child does not at first distinguish between "just" and "unjust" punishments but resents them equally. By taking over its parents' standards it gradually succeeds in suppressing its hostility in the case of "just" punishment. The reaction of most people to "unjust punishment" is out of all proportion because the hostility suppressed in connection with deserved punishments is then released in full force.

I analyzed a patient who had had numerous convictions for exhibitionism. He was an irascible Irishman, full of grievances and prone to fighting at the least provocation. As a child he had been a "sissy," and after joining the Navy he became tough. Both his fighting and his exhibitionism served as assertions of his manhood. That he had been sentenced to prison strongly reinforced his sense of inferiority and made him morbidly sensitive.

Against this general background, each of his querulent grievances could be analyzed individually. On one occasion he complained bitterly—and had almost had a fight over it— because the girl in the canteen served others before him. I inquired whether as a child he ever had been kept waiting for meals. He denied it. I persisted; "Surely every child is kept waiting sometimes." Then he told the story of his childhood. His father lived with a woman not his wife, who brought the boy up. His foster mother spent many hours in bars flirting with men and neglecting the children. The boy was attached to her and tried to hide these facts from his father. He was very much ashamed of his foster mother's flirtations and of the quarrels at home. He was very sensitive lest somebody at school might allude to them, as later he was quick to read an allusion to his prison past even into harmless remarks.

It is essential to discover the element of justification in

every querulous grievance. Neither the analysis of the instinctual factors nor of their defensive function is by itself likely to cure the trouble. The apparent paradox is easily explained. This pathological mode of reaction is the patient's weapon against a painful reality and guilt, and the analyst's efforts to induce the patient to face facts he finds intolerable only increase his need for defense, i.e., his pathological behavior. The usual attitude of adults is to minimize the child's grievances or to blame it for "making a fuss about nothing." It is extremely rare for an adult simply to acknowledge his guilt without trying to explain it away or turning the tables on the child. This attitude not only increases the child's guilt but interferes with its sense of reality. If an analyst does not take the patient's complaints at their face value but regards them only as a defense, or as an expression of his guilty instinctual impulses, and fails to distinguish sufficiently in his interpretations between reality and fantasy, he will seem to the patient to be repeating the parental attitude of putting all the blame on him and not listening to his complaints.

The querulent patient reproaches others with his grievances, a reaction to the accumulation of guilt connected with serious or trifling incidents. Such patients at once assume that they are to blame, whatever happens. A characteristic example was a patient who could not hear anything when telephoning, and immediately began to fear she was becoming deaf. Only later did it occur to her that perhaps the telephone was out of order, which in fact it was. On the second day of her analysis she looked, when leaving, for the doorknob on the left side instead of on the right, and asked what unconscious motive she might have for making the mistake. She was tremendously relieved when I said that the mistake was due to the fact that the knob was not on the side that it usually is. Her former analyst's assumption that every mistake, every misfortune, and most illnesses were her fault had increased her guilt considerably. This patient was greatly impressed because I went to some trouble to change her appointment to assuage her fear that others might find out that she was being analyzed. The fact that I gave consideration to what she regarded as unreasonable oversensitiveness substantially diminished her querulent attitude. Children who are told not to make a fuss about what appears unreasonable to the adult displace their resentment to the few "rational" injuries they are permitted and overemphasize them to a ridiculous extent.

It is essential to consider the patient's feelings, but to humor him indiscriminately or simply to agree that his grievances are justified would be of little therapeutic value. The patient tries so desperately to convince others that his grievances are legitimate because he himself does not believe that they are. His allegations and denunciations are voiced loudly to drown his own doubts. The intensity and endless repetition of his complaints is partly due to the fact that he is not voicing his real grievance but a displaced one. Each repetition of the complaint is a fresh and unsuccessful abreaction. Often, too, the patient's grievance is fully justified, but he is too guilty to allow himself to realize this, and he overcompensates for his doubt by a belated and exaggerated insistence. In a sense, querulance is an attempt to establish that one's grievance is justified, thus to recover one's sense of reality. But often, paradoxically enough, the assertion of a grievance itself expresses denial of it. Denial by assertion or exaggeration seems to me an important defense mechanism. I have been impressed at seeing how upset some patients become when I agree that their complaints—which they had reiterated endlessly with the greatest vehemence—were justified. Having voiced their grievances they ceased to believe in them. They frequently put themselves in the wrong by attacking the person (against whom they had a justifiable grievance) for the wrong thing or in the wrong way, thus preventing others from taking an objectively critical attitude, or inducing them to defend the person wrongfully attacked. Because of the complicated mechanisms of displacement, denial, and asseveration, it seems essential in the analysis to isolate any elements of justification for the patient's grievance and to acknowledge their existence. It is our task to strengthen the patient's sense of reality, to give him the right to complain, and to avoid increasing his guilt by invidious attitudes or interpretations.

A patient had a querulent attitude toward her husband, in accordance with her general attitude. I had the impression that her reproaches were on the whole justified and that their intensity was due to her having had too much to contend with for many years. After having analyzed her fear and guilt toward her husband, who was largely a substitute for her mother, she gradually came to the conclusion (to which others had come long ago) that he was an impossible person and separated from him. Her querulance had been partly a defense against becoming completely indifferent to him and to giving him up.

Often grievances become justified if viewed in relation to their whole setting. Measured by normal standards, the grievances of the prostitute when her father refused to comply with her increasing demands for money were unreasonable. But as a child she was blamed for any striving for independence and deeply reproached at the bare mention of the idea of earning her living later on. For her parents' sake she renounced her independence and perpetuated her childishness into adult years by developing severe inhibitions. It was therefore quite logical that, after having sacrificed so much, she should deeply resent any suggestion that she should work, and demand money from her parents to compensate her for all she had sacrificed. But the loss of her happiness and independence could not be compensated by money so she always had to repeat her demands, and her reaction, when she met with a refusal, was due to the hostility aroused by her submissiveness, and by being cheated even out of a price for it.

This patient had reacted with a phase of intensely querulent and unreasonable behavior to being put on probation, and no interpretation, reasoning, or reassurance seemed to have any effect. The first change came when I admitted that I had been wrong in advising her to accept probation, and that I had been responsible for her relapse into stealing, and thus indirectly for her being put on probation. She reacted to this by admitting to her friend that she had been in the wrong, a thing she could not have done otherwise. The fact that I could bear to be in the wrong made it possible for her to tolerate guilt. Her father, a Victorian, consistently impressed upon her that she had no rights whatsoever and that he was under no obligation to her. He would never admit having been in the wrong, made a point of not apologizing to or thanking her, was harsh and unforgiving. Giving the patient the right to complain often diminishes his need to complain. A querulent attitude is largely a struggle for one's right to have grievances.

The same patient, while violating every law and social code, was, when she got the chance, most severe in her condemnation of everyone who did not behave perfectly correctly toward her. However badly she behaved toward a person, she never considered it a reason for understanding or forgiving a minor slight. But that was just how her parents had treated her. They made most exacting demands upon her, never overlooked her shortcomings, and never admitted their own.

A pathological grievance is always partly a displaced one. We must, however, pay as much attention to the substitute as to the original. The former is not chosen merely for its symbolic meaning. Little is said in this paper about the symbolic significance of the patient's grievances since these are obvious to every analyst. The danger is that we should remain satisfied with having understood the symbolic meaning and so come to overlook the reality aspect of the grievance. A patient who after thirty years cannot get over the fact that as a child she was once not allowed to have a banana, although her sister was given one, obviously suffers from penis envy, but she may have been quite right in concluding that her parents preferred her sister. Instead of saying this, however, she only remembers with a painful sense of grievance an unimportant incident (according to adult standards) when her sister was given preferential treatment. It is essential to understand what an event which appears trifling to an outside observer means to the patient consciously or preconsciously—and not only symbolically. Thus it may have had the effect of a last straw, or it may be a detail typifying a whole attitude. If a patient reacts excessively to "trifles"—with tantrums, querulance, or depression —it is because these trifles are all he has ever had. A patient who does not believe in analysis is likely to cling to every minute that is his due, and one who has no satisfactory contact with the analyst will set his heart on securing a few extra minutes for which he does not pay. A child may go on crying for a toy even after it has got it. This reaction will appear less unreasonable if we realize that the fuss it makes is not so much about its toy as about the happy mood it has lost. At first it cries for the toy, but soon it starts to mourn for its mood, which has become poisoned by hate and fear and which it cannot recover even after it has been given the toy. The reaction of querulent patients is more easily understood if we remember that they are upset not so much by the actual frustration, which may be a minor one, as over the happy mood, pleasant fantasy, or idea of grandeur which has been shattered by this; the patient's complaint that nothing can remedy the wrong he has suffered is thus subjectively justified. The more unhappy and unstable the patient is, the more precious his rare happy moods become and the more difficult will he find it to recover them if he has been upset. In making a fuss about nothing, the patient often repeats his parents' way of treating him, as he does when he claims that he is not interested in the specific case but in the "principle." The fact that the patient is impelled to create certain grievances in order to justify his hostility or rationalize his feelings of being hurt, etc., should not be forgotten.

I consider that the complete picture of the querulent reaction consists of (1) the grievance, (2) the querulent complaint, and (3) the idea of compensation or hoped-for revenge. Generally the sadistic or libidinal content of the compensatory fantasy is rather blurred by repression or rationalization in the shape of demands for money or for an apology. The more the querulent aim is repressed, the more querulent complaining becomes an aim in itself. The repression of libidinal aims leads, as usual, to a regressive increase of sadism.

The unconscious content of the fantasy of compensation corresponds to the original grievance. The schizophrenic patient who could not get over the fact that because of her low intelligence quotient she was not accepted in a particular class in school, bit the pillow in her fits of rage. Her grievance was that she had no penis, and was not loved by her mother. Both these complaints went back largely to unsatisfactory weaning experiences. Her oral disturbances led to severe eating difficulties, and at a later stage to intellectual inhibition. In biting the pillow (breast or penis) she was expressing the oral-sadistic wishes, the fulfillment of which would have remedied her oral grievances.

Money demanded in compensation is not only a rationalization but also a symbolic expression of libidinal wishes. The symbolism of money is a very varied one; it can be a substitute for feces, food, a protecting parent, a baby, the penis, sexual pleasure, etc. The patient, who wanted to start legal proceedings against his analyst (a substitute for his nurse who probably seduced him) in order to recover the fees, avoided spending money on anything that gave him pleasure in order to be able to continue analysis. By demanding the money back from the analyst (the nurse) he was not only turning the tables in respect to his training in cleanliness, but demanding the pleasure (sexual) he had lost from the person who had seduced and then left him.

The prostitute who always hoped to obtain vast sums of money to compensate her for her various grievances derived such satisfaction from these fantasies that she sometimes tried to convert them into realities by embarking on litigation. The clinical fact that she was a prostitute, a thief, homosexual, full of penis envy and hatred toward men, and full of violent resentment against her parents, makes it a plausible supposition that money symbolized for her power, her father's love, a penis, semen, a baby, her mother's milk, sexual pleasure, and every other type of libidinal gratification.

The unconscious situation of grievance may correspond, in my experience, to any important situation in the child's life:

1. Weaning: the prostitute intended to take proceedings against her bank over a delay of two days in paying her allowance; the patient who feared that I might cut short his time or give wrong interpretations (bad food).

2. Training in cleanliness: the prostitute's reaction to bills; wanting the analyst to refund the fees; another patient's querulent hate against a certain "dirty, filthy, disgusting" person identified with excrement.

3. Guilt and interference with masturbation: the querulous reaction of the same patient on being interfered with while daydreaming; intention to take the analyst (substitute for his nurse) to court.

4. Castration fear: querulous reaction to my interpretations, regarding them as attacks; substitute for beating or castration; frequently displaced to politics, championing the cause of the oppressed.

5. Penis envy: schizophrenic patient's grievance at not being allowed to enter a class in school because of low intelligence; the prostitute's plea that homosexual women should be treated like men.

6. Homosexual frustration: schizophrenic patient feels badly treated by teacher; several patients disappointed or disillusioned by friends or superiors.

7. Oedipus frustration: a litigious grievance concerning inheritance when the patient reproached his mother for taking sides with his brother (father substitute).

8. Jealousy of brothers or sisters: a patient's grievance that his naturalization takes longer than his friend's, accompanied by fear that he is not wanted; feelings that brother is being preferred.

9. Interference with scopophilic impulses, etc.: grievance of schizophrenic at not being allowed to enter class in school; grievance that I give wrong interpretations, or at getting a stupid, or not getting an immediate, answer.

10. It may also correspond to situations that do not represent major injuries to primary libidinal urges.

The fantasy compensation expresses equally varied libidinal wishes, and the sadism expressed in querulance is also derived from manifold instinctual sources. The fact that querulance is most frequently found in borderline cases (although it may be observed in certain hysterical types), and that its mechanisms are allied to paranoid, manic, and obsessional mechanisms, are indications that it is mainly related to pregenital phases. Thus even when the grievance corresponds to phallic or Oedipus frustrations these would seem to have their effect largely by activating earlier pregenital ones: the patient who in his grievance that his naturalization took longer than that of his friend expressed his reactions to his brother's birth; he had been very abruptly weaned owing to his mother's sudden illness, and had been unable to get over this; the fear of losing his mother's protection and love was reactivated by the birth of his brother and found expression in his various paranoid anxieties.

I do not believe any particular instinctual frustration or fixation can be regarded as being specific for querulance. Unconscious homosexuality is sometimes an etiological factor, but by no means always. The grievance of the schizophrenic against her teacher sprang from frustrated unconscious homosexuality. The prostitute became manifestly homosexual in the course of her analysis, and this change neither diminished nor increased her tendency to querulance. Her grievances, which were concentrated either consciously or unconsciously on her friend, sprang from her suppressed hostility. Her annoyance over the neon light expressed her reaction to parental intercourse and her wish to induce her mother to have intercourse and be destroyed by it (to induce her friend to touch the electric wire); her desire to remove the neon light and the electric wires on the stairs represented an attempt to rid herself and her mother of the dangerous penis.

A serious disturbance of pregenital development seems to be present in every case of querulance, but to bring about this particular symptom a number of secondary factors seem necessary: lack of humor and nagging on the part of the parents, harsh ideas of justice combined with actual injustice, giving the child much cause for feeling aggrieved while denying him the right to complain. Characteristic for querulance is a particular combination of the mechanisms of projection, denial, and isolation. The sadism expressed in it belongs to equally varied instinctual sources: oral sadism was clearly shown in the case of the schizophrenic who bit her pillow in her querulent fits of rage; anal sadism, in another case, in which the patient used exclusively anal invective against the object of his reproaches. The prostitute once went to bed when she was upset and talked ceaselessly at her mother for twenty-four hours. Litigating and complaining are substitutes for screaming or making scenes about parental nagging and beating. The endless repetition of the complaint represents the refusal to make the smallest concession (anal obstinacy and mastery).

It is known that speaking may symbolize oral and respiratory attacks, anal and urethral ejection and vomiting, as well as genital activities. Endless and stereotyped but not unfriendly criticism of my clothes and the way I did my hair by querulent male patients stood midway between hostility and open sexual interest. Querulance is a substitute for and sometimes the only means of an object relationship, and that interest in the external world is, in some patients, expressed almost exclusively through their symptom. In this they are often only modeling themselves upon their parents whose only way of showing an interest in them had been by criticizing them.

In the antisocial tendencies which find expression in querulance, the patient is usually the only person who is unaware of the sadism revealed by his behavior: he "only said" or he "only tried to prove his right." The mechanisms of "denial" and withdrawal of affect are characteristic and difficult to influence. The prostitute who was, as she thought, innocently and through sheer bad luck always getting involved in litigation, allegedly much against her will, became for the first time conscious of the satisfaction it gave her when a doctor sued her for not paying his fees. It excited her greatly to imagine how much trouble and time the doctor had wasted by taking her to court and how his efforts would all come to nothing as she would eventually avoid paying him.

In remaining unaware of the sadism expressed by his querulance, or that his sense of grievance is excessive, the patient emulates (or caricatures) his parents, who were usually equally unaware of their nagging behavior and of making mountains out of molehills. It is a sign of his loss of capacity for emotional contact that the patient is unable to see other people's points of view. All that matters is that he has been wronged. He genuinely believes—in his condition of pathologically heightened narcissism—that the wrong he has suffered involves the whole of mankind and eternal principles of justice. He is unable to believe that any good may reside in a person who has shown himself capable of hurting him. Identification with his superego leads to an exalted conception of himself and protects him from guilt and from having to acknowledge reality. The patient often projects his own id onto the person he condemns, but strictly isolates any connection between himself and him. The patient denies his own sadism and any wrong he may have himself committed. He is all white, his adversary all black. He isolates the sense of grievance from everything else; hence whatever good the other person may have done him is of no account. It is first and foremost the mechanism of isolation which protects him from yielding to reasonable argument even if he admits its justification.

One patient proved an exception to this rule. She was very intelligent, had a good sense of reality as well as a sense of humor, and was aware of the pathological nature of her querulance. Nobody could have put the case of her adversary better than she did herself, but this did not prevent her

from displaying a most violent and unreasonable querulance; on the contrary, she felt that the knowledge of how
understanding she had been was an additional justification
for her querulance. "Understanding" was the main expression of her positive feelings toward others. Having done so
much for them as to understand them, she was free to
express her hostility querulently. Her bitterest reproach
against her parents was not that they hurt or bullied her, but
that they were completely lacking in understanding. Her
ideal was that of a just and unforgiving God, in contrast to
her weak father, whom she despised, and to her aggressive
and querulent mother, who was equally without understanding or fairness. This patient's mechanism of denial was
not marked (this accounted largely for her good sense of
reality), but her mechanisms of isolation and withdrawal of
affect were all the stronger. Owing to the strength of her
isolation mechanisms, her insight was perfectly detached
from her emotional reactions.

ON THE MECHANISMS OF SPACING AND CROWDING EMOTIONS

OTTO E. SPERLING

(1948)

Born and brought up in Vienna, Otto Sperling was intrigued as a high school student by the exciting new discoveries of psychoanalysis and sought Freud's advice about becoming a psychoanalyst. Following his suggestion, Sperling attended medical school, underwent psychiatric residency training, and became one of the first students at the newly founded Vienna Psychoanalytic Institute, where he was supervised by Helene Deutsch, Paul Federn, and Edward Hitschmann. This same spirit of discovery runs as a thread throughout his prolific contributions to the psychoanalytic literature over the years.

In this paper, Sperling makes a unique contribution to the study of disturbances in affects by describing a particular defense against affects: the mechanisms of spacing and crowding emotions.

Sperling reminds us that Freud emphasized the importance of defenses against emotions prior to his elaboration of defenses against instinctual drives. The defenses Freud named were repression, postponement, displacement, isolation, change of quality, projection, and introjection. The special defenses against feelings of guilt were sharing of guilt,

173

borrowing of guilt, and regression; against anxiety, denial, active anticipation, turning from passivity to activity, libidinization; against sexual drives, asceticism and intellectualization.

Sperling discovered that certain individuals, out of a fear of an excessive emotion, subdivide an affect and experience the separate parts at different times. "The emotions have to be separated and spaced in order to avoid a traumatic affect, the danger of which is very real." Separating and subdividing emotions, Sperling observed, is often found in latent schizophrenics in whom excessive emotions seem to mobilize their psychosis. This mechanism, however, is not confined to severe neurotics or psychotics, but is part of the psychopathology of everyday life.

The opposite of spacing emotions is the mechanism of "crowding" emotions into one simultaneous climax. The explanation for this may well be the observation that this is a manifestation of a counterphobic attitude: through actively initiating, the greater psychic pain of passively anticipating and enduring is overcome. Often, the two mechanisms, crowding and spacing emotions, coexist.

Defenses against emotions are more basic and archaic and were studied earlier than defenses against instinctual drives. As early as 1900, in *The Interpretation of Dreams*, Freud mentioned several defenses against affects, namely, repression, postponement, and displacements. Later, he described isolation, change of quality, projection, and introjection. There are special defenses against feelings of guilt, for instance, sharing and borrowing of guilt, and regression. Against anxiety there are additional defenses, e.g., denial, active anticipation, in the turning from passivity to activity, in libidinization, etc. Asceticism and intellectualization, which Anna Freud (1936) describes as defenses against the sexual upsurge in adolescence, are at the same time defenses against the sexual affect.

In this paper I describe a mechanism which I have been able to observe in a number of cases whereby, out of fear of an excess of emotion, the affect is subdivided and the parts experienced at different times. In the psychological sphere this is similar to certain surgical operations which are performed in two parts, with an interval during which the patient may recover. In trying to explain this mechanism, I am faced with the difficulty which complicates every psychoanalytic study, that of overdetermination. It is usually the mechanism of isolation which is also involved.

Jean, who suffered from various phobias, was engaged, and had to arrange the date for her wedding. She would have liked to elope, but her parents insisted on a formal wedding. For her a formal wedding meant a theatrical performance which she contemplated with some stage fright; but the actual wedding meant more to her—namely, arriving at a decision after a long period of doubt as to whether she was making the right choice of a husband. Besides this there was a fear of defloration. About three weeks before the wedding she persuaded her fiancé to get married in court, clandestinely. Thus the affect connected with making the decision and with defloration was separated by three weeks from the affect connected with the official wedding. She arranged for this subdivision out of fear that her emotion would be unbearable if there were no interval.

As a child, up to the age of six years, she had two mothers, her real mother and an unmarried aunt. When this aunt, whom Jean preferred, had to leave the house because of a quarrel with Jean's mother, Jean made it difficult for her mother by developing an anorexia. This situation was repeated at nineteen, when she had two suitors. She preferred Peter, loved him masochistically but without permitting any physical contact, and rejected him. With Saul she had clitoral sexual experiences, although she felt only an obligation and no love, and married him after years of indecisiveness, doubting all the time whether she should not have married Peter.

The separation of tender love and sensual love was, in this case, not only motivated by the mechanism of isolation. Freud (1912) gives two motivations. First, the object of tender love is a substitute for the incestuous object, in this case the mother. The sensual love has to be diverted to another, a degraded object, in order to prevent the realization that it was really the mother who had been desired in a sensual way. Like repression, isolation is directed against conscious knowledge. While in repression the whole story is eliminated from consciousness, in isolation only the knowledge of the connection of the isolated facts is unconscious, in Freud's cases the connection of the mother with sensual desires.

Freud adds a second motivation for the separation of tender and sensual love; namely, perversions, the gratification of which would be possible only in the degraded object, not in the loved one. A third motivation was found by Eidelberg (1934), who saw this separation brought about in two cases by the mechanism of identification. Identification with an overestimated partner made these men impotent, but where identification did not take place, either because the object was degraded or because of a similarity to the father, sensual relations could be established.

In the case of Jean and in several similar cases I could find a fourth motivation; namely, the avoidance of too much emotion. The simultaneous fulfillment of sensual with tender love seems to them more happiness than they can bear. The emotions have to be separated and spaced in order to avoid a traumatic effect, the danger of which is very real. Grinker and Spiegel (1945) found that it is the intensity of anxiety which brings on war neurosis. In the case of Jean the fear of childbirth was an emotion which she could not subdivide, and a few weeks before childbirth she broke down with a severe depression.

Doris, who suffered from compulsion neurosis, fell in love with her future husband and married him after overcoming a number of obstacles. They could not live together long because he was drafted into the Army, but he was stationed in this country and they were able to see each other occasionally. She remained faithful, in spite of various temptations, until she received a telegram from her husband that he would be able to see her at a certain place. The day before she was to meet her husband she had sexual intercourse with another man in whom she was not at all interested. This experience later bothered her conscience and she could not explain it to herself, especially because before her marriage she had been relatively inhibited sexually, and later both with her husband and in this extramarital episode. In the analysis of the frigidity, the fear of becoming insane from too much emotion was very important. Her mother and one of her sisters were schizophrenics. By her unfaithfulness she made sure that she would not feel too happy in seeing her husband. As might have been expected, she split her transference in her psychoanalysis by finding a married Austrian refugee whom she encouraged to read poetry to her.

Richard was very aggressive in his career, and very sexually agressive with women. He felt that he owed his successes to a kind of sacrifice. On the way to meet a woman, he had to vomit, sometimes in the street, sometimes in restaurants. Before he vomited he was excited, tense, afraid of rejection, and afraid of vomiting. Afterwards he felt calm and became master of the situation. During the psychoanalysis he changed his symptoms and would masturbate before the date, with the same effect. His sexual drive had then lost most of its urgency and he could have sexual intercourse with the woman cold-bloodedly. During this intercourse he could reach an orgasm, but much of the excitement was gone since he had separated most of his sexuality from the triumph of conquest. In this case vomiting had the same effect of a discharge of excitation as the masturbation.

In some cases of ejaculation praecox, besides the well-known unconscious motivation, the mechanism of spacing emotions may play a part. In the first premature ejaculation most of the sexual tension would find an outlet, while the affectionate side of the relationship would play a part in the second attempt.

From the therapeutic point of view the observation of the spacing mechanisms in our patients should be of a certain value as a warning signal. If the patient is so careful in the handling of his emotions, interpretations will have to be allocated in such a way as to avoid traumatic emotional upheavals.

In general I have found the mechanism of spacing emotions most often in patients with depressions, phobias, and masochism. These people avoid strong stimulations in the nonsexual sphere also, for instance, baseball games, races, betting and gambling, as too exciting. They avoid mass entertainments such as fairs, parades, funerals, barbecues, and amusement parks as garish and ostentatious. They might regard Wagner's operas as "too much brass," popular music as "too sweet," and detective stories as "too gory"—or they might read the ending first in order to reduce the suspense. The fear of excitement could be traced back to traumatic experiences in childhood such as operations without anesthesia, sexual seduction, separation from the loved objects, and observation of parental sexual intercourse.

The mechanism of spacing emotions can best be appreciated by comparing it with its opposite, the mechanism of crowding emotions into one simultaneous climax. Let me cite an example. Paul was married to a jealous woman. He started an affair with another woman whose husband tried to divorce her on the grounds of her infidelity. That was not enough; their sexual intercourse had to take place on a stairway in a strange building where they could have been surprised at any moment. He had to combine the sexual excitement with the defiance of the dangerous rival, of his wife, and of public order. It was not a necessary condition for his sexual enjoyment, nor a perversion, but an added stimulation for which he longed. As long as his partner was willing to forgive him his chicaneries he felt all right. When she broke off the relationship he went into a depression, and it was for this reason I saw him. In the psychoanalysis this crowding of emotions could be understood as a manifestation of his counterphobic attitude. He re-enacted his traumatic Oedipus experiences, risking discovery and being punished for his relationship with his mother substitute in order to demonstrate that "I am not afraid any more." The fact that he had to prove it, and the obsessive manner in his search for the previously feared situation, show that he was still fixated to the trauma. The active repetition, however, of what had previously been experienced passively neither helped him to forget the trauma nor prevented his later breakdown. These repetitions had already begun as a child of ten with a seduction of his younger sister and challenging her to tell it to father. In school he was ambitious and successful, but his experiences there centered on climactic examinations crowded at the end of the term. Playing chess or cards did not give him pleasure unless he combined it with gambling for high stakes. Characteristic of his technique in playing chess was his centering his defense and attack on one pawn. In business he was successful in the arrangement of large-scale speculative deals. In his previous extramarital relations he had arranged orgies. In his relationship with his wife, whom he called "Mom," he had conscious fantasies of incest. When he had to get a new set of teeth he had all his own teeth pulled in one sitting.

I have found the crowding of emotions frequently in psychopathic personalities, but I have no doubt that it is very common in that group of normal persons which has been characterized, first by F. von Schlegel and later by Nietzsche (1920), as Dionysian. It is characteristic that Wagner's music drama shows this crowding of emotions in the combination of architecture, scenery, music, voices, drama, philosophy, religion, nationalism, even incest, all combined in one morsel.

In the normal person I have often found the two mechanisms of crowding and spacing emotions coexistent. Some emotions are subdivided, some are climaxed. One interesting example was mentioned by Greenson (1949). Some of the inmates of Japanese prisoner-of-war camps would divide their rice portions in order to eat several times a day. Others would save several rations so they could have a big meal once in a while, and the feeling of satiation. Both Margaret Fries (1935) and René Spitz (1945-1946) have demonstrated that the infant wants to crowd the experience of food intake with the experience of warmth and affection from the mother.

The more I followed up these mechanisms in my patients, the more convinced I became that, disregarding the extreme cases which represent examples of phobia and counterphobia, this managing of emotions is normally a basic function of the psychic apparatus, representing Freud's dualism of basic drives. The psychic apparatus, in the service of the death instinct, works in the direction of mastering and eliminating stimuli from within and without, in this way keeping psychic tension at the lowest possible ebb. Subdividing and spacing can easily be recognized as a mechanism of the death instinct. In the crowding of emotions there appears to be a manifestation of Eros (life instinct).

ANXIETY AND THE CAPACITY TO BEAR IT

Elizabeth Zetzel

(1949)

As a backdrop to this important contribution, Zetzel, in this paper, reviews the history and development of analytic thought regarding the essential nature of anxiety, describes two types of anxiety—primary and secondary—and provides a lucid description of the basic instinctual drives and their significance for the development of anxiety.

As a result of her work with World War II combat veterans, Zetzel proposed that the development and toleration of secondary anxiety is not only inevitable but desirable both as a stimulus for early infantile development and as an essential prerequisite for the construction "of adequate defenses in all danger situations, whether they arise from within or without." She discovered a group of patients who had successfully avoided any awareness of fear or anxiety, denying and repressing the existence of danger situations both external and internal. However, they neither developed nor tolerated anxiety, either partially or in disguised form, as do patients suffering from somatic diseases. They did not develop traumatic war neuroses, nor, on the other hand, were they able to acknowledge by phobic symptom-formation their awareness of threatened danger situations. Ultimately, after prolonged severe stress, they tended to develop severe emotional breakdowns, and of even greater im-

portance, their symptoms proved to be highly irreversible no matter how long the therapy.

Paradoxically, these patients give a history that they were notably "well adjusted prior to breakdown." Able to experience severe enemy action for an appreciable length of time without developing symptoms, they had not been aware of any change in their condition up to the time of the particular traumatic incident that was their "undoing." The "trigger" was often a very slight traumatic experience occurring after enduring many more serious and even grave threats to life itself. Subsequent to this incident these patients did not feel or appear anxious, nor were they able to work through their traumatic experiences by anxiety dreams. Instead, after a rather swift initial recovery, a more ominous clinical picture gradually appeared; they became depressed, somewhat paranoid, and markedly hypochondriacal.

Zetzel brings to our attention the prophylactic value of previous anxiety with respect to relatively irreversible actions following frightening experiences. These patients had failed to develop and cope with secondary anxiety related to unconscious castration fears and other early fears. There is no question in her mind that secondary anxiety was indispensable both as an aid to development and as a protection against psychic disaster in life. It is of fundamental importance to promote growth of the ego.

A companion piece to Zetzel's valuable observations on the capacity to bear anxiety was her 1965 paper, "Depression and the Incapacity to Bear It." This later paper was an expansion of the theoretical propositions first set forth in the paper reproduced here. Those who "bear" depression without falling ill demonstrate an ability to control primitive, aggressive instinctual energy and therefore show an earlier onset in the capacity to tolerate delay and frustration; they show an absence of early fixations, which determine, of *course, vulnerability to ego regression, a crucial factor in the severity of illness; and they are characterized by a mature, passive acceptance of the inevitable, which is a prerequisite for remobilization of adaptive resources.*

The first aim in this paper is to review briefly the history and development of analytic thought regarding the essential nature of anxiety in order to state as clearly as possible those aspects of theory which, although still incomplete, appear to be relatively noncontroversial, in that they are compatible with considerable differences of opinion in respect to other basic concepts. In contrast, I also wish to define other important theoretical concepts, particularly with regard to the nature and origin of internal danger situations, which appear far more controversial and in respect to which differences of opinion tend to give rise to unavoidable theoretical controversy.

The second aim, owing to the fact that my own interest in this subject was originally stimulated by my opportunity during the war of examining a large number of anxious soldiers to a greater or lesser depth, has a more direct clinical bearing. I should like now to use this opportunity of carrying a little further my previous tentative conclusions that the presence of anxiety symptoms both in childhood and in adult life is often of good prognostic significance, in that individuals who had been capable of tolerating relatively great amounts of anxiety during the course of development proved on the whole less liable to develop relatively irreversible neurotic reactions in the face of traumatic war experiences.

From its earliest period, psychoanalytic theory regarding the nature of anxiety has approached the subject from two points of view. In the first place, the relationship of anxiety to instinctual frustration has been stressed. Although Freud made considerable modifications in his conception and orientation in this respect, he continued to stress the close relationship of anxiety to quantities of frustrated instinctual tension. The importance of this aspect has always been generally accepted by analytic writers. Fenichel (1945), for example, frequently refers to the pathogenic effect of what he calls "dammed-up" states, a term also used by Anna Freud (1936) in *The Ego and the Mechanisms of Defense*, and Ernest Jones (1911), too, has from a very early date stressed the vital significance in relation to the emergence of anxiety, of mounting instinctual tension for which no discharge is available.

On the other hand, Jones in particular has always considered anxiety from a biological point of view, emphasizing the close relationship between anxiety and fear.

In what may be regarded as his definitive statements on the subject in "Inhibition, Symptoms and Anxiety" (1926) and in the "New Introductory Lectures" (1933b), Freud also distinguished between two types of anxiety. He recognizes and explicitly states the value of anxiety as a response to an internal danger situation. At the same time, however, he does not abandon his earlier emphasis on the importance of accumulations of excitation which cannot be discharged. He thus gives the name primary anxiety, or the traumatic factor, to the condition which, he states, is directly brought about by helplessness in the face of overwhelming instinctual excitation. Secondary anxiety, in contrast, is a defensive reaction which becomes manifest as a signal that a danger situation may arise.

I shall in this paper accept Freud's distinction between two types of anxiety, and define primary anxiety as the direct result of such helplessness in a situation of overwhelming excitation as to constitute a traumatic event. Secondary anxiety, however great, is defined as a defensive reaction brought about by fear in the face of an internal danger

situation. In considering the capacity to bear anxiety, therefore, this double orientation must be borne in mind. Let us
assume that instinctual excitation or tension of any kind will
at some point reach a pitch sufficient to precipitate traumatic
or primary anxiety. One might postulate three possible
stages in this development. In the first stage, while instinctual tension remains well within the individual capacity for
its toleration, it will not constitute a danger situation, but
will be experienced as a specific tension, for example sexual
desire, without anxiety. In the second stage, the instinctual
tension will have reached a pitch nearer to the breaking point
of the individual so that an internal danger situation is
created. At this point true anxiety of the secondary type will
be experienced. Finally, after the tension reaches a pitch
which cannot be tolerated, either with or without inter-
vening secondary anxiety, a traumatic event will occur,
characterized by the appearance of primary anxiety.

In discussing anxiety, therefore, we have a double task:
first we must consider both the origin and psychogenesis of
instinctual frustration, and second we must formulate and
describe the way in which this frustration presents itself as an
internal danger situation. We must, that is to say, first
consider briefly the various views regarding the basic
primary instincts and the conditions determining their frustration; and in the second place the specific internal danger
situations which arise in the course of mental development.
With regard to both these questions we approach controversial matters, since with respect to instinctual tension and
in respect to internal danger situations the part played by
aggressive instincts is a matter of considerable differences of
opinion. To put the extremes of the controversy in its
simplest form, we must ask and answer the question: Is
anxiety, either partially or wholly, produced by or in
response to primary aggressive impulses? or, on the other

hand, should aggression be regarded as mainly secondary, arising either as a result of external frustration or as a direct response to anxiety itself? Some stress the vital relationship of anxiety to primary aggressive or destructive impulses. Others doubt the existence of primary aggression as an independent pathogenic factor, relating its appearance rather to external frustration of primitive instinctual impulses. In between these two extreme points of view, Loewenstein (1940), in a paper entitled "The Vital or Somatic Instincts," makes a case for the reinstatement of the self-preservative instincts as primary; and Freud states in "Inhibition, Symptoms and Anxiety" (1926) that "what we are concerned with are scarcely ever pure instinctual impulses but mixtures in various proportions of the two groups of instincts" (p. 125). In his paper on "Psychoanalysis and the Instincts" Jones (1936) also concludes that "the eroticizing of aggressive impulses is a remarkably general process which accounts for much of the complexity of life. For these reasons it is extraordinarily difficult to detect spontaneous activity of the aggressive instinct in isolation, and I do not myself know of any unequivocal example" (p. 169).

A full discussion with regard to the nature of the basic instincts would obviously be impossible within the scope of this paper. It is, however, essential to recognize that the question of the nature of the aggressive instincts is pivotal in this connection. There would, I think, be general agreement that in respect to clinical conditions and in the course of every analysis, anxiety can be seen either as a response to, or as a cause of, aggressive impulses which are either conscious or threatening to become so. We are all familiar, that is to say, with the child who becomes aggressive because he is anxious. Anna Freud devoted a chapter to this type of aggression in *The Ego and the Mechanisms of Defense* (1936) under the title "Identification with the Aggressor"; and

Theodor Reik published a paper entitled "Aggression from Anxiety" in which he expanded this topic at some length, stating that: "We have hitherto underestimated the significance of the mechanism whereby anxiety is transformed into hatred, and so into aggressive tendencies" (Reik, 1941, p. 9).

This agreement with respect to clinical manifestations does not, however, by any means imply any real consensus, either with regard to the existence of aggression as a primary instinct, as to whether this aggression is in the first instance directed toward the self, i.e., the death instinct, or toward the outside world. Nor is there agreement as to the degree and manner in which the instincts are regarded as inherently dangerous. To restate the points of view held by some of the analysts who have made important statements on the subject, Klein states, in her paper on schizoid mechanisms: "I hold that anxiety arising from the operation of the death instinct within the organism, is felt as fear of annihilation (death), and takes the form of fear of persecution" (Klein, 1946, p. 100). It is clear that in her opinion the ultimate source of anxiety is attributable to primary destructive impulses directed toward the ego. Anna Freud, without being specific regarding the nature of the instincts concerned, definitely includes dread of the strength of the instincts as an important cause of deep anxiety. Whatever the orientation toward the basic instincts, there is no doubt that the conception that sexual and aggressive impulses which cannot be tolerated become manifest as primary anxiety is still fruitful as a means of increasing our clinical understanding of traumatic states. It is important to realize, however, that although this conception was first expressed in relation to sexual impulses, modern developments have led to greater emphasis on the part played in early anxiety states by aggressive and destructive tendencies. Since, moreover, the conception of frustration as a source of instinctual tension plays an important part in this theory, the hypothesis that aggression, tension, and anxiety react in an increasing vicious circle under unfavorable circumstances can be easily correlated with this point of view.

So far, then, I have briefly considered the nature of the primary instincts which, when frustrated, produce instinctual tension. When this tension becomes intolerable, primary anxiety, or a traumatic state, results. While, however, this frustration is present in lesser degrees, the consequent tension is, according to Freud's conception, experienced by the individual as an internal danger situation. The biological response to danger situations, whether internal or external, is to develop fear. Secondary anxiety, thus defined as the purposive response to an internal danger situation, is a conception of the utmost importance. To put the problem again in the simplest form: Assuming that instinctual frustration is the determinant of an internal danger situation, how much are we to attribute this danger situation to an external environment of a frustrating kind, and how much are we to regard it as something inherent in the nature of human psychological make-up? This problem is closely related to the topic I have just discussed—that is, the nature of the primary instincts themselves. The emphasis here, however, is somewhat different. In my former remarks, I briefly outlined one of the sources of differences of opinion regarding the relationship of frustration to instinctual tendencies. Here, however, I am more concerned in considering our orientation toward internal danger situations. I do not by any means wish to minimize the importance of external reality or the relationship of anxiety to external frustration or danger. My thesis, however, is not so much that external events are unimportant, as that their pathogenic action lies in the internal situations brought about when accumulated instinctual frustration, however originated, reaches a pitch sufficient to constitute an *internal* threat. Here, too, we are concerned with important differences of opinion as to how far this instinctual frustration may be attributable to external situations, and to what degree frustrations are inevitable owing to the fact that the instincts themselves are essentially dangerous. Freud himself, although accepting the conception that instinctual frustration is the determinant of an internal danger situation, tended to imply that this situation was brought about not so much by fear of the instincts themselves as in relationship to a possible resultant external threat, particularly that of castration (Freud, 1926).

I have distinguished between internal danger situations directly attributable to instinctual frustration and internal danger situations which on analysis can be interpreted as related to threats arising from internal objects. It will be obvious, however, that this separation is artificial, and only justifiable for purposes of description. Although there are, as I have emphasized, considerable differences of opinion both as to the nature of the instincts concerned and with regard to the structure and significance of internal objects preceding the definitive and generally accepted superego, there is no difference of opinion as to the fundamental inseparability of instinct from internal object. Freud, for example, in the "New Introductory Lectures," states:

> There is no doubt that when the super-ego was first instituted, in equipping that agency use was made of the piece of the child's aggressiveness towards his parents for which he was unable to effect a discharge outwards . . . , and for that reason the severity of the super-ego need not simply correspond to the strictness of the upbringing. It is very possible that, when there are later occasions for suppressing aggressiveness, the instinct may take the same path that was opened to it at that decisive point of time [1933b, p. 109].

I have not, so far, attempted to make any distinction between conscious and unconscious anxiety. The concept of unconscious anxiety is one which presents a number of theoretical difficulties, although a great deal of analytic theory is based on its existence. In considering this problem it is important to specify the type of anxiety under discussion. With regard to primary anxiety it is difficult to be definite. In those situations which have been described as traumatic—the infant at birth and in other situations of total helplessness in the face of overwhelming excitation; the adult when this situation is repeated in a traumatic experience— the physical and mental manifestations obviously affect the whole of mental and physical life. When, however, instinctual tension of this type is present in less intolerable quantities, it may be guarded against by a number of different defenses. Accumulation of inner tension has been defined as the determinant of the internal situation to which secondary anxiety is the biological response. Secondary anxiety so defined, since it is associated with the mental and physical changes which are the inevitable accompaniment of fear in any danger situation, external or internal, will, when it is developed and tolerated as such, produce conscious manifestations. There are, however, a number of other defenses against this threatened internal danger situation which either prevent the emergence or disguise the subjective experience of true secondary anxiety with full awareness of its mental and physical aspects.

The thesis I wish to offer for discussion is to the effect that the development and toleration of secondary anxiety as such is not only inevitable but also desirable, both as a stimulus to early infantile development and as an essential prerequisite for the construction of adequate defenses in all danger situations, whether they arise from within or from without. The physical and mental manifestations of this type of anxiety are closely related to the physical and mental accompaniment of normal fear, that is, fear in an objective or external danger situation preparatory for action. According to most accepted physiological and psychological theories, the physical and mental changes developed in this situation are definitely purposive in that they prepare the individual to deal with a threatened danger. Psychologically, that is to say, the anxious individual will be conscious of some feeling of anticipatory dread, mental alertness, and tension. Physically he will produce some or all of those physical changes which in an external danger situation would equip him either to fight or to take flight. A good example of the stimulating effects of this type of anxiety in a real-life situation we must have all experienced is that associated with examinations. This situation can also be used to illustrate the difference between anxiety as a stimulating and as an inhibiting factor. Where the anxiety retains the quality of normal purposive fear, the examinee, although subject to some uncomfortable physical sensations, is usually aware of noticeable mental alertness, ability to use his resources to the best of his power, and moreover to sense and avert the traps presented to him by a wily examiner. When, in contrast, for any reason anxiety loses these qualities and resembles rather the helpless manifestations of the infant presented with a situation with which he cannot cope, the mind becomes blank, the individual tremulous and distressed, and unable to use his resources in any purposive way.

When we try to disentangle the psychopathological differences between these two reactions, we are faced with a number of difficulties. Although the examination situation does not present an actual objective threat to the individual, it must nevertheless be regarded as a real danger in that failure must be assumed to involve real disadvantages. We must assume, therefore, that the individual differences responsible for bringing about these well-recognized different reactions to an examination situation are complicated. There is in fact considerable analytic literature on the subject of examinations, which was summarized in a paper by Flugel (1939). Although in this paper a number of interesting interpretations of the examination situation are given, the emergence of the type of primary anxiety I have here described is not stressed. I feel, however, that the distinction between these two groups is particularly clear in the examination situation. In the first group, the danger situation is recognized and accepted as a challenge which can be prepared for and coped with so that the anxiety acts as an ally, whereas in the second group the tension and excitation produced, far from helping, inhibit the individual and prevent him from coping with the situation. In the successful individual, it might be argued that these manifestations should not be described as due to anxiety so much as to normal fear. I use the example, however, as an illustration of the stimulating effects of fear in a danger situation—effects which I believe to be qualitatively comparable to secondary anxiety developed in relation to internal unconscious danger situations. Between the type of anxiety or fear which is entirely successful in its stimulating effects and the type of anxiety which is entirely inhibiting there is a wide range of conditions which comprise the various types of clinical anxiety, and the defense against them. To give a few examples: if we assume that the optimum which we describe as normal fear produced only an amount of anxiety sufficient to act as stimulus without causing any significant subjective distress, we must next consider the individual who, although he develops more anxiety than he can deal with comfortably, is nevertheless able to tolerate this as anxiety, without being overwhelmed, without developing incapacitating physical symptoms, and without developing an examination phobia. Next we must consider the type of individual who in association with a degree of anxiety greater than the optimum readily expresses his anxiety in the form of somatic symptoms. This type of candidate will at the mild end of the scale only be aware of symptoms such as palpitations, frequency of micturition, dryness of the mouth, and the like, while at the more severe end of the scale he may produce sufficient physical symptoms to interfere with his success. Finally, we must consider the individual who, because of the degree of anxiety aroused by the thought of an examination, develops an examination phobia.

The same range may be applied to the various responses to internal danger situations which stimulate anxiety related to unconscious sources. At the one extreme we have individuals who are able to tolerate considerable anxiety as such, when the danger situation is one which must be recognized and when no positive defenses are available at the time. Next we have the important group of individuals who, although they retain the subjective awareness of a danger situation, are not able to contain this danger situation within themselves—i.e., to recognize the danger as arising from within— but who project it onto the external world in the form of a phobia. This type of anxiety is so well recognized and understood that I do not feel that any further discussion is indicated at this point. It is important, however, to stress the fact that this group of individuals, although they manage to avoid the subjective experience of very great quantities of what Freud has described as free-floating or unspecific anxiety, nevertheless do not deny their awareness of a danger situation in spite of the fact that they project an internal danger onto the outside world.

Next in this range of diminishing awareness of internal danger situations we have the group of individuals in whom the physical responses to anxiety play a more prominent part than the mental. These individuals are much less aware of fear than of its bodily concomitants. To consider this problem in detail would obviously take us far afield, since it involves the whole question of bodily compliance, the way in which different organs can take on special psychological significance and the way in which bodily changes at first produced by anxiety may be perpetuated, or disguised, by hysterical mechanisms. The degree and manner in which the total manifestations of anxiety, both physical and mental, may be split up as a defensive measure, are obviously of considerable interest. Zilboorg (1933), for example, in a paper entitled "Anxiety without Affect," has described an interesting case in which a patient produced the physical manifestations of an acute anxiety attack without emotional concomitants. Usually, dissociated physical manifestations of anxiety are of a more chronic nature, and it is well recognized that the type of personality who tolerates considerable quantities of anxiety in its physical manifestations over a long period often tends to be predisposed, either as a result of cumulative stress or in some new situation which increases the quantitative tension, to develop one of the organic diseases which are recognized to be psychosomatic in origin.

Not infrequently, patients who develop psychosomatic disorders deny much awareness of conscious fear. Unlike phobic patients, they do not retain an awareness of a danger situation, even though they may experience many of the bodily concomitants of fear. During the war, for example, many patients of the effort syndrome type denied any experience of the emotion of fear or anxiety. This group, therefore, passes by imperceptible shades into the last group, the one I am most concerned with; namely, those who have successfully avoided any awareness of fear or anxiety, denying the existence of danger situations both external and internal. Individuals of this group, that is to say, at the point when instinctual tension reaches a degree sufficient to constitute an internal threat, successfully deny or repress the danger situation. Unlike the other groups I have described, therefore, these individuals neither develop and tolerate anxiety—even partially or in disguised form—as do patients suffering from psychosomatic disorders; nor, on the other hand, do they acknowledge by phobic symptom formation their awareness of threatened danger situations, whether external or internal.

To illustrate this point I refer to a short study I made in 1942 of a particular group of patients, characterized by an apparent personality change after one specific terrifying war experience. The previous personalities of these patients all showed certain features in that they all tended to have experienced little, if any, conscious anxiety. The patients of this group could not, however, be described as typical of the counterphobic group described by Fenichel (1939a), nor had the previous personality structure apparently been grossly abnormal. In one case of this type there was every evidence to suggest that both with regard to sexual life and with regard to capacity for sublimation the patient had been notably well adjusted prior to his breakdown. In a typical case the individual concerned had had no previous breakdown and had often experienced severe enemy action for an appreciable length of time without developing symptoms. He had not been aware of any change in his condition up to the time of the traumatic incident. In each case the traumatic incident consisted of a terrifying experience which had the specific quality of involving some undeniable physical threat. A London fireman, for example, had been on fire-fighting duties during all the worst London fires, and suddenly developed acute and inhibiting anxiety symptoms after receiving a very slight injury to his hand when a falling beam in a burning building touched him. Others gave similar histories. The striking thing about this group of patients, however, was that the course of recovery after the traumatic experience differed from that of the more typical war neuroses. These men, that is to say, did not work through their traumatic experiences by anxiety dreams, nor did they remain conspicuously anxious. Instead, after a rather quick initial recovery, they became resentful, depressed, somewhat paranoid, and markedly hypochondriacal. They tended to look back at their former personalities and general health with a sense of mourning and grievance. They also showed a striking incomprehension and bewilderment in respect to their symptoms, which were colored throughout by a subjective change both in respect to themselves and to the outside world. This type of patient did not make a full recovery even after considerable treatment, and it therefore appeared that the change brought about by the unfamiliar and totally unprepared-for appearance of severe fear or panic, related to recognition of an external danger situation, was more or less irreversible.

I have described this group of patients for several reasons. In the first place it was these men who first brought to my attention the prophylactic value of previous anxiety in respect to relatively irreversible reactions of this type, following frightening war experiences. The other groups I have described—namely, those who had shown evidence of free-floating anxiety, psychosomatic symptoms, or phobic anxiety—frequently broke down with severe symptoms following battle experience. Only, however, after prolonged stress such as to exhaust the whole individual and reduce his capacity to endure instinctual tension and/or accumulation of overwhelming quantities of excitation which had resulted in the emergence of demonstrable primary anxiety, was a comparable clinical picture produced. Even then, moreover, the tendency toward spontaneous recovery was more in evidence. Usually, however, the clinical picture presented by patients giving a history of previous anxiety was that of quantitative increase in their previous symptoms unaccompanied by any marked qualitative personality change. In my earlier paper I described one case in considerable detail, stressing not only the previous evidence of phobic formation in his character, but also the fact that the specific traumatic experience leading to his breakdown was similar in every respect to the type of experience which I have described here. It was, that is to say, an experience which reactivated obvious castration fears. During the course of the war I saw a number of other patients who showed a very similar psychopathology, with no persistent subjective changes, who frequently recovered to a sufficient degree to return to full military duty. For those patients who developed relatively irreversible internal changes of a regressive type, the failure to develop and cope with secondary anxiety related to unconscious castration fears appears to have been of decisive importance. Since, moreover, it is generally agreed that castration fears are integrally bound up with instinctual urges, both libidinal toward the mother and aggressive toward the father, it is evidence that this omnipotent denial of external danger was determined by relative intolerance of the instinctual conflicts involved in the genital Oedipus situation. This relative intolerance was demonstrated by the manifest depression, tension, and inability to cope with the changed internal situation resulting from a traumatic experience, which made untenable the previous mechanism of projecting an internal danger situation to the outside world and then denying it.

The fact that war experiences of an identical unconscious significance produced such different clinical results in these groups of patients illustrates the complex problem with which we are faced in considering the problem of anxiety. As I have suggested throughout this paper, we are concerned with two questions, namely, the capacity of the organism to tolerate instinctual frustration and the capacity of the ego to recognize, tolerate, and deal with the threatened internal danger situation arising as frustration increases. At this point we must again ask ourselves the relationship between these two problems. Throughout analytic literature there is an implied contrast between manifestations of anxiety which serve positive purposes and those which take inhibiting, paralyzing forms. In between these two extremes I have described the types of clinical condition usually considered under the heading "anxiety states," in which, although the anxiety retains the quality of a defensive reaction, either the quantity of the anxiety or the type of defense used by the individual results in relative distress. It seems, therefore, impossible to draw a sharp distinction between useful and useless anxiety.

I would suggest, however, that three grades may be described; namely, first, anxiety tolerated as such during critical periods of development until positive modes of defense become available. Under optimum conditions this purposive anxiety is characterized by the stimulating qualities of normal fear, but should nevertheless be defined as anxiety, since the danger situation is predominantly internal and unconscious. Second, there is the group in whom the anxiety reaches a degree, or is dealt with by a type of defense, which must be regarded as pathological, but which must nevertheless be regarded as serving a useful purpose in that these manifestations of anxiety, either phobic or psychosomatic, are preferable to the disaster against which they are erected as a defense. As both the instinctual tension constituting the danger situation and the secondary anxiety thereby stimulated increase toward the limit of individual tolerance, the purposive quality of the anxiety becomes to a greater or lesser degree overshadowed by the impending disaster. The anxiety, that is to say, becomes less and less effectively purposive, and comes more and more to resemble the inhibition of a panic situation. Finally, we have the situation in which the defenses have broken down and in which the individual becomes helpless in the face of overwhelming excitation. This traumatic experience represents a psychic disaster brought about by a type of anxiety manifestation not only quantitatively but qualitatively different from the other groups. This qualitative difference is demonstrated not only by the inhibiting, paralyzing nature of the acute symptomatology, but also by the regressive aftereffects indicated in the particular group I have described by development and persistence of depression, hypochondriasis, and mild paranoid tendencies—symptoms in brief more aptly described as produced by the reaction to a disaster than as a defensive measure against a threat.

The significance of trauma in this sense, as the disaster against which anxiety is erected, is hinted at throughout analytic literature. Freud, for example, considered that the prototype of this traumatic experience is the situation at birth, and thus developed the conception of primary anxiety which I have accepted as the basis for my paper. The relationship of birth to specific subsequent anxiety symptoms has also been discussed by Greenacre (1941), who has published two papers on the subject. Fenichel also, as I have already stated, frequently refers to the pathogenic effect of dammed-up states which he describes in very similar terms, contrasting this type of helplessness with purposive fear. It is clear that analysts of every theoretical orientation would agree that the traumatic experience is closely related to helplessness in a situation of overwhelming excitation, in which the individual not only feels abandoned by all good objects but facing attack and extermination by all bad ones, be they external or internal.

In the earlier paper to which I have already referred, I described some clinical evidence which suggested that, in the group of patients I have described, the failure to develop anxiety, although related at a genital level to denial of castration fear, was ultimately determined by the previously denied recognition of this original danger situation so that once danger became inescapable, regression to the earliest level became inevitable. This implied argument to the effect that secondary anxiety is indispensable both as an aid toward development and as a protection against psychic disaster may at first sight appear paradoxical. Whatever one's orientation toward the basic instincts, and whatever the emphasis laid on external and internal factors, danger situations in infancy will nevertheless first appear in relation to instinctual tension and frustration—i.e., in relation to an internal situation. Danger situations thus determined are, in my opinion, inevitable even under optimal external conditions, and however well they may be dealt with by the various mechanisms at our disposal, they are not eliminated as potential sources of further danger. The conflicts which have determined them remain buried in the deepest levels of the unconscious from the cradle to the grave, so that under unfavorable conditions, either externally or internally determined, they may be revived at any period of life. Secondary anxiety, defined as the appropriate biological response to these internal danger situations, is thus indispensable at every stage of development.

Not only do I believe that the capacity to develop and tolerate secondary anxiety is decisive for the achievement of mental stability and health, I should also like to suggest that it is closely related to an allied subject of vital clinical importance, namely the limitations of analysis as a therapeutic process. In this connection, the double orientation I have been stressing throughout is also apparent. I would suggest that patients who tend to develop anxiety with the inhibiting qualities of the primary type whenever tension increases have not only been so hampered from the dawn of life as to have failed to reach a level of ego development at which secondary anxiety was developed, but also tend in the analytic situation to repeat this traumatic experience with manifestations such as to raise considerable doubt as to their capacity for ultimate satisfactory development. What I wish to stress is what I believe to be the qualitative difference between two types of anxiety, emphasizing the failure of the psychotic to develop or tolerate stimulating or purposive anxiety of the secondary type. Zilboorg, in the paper I have already quoted, also hints at the possible close relationship between psychotic and primary anxiety, suggesting that the physical tension, perplexity, and distress preceding psychotic regression may also represent a repetition of the birth trauma.

In respect to neurotics, I believe that the capacity to recognize and tolerate the existence of an internal, unconsciously determined danger situation by developing secondary anxiety is decisive. In my opinion this capacity is very closely linked with the problem of psychological insight. If, as I have suggested, anxiety is defined as the response to an internal danger situation, the capacity to develop and tolerate anxiety, associated as it must always be with an unconscious conflict, is very closely related to the capacity to recognize and tolerate the instinctual conflicts and tension which constitute the internal danger situation which threatens. The more an individual has been able in an internal, unconsciously produced danger situation to develop and tolerate anxiety as such, the more one finds in analysis that he is capable of facing and resolving the conflict which determined it. Conversely, the more the individual has tended to defend himself against anxiety by the development of hysterical symptoms, severe psychosomatic symptoms, or by the omnipotent denial of danger, the less will he be capable of tolerating insight in its literal sense of looking within. I should like to suggest that, with respect to the analysis of neurotic patients, this capacity of achieving and tolerating the anxiety associated with insight is of decisive importance.

To conclude, I have tried in this paper to recapitulate briefly the historical development of analytic theories regarding the nature of anxiety, stressing the importance of the distinction between primary and secondary anxiety. It seems to me that the distinction between anxiety as a manifestation of something which has not been tolerated, resulting in psychic disaster, and anxiety as the purposive response to a threatened danger which has not yet taken place, throws considerable light on many clinical problems. I have suggested that for favorable development two factors are essential. First, a sufficient capacity to endure instinctual tension to allow the threat of a traumatic situation to develop, and second, an ability to recognize this threat by developing anxiety of the purposive, biological type, which may be utilized as a means of securing and maintaining satisfactory development and mental health.

PATHOLOGICAL GENEROSITY

Hilde Lewinsky

(1951)

It is often difficult to distinguish between character traits and affects when the former exert an influence of tremendous significance on the interpersonal relationships of our patients. The emotional life of an individual can become so overwhelmed by the motivational strength of a character trait that it lends a particular affective coloration to the personality. Thus, character traits blend into affective states. Pathological generosity is an example. Other examples are obstinacy, severe frugality, and extreme submissiveness.

Pathological generosity is an emotional state characterized by a profuse and overwhelming desire to give to others not only material things, but thoughts, interests, and care. There is an obvious narcissistic gratification in generous giving, and those prone to it are unable to bear frustration without resultant neurotic reactions of despair and hate if they feel rejected. Instead of feeling unfriendliness or hatred for rivals, they behave in a generous and helpful manner, all the while feeling a "feverish love" for the object of their munificence.

These patients never visit any of their friends without taking them some present; they feel they would otherwise not be welcome. "Beneath this erroneous conception of reality they believe in an 'ultimate success through giving.' They prefer giving a half crown to lending and losing a

shilling." In giving, they are driven by the need for acknowledgment; in lending and losing, they would only feel cheated
out of recognition. Ensuing bitterness testifies to the failure
of this quest and to a still existing hope. Their hours are filled
with reproaches and complaints that other people were "not
generous, had let them down; in short, they had not been
repaid."

Pathological generosity is also a defense for people
unable to bear frustration upon rejection without neurotic
reactions of despair and hate. This leads to a fear of refusing
others. Simultaneously, there is unconsciously a need "to get
something for nothing" in order to heal a narcissistic wound
of childhood.

Lewinsky describes a patient whose major trauma in
childhood was the awareness that she was a disappointment
to her parents and had fixed it in her mind that she could not
possibly be loved for herself, "only for what she would
give."

Unconscious motivations responsible for pathological
giving are: collecting of goodness around one; an erroneous conception of reality, i.e., belief of ultimate success
through giving; and an identification, not with the receiver
of gifts, but with the gift itself. In a sense, the individual
is present through his gift. The gift thus functions as a symbol.

Schematically, the development of this not-uncommon
affective state is as follows. The hopelessness of desires in the
oral and anal stages leads to sadism. However, nothing can
be attained through the sadistic approach, and the child
engages in "the illusion of ultimate reciprocity," a term
introduced by Lewinsky. The end result is pathological
generosity, which is a technique to gain through the use of
negation, denial, and reaction formations what was so
cruelly denied in childhood.

In his paper on "The Spending of Money in Anxiety States," Abraham (1917) drew attention to the fact that the young science of psychoanalysis was more interested in understanding meanness than in its apparent opposite. Four years before Abraham's paper, however, Ernest Jones, in his article "The God Complex" (1913), had already described a syndrome in which spending, giving, and generosity played some part. In this paper, the desire for omnipotence, including omniscience, took the central position, and generosity, in connection with the God complex, was explained as being due to the relative unimportance of the gifts in comparison to the fantasied possessions.

Furthermore, such apparent virtues would not be in the foreground of practical analytic work. The patients approved of them. Later, character analysis, trying to deal with new groups of patients, directed its searchlight on the so-called virtues as well. But even so, generosity did not arouse as much interest as, e.g., overcleanliness.

Wherever generosity was mentioned, it was described as a reaction formation against greed, following Freud (1905c) in his description in the "Three Essays."

Anna Freud (1936), dealing with *The Ego and the Mechanisms of Defense*, put greater stress on this trait. She clearly showed that the simple explanation of reaction formation did not fully cover the syndrome.

From another angle, the problem of "giving" found an important place in the description of the mental make-up of the individual.

In all her writings since 1927, Melanie Klein stresses the aspect of reparation based on depressive and persecutory anxiety. Naturally giving plays a great role in reparation. An attempt at omnipotent reparation by special generosity is then due to the feeling of overgreat destructiveness, which can be repaired only by overmuch giving (1945). Throughout Melanie Klein's writings there are numerous examples of the symbolic values of the gifts, representing the children robbed from the mother, the father's penis, etc.

The two patients from whose analysis I propose to give you some extracts were in treatment with me during the war. During that time the economic aspects of life were much in the foreground. Individuals who in ordinary circumstances might be considered mean would probably excel in their savings groups. My two patients, confronted with this altered reality, found themselves obliged to acknowledge their symptoms.

The two women had in common: (1) father fixation; (2) penis envy; (3) a reduction of orgastic potency and occasional incapacity to reach a climax (W. Reich, 1927).

The penis envy had in both cases been strongly supported by the parents, who were very much disappointed about the sex of the children. One patient, A, was an only child and the parents had wanted a boy. A's parents, living in South Africa, sent A to England at the age of two years, to be brought up by a maternal aunt. The other patient, B, was conceived shortly after the death of a son of eight years, who had been the second child of her parents, the first being a daughter. B's parents had fervently hoped to replace their son.

In the object relations of both women, giving played an immense part. This giving was not necessarily only of a clearly material character, but extended to thoughts, interests, care, etc. Both managed to get themselves repeatedly into relationships where their giving was so profuse that the recipients, even if they wished to reply, felt too overpowered to do so.

The analysis of the situations in which generosity occurred provided four main types of giving, which I call: (1) propitiatory; (2) assertive; (3) fetishistic; (4) deceptive.

The first type, propitiatory giving, is self-explanatory. For instance, A would never visit any of her friends without taking them some present; she felt that she would not otherwise be welcome, just as she herself had not been welcome to her parents.

Assertive giving: Anna Freud (1936) in *The Ego and the Mechanisms of Defense* describes the case of a girl who in a phase of exhibitionistic desire and penis envy would constantly make empty promises, thus disappointing the other siblings. Clearly, this form of boasting led to unpopularity and could therefore not be used by my patients, whose original aim was to be loved. As neither of them could boast of the cherished possession of a penis or of the father as a lover, they tried to reassure themselves on the anal level of possessions and by urethral ambitious endeavors. But as they wanted to be loved, not to be envied, their constant boast "I have" or "I can" had to become "I have something for you" and "I can do so-and-so for you," and the assertions had to be proved by generous actions. With both patients the underlying idea was that they—the children—were as good as boys and should therefore be loved accordingly. At the same time, they tried to prove their goodness to themselves. I think it is interesting in this connection that the word "generous" means "of noble birth."

The need to substantiate the assertions in "kind" was supported by their own inability to bear frustration without neurotic reaction; their despair and hate about any "No" led to a fear of refusing others. In adolescence, forms of behavior developed which appeared nymphomanic, "the girl who could not say no." In reality, the desire for flirtation with its possibilities of narcissistic gain was much greater than the desire for intercourse. Only in analysis, as a woman of thirty-six, could A deal with her horror of being considered a flirt. She sharply criticized any woman who used the desires she aroused for her own advantage; she railed about the unfairness of such behavior. Clearly the unfairness consisted mainly in others doing what she did not dare to do herself.

Naturally there were strong narcissistic gratifications in my patients' generous giving. One rather more obscure narcissistic source was built on the following early experience. The little girl B was on holiday; she wanted to join in the play of other—older—children. They played shop. She produced a box of chocolate cigars and naturally had a very quick turnover; her "shop" was beleaguered and she soon "sold" the lot. She delighted in the game and her popularity. After a very short time she found herself without chocolate cigars, without further customers, and with a great heap of money in the form of pebbles. She was heartbroken. Naturally the whole situation was possible only on a neurotic basis, as the child was above the average in intelligence. The oral, anal, and phallic significance is clear. The experience worked as a trauma. The narcissistic wound to her own "simple-mindedness" for having believed herself popular and liked had to be dealt with. It could not be made good by a new box of chocolate cigars from the parents.

According to Freud's (1915a) description in "Instincts and Their Vicissitudes," there are two ways of turning an instinct into its opposite: (1) by change from active to passive or vice versa, and (2) by change of context. The described situations could be dealt with: (1) by not wanting to play at all, or (2) by either wanting something for nothing or giving up the expectation of getting anything in return.

The first way, not wanting to play, is alien to the child. The second, wanting something for nothing, would not heal the narcissistic wound. However, she retained a great hankering after this form of reaction, which later showed itself in a desire for gambling. Giving something for nothing seemed the only way in which she might forget her "stupidity." This experience, added to the awareness that she, as a girl, was a disappointment to her parents, has fixed it in B's mind that she could not possibly be loved for herself, but only for what she could give.

In B's case, she could not collect friends without giving, so that these friends could not be a substitute for the "ever-bountiful" mother-breast. On the contrary, in the vicious circle of her neurotic responses, B felt in constant need to be such a substitute to others.

A's and B's generosity appeared to contain all the elements of the manic position as described by Melanie Klein (1940) in "Mourning and Its Relation to Manic-Depressive States." There certainly was a desire for triumph closely bound up with contempt and omnipotence, and further the desire to control the object. The sadistic gratification of overcoming and humiliating the object was, however, repressed. Thus, the benign circle started by the act did not appear to be broken, and the patients were glad to be in a position in which they turned the tables and showed up the cupidity and greed of others.

The third type of giving, which I called, for want of a better word, "fetishistic," took place on various occasions when one would have expected the patients to feel hate and envy.

Following the pattern of the Oedipus situation, both women repeatedly had love relationships in which the man, through continuing his affair with them, had another woman whom he preferred. Instead of hate of and unfriendliness toward the rival, they felt and showed a form of feverish love and behaved in a generous and helpful manner, e.g., by preparing a meal for the other woman's arrival, putting out flowers, etc. The identification with the man played a part in this behavior, but a more important component was their erroneous conception of reality, their belief in ultimate success. Their behavior calls to mind W. Reich's (1927) description, in *The Function of Orgasm*, of a boy's attempt at conquering his mother. This boy had not taken up the fight with his rival (his elder brother) but shortly before puberty he decided to conquer the love of his mother, who idolized her eldest son, by agreeing with this idolization. He had made the comment quite often that his mother loved those people who praised her eldest son and hated those who were against him. The generosity shown in such situations could also be explained as an attempt at reparation for the damage done to the parents. But both women emphasized that there was no other chance to keep even the little they had. Their choice was not between "all" and "nothing," but between "precious little" and "nothing." Following this trend of thought, A said: "I want all but can't have it; I can't bear to have nothing; I must try to keep the little I have got. I want to keep this small space in his life."

"What comes into your mind about it?"

"A cot in my parents' bedroom."

This association led to the working through of her desire to watch the parental intercourse. The main determinant for the presents given in this triangular situation became clear: the patient identified herself not with the presentee but *with the present*, trying to be present through her gift. The idea is closely connected—though it works in the opposite direction —with that degree of fetishism described by Freud (1905c) in the "Three Essays." Freud quotes from Goethe's Faust: "Get me a kerchief from her breast,/A garter that her knee has pressed."

The desire to be the child with the parents appears at first to correspond to the wish to be the good child as Melanie Klein described it in *Love, Hate and Reparation* (Klein and Riviere, 1937). Ultimately in making sacrifices we play the part of a good parent; we also play the part of the good child toward his parents, which we wished to do in the past and are now acting out in the present. But the power of this desire does not originate in any intention to be a "good child" as the parents understand this expression, but—on the contrary—to see what the child was forbidden to see. Infantile curiosity was the powerful motive in the generosity shown in these triangular situations, e.g., in giving an entirely uncalled-for present of food and wine to such a couple, A felt able in a vague way to know what this man and this woman would do when they were together. She realized this later when she found out that the people had not used her gift. Her curiosity was very strong. To be "in the know" made her feel less insignificant and allowed her to pretend to benevolent omniscience: whatever went on happened with her knowledge, equivalent to "her permission"; thus she denied that she had no power to alter it.

When working through this material, A laughingly connected another of her generous gestures with the same forbidden wish: often, on holidays, she had offered to take snapshots of couples or of groups, in order to allow the would-be photographer to join in the group picture. Here she certainly played the good child who helped the parents to be together and who had the gratification of seeing them together through her grace. The desire to be in the picture herself in place of the mother remained frustrated.

The fourth type of generosity I called deceptive. It was the only form of faintly anonymous giving which occurred in these patients. The deception—in contrast to that of the impostor—was not to the disadvantage of the deceived. One example: B, who works in an office, is sent by her superior, for whom she has a "passion," to buy an inexpensive fountain pen. B buys a first-class pen, and asks the shop assistant to give her a bill for sixpence less than the price her superior had allowed her to spend; she pays the rest herself. The narcissistic gain is great, she is pronounced a "wizard," and, although she herself knows that she cannot really produce these magic results, she can prove to herself that cupidity paralyzes the judgment of reality in others.

As the need for giving was extraordinarily strong, I was not astonished to hear from A that she had frequently stolen in order to be able to give. We meet this combination relatively often in child-guidance clinic work, where the history starts with stealing and giving the stolen goods to other children. In such giving away of stolen goods, the attempt to sidetrack guilt is clearly important. The overrating of material possessions is also clear. But the desire to be thought of as powerful played the main part, at least in the case of A. A later managed to become a valuable officer in the Control Commission in Germany, where the giving out of material comforts and forceful "scrounging" for her protégées was a permitted and important feature of her work.

In "Manifestations of the Female Castration Complex" Karl Abraham (1920) has described the character and behavior of frigid women with strong penis envy. He says that they tried to get the present of the penis by violence. Their vengeful attitude finds an expression par excellence in frigidity: to disappoint the man, to raise false hopes. The reason why A and B dealt in a different way with the same desires lay in their still existing hope. I was able to show them the pathology of their giving through their attitude to lending. Here their attitude was the opposite of the proverb "Better give a shilling than lend a half crown and lose it." They much preferred giving a half crown to lending and losing a shilling. By giving something they would get a reward either in their own minds or actually in the acknowledgment of the recipient; in lending and losing they felt cheated out of any recognition, out of any thanks. Their bitterness gave the clue to their still existing hope. Hours were filled with their reproaches and complaints that other people were not generous or had let them down; in short, that they had not been repaid. Their firm belief in an ultimate reciprocity came to the surface. This belief was so elemental that I thought it worthwhile to inquire into the aspect of generosity as seen in primitive peoples.

Money-Kyrle (1939) in *Superstition and Society*, describing the Normanby Islanders, says that they like to appear generous, for generosity is part of their group ideal, but they are really very greedy. Generosity has been described as an essential part of the social system of the Trobriand Islanders. Generosity is the highest virtue to them. Generosity is not, however, a one-sided affair in their social system but in this and in all the manifold activities of economic order, the social behavior of the natives is based on a well-assessed give and take, always mentally ticked off and, in the long run, balanced.

At the other end of civilization we find traces of the reciprocal attitude in all social manners. All ethics, and especially Christian ethics, stress the expectation that generosity will be generously repaid. Melanie Klein (1927) in "Criminal Tendencies in Normal Children" emphasizes that in the unconscious the Biblical precept "An eye for an eye" is at work. This precept—though here meant in a retaliatory fashion—is an equivalent to "Do unto others as you want to be done to." That Christian ethics, for instance, would lend themselves to be used as the means of a technique was illustrated by another patient of mine. Having heard the maxim of the Sermon on the Mount that "The last will be first," he always used to work his way to the end of any queue.

In the case of altruism described by Anna Freud (1936), the old desires of the patient had not been repressed, but were projected. In both my patients the mechanism of projection dealt only with the principal question: that everyone would like to be loved, to be spoiled, to be looked after. In the particular instances of giving, A and B were on the whole thoughtful of the loved person's wants. But even so, they were sure that they could never bring themselves to give what was really expected of them. This feeling was not entirely due to having disappointed their parents by being girls. In her analysis B found out the early prototype for her depressive conviction. As a child she had clamored for her mother's presence, wanting to play with her, to have her near, and had told the mother that she wanted her so badly because she loved her. The mother had answered: "If you love me, you be a good girl and leave me alone." B managed in her adolescence to get the same reply from a teacher, whom she pursued in a "crush": "If you really love me, prove it by leaving me alone."

It is understandable that both A and B, hysterics on an anal basis, found this concept of love beyond their strength. Their thoughtfulness in giving was a compromise. In contrast to Anna Freud's case, my patients did not feel forbidden to get anything for themselves. But what they wanted could only be given by someone else and, in order to be really satisfactory, should be given without their asking for it.

B, explaining her difficulties in asking for something from others, exclaimed in tears: "What is the good of telling someone 'Please kiss me spontaneously'?" What they hoped to induce by their pathetic and pathological generosity was to turn the clock back: either to be made male and thus be welcome to the parents, or to be assured and convinced of their welcome as female.

Summary

Giving as concerned in pathological generosity has its roots in oral and anal fixations. It is due to an acknowledgment that the direct satisfaction of the greed for love, for a penis, etc., cannot be attained through the sadistic approach. Owing to an incapacity to face the hopelessness of the desires, the illusion of ultimate reciprocity is introduced. The patients used generosity unconsciously as a technique comparable to homeopathic magic. There were indications that they attempted satisfaction of infantile curiosity by identification with their present.

ON BOREDOM

Ralph R. Greenson

(1953)

*Boredom is characterized by: a state of dissatisfaction
and a disinclination to action, a condition of longing and an
inability to express what is longed for, a sense of emptiness,
an attitude of passive expectation that the external world will
supply satisfaction, and a concomitant distortion in the sense
of time.*

*If we are to classify boredom developmentally, we
would say it is derived from the early preoedipal period. It is
a manifestation of ego regression and is a primitivization of
ego function.*

*This paper, a model of psychoanalytic writing, covers
three important facets of this affect: the thinking disturbance
involved, the vicissitudes of oral impulses, and the defenses.
A carefully documented case history of a 29-year-old woman
whose chief complaint was that she was "terribly bored" is
used to demonstrate these aspects of the condition. Greenson
quickly and correctly perceived that the patient was able to
conquer her boredom during the early phases of an intense
positive transference. On other occasions, boredom lifted
only to produce acute depression, at which time there was an
attempted suicide. With the removal of the depression, the
patient again fell into boredom. Sexual acting out was shown
to originate from a desire not for sexual satisfaction but for
emotional warmth. Boredom was a defense against other*

affects and not against memories, since she was able to remember vividly much material which would be most unusual in a neurotic patient. There was a severe disparity between vivid dreams and monotonous recitations, without significant associations, regarding her feelings or thoughts throughout the analytic sessions. Her fantasy life was nearly impoverished.

The patient showed little reaction to a vivid dream life at the level of consciousness. Greenson observed that vivid dreams were allowed so long as motility was blocked by sleep. During the apathetic, boring intervals characterized by an apparent absence of drives, he noted remnants of libidinal strivings, e.g., sensations of hunger, a preference for cunnilingus in sexual relations, an undue need for alcohol, and promiscuity. The patient's primary libidinal orientation focused on her oral strivings. What was most deeply repressed and what was to constitute the most re-sistant unconscious impulse was her searching for an oral reunion with her mother.

Greenson's complex and detailed psychodynamic picture of the patient who struggles with boredom might be schematically presented as follows: In the struggle against impulses, the patient tries to give up object relationships. He therefore regresses to identifications in various forms. These identifications prove threatening, and the patient attempts to renounce all actions reminiscent of the mother and becomes withdrawn and narcissistically oriented. This constitutes a narcissistic withdrawal and results in a feeling of "not being there" or of "being gone." This situation serves the purpose of denying the existence of one's body and the incorporated mother-images. Simultaneously, suffering is experienced and a severe sense of nothingness ensues. An attempted solution is the search for new objects through promiscuity. When this impulse-ridden behavior ceases, the patient experiences boredom, emptiness, and a longing to fill up the emptiness. (Greenson described the psychology of apathy in a previous paper [1949] as a monument to the total defeat of all desire and longing.)

Distortions in the perception of time sense are a common phenomenon in numerous pathological affective states, e.g., nostalgia, disillusionment, and depression. Greenson thinks it has a particular importance in boredom. He suggests an explanation of the agonizing slowness of the passage of time in patients who are bored. Hartocollis (1975) has written an illuminating paper on this subject.

I

Boredom is a phenomenon which is easier to describe than to define. The uniqueness of the feeling of being bored seems to depend upon the coexistence of the following components: a state of dissatisfaction and a disinclination to action; a state of longing and an inability to designate what is longed for; a sense of emptiness; a passive, expectant attitude with the hope that the external world will supply the satisfaction; a distorted sense of time in which time seems to stand still. (The German word for boredom is *Langeweile*—which, literally translated, means "long time.")

Boredom is seen to occur in healthy people as a transient state. In the neurotic, boredom usually does not play an important role since the patient is preoccupied with anxieties, depressions, frustrations, obsessions, etc. In the psychoses, boredom proper is rarely described, but we do see similar reactions in apathy and in the depressions.

It is the purpose of this presentation to investigate, on the basis of clinical material, the various dynamic and structural factors responsible for the state of boredom. The most systematic and comprehensive analysis of this subject was made by Fenichel (1934a). In that paper Fenichel demonstrated that the bored person is in a state of dammed-up instinctual tension, but the objects and aims are repressed. He described two forms of boredom, one characterized by motor calmness, the other by motor restlessness; but he found in both the same essential pathology. He, and later Spitz (1937), depicted the peculiar role of monotony in producing both states of high excitement and boredom. In addition, Fenichel indicated the importance of orality, and sketched briefly some connections between boredom, depersonalization, and depression. Other writers, namely, Ferenczi (1919), Spitz (1937), Winterstein (1930), and Bergler (1945a), have contributed to one or another aspect of this problem. This paper will be limited to a further exploration of boredom, emphasizing particularly the disturbances in the thinking processes, the vicissitudes of the oral impulses, and the defense mechanisms involved in this syndrome.

A twenty-nine-year-old, attractive married woman with four children entered analysis with the chief complaint that she was terribly bored. For the past five years her main preoccupation had been trying to fill up her empty life. Her husband, her children, her many acquaintances, her social activities, all bored her. She had attempted various hobbies, took lessons of all sorts, had begun drinking, had become promiscuous—all to no avail. Her life remained empty. She could not get emotionally involved with anybody or anything, and her only aim was to kill time, to push the hours away, hoping the intolerable boredom would somehow vanish. About a year before coming to treatment she had gone through an acute depression, but after a suicide attempt with sedatives the depression disappeared and the old feeling of boredom returned.

The relevant part of the patient's present situation can be reported as follows. Her husband was a kindly man whom she had married ten years previously because he was wealthy and good to her. She was fond of him but had never loved him. In recent years she noted an increasing resentment toward her husband because of characteristics in him which she considered "motherly." He was overprotective toward the children, extremely emotional with them, and completely inconsistent. The patient herself was fond of the children but only in a rather distant way. She was unable to become really emotionally involved with them and felt much more like their sister than their mother. She had no idea of how to spend time with them, how to talk to or play with them. She hired a nursemaid to care for them and rarely saw them.

The patient's recent sexual history revealed that she had been faithful to her husband for many years and had started having extramarital affairs only when her boredom became extreme. She enjoyed these affairs because of the intrigue; they were interesting and diverted her mind. Her sexual satisfaction was greater with her husband, however.

Since the onset of the boredom, the patient had taken to drinking quite heavily and consumed about ten to fifteen alcoholic drinks per day. She did not consider herself an alcoholic since, in her social sphere, this quantity of drinking was usual. Her own reason for drinking was that it made her feel pleasantly quiet and made the time pass quickly.

The significant past history of this patient disclosed that her father had deserted the family when the patient was two and a half years of age and she was abandoned by her mother at three. From that time on the patient lived with grandparents, aunts, and uncles, being shifted about at irregular intervals. From time to time her mother would visit and spend time with her.

The patient's mother was a warmhearted, irresponsible, promiscuous, alcoholic woman. In the first years of her life the patient yearned for this mother because she was so warm and giving in her ways, in contrast to the cold, austere grandparents. Later on she turned against her, felt great conscious hatred toward her, and was determined never to become the kind of woman her mother was. During the course of the analysis the fear of becoming like her mother was uncovered to be one of the dominant anxieties in the patient's life.

The patient's early sexual history is noteworthy because of the many traumata and because of the ease with which she was able to recall these experiences. From age two she could remember primal scenes; at age four she experienced cunnilingus with dogs; somewhat later there were doctor games and before six clitoral masturbation. At twelve there was a resumption of masturbation, at fifteen the first heterosexual experience. She had an abortion at age sixteen, syphilis at seventeen, a homosexual affair at eighteen, and indulged in various perverse acts until nineteen, when she was married. Most of these activities were pursued because they were a means of establishing an interpersonal relationship. The patient felt she had little else to offer anyone and she was grateful for any emotional warmth shown her. The search for sexual satisfaction was an unimportant factor in this behavior.

II

The analysis began with the patient pouring forth a flood of memories with much painful affect. It was striking that these memories had not been repressed but were readily available. With the production of these memories and the affects connected with them, the boredom vanished; instead, the patient became tearful and depressed. This, however, she felt as a relief from her usually torturing boredom. Within two weeks after the recital of the many traumatic events, the boredom returned, and it was now possible to study more minutely what this boredom represented. It quickly became clear that in the bored state the affects connected to the traumatic events were repressed. When she was bored it was possible to get her to describe a traumatic event, but this was done without any emotion. The initial welling up of strong affect was possible because of a strong early positive transference. The return of the boredom indicated the re-establishment of the old defenses, directed against affects primarily, not against memories.

During the bored state the patient would describe her feelings as follows: "I can't get with it. I'm nowhere. I'm gone. I feel empty. I am constantly hungry but I don't know what for." During these periods she would drink excessively, usually awakening with an amnesia for the evening's events. At these times the patient would experience short-lived, acute obsessional ideas concerning the fear of becoming fat, and would go through periods of alternately starving herself to undo this and stuffing herself to celebrate her accomplishment. Wulff (1932) has described a picture of food addiction with this manic-depressive undertone. She consumed a great deal of time looking at her image in the mirror, carefully scrutinizing her figure to determine any minute changes. She squandered hours in beauty parlors, at hairdressers, and had massages. In the evenings she would watch television for hours on end. It was at these times that she hungrily searched for a sexual affair because it would give her something to think about.

During this phase of the analysis it was characteristic for the patient to report in exact detail the trivia of her everyday life. It was particularly striking that she was never silent, and although she would describe activities and happenings, she never voluntarily talked of her emotions or thoughts. Her statement, "I can't get with it; I'm nowhere," represents her awareness of the fight against feelings, impulses, and fantasies. The struggle against the fantasies was a key point of her defenses. This patient would experience the most vivid night dreams, yet her associations went to the day remnants and then on to the minutiae of her everyday life. There was no link from the night dreams via associations to fantasies, or thoughts, or memories. Yet she was apt to describe other people's fantasies very readily. She could imagine what her friends might be imagining. Her night dreams were so vivid that she usually felt them to be real. Often her husband would relate that she spoke or acted out something in these dreams. The content of these dreams dealt primarily with some traumatic event of early childhood; but her defenses when awake rendered the recital of these dreams a monotonous performance.

The absence of fantasies was most vividly demonstrated in the patient's sexual life. In order to reach orgasm it was necessary for her husband to tell her stories of some sexual perversion which he had committed or imagined in the past. The epitome of this kind of behavior was using pornographic motion pictures projected on a screen in the bedroom prior to intercourse. Even in masturbation the patient would get bored because she had "nothing to think about." (In the past, however, she had been able to obtain autoerotic satisfaction by imagining cunnilingus being performed on her, usually by a dog or a woman.)

The impoverishment of the fantasy production was also manifested in the patient's language. She spoke in a very simple slang and used a minimum of words. Her description of her bored state was typical. "I'm gone. I'm nothing. I'm nowhere." An evening's conversation with friends was dismissed with "Some friends dropped over for some routine dialogue." If she changed her coiffure, she would ask the analyst, "How do you like my new *type*?" If the analyst made an interpretation which was meaningful, the patient would simply say "Bong!" If the interpretation seemed farfetched, her response would be "No bong." Her language contained a minimum of metaphor and verbal imagery. Metaphor is personal and individual, and is determined by the speaker's specific past history (Sharpe, 1940). In this patient's language one sees her struggle against individuality, against her own past history. Further, the concreteness and the condensation character of her speech have the qualities typical of the primary process rather than the secondary process. The patient's responses to interpretations, "Bong" and "No bong," are typical examples of this. It seems that her ego could use the primary process and not only be over-whelmed by it. Freud (1905b) in his explanation of wit and Kris (1950) in his paper on preconscious mental processes describe related phenomena. (See also Freud, 1915d; Gold-stein, 1944).

The inhibition of fantasy life of bored people has been stressed by Fenichel (1934a) and Winterstein (1930). The analysis revealed that fantasies (even thinking and feeling) had to be fought against since they were a threat. Freud (1915d) described the unique position of fantasy among the mental phenomena, in that it possesses qualities of both systems *Pcs.* and *Ucs.* Kris (1950) stressed the point that in fantasy more libidinal and aggressive energy is discharged than in effective thinking, where neutralized energy is used. Fantasy is closer to the id and primary process than reflective thinking. Thus fantasy is closely linked to both voluntary motility and involuntary discharge. In addition, since visual imagery was particularly exciting for this patient, as mani-fested in her sexual practices, it was imperative that fantasy be curtailed. It is pertinent to recall that the patient's night dreams were extremely vivid; most of the time they felt real to her. This can be construed to mean that as long as motility was blocked by sleep it was possible for her to endure strong visual imagery. Furthermore, fantasy depends on and leads to memory. For this patient, to remember meant either to feel the traumatic abandonment of early childhood or the guilt feelings and anxieties derived from her later experiences. Thus the motive for the ego's inhibition of fantasy seems to be based on the fact that fantasy could lead either to dangerous actions or to painful remembrances. Throughout her analysis one could see the transition between states of boredom which, when lifted, led either to severe depressive reactions or to impulse-ridden behavior.

The method by which this inhibition was achieved is more difficult to formulate. The answer seems to lie in the shifts of cathexis required for the perception of preconscious thought. The censorship systems between systems *Cs.* and *Pcs.* prevent the necessary hypercathexis or the connection to verbal imagery, thus blocking the gateway to consciousness and to motility (Freud, 1900; Rapaport, 1950; Kris, 1950). In general, one sees in this patient a severe disturbance in the thinking processes of the ego. The contrast between the vividness of the dream imagery and the emotional impoverishment of the waking thoughts indicate the patient's struggle against perceiving her fantasies. It also indicates the losing struggle, in the sense that the dreams seemed more real. This would indicate the weakness of the ego's ability to defend itself from the affects attempting to break through into consciousness. Freud (1940) and later Lewin (1950) describe such phenomena in discussing psychotic states.

III

Despite the seeming absence of drives during the apathetic, bored intervals, it was possible to discern some remnants of libidinal strivings. The most prominent feeling in this patient was the sensation of emptiness, which she construed to mean hunger. She was afraid to eat, since eating would make her fat, and being fat would make her like her mother. She was also unable to accept being a mother, for this meant she would be *her* mother. As stated above, she did not feel like her children's mother, but rather like an older sister. The many-sidedness of this struggle was evident in her frequent failures at dieting, her marrying a "motherly" man, and in her preference for cunnilingus. To be fat meant to be well fed, contented; but it also meant to be like mother, to be dirty, to have a vagina, and to be unlovable. To be thin was to be clean, to be a penis, and to be worthy of love. Yet thinness meant to be empty and to be constantly hungry. The few times in her life when she was relatively content were when she was pregnant, for then she was full, but not yet a mother. After delivery she was impelled to combat the awareness of being a mother.

The drinking was, at first, a defense against the impulse to eat. Later on it was a means of becoming unconscious, i.e., to have an orgasm. Drinking meant she was able to indulge in sexuality without having to remember her fantasies. Drinking also gave her a feeling of having something in her without feeling unpleasantly full. The patient claimed that when she drank she felt quiet. Finally, drinking also meant to be like her mother, and thus eventually was also intolerable.

The promiscuity which was prevalent before the analysis was basically a means of maintaining some semblance of interpersonal relationship. In her homosexual relationships, the patient usually sought strong, protective women, who would do things for her sexually. The promiscuity and the homosexuality had to be renounced when they became linked to the patient's conception of her mother.

The analysis revealed the patient's primary libidinal orientation focused on her oral strivings, which is in accord with Fenichel's findings. On the surface the libidinal aim was passive, i.e., the wish to be sucked. For the patient this symbolized the greatest token of being loved; it was a means of simultaneously gratifying libidinal and narcissistic needs. It was an attempt to undo the traumatic deprivation of her early childhood. It was interesting that when cunnilingus was being performed upon her she felt like the little one who was being cared for by the adult—man or woman was unimportant. But beneath this passive oral impulse there was an active oral striving to "melt" her mouth into the genitals of another woman (Fenichel, 1934a). At these times she would describe her aim as wanting to lose the awareness of the boundary between her mouth and the woman's genitals. This was the most deeply repressed and the most resistant unconscious impulse. This patient, despite her conscious hostility and contempt for her mother and her fear of becoming like her mother, unconsciously was searching for an oral reunion with her mother. She wanted to re-establish the infantile unity of mother and child via the mouth. The acute depression one year prior to the analysis was precipitated by a sudden, irrational jealousy of her husband's relationship with a woman very similar to her mother.

It was possible to observe how this patient, in her struggles against these impulses, had attempted to give up object relationships and regressed to identifications in various forms. Then, when these identifications proved threatening, she attempted to renounce all actions reminiscent of her mother, became withdrawn and more narcissistically oriented. The looking in the mirror, her preoccupation with her body, the occasional choice of homosexual partners who resembled herself, all pointed in this direction. This narcissistic withdrawal, however, brought with it the feeling of not being here, of being gone, which also was painful, but which served the purpose of denying the existence of her body with the incorporated mother image. Her attempts to escape from the nothingness then led back in the direction of unconsciously seeking a relationship to a woman, or a man, like her mother. Thus this patient vacillated between different kinds of object relationships with men or women who were mothers in some aspects of their relationship to her, but she could not maintain one where motherliness and sexuality were combined. When the awareness of the motherliness became too clear, she then resorted to finding new objects for sexuality, which led to promiscuity, only once again to be reminded of her mother. The vicissitudes of the patient's attempts to cope with her oral-incorporative urges toward her mother are reminiscent of the struggle between superego, ego, and introject in psychotic depressions (Freud, 1917; Abraham, 1924a; Fenichel, 1945; Lewin, 1950). Part of the object relationships of this patient were aimed at finding a good introject in order to neutralize the bad introject which had already been incorporated. This is similar to the question of good food versus bad food (Rado, 1933), which obsessed her during her struggles with eating.

Apparently, one of the ways this patient was able to avoid a psychotic depression was by discharging different oral-incorporative impulses in eating, fasting, drinking, homosexuality, cunnilingus, and pregnancy. However, she was not merely an impulse-ridden personality; her main complaint was boredom. Most of the time she did not feel driven. On the contrary, she complained of feeling empty, and longed to fill up the emptiness. A further study of this feeling of emptiness and the mechanisms responsible for it provides the key to the understanding of her boredom.

IV

The feeling of emptiness, combined with a sense of longing and an absence of fantasies and thoughts which would lead to satisfaction, is characteristic of boredom. In patients who suffer from apathy we also find a feeling of emptiness, but here there is no more longing and a far greater inhibition of the ego's thinking and perceptive functions (Greenson, 1949). In the depressions, too, there is a feeling of emptiness, but it is the world which is felt as empty; the self is sensed as heavy, weighted down, or low. Further, in depressions there is a rich, though morbid, fantasy life concerning specific objects or their derivatives.

The emptiness in boredom is in the first place due to the repression of the forbidden instinctual aims and objects, along with the inhibition in imagination. However, there seem to be additional determinants for this empty feeling. Emptiness represents hunger. When bored, the patient ate, drank, looked at television or in the mirror. Most bored persons resort to oral activities. The bored individual's feeling of emptiness is similar to the experience of the child waiting hungrily for the breast. The aim and object, sucking, breast, and mother, are repressed, however, and only the feeling of emptiness remains. It seems that we are dealing here with the substitution of a sensation for a fantasy. Instead of having imagery involving derivatives of her mother and her longing, the patient regressed to a more archaic thought form and perceived, instead, a sensation of emptiness. This is a manifestation of ego regression, a primitivization of ego functions, to use Kris's term. This phenomenon brings fantasy closer to the id and the primary process. The emptiness is not merely a sensation, however, it is a psychic representation (S. Isaacs, 1948). This conception may be expressed thus: the emptiness represents the hungry child with the image of "no-mother," "no-breast," "mother-will-not-come." (This may help to explain the agonizing slowness of the passage of time in these patients. The experience of time seems to be dependent upon delay of impulse discharge. Excessive discharge delay seems to slow down the passage of time, whereas quick impulse discharge makes time seem to pass quickly [Fenichel, 1934a; Rapaport, 1950].)

If we return to the problem of the feeling of emptiness, it seems plausible that the formulation of the hungry child with the image of "no-mother" may also represent an attempt to deny that the mother was incorporated within the patient. It may be that through the boredom the patient was saying: "It is not true that my mother is within me. I'm just a little baby waiting hungrily for some satisfaction." The denial of the introjection appears to be the decisive defense mechanism which made it possible for this patient to develop boredom and at the same time to ward off a severe depressive reaction. The mechanism of denial is further illustrated by the fact that the bored person often claims to be in a state of lack of tension, and boredom has been described as a displeasureful lack of tension. The denial seems to becloud the fact that the patient is full of tension, but it is a special kind of tension—the tension of emptiness. "The bored person is full of emptiness." Another aspect of the denial can be seen in the readiness of bored persons to describe situations and people as boring rather than to acknowledge that the bored feeling is within. "It bores me" is more ego syntonic than "I am bored." When one is bored, even the most exciting events can be felt as boring. (At this point one might speculate upon the connection between boredom and elation, which also makes extensive use of denial mechanisms [Lewin, 1950].)

The feeling of emptiness is thus seen to be overdetermined. The mechanism of denial is an important factor in producing this sensation. In this way the ego has attempted to ward off the awareness of strong oral-libidinal and aggressive-incorporative impulses. This defense succeeds, since it temporarily prevents the outbreak of a severe depression or self-destructive actions. This defense failed in the case of severe boredom, since the self-inflicted deprivation stirred up feelings from the traumatic deprivation of early childhood and therefore brought with it the feeling of being overwhelmingly bored, which was also intolerable.

V

The crucial therapeutic factor in this case was the transference. The patient was able to develop a strong positive transference which eventually led to a change in the character of the incorporated objects, which were now reliable and permissive. Gradually she was then able to tolerate object relationships on a higher libidinal level.

An interesting aspect of this improvement was seen in the patient's reactions to the purchase of a new and beautiful home. The patient's attitude to possessions is noteworthy: if she bought something which she liked and considered beautiful, it was not merely her possession, it was she. She would exhibit a beautiful vase to her friends with the phrase, "Look at me." She would exclaim when she saw a pretty dress she wanted, "This is me." She did not like her rented home. The patient's attitude to possessions is noteworthy: disavow. It was big, rambling, i.e., fat, sloppy, like mother. The new and beautiful home was sleek, pretty, and thin; for her it meant, "The new me, the me I want to show." Whereas previously she had often felt homeless despite her luxurious setting, with the purchase of the new home with which she could now identify, she now felt "at home." It should be emphasized that the patient's utterances about her possessions were always said with tongue in cheek, as though part of her ego were well aware of her ego boundaries.

As the apathetic bored state disappeared and fantasies began to return, one could then discern a different kind of boredom: agitated boredom. There persisted some feeling of emptiness, but with the perception of fantasies the patient began to do things. The actions undertaken, however, were not satisfying, and there was an atmosphere of restlessness and dissatisfaction in these activities. Fenichel (1934a) and Spitz (1937) have described the fidgetiness in children who are in a high state of conflictual excitement about the parental night noises they hear. A similar condition can also be observed in the agitated boredom of the prepuberty child. In the patient under discussion it seemed that the agitated boredom was due partly to her dissatisfaction with the available activities. In the transitional phase the real aims and objects of her instinctual demands were still not accessible to her. Nevertheless, since body sensations had begun to become capable of translation into visual imagery and thought, the gateway to motility was opened. In a sense, however, the images and thoughts were still deflected and distorted by the persisting censorship, and therefore led to the "wrong" fantasies and therefore to dissatisfying actions. Many people suffer from boredom of this type. They are characterized by a great need for "diversions and distractions." The very meaning of these terms confirms the persisting censorship between impulse and action. These people do not enjoy true satisfaction and therefore have to resort to frequent "distractions."

VI

On the basis of the foregoing formulations in reference to the clinical case cited above, it now seems possible to attempt to explain the occurrence of boredom in normal people. One might construct the following sequence of events: At the behest of the superego, certain instinctual aims and/or objects have to be repressed (Spitz, 1937). This step results in a feeling of tension. At this point, if the ego has to inhibit fantasies and thought derivatives of these impulses because they are also too threatening, we have as a consequence a feeling of emptiness. This is perceived as a deprivation, a self-administered deprivation. We thus have a combination of instinctual tension and a vague feeling of emptiness. The instinctual tension is without direction due to the inhibition of thoughts and fantasies. Tension and emptiness are felt as a kind of hunger—stimulus hunger. Since the individual does not know what he is hungry for, he now turns to the external world, with the hope that it will provide the missing aim and/or object. I believe it is this state of affairs which is characteristic of all boredom. (If fantasies or other derivatives of forbidden impulses should break through into consciousness, there would be no boredom but either frustration, anxiety, depression, or obsession, as we see in other neuroses.)

Boredom can occur on any level of libidinal organization. However, the hypotheses set forth above, the clinical case herein described, and the general experience that boredom occurs more frequently in depressed patients indicate that people with strong oral fixations are particularly predisposed to boredom. The explanation for this lies in the role played by deprivation in the production of boredom as well as in the related states of depression and apathy. Depressed people feel deprived of love, either from an external or an internal object, or both. In apathy, too, traumatic deprivation plays a decisive role—only here the external world is responsible. In boredom we find a self-administered deprivation; the loss of thoughts and fantasies which would lead to satisfaction. Depressed persons are full of fantasies in their struggle to regain the unloving object. Apathetic persons have given up the struggle, and their fantasy life is restricted to factors concerned with the question of survival. In boredom there is a longing for the lost satisfactions similar to what one sees in the depressions, along with the feeling of emptiness characteristic of apathy.

CRYING AT THE HAPPY ENDING

Sandor S. Feldman

(1956)

Dr. Feldman's sustained interest in the affects and their expression is indicated by two papers on blushing (1941, 1962) and a volume on the nonverbal expression of affects, Mannerisms in Speech and Gestures in Everyday Life, *first published in Hungarian and later in English (1959).*

The present lucid essay is not concerned with crying and tears usually shed upon experiencing tense or perilous situations, or physical or mental pain, but with crying that follows exposure to happy events in one's own life or in the lives of others. This type of reaction, often referred to as a paradoxical affective response, remains "paradoxical" only insofar as and as long as its true unconscious motivation remains hidden from our understanding.

Three case histories demonstrate the unconscious motivation behind such occurrences. In the first instance, a patient, having suppressed tears for more than two decades, broke into violent weeping when someone was "good" to him, reminding him of the only person who had taken care of him and loved him after his mother's death. "Now that things turned to the good, the suppressed tears were released."

In a second instance, an aggressive businessman burst into sudden loud crying and sobbing while viewing a motion picture in which two men fell into each other's arms in becoming reconciled after a period of long and bitter hatred. The unconscious reason for this affective release was a conviction that he would never be loved because of childhood deprivation of love. These circumstances, the man believed, had turned him into someone who had allowed hate and hostility to dominate all his relationships. This lifetime attitude of sadness and severe guilt for his cruelty to others in his own business life convinced him that he was doomed to unhappiness. In identification with the figures in the film, he experienced the sadness, not the joy, of their happy reconciliation.

In a third instance, a man, while gazing at a lovely and sentimental picture depicting a happy child-mother relationship, cried uncontrollably. He was overwhelmed with the realization that his fantasies of future gratification were no longer attainable.

The concept of "delay of affect" is central to the phenomenon of crying at the happy ending. First coined by Weiss (1952), this term was reintroduced by Feldman in the present paper. The tears and crying are due to sadness once delayed, but now expressed. As long as the wish for a happy solution has not become a reality, one suppresses sadness, and whenever everything "turns out well," one permits oneself the discharge of the repressed emotions and affects.

The brevity of this communication does not do justice to the importance of this widespread psychological and social phenomenon. The writer is aware of this fact and expects that the reader will be overwhelmed by reactions stimulated by his own experiences. Some might find the writer's interpretations and suggestions difficult to accept, insufficient, and not covering the subject. However, the conclusions are based on careful, long, and painstaking analyses of patients who—in the course of their treatment for other purposes—presented this phenomenon. Encouraged by his findings, the writer took the liberty of applying this knowledge to events and cases he did not have the chance to investigate through personal interview.

In our culture, tears are usually shed as a result of physical and mental pain, grief, sentimental experiences, exalted scenes, and at the happy ending of a tense or perilous situation. Tears caused by violent laughter or cough have no psychological origin. According to Darwin (1873), they are the result of muscular and vascular processes due to those actions.

A man who by cruel fate was stricken from childhood on by several different physical infirmities, who in addition to these traumatic events lost his mother when very young, and was harshly terrorized by a threatening and dictatorial father, developed a painful and paralyzing neurosis. At the end of his long analysis, which he felt helped him a great deal and opened for him the possibility of a happy life, he said to me: "Thank you, you were so good to me." He then burst out crying, which he could hardly suppress, and in embarrassment left hastily. Right or wrong, crying in men is considered a weakness.

Why did this man cry when he expressed his gratitude at the happy ending of a long and painful journey of his life? Was he happy? Of course he was. Was he full of joy? Of course he was. The question is whether he cried *because* he was happy or for some other reason which was stirred up *at the occasion* of the happy ending. In the writer's opinion, the latter interpretation is the correct one. This man suppressed tears for more than two decades. Now that things turned to the good, the suppressed tears were released. True, he was helped a great deal, but would everything from now on in his life be without pain and trouble? Hardly! Life is tough even when one has become well. Furthermore, the separation from one who was "so good" to him reminded him of the only person who had loved him and taken care of him after his mother's death. This person also died at an early age. He was sad and in pain that, again, he was to be separated from a kind and loving person, his therapist.

A tough and aggressive businessman burst into sudden, loud crying and sobbing when he observed in a motion picture that an unhappy misunderstanding between two good friends, followed by a period of long and bitter hatred, was happily clarified, and as a result of this they fell into each other's arms. This man was ruthless and more than unfair in his business life. He did not permit himself to have feelings of kindness toward anybody except the few members of his close family. This hard exterior was but a front, for deep down in his heart—like everybody—he craved to love and to be loved. When in the motion picture he saw that hatred, hostility, and cruelty gave way to love and brotherhood, despite feeling happy that things turned out well, he still felt that he was a loser. This made him sad and therefore he cried. It was the sadness that made him cry and not the joy of the happy ending. It should be emphasized that he was happy and joyous, but he cried because of the above-mentioned reasons and not because an unhappy situation was happily resolved. Furthermore, the story with the happy ending also made him feel guilty for being so cruel in his professional life.

A male patient related in his analysis that his eyes became watery when he looked at a commercial advertisement presenting a lovely and smiling mother bending over a healthy, happy, and smiling baby. This man had grave emotional difficulties in his marital life; he could not tolerate any justifiable criticism; he wanted, like a child, unconditional love. The picture which moved him so deeply did not portray a sad event but a happy one. Didn't he like the picture? Of course he did. Was he not happy to see the happy scene? Of course he was. Why then did he cry? It was disclosed in his analysis that the lovely and sentimental picture made him sad because he realized that in reality the happy child-mother relationship was no longer attainable. He had to realize the sad fact that he was a grown-up man and had to face all the consequences of reality, i.e., that his wife was entitled to expect certain nonsexual and sexual gratifications from him in order for her to consider him a normal husband. He found the picture lovely and charming. On the other hand, the picture stirred up feelings of frustration, which made him sad; the joy was there, but the tears were caused by associations which led to sad events.

The heroic captain orders all men to abandon a badly damaged ship, but he remains on it until the last moment, after all hope to save the ship has been given up. He himself is saved only after several trying days. His wife, who followed his plight by radio announcements, learns of his rescue, and cries with joy. There is no doubt that she was full of joy and happiness, but is it true that her joy and happiness over her beloved husband's rescue made her cry? For this case we can readily accept the interpretation which Weiss (1952) offered in a fascinating brief paper. He states that in such a case we encounter the phenomenon of the "delay of affect." As long as one worries about the fate of the beloved one, as long as the wished-for happy solution does not yet take place, one suppresses the sadness. When everything turns out well one permits oneself the discharge of the repressed sadness. Weiss too thinks that it is not the joy that makes one cry under the above-mentioned circumstances but —in the last analysis—the tears are due to sadness. Furthermore, Weiss realized that the "delay of affect" is not the only explanation, and that there are other possible causes for crying at the happy ending. The writer of this paper has already presented two theories: one, that the happy ending reminds us of the lost happy past; the other is that the happy ending makes one realize that there is a kindness, love, and goodness that one could exercise but does not. The latter instance could be seen in the case of the "tough business-man."

Parents go through many emotional tribulations until their child grows up, goes through school, and reaches the happy day of graduation. When they see (as it happened to the writer himself at his daughter's graduation) their child marching solemnly toward the platform—they burst into tears. They say that they cry out of joy and happiness. They say this because they feel happy and, therefore, in the writer's opinion, it appears to them that the tears are tears of joy and happiness. The graduate usually does not cry, only the parents, relatives, friends, and perhaps some emotional and sentimental strangers. But is it true that those tears are tears of joy just because they appear *when* one feels happy and joyous? Isn't it justified to apply Weiss's explanation—at least as one possibility—that for long years the parents, relatives, and friends suppressed a great deal of worry about the future of their child, and now, at the happy ending, they release their accumulated apprehensions through their tears, and call it "tears of joy" and "tears of happiness"?

The beautiful bride stands at the altar with the hand-some bridegroom. She is happy; it is the happiest day of her life. This is the moment she dreamed of for so long. The dream comes true. The bride usually smiles or not, but does not cry. (A middle-aged woman told me that she cried at her wedding because she was not sure whether she loved her husband and was afraid that she wouldn't be happy in her marriage.) The bride's parents, relatives, etc., might cry; they usually do. When asked why they cry, the answer is always that they cry because they are happy, that they are overwhelmed with joy. They feel that they are happy for her and the tears are tears of joy. Some say that they cry because they lose their child through marriage. The writer believes that they cry because they feel that up to this time the child was safe and protected by them, but from now on the bride especially is heading toward a difficult and uncertain future. Behind the present happy and joyful event looms the sadness over the uncertain future of the beloved child.

A male patient had a brilliant brother who excelled in his studies, in sports, and in his social relationships. The patient, on the other hand, was timid, shy, and anxious. His brother once praised him and the patient burst into tears. During the course of his analysis it was realized that he cried because he was sad that the praise came so late and did not happen earlier. He was happy when the brother praised him, but the tears came not for the good he received but for what he had *not* received in the past.

When this man was five years old his mother gave him an old tennis racket. He started to cry. His mother was puzzled and couldn't understand. Was he happy? He was. But still he had to cry. The tears were tears of sadness. He had had very little contact with his mother and for long years he had been taken care of by a nurse. Mother's kindness reminded him of the dormant, painful, and sad fact that she had not given him attention. The tears were not tears of happiness but tears of unhappiness. This bright and essentially strong man could not use his excellent capabilities because he had to withdraw to his fantasies in which he compensated for his inner loneliness.

A female patient cried when she observed a little boy who was overwhelmed with joy when his parents presented him with a pair of new shoes. The patient knew that the boy's parents were poor and that the shoes were of cheap fabric. She knew that the boy was unaware of the fact that

there were must better shoes available for those who had
the money for it. The little boy was happy because he
thought that the shoes were wonderful, the best shoes in the
world. The patient understood and appreciated the happiness of the child; nevertheless, she was sad because of what
the child was missing. Her tears, again, were not tears of joy.

The Bible offers the most moving and wonderful example of our problem with the story of the meeting and
reconciliation of Jacob and Esau. After a long period of bitter
rivalry and hatred which separated the two brothers, they
met. The Bible (Genesis 33:4) says: "And Esau ran to meet
him, and embraced him, and fell on his neck, and kissed
him; and they wept." The hatred gave way to love. Why,
then, did they cry? There is a very unusual kind of printing
in the original Hebrew text: above all the letters of "kissed
him" (*vajishokaehu*) there are dots. The writer, who in his
early childhood loved to read and study the Bible, asked his
father, who was a profound scholar in this field, what the
dots could mean. He told the writer that despite the reconciliation Esau still hated Jacob and when he kissed his
brother the impulse to bite Jacob flashed through his mind,
but he checked it; the dots above the letters are symbolic
marks of the teeth. In his commentary to the Bible, the Chief
Rabbi of England, Dr. J. H. Hertz (1938), remarks about this
that "The Rabbis doubted whether the kiss of Esau was
genuine or not." There are two possible explanations for the
weeping at the joyous and happy ending. The brothers cried
because at the moment of the reconciliation they were reminded of the bitter hatred in the past, or they felt that the
reconciliation was not a genuine one. Possibly both feelings
were present.

After long and strenuous preparations, competing for
the title of Miss America, a few girls stand on the platform
waiting for the final decision of the judges. The name of the

winner is announced and, often, the winner faints or cries. Engel (1950) explains one of his patient's fainting as "an hysterical conversion symptom: as a substitutive expression of the emotional tension of sexual excitation which could not find adequate outlet through full-fledged motor behavior" (p. 74). Engel's explanation would take care of the fainting. What was the cause of crying? After all, Miss America wanted to win, and she was happy to be the winner. If asked, she would say that she was crying because she was happy. The writer never had the pleasure of analyzing Miss America. He can only guess, on the basis of his analytical investigations of other similar cases, what the hidden motive of the crying might be. The writer suggests that she cries because she knows that this is a passing glory: time comes and age will destroy the glorious features of youth. But probably there are other additional and individual reasons for the crying. Since this paper was read, the writer was informed by two reliable persons that when they watched the television presentation of one of the beauty contests they distinctly heard the sniffling winner whispering to herself, "Daddy knows." The father died a year before the event. Is it farfetched to assume that the tears were caused by the sadness that her father could not witness the glory of his daughter?

According to Darwin (1873), children cry out loudly when they are hungry or in some other distress. They cry out for aid and protection. Through a chain of physiological connections the crying affects the lachrymal glands and they secrete tears, and it has come to pass that suffering readily causes the secretion of tears, without necessarily being accompanied by any other action.

Shedding tears is a protective reflex action when the eyes are endangered, i.e., by irritating foreign bodies. The protection of the eyes for the purpose of self-preservation and libidinal gratification (looking and being looked at) seems to have become the model of protection for any kind of insecurity. This could be pain, hunger, or any kind of distress like mourning, sadness, grief, or whenever a sudden increase of psychic-emotional energy thrusts itself on the mental apparatus. It is possible that even a sudden eruption of a happy emotion becomes so painful that it has to be removed: the mental apparatus cannot tolerate such a great tension and attempts to get rid of it by primary reflex-defense mechanism, by shedding tears. The alternate crying and laughing in an intense and sudden happy or unhappy situation might become understandable. Even happiness can be painful if it is too intense.

Some people cry at the pleasurable gratification of orgasm in sexual union; some people experience great embarrassment when they confuse words "funeral" and "wedding"; others cannot help smiling when they express their sympathy to mourning persons, etc. Probably the attraction of opposing poles in thoughts and feelings is a fundamental characteristic of our mental behavior. Masserman (1954) would call this the "inner dialectic of human behavior" (p. 311). One of the writer's close relatives, apparently feeling the need to tell her experience to another human being, related that after the greatest suffering and blow that could be inflicted on a human being, losing a child, going home after the funeral she and her husband felt a strong urge to conceive another child, which was born to them nine months after the date of the funeral. The same urges have been reported to the writer by many persons who attended funerals. The idea of life stirs up the idea of death and vice versa. The most striking example is crying after hearing the news of unexpected recovery of gravely hurt or sick close relatives. The good news is received with profound joy and happiness and is followed by crying. In many cases, one can observe a "composite" facial expression: crying and smiling. The painful concern about the fate of the injured or sick persons was checked and controlled for a long period of time: the hope for a happy ending kept the tears at bay. Now that the unexpected but hoped-for recovery has taken place, the undischarged tears are permitted to come to the fore.

SUMMARY

Analytic observation encouraged me to assume that crying at the happy ending is due to a "delay of affect" (Weiss, 1952); to sad events the memories of which are stirred up by the happy ending; to guilt ("How sad it is that we are bad, though life shows that one could be good"). The writer offers another possibility as an explanation for the crying at the happy ending. As children we are happy, we are loved and protected, and despite our pains and frustrations we believe that life is essentially joyful. As children we do not know that the time will come when death will put an end to our happy object relationships. As children we think that the world consists of children, young people, and old people; we believe that we shall stay young forever. Gradually we realize the bitter truth, but we still cling through hopes, illusions, and temporary happy events to the idea that life is a happy proposition and we shall always be together with our beloved ones. Even those who believe strongly in a life hereafter cry (with some exceptions) when they have to separate from the earthly forms of those whom they dearly loved. When something makes us happy, especially when a sad and painful situation turns out well, making us joyous and happy, the fundamental knowledge and feeling that this is only temporary and not lasting breaks into our mind and makes us cry.

Small children do not cry at the happy ending: they

smile because they do not yet accept the fact of death. Crying at the happy ending probably starts when death is accepted as an inevitable fact.

We do not cry only for the past unhappy events which are over anyhow, nor for happy events which we cherish, but we do cry that the happy childhood with its illusions is gone and we cry for the sad end which is sure to come; the separation from the beloved ones.

There are no tears of joy, only tears of sorrow.

ON POUTING

CARL P. ADATTO

(1957)

Facial expression is the voluntary and/or involuntary equivalent of an unverbalized affect, and an affect may be expressed through the facial-mimetic musculature alone. The development of facial-mimetic expressions is an indicator of the state of early ego development and the formation of object relations. In addition, specific expressions assume the role of important psychic functions as described by Spitz (1965) with regard to smiling and Kris (1940) with regard to laughing.

The analysis of pouting in Adatto's patient helped him to come to terms with a great deal of infantile material and his current problems both in the external world and in the transference. The patient became depressed and especially angry whenever his wife became pregnant. Under such circumstances he either made intense demands upon her or engaged in pouting, both during and outside the analytic sessions. The aim of the pouting-filled silence was to force the mother to pay attention. In his history, the patient portrayed himself defensively as the favored child to whom everything should be granted without effort.

Pouting is not only an expression of an oral conflict, but is a mode of communicating this conflict to people around oneself. "The thrusting out of the lips seems to be a literal reaching out for the breast and the milk. It also represents an attempted denial of the fact that one does not have the breast. It is as though one is saying 'I actually have the breast in my mouth.'"

In my own clinical experience, behind the mask of frequent pouting in a thirty-five-year-old housewife who had made four unsuccessful suicide attempts before entering psychoanalysis lay severe unconscious repressed rage not yet turned against the self. Pouting proved to be a time-limiting phase of "intermediate" demand and aggression before the onset of severe depression. It thus had an intimidating and coercive function which usually did not achieve the desired result.

Pouting is an affective reaction representing a "wish for oral gratification and is a reaction to frustration." As such, it is a regressive wish to return to a state of satisfactory maternal contact.

It seems to me that the value of knowing the meaning of a certain affective expression is nowhere better illustrated and exemplified than in this short essay. An affect, when clearly understood, constitutes "psychoanalytic shorthand," equivalent to the lengthy careful historical reconstruction of certain aspects and vicissitudes of a patient's early life.

The expression of affect through the facial-mimetic musculature originates as an archaic and infantile mode of expression, conveying the biologically inherited and environmentally determined aspects of the individual. Fenichel (1945) states that among adults it still governs many of their relations with one another. "Even when full emotional spells have become rare, the facial expression signifies an involuntary equivalent of affects which, by means of empathy, informs spectators of the nature of the subject's feelings" (pp. 318-319). In addition, the connection of facial-mimetic expressions with early ego development and object relationship in infants has been discussed by Spitz and Wolf (1946), Hendrick (1951), and Kris (1940) in regard to smiling and laughing. Specific facial-mimetic expressions thereby assume the role of an important psychic function, and because of this need to be subjected to analysis. They offer a readily available source of learning something of the vicissitudes of the individual's development, even though the patient's position on the couch does not permit a full view of his face.

Pouting falls into this category of behavior, combining a mimetic muscular attitude, the expression of the affect of sullenness, and silence. The dictionary definition of the verb "pout" is as follows: "To thrust out the lips, as in displeasure; hence, to look sullen."

The analyst often is rewarded with a lucid insight into the development of a particular phenomenon, which in turn furthers his understanding of similar phenomena. This paper will present a fragment of a patient's analysis which brought out the meaning of pouting in terms of the infantile period, the current problem, and the transference.

The patient, a young lawyer, had been married for about two years and in analysis for one year when his wife became pregnant for the second time. During the first year of their marriage she had a pregnancy which terminated in a spontaneous abortion, to which he reacted with moods of depression, and outbursts of anger toward his wife. There were no somatic or sleep disturbances accompanying the depression, but this symptomatology was in part the reason for his seeking analysis. At first he reacted with much pleasure to the current pregnancy. The analysis to this point had progressed rather smoothly, and he had been making good initial progress in understanding the origins of the verbal attacks he would make on clients who did not accept his advice without question.

During the analysis from time to time he had doubts

whether he was wise in pursuing this therapy because he could use his time and money to better advantage. Usually this centered around specific anxieties which, when analyzed, stimulated the analysis further. After the fourth month of his wife's pregnancy, when fetal life became evident, his behavior changed perceptibly. He produced little pertinent analytic material, was frequently late for appointments, and began to complain steadily about his wife's poor housekeeping habits. Even though he was fully aware that his wife's pregnancy made demands on her, he isolated this fact from his tirades against her. He also complained that the senior partner of the firm did not appreciate his hard work. He became moderately depressed and felt that no one was on his side.

One day as he left the session he blasted the analyst with a verbal attack about how little he had gained from his analysis, and in particular from the session of that day. The next day he was late for the session, and exhibited a definite pouting, as indicated by his sullen attitude and thrusting out of the lips. This persisted while he was on the couch, and for several days while he talked about the same theme of how little he was getting and how hard he was working. Finally he was confronted with the observation that he had been pouting during this time. This created a sudden change in his behavior, from sullenness to much curiosity about the fact that he was completely unaware of his pouting. He pursued the point by commenting that this was a common mode of expression during his childhood, and the object of much chagrin on the part of his mother. When other methods of communication failed to reach her, the silent pouting would ultimately elicit some concern on her part, and she would become attentive.

This stimulated the recall of a memory which took place when he was about three years old. He and two older sisters were in the room with their mother watching her breast feed their baby brother. He remembered that his mother playfully shot milk from her breast at them with the implication that they could have some too. The abundance of the maternal milk impressed him, but he recalled being angry and unhappy.

He himself had been breast fed also with the same abundant milk, had been weaned easily, and had evidently enjoyed a highly satisfactory period until the birth of the brother. He had been indulged and looked upon then and later as the favored child. During the analysis he had viewed his father as being a more favored person than he himself, because the mother would not hesitate to look after the father before she would attend to the children. However, at this time, he recalled that his father would have outbursts of anger when the mother was taking care of the younger children. He now reformulated his opinion, feeling that the baby came first in the mother's attentiveness.

In addition, he confided that he had always felt he was favored by the mother because he was so much like her. Again and again he denied the fact that the other siblings meant much to the mother, and many of his actions seemed to stem from the premise that he was a favored person. Throughout life he had assumed that what he received was his just due; persistent refusals or rejections had usually elicited strong reactions of rage and a feeling of depression. In relation to his clients he also expected to be taken care of, but would also play the role of the mother with plentiful milk, and become upset if they refused his offerings. This duality permeated his character structure.

The analysis of the pouting opened up an understanding of the structure of his oral aims and led to new insight. It became clearer to him that in the outbursts toward his wife he was again acting out the wish for the maternal breast and its frustration, as condensed and dramatized in this memory. He was threatened by displacement again, and signaling the objects around him that he was in the old dilemma. The failure of gratification of infantile needs in the analysis produced a parallel transference reaction which could be analyzed once he was content to be satisfied with analytic interpretation. This steppingstone in the analysis afforded an excellent opportunity for the patient to get a clearer picture of his instinctual needs as well as his archaic and infantile approach to gratification of the needs.

Pouting, in this instance, afforded a timely occasion to analyze an infantile mode of expression which was persisting during adult life, and presenting a facet of his early neurotic pattern. In this individual pouting can be looked at as both an expression of an oral conflict and as a mode of communicating this conflict to the objects around him. The thrusting out of the lips seemed to be a literal reaching out for the breast and the milk. In addition, it represented a denial of the fact that he was not the infant being fed at the breast. It was as though he were saying, "I actually have the breast in my mouth." This defense of denial would hold him in good humor when he would begin to feel the frustration of his oral longings, and account for his feeling that he was a favored person even when he was not. In fantasy he had the breast all the time. However, when reality again superseded and he felt the frustration which no longer could be warded off, he would react with anger and depression.

The sullenness in this patient seems to be a throttled-down anger. He had some solace in the fact that the siblings and father were also denied. In addition to being a reaction to not having the breast, it was an acceptable means of finally breaking into his mother's awareness. She would eventually respond to the signal and gratify him once again. This in turn would reinforce his feeling of being important as a consequence of getting the breast again. The persistent repeated satisfactions during life undoubtedly accounted for the continuance of pouting as a mode of communication.

It was noted that often he would become sullen without thrusting out his lips. But it was the combination of the two that had special meaning to the patient, and enabled him to experience and understand the true meaning of his behavior.

In conclusion, pouting, like any other expression, reflects the vicissitudes of the individual's development. In this person pouting seemed to be a wish for oral gratification and a reaction to frustration, having previously experienced adequate gratification during the oral period of development. As such it represents a regressive wish to return to a state of satisfactory maternal contact.

ON SMUGNESS

Jacob A. Arlow

(1957)

One of Arlow's early psychoanalytic achievements was his study on smugness, which was awarded the Clinical Essay Prize of the Institute of Psychoanalysis in London in 1955. To extend our knowledge of the affects, we must proceed from a sound theoretical point of view, keeping in mind (1) the gradual fusion of early affect components and their development into complex adult emotional attitudes; (2) the correlation between affective development with instinctual development; and (3) the interrelationship of ego and superego.

Arlow describes smugness from the dynamic and structural points of view, and "the final affective expression, in the mature, highly differentiated psychic organization, [is shown] to develop from a series of intersystemic and intrasystemic tensions" (Jacobson, 1971, p. 13). Smugness is an acute or chronic emotional state characterized by "complacency, self-centeredness, and self-satisfaction." An aura of neither wanting nor needing anything or little from the environment is perceived by others as superiority, self-righteousness, self-containment, and independence; it elicits hostility and occasionally envious fascination from onlookers.

For much of his paper Arlow turns his attention to the latter, to the study of the reactions of his patients to those they perceive as "smug." The type of patient who finds the smug person difficult to tolerate is very often severely disturbed, suffering from both oedipal and preoedipal conflicts (a severe sense of oral deprivation). Those who over-react to the smug are often greatly preoccupied with social climbing, have a deep need to overcome feelings of social inferiority and low self-esteem. They suffer from an insatiable oral greediness, a fear of poverty, represented by unconscious fears of starving or being abandoned. The latter leads them to unreasonable demands to be fed or for narcissistic supplies. They may present a deep sense of disillusionment at being considered inferior to other siblings during childhood. They demonstrate an extreme callousness to others and usually suffer especially intense castration anxieties which regressively reactivate and accentuate their own oral conflicts. They respond with violent rage to those who are "smug," and they perceive these individuals to have slighted them. The calm, self-satisfied demeanor of the smug person represents to them the fulfillment of their own hidden wishes, namely, to achieve a "tension-free sense of satiety comparable to falling asleep at the mother's breast."

Arlow predicts that the clinical conclusions drawn from the strong overdetermined reactions of persons in response to smug individuals may well cast further light on the mental state of smug people themselves. However, the question is difficult to answer, for genuinely smug people do not usually come for analysis, although patients frequently report incidents or experiences in which they have felt smug themselves or in which other people have considered them to be so.

Besides depicting the parental background of several smug patients (and those who envy the smug), the unconscious meaning of smugness, its connection with past childhood events, and the consequences on character develop-

ment, Arlow suggests that much can still be learned from a study of the object relations and narcissism of those who are smug.

Some degree of negative response is practically the universal reaction to smug people. To be characterized as smug is never considered a compliment. Such a characterization invariably denotes not only a sense of disapproval but a feeling of active dislike or hostility.

According to the Oxford English Dictionary, the origin of the word "smug" is obscure. Originally, its meaning related to neatness or primness in dress. Only during the past few centuries have the current connotations of offensive self-satisfaction, complacency, and self-righteousness become associated with the word. There is, furthermore, an additional, although hardly popular, sense in which the word appears in the literature, i.e., to steal or to grasp, a meaning which some think may be connected with the root of the word "to smuggle." In the course of this paper it will be demonstrated how these two very different meanings may be derived from a response to a typical situation in which the prototype of the smug person is regarded as a grasping thief.

The smug person is not actively aggressive or malicious toward others in his smugness. If anything, he tends to be withdrawn and self-contained, undemanding in regard to his environment, and above all, seeming to want or need very little from it. Why so complacently self-satisfied a person should evoke such hostility is not completely clear.

In the course of psychoanalytic practice, however, it is not uncommon to observe patients in whom a most intense hostility and violent hatred are provoked by an encounter with a smug person. The smug object of this outburst may be and often is a relative stranger of no particular significance in the patient's life, a passing acquaintance from some casual social meeting. This fact serves only to accentuate the irrationality of the patient's response, a response whose intensity betrays all the indications of an exaggerated reaction. Both the irrationality and the exaggeration naturally lead to the suspicion of some unconscious determinant for such behavior. The analysis of such attitudes, furthermore, should reveal not only the significance of the predisposition on the part of certain individuals to react so acutely to smugness (in others) but may perhaps afford some insight into the more common, milder responses felt by most people toward their smug fellows. The phrase "smugness in others" is used advisedly, for it is by no means unusual for those very individuals who berate the complacently self-satisfied to learn to their chagrin that they themselves have been guilty of creating the impression of smugness in regard to themselves.

Listening to the descriptions which patients give of smug people and how they respond to them, we obtain a strikingly similar picture. Complacency, self-centeredness, and self-satisfaction are their most prominent attributes. The quality of self-righteousness holds a relatively secondary position, but an important one, especially for certain patients. The sense of self-containment which the smug person imparts is interpreted as a self-centered withdrawal of interest from other persons. The smug person is independent. He seems in need of no one. This element arouses envious fascination. But beyond that, the smug person acts as if he were oblivious of his surroundings, even unaware of the people in the immediate vicinity, or aware of them only in a general, undistinguishing way. It is this aspect of the smug person which is most intolerable and infuriating to such patients. Their sense of self-esteem is offended; the blow to their narcissism is compounded with a sense of futile and injured rage. The mere presence of a smug person, they complain, is something they cannot endure. They feel in turn angry, inferior, insignificant, and frustrated. Nothing and no one, they say, can impress the smug person. His mind is closed; he cannot learn; he will not change. It is the universally expressed wish of these patients to puncture the barrier of complacent repose, to disturb the equilibrium of self-satisfaction—often by slapping the smug and vapid face, for of all the features of the smug person the facial expression seems to be the most irritating. His countenance is described as clothed with a look of cold, empty haughtiness, or the lips are said to be touched by a very faint, amused smile, as if the subject were enjoying some private communion of self-appreciation.

Several especially articulate patients distinguish between their reactions to the smug and to the conceited person. The latter they regard as a sort of fool, one who pretends to an unjustifiably exaggerated evaluation of himself, but is by no means convinced in this estimate. It is for this reason that the conceited person tries repeatedly to call the attention of others to his actual or imagined superiority. He needs witnesses to overcome his own doubts concerning his worthwhileness. Not so the smug person; he requires no external confirmation to ensure his sense of self-satisfaction. That is brought about by his own fiat. He enjoys himself publicly, unabashedly, and without concern for the judgment of others. In some instances this last point serves to differentiate the response to successful but generous or modest persons. Such individuals have the good taste, or, perhaps more accurately, are moved by their more highly developed sense of guilt, to refrain from giving offense to others by ostentatious self-satisfaction which humiliates the less successful by treating them as if they did not exist. Such people have a regard for others' feelings.

The type of patient to whom the smug person is so sore

a trial and the typical derivation of this attitude are illustrated by the following clinical excerpts.

CASE 1

Quite the opposite of the smug person delineated above was Mrs. A. She was an intensely unhappy married woman of thirty-seven, who, in spite of a fairly well-to-do economic position, felt poverty-stricken, deprived, and dissatisfied. Although she drove a brand-new convertible car, belonged to a fashionable country club, and sported an attractive French poodle, she identified herself with a rejected Negro child whom she had seen in a movie, a child who had been abandoned in the slums of Harlem. At the beginning of the analysis, which was undertaken for marital discord, social anxiety, and insomnia, her major preoccupation was "Who snubs me? Whom do I snub?" Her devotion to social climbing was motivated by a need to overcome her social anxiety and strong feelings of social inferiority. For this reason she sought out the company, if not the friendship, of the successful, the famous, and the notorious. She worshipped the secular pantheon of celebrities, seeking to recover her self-esteem through identification with these latter-day demi-gods. It was indeed her secretly cherished dream that her analysis in one way or another would transform her into her ideal, a Greek goddess of unsurpassable beauty whom everyone would fall down and worship. Such a person would be perfectly poised, composed, and independent. Her love life was dominated by narcissistic object choices of men she thought to be cold, disdainful of others, and aloof.

Her difficulties stemmed from an insatiable oral greediness, which from earliest childhood disrupted her relationships. Her father was a bold, driving, sadistic, and successful man, who, though close to the age of eighty, still dominated and humiliated his family, his relatives, and his business associates. The mother was described by the patient as very beautiful but self-centered and selfish. The patient herself was the seventh of eight children—the eldest a girl, then five boys.

When the patient was three years old a sister was born. Following the delivery, the mother developed very serious complications which caused her to be hospitalized for many months. During this time the patient was in the charge of her older sister, who doted upon her but who was, nevertheless, an exacting parent substitute. Scarcely had the mother returned from the hospital when this sister married and left with her husband for a distant city. This fresh disappointment, coming so swiftly upon the heels of her disillusionment in regard to her mother, was something which the patient could hardly overcome. Although at this point she turned to her father with furious demands to supply her with all she felt she needed, she continued to yearn for her sister and replaced the object of her affections, now lost in reality, with an identification. In her analysis it was possible to see innumerable ways in which she imitated and identified with her sister, but in her dreams the object relationship, as it were, was restored. She saw herself repeatedly in the company of her sister (or sister substitute) who fed, dressed, and nursed her. From a strictly statistical point of view more than seventy-five percent of the patient's dreams were concerned with feeding and being fed. Variations on this theme were connected with the ideas of sleeping and dying, probably because at the time of the analysis the patient's older sister was already dead. Her fear of poverty represented an unconscious fear of starving to death or of being abandoned, just as her unreasonable demandingness for position and narcissistic supplies reflected her insatiable hunger. For example, when she heard that her husband had been separated from the firm in which he held a partnership, she went to the local grocery and impulsively bought fifty dollars worth of canned food to be stored in the larder. Following this she became elated and, denying her deep-seated fear of starvation, began planning a series of elaborate and expensive dinner parties which she could ill afford.

To compound the insult the younger sister developed into a very beautiful child, the delight and pet of the entire family. Each year the patient celebrated the birth of this younger sibling by getting depressed. In connection with one of these episodes the patient recalled that, as a child, she had hurled a cat out of a window and killed it. She unconsciously identified her adopted daughter with her younger sister, persistently making slips of the tongue in which she interchanged their names. Her attitude toward her daughter was a mixture of identification and ambivalence. When identified with her she could refuse her no demands, and no criticism directed at her daughter from whatever source would be countenanced. On the other hand, she would expect her daughter to epitomize in reality all the qualities which she herself prized. She was at the same time capable of extreme callousness and cruelty toward her daughter, compensating for this by various acts of ingratiation and self-punishment. From her husband she expected an all-giving mother-father image from whom she would passively receive various token substitutes for the breast-penis to help her achieve once more the golden age of her childhood, before the birth of her sister, when she enjoyed a sense of narcissistic fusion with the mother, a sense of complete passive gratification which admitted of no rival. The patient acted out the impulse to be breast fed by unconsciously seducing her eight-year-old daughter to suck at her breast.

Mrs. A experienced a violently rageful reaction when she met a smug but beautiful girl married to a wealthy man. She said, "I was furious. I wanted to slap her face. I couldn't stand the looks of her. I know why I didn't like her; she was so smug, so self-satisfied, so pleased with herself—like a cat who had all the cream, licking her chops. She looked as delighted as though she had swallowed the whole world— maybe she did, because the world does not exist for her; nothing exists for her but the good feeling she has for herself. She did not even notice me. I don't think she even knows that I exist. She doesn't need me; she doesn't need anyone. She made me feel so small, so insignificant. I felt like an outsider, so dissatisfied with myself. What a contrast between her and me! I am never satisfied; I am always hungry. It makes me think of the time when I was in my bedroom sulking while my mother was in the kitchen, busy feeding my younger sister. I was so furious, so envious." (This memory consistently reappeared in the analysis in association with oral envy and rage over oral deprivation. The incident referred to had taken place when the patient was a little over four years of age, at a time when she combined her resentment at oral deprivation with her penis envy, blaming the frustrating mother for both.) The patient's associations then continued, "It makes me think of the time when I first saw my mother and sister in the bed after my mother returned home from the hospital. How unhappy I felt when I saw my sister sleeping so quietly next to my mother, so peaceful, so at rest. I wanted to get into bed next to my mother and push my sister out. I was so hungry for my mother's love. That is the picture that always comes back to me at times like this."

It is clear from this material that the patient's reaction to the smug person is based upon a very intense feeling of envy. The calm, self-satisfied repose of the smug person represented the fulfillment of the patient's own wishes, namely, to achieve the tension-free sense of satiety and to fall asleep at the mother's breast. The smug object of her hostility was unconsciously identified with the well-fed younger sister, satisfied and self-satisfied, now blissfully withdrawn into sleep after having nursed her fill at the mother's breast. The sense of withdrawal of cathexis from the external world is reflected in the patient's statement that for the smug person the world does not exist because she has swallowed it. To the patient, furthermore, the smug person represents a usurper, a younger sibling who has stolen her rightful place at the mother's breast. The outraged sense of injustice which the smug person stimulates is associated also with the need to inhibit the wish to push aside the usurping rival. This attitude becomes more explicit in the next case presentation.

CASE 2

Dr. K, a forty-three-year-old physician, suffering from a character neurosis, was chronically depressed, inhibited, and pessimistic. Since any emotional display was most unusual with him, it was all the more striking when he responded with violent rage to an encounter with a colleague whom he considered smug.

The patient's passive oral wishes had a complicated structure stemming from both preoedipal and oedipal conflicts. The father was ineffectual and rather unsuccessful, while the mother was an active, capable, professional woman, apparently with a good deal of musical and artistic talent. To the patient the mother unconsciously represented a phallic woman, and in some of his fantasies intercourse between the parents consisted of the mother nursing the father as she had the younger sister.

An especially intense castration anxiety had regressively reactivated and accentuated oral conflicts, but for other reasons such material would inevitably have dominated the patient's productions. In the first place, he had come to me after a number of years of what he considered an unsuccessful analysis with a woman therapist. Actually, one of the patient's goals in treatment, which in his mind was associated with economic security, was beyond his therapist's capacity to fulfill. Secondly, during his course of treatment with me his mother was dying of cancer of the breast. Because he had administered a course of hormone injections to her some years before for menopausal symptoms, the patient kept reproaching himself with the thought that in some way he was responsible for his mother's developing cancer.

After having been breast fed for a year, he had been weaned suddenly and precipitously in order that his mother might enter upon her professional studies. A devoted grandmother took care of him, but his reaction to weaning was, nevertheless, most severe. He lost his appetite, became constipated, would not sleep, and cried so piteously and so continuously that the distraught grandmother permitted him to suck at her dry breasts in order to quiet him. The patient thus had what Abraham (1924a) characterizes as a "primal depression." No sooner had the mother completed her professional studies than a younger sister was born. The mother was particularly attached to this younger sister for several reasons, one being that this sister suffered from a hereditary form of deafness transmitted to her by the mother. The patient's lifelong complaint had been that his sister got everything and he got nothing. As he put it, "No red carpet was ever rolled out for me. I always had to get in through the back door." At a relatively late age he married a girl who was more or less picked for him by his mother, and whom he knew to have prospects of inheriting money from her parents. Toward his own two children the patient was extremely overprotective, living in constant dread lest they fall out of the window. Professionally, he was convinced that he would never succeed, and that with the first worsening of the economic situation he would lose his patients and have to face the danger of starvation.

The reaction to the smug colleague came about in the following way. During a period when the patient was feeling more than his usual concern about not having enough patients, he felt that a colleague, Dr. X, was influencing the relatives of one of his patients to withdraw the patient from treatment with Dr. K. In reporting this incident my patient became very furious, but did not think of doing anything about the situation. I pointed this out to him and suggested that he could get in touch with Dr. X in order to ascertain the true nature of his interest in this case. On the following day he returned and reported a fantasy which he said had filled him with a very positive feeling of satisfaction. He felt that both he and Dr. X were in analysis with me and that I was taking his part. "For a change," he said, "somebody is on my side against a greedy, grasping rival instead of the way it has always been—vice versa." He then added, "I have known Dr. X for some time. I cannot stand him because he is so smug." In explanation of this remark the patient stated, "He is selfish, egocentric, self-satisfied, greedy, and grasping. He never feels guilty; he doesn't consider that he does anything wrong. He is a snob. He makes you feel inferior and frustrated. He is like all smug people. You cannot influence them; you cannot teach them. They are close-minded. They are not gentle. It reminds me of another one of my colleagues who asked me what kind of music I liked. When I said I liked Dvořák he looked down his nose at me. He is the kind that likes fourteenth-century music played on obsolete instruments."

The patient went on to say, "Smugness is a disease. I never allow myself to be satisfied. There is a danger in being smug. I didn't show off my medals and decorations. I don't have an attitude of 'Pull open your jacket and show off your fat belly with your Phi Beta Kappa key,' but Dr. X is that way. He beat me to several jobs. He is the fair-haired boy and now he is sitting pretty. He had plenty of patients and he is eating off the fat of the land. When we were in the Navy we both took a course at the same hospital. He walked in and smugly displayed his service coat with the "fruit salad" (military slang for campaign ribbons) on it. Whenever there was a job open and we both tried for it he beat me to it. He got my place. I can't tilt at windmills. He has everything; I have nothing."

The use of oral images—"fat belly," "fruit salad," "living off the fat of the land"—was pointed out to the patient. In response he stated, "Yes, he reminds me of a stuffed fat baby drifting off to sleep. That is why you can't teach smug people anything. They are asleep but they don't know it—which reminds me: I got up early this morning; I could not sleep; something is wrong, I don't feel anxious, but . . . I'm always dissatisfied. I set high goals and I never reach them."

The patient's associations then turned to gifts. A rich cousin of his had just had his home decorated most expensively through his father's generosity. This cousin as a boy had had hundreds of dollars worth of electric trains and tracks. The patient complained that his son had only a very small set of trains. An uncle in Florida gives his son thousands of dollars a year in gifts in order to avoid inheritance taxes. Now he gives gifts to his adopted grandchildren. The patient reported that he had had the thought, "Why give the money to strangers or the government? Why not give it to his nephews or nieces? I wonder . . . am I in his will?" He began to berate his father-in-law for being so generous in his charitable contributions. He attacked professional solicitors for charity as racketeers who pocket the money for themselves. He gives to charity reluctantly, he said, because "everyone takes from me, but who takes care of me?" He then recalled that his mother had recently received two beautiful ash trays as gifts, and that he had had the thought that when she died she would leave these ash trays to his sister and not to him. Suddenly he checked himself and asked, "Why all this talk about my hunger for gifts and what I want from my mother? Good heavens!" he exclaimed, "today is my sister's birthday."

Only with great reluctance did thoughts of his sister's birthday find expression. If she had never been born he would have had everything. He had sent her a birthday gift grudgingly. When he gave her husband a bottle of "Black Label Schenley" he had the thought, "Poison has a black label on it, too." He added, "This week I have been more liberal in prescribing drugs for my patients. I used to be afraid of prescribing drugs for fear of poisoning someone. I was also afraid that some patient would have an idiosyncrasy to a drug and die. Even aspirin would frighten me; the patient might develop tinnitus and deafness. My sister is deaf."

Subsequent associations referred to his earliest recollection of his sister when she first came home from the hospital. He had to be quiet in order not to awaken the new baby. Upon seeing his mother nurse his sister he had apparently tried to suck her breast because he recalled an incident—obviously a screen memory—in which his mother's breast has been pumped of milk, the milk placed in a "gravy boat" with a long spout from which he then proceeded to suck. He did not like the taste of the milk, and as he spat it out his mother laughed at him. (It was indeed with the analysis of his reaction to smug people that the dramatic information about sucking his grandmother's dry breasts and other material relating to cannibalistic fantasies were first obtained.) He complained at the injustice of the favored treatment which his sister had received, comparing her again with the smug Dr. X. Both were greedy, grasping, sated, and untroubled by feelings of guilt. He felt himself to be dissatisfied, hungry, and conscience-stricken.

To summarize the material: The fantasy that both he and Dr. X were in analysis with me and that I was favoring him and protecting his economic security was a wish-fulfilling transference fantasy marking the date of his sister's birth. I represented the mother, and the smug Dr. X was identified with his newborn younger sister. In the fantasy, however, the relationship is reversed. The patient is the favored one, receiving the gifts. He is the newborn child, happily asleep at the mother's breast. Since hunger and frustration are necessary concomitants of wakefulness, object finding, and learning, it is clear why the smug person, identified as he is with the sated, sleeping nursling, is characterized as close-minded, unteachable, and not amenable to influence.

In this material, furthermore, the patient identifies the pangs of conscience with the pangs of hunger. For the smug person there is no tension between the ego and the superego, a state which may be compared with a sense of fusion between the sated nursling and his object. The loss of self-esteem which accompanies feelings of guilt may be genetically related to the sense of helplessness of the "abandoned" child. Thus the inwardly perceived effects of the superego, which in certain respects behave like an internal persecutor, may have as their prototype not only the unpleasant sensations stimulated by the fecal mass (Stärcke, 1920; Van Ophuijsen, 1920; Arlow, 1949) but also the painful affects of hunger. One cannot feel smug and guilty at the same time.

The relationship between satiety, sleep, and smugness was explicitly stated by a young male patient, a "borderline" case with severe oral conflicts characterized by insomnia, alcoholism, and sexual promiscuity. He was most intolerant of smug people, going out of his way wherever possible to upset their composure and to irritate them. One evening he discovered that his mother, a barbiturate and alcohol addict, had stolen from his cabinet a bottle of liquor which he prized. He became furious with her and, in recounting his reaction during the analytic session on the following day, said, "I asked her if the liquor were mine, where she got it, why was she drunk. My words did not disturb her. She did not even hear me. She had that glassy stare, that smug, unseeing look of the self-satisfied drunk. This I could not stand. I began to scold her, shouted at her at the top of my lungs—no effect. She was asleep with her eyes open. This made me even more furious. 'I will wake her up,' I said, 'even if I have to slap her face.' I remember now where I saw that look before. It was on the face of a fellow who went to military school with me. I used to get food from home which I would save in a strongbox. Once I found that the strongbox had been forced open and the roast turkey which I had hidden was gone. I knew who had eaten it; I went after him and found him on the drill field. He looked so smug and so smart. He did not even notice me. I hauled off to sock him and I would have killed him if the gang hadn't stopped me." The patient used to save his food in order to eat alone in a secret cave which he had found in the meadows near the boarding school. This solitary play represented an acting out of the intrauterine fantasy which appealed to the patient, who had enjoyed the special status of an only child until the age of eight, when he was enrolled in the boarding school and was suddenly confronted with a multitude of boarding-school siblings. Following Lewin's (1946) idea about the relationship between satiety and sleep, we may speculate that the state of self-contained smugness corresponds to a waking representation of sleep in which cathexes are practically completely withdrawn from the external world and reinvested in the subject's own self-representations.

It is an inevitable experience for the analyst, in the course of therapy, to be accused sooner or later of being smug and complacent. Such an accusation comes rather characteristically from women with intense penis envy and strong oral dispositions. In the transference relationship of several patients of this type, the analyst was identified with the evil mother, charged with depriving the little girl and frustrating her oral needs, a factor which Freud emphasized in his later studies of female sexuality. The smug possessor of the phallus is equated with the favored child who has been generously and appropriately fed. Feelings of this kind not unusually emerge at the time of the menses. In the course of one session during her period, a patient attacked the following individuals in turn for their smugness: the analyst, her husband, a very masculine girlfriend who was an excellent athlete and much too fat, and a former patient who had completed her treatment and was now contentedly pregnant.

The patient had been weaned early because at the age of four months she had developed colic, food allergy, and eczema. It was many months before this condition could be brought under control. During this time she became sleepless and hungry and cried a great deal. In addition, in order to prevent scratching, her hands had been pinned to the bedclothes. These feelings of deprivation were combined with her hostility toward her mother during the phase of penis envy. She had wanted to have curly hair like her brother. Her mother had told her that if she ate lots of raw carrots the desired transformation would come about. She followed her mother's advice faithfully, only to come to ultimate and bitter disappointment. In this patient's thinking the brother, the husband, the analyst, the woman athlete, and the former patient were all smug because they had a penis which they had acquired through being properly cared for and fed. She equated being castrated with being hungry, sleepless, and dissatisfied. On the other hand, being phallic and pregnant were the same as being sated, asleep, and smug. The self-contentment of pregnant women, incidentally, is perhaps the one situation in which the term "smug" is used with a minimal sense of opprobrium. The relationship of the self-satisfied repose of the pregnant woman to fantasies of an oral nature is too well known to be expanded upon at this point. A necessary precondition for the enjoyment of this state by the pregnant woman is freedom from guilt over the oral fantasies involved. The investment of the superego with oral-sadistic drives is the link which connects the sense of painful self-judgment with the feeling of hunger.

Up to this point the material has been drawn almost exclusively from the violent reactions of envious patients to smug persons. How accurately does this model as projected by these patients reflect the mental state of smug people? It is difficult to answer this question because genuinely smug people, if such exist, do not as a rule come for analysis. There are, however, a number of situations which afford at least a partial or suggestive answer to this problem. To begin with, the state of being smug is only a temporary frame of mind, usually evoked in a very definite context and serving various intrapsychic purposes as a result of a complicated genetic development. Occasionally patients do report experiences in which they felt smug or in which other people considered them so. It will also be recalled that earlier in this paper a number of the patients who reacted with such intensity to smug people were themselves accused on several occasions of being equally offensive in the same fashion.

The type of smugness which patients most often are prepared to ascribe to themselves is the sense of self-righteous complacency felt at the debacle of some unfair, greedy, grasping competitor. The spectacle of fate punishing the guilty not only justified their own renunciations but was accompanied by a feeling of elevation of self-esteem from a sense of superego approval. A professional man reported that he felt smug on reading in the newspapers that two of his professional rivals had been apprehended perpetrating some illegal transactions. He stated that he disliked them both because they were smug. "Now that they are in trouble, I can almost feel smug. I don't like smug people. They are selfish, grasping, without the gnawing sense of guilt. They do not realize their potential. They do not help others. They get their success the easy way." One of the professional rivals was described as being condescending toward the patient: "He has had more than his share of success. He got it illegally. I used to get furious if anyone were condescending toward me. For example, X was smug and very condescending toward me. He pushed me out of my position in the office. He studied my records and methods in order to supplant me." Further associations indicated that these two dishonest professional rivals had been considered "white-headed boys." The patient stated that before a younger sister had been born he had been the white-headed boy. Subsequent associations revolved about the theme of sibling rivalry, nightmares which followed the birth of the younger sister, and various methods which the patient had used to torture the young usurper.

Certain aspects of the mood of smugness resemble a quiet form of elation. This mood of quiet elation, this diminution of tension between ego and superego, is often conceived of in terms of oral rewards. For elucidation of the oral component of elation we are indebted to the observations of Lewin (1950). Similar observations on the feeling of triumph were made by Fenichel (1936b) and Helene Deutsch

(1927). The woman patient mentioned above, who had been told that her hair would grow curly like her brother's if she ate carrots, demonstrated this connection between smugness and triumph. After having got the better of a male competitor she reported that she felt very smug, no longer hungry or dissatisfied with herself, quietly complacent "like the cat that ate the canary." Because of her strong oral fixation, almost every success which this patient experienced was felt in terms of oral gratification.

A coldly aloof, self-satisfied air of complacency may be used in a hostile and defensive fashion to humiliate competitors and to demonstrate one's invulnerability, indifference and independence from potential love objects who have the power to rebuff, reject, or humiliate. Such smugness imparts the hostile connotation "I do not need anyone; anything I need I can find in myself." The hostility intended by this type of smugness may not be conscious, but the attitude of being a completely self-satisfying and emotionally self-contained unit usually is. Such an assumed air of smugness often serves as a defense against painful feelings of social anxiety and inferiority in narcissistic patients. Two such patients had affected this pose. For the reasons already elucidated earlier in this paper, they both despised and were extremely irritated by smug people. To one of these patients, nevertheless, it came as a shocking surprise that she had created the impression of smugness on several occasions when she actually was aware only of defensively withdrawing into herself because of her anxiety. During such times this patient, the first one reported on in this paper, would become extremely hostile to her unresponsive and threatening environment, and would entertain the fantasy that she was indeed the invulnerable and independent figure of a Greek goddess, the ideal to which she aspired. The second patient, an attractive model whose system of security was being undermined by the fading of her beauty, was constantly aware of the impression which she was creating and of the method which she used to create this impression. She was an "as if" personality (Deutsch, 1942) who was completely dependent upon her environment for her own sense of self-esteem. When she entered a new social situation which she felt she could not master, she knew that, by standing off alone in some prominent position and acting like one aloof, distant, and self-absorbed, she would inevitably arouse the interest and attention of a number of people. When such attention was not immediately forthcoming and the patient felt herself growing anxious, she would imagine that she had a very long, full breast which she could put into her own mouth and suck. In this manner she could become completely and happily detached from the unresponsive or unfriendly environment, and it was at such times that she imparted the impression of her smugness to observers. Another version of this fantasy of being a completely self-contained emotional unit appeared in a dream in which the patient saw her house tenanted by all the outstanding figures in the artistic, theatrical, literary, and entertainment worlds. While it is undoubtedly true that this type of smugness is the end result of a complicated genetic development in which an air of hostile repudiation of dependence on the environment is outstanding, it nevertheless remains a fact that the capacity of such individuals to inflict pain on those who observe them through an assumed air of smugness is related to the narcissistic mortification which they thus inflict upon their observers and by the sense of envy which an air of self-containment is capable of arousing in most people.

Support for these conjectures comes from a recent study by Rangell (1954) on the subject of "poise." From clinical, neurological, and biological considerations, he emphasized the role of the mouth and the perioral areas in clinging, supporting maneuvers for the purpose of maintaining narcissistic and other forms of equilibrium. One of his patients, for example, could maintain or regain her social poise through the reassuring presence in her hand of a cocktail glass.

A comment on object relations and narcissism is pertinent at this point. The narcissistic type of object choice characterized almost all the patients reported on. Several of them were attracted only to smug people as love objects. A. Reich (1953) has shown how the regressive reinstitution of this type of object choice may be used especially by women with problems of penis envy to fend off feelings of narcissistic mortification. The choice of object follows the prototype of the archaic infantile ego ideal, usually an omnipotent parental figure. While mortification at the advent of and the loss of love to a younger sibling were pre-eminent in this material, other forms of narcissistic mortification, viz., penis envy, frustrated oedipal wishes, etc., serve to reinstitute in a regressive fashion a fantasy of securing invulnerability to disappointment and humiliation through identification with the sated nursling. The material presented suggests that the model of omnipotence may be derived from the invulnerability to stimuli or to narcissistic mortification which the young child imagines to be the happy state of the sated, sleeping nursling.

CONCLUSION

Those who have known severe hunger and its later representations, i.e., absence of narcissistic supplies, most bitterly resent smug people. They find it most unjust that others should enjoy what they have had to renounce and can no longer experience. The ideal prototype of the smug individual is fantasied as the well-fed nursling falling asleep at its mother's breast. Smugness represents oral satiety with incorporation of the good object. The object may be represented in current experience by fame, success, etc., but it is ultimately identified with the penis-breast and milk. Smugness implies a temporary diminution of tension between ego and superego plus a relatively large and transitory withdrawal of the cathexis invested in objects. The freedom from tension and withdrawal of object cathexis correspond to the state of affairs which may be assumed to hold for the infant happily asleep after feeding. In this respect, smugness is in the nature of a waking representation of sleep. (It probably differs from mania in the easy reversibility of the process of cathexis of self-representations back to cathexis of object representations.) The various attributes ascribed to the smug person—his self-satisfaction, self-absorption, lack of awareness of the environment, the pleased look on his face and lips, the absence of guilt, his greediness and grasping, and his inability to learn—are derived from this situation. Hunger is the awakener, the source of frustration which directs the individual once again to the world of objects where the process of learning can develop. Guilt over oral greed interferes with the ability to be smug. Some negative reaction to smugness is present to some degree in everyone—to the extent that all human beings in some measure yearn for the tension-free sleep they enjoyed in their mothers' arms. It is an early and undoubtedly basic narcissistic mortification that the individual must awaken and know hunger while others seem to sleep their lives away in blissful satisfaction.

ON ARROGANCE

W. R. Bion
(1958)

In this short paper, the clinical material of which can be likened to an excerpt from a detective thriller, Bion provides a striking example of how the appearance of new affective states during analysis may be of crucial significance for the outcome of therapy. During the course of analysis, Bion's patient developed a triad of emotional attitudes: curiosity, arrogance, and stupidity. They were part and parcel of a regressive picture involving a severe negative therapeutic reaction and impending psychotic disorganization.

The sudden appearance of this triad in one in whom "psychotic mechanisms are active" is a signal that one is dealing with a "potential psychological disaster." In my own clinical experience, chronic arrogance is quite often seen in those of paranoid disposition.

Scattered references to curiosity, arrogance, and stupidity often appear during the analysis of apparently neurotic patients and especially those in the midst of a negative therapeutic response. They are then projected onto the analyst. The clue to such a development was afforded one day when one of Bion's patients wondered that Bion "could stand it." This was a projection whose meaning was that there was "something" that the analyst was able to tolerate but that the patient could not. The patient is engaging in a wholesale flight from unacceptable ideas through denial and projective identification. It is the primitive superego of these patients that negates their own use of projective identification. The clue to an approaching psychotic picture was provided by the emergence of widely separated references to curiosity, arrogance, and stupidity. "The stupidity was purposeful, and arrogance not always called by that name was sometimes an accusation, sometimes a temptation, and sometimes a cry."

My own clinical practice provides another example. One of my patients, a homosexual who had begun to engage in homosexual activities at the beginning of therapy, developed the triad of arrogance, stupidity, and curiosity. His desire for homosexual contact had been suppressed at great psychic cost, manifested by depression and severe social withdrawal for over a decade. Its enactment provided him at first with great psychological relief. Simultaneously longing to cease homosexual activities, he actively immersed himself in them. As summer vacation approached, he became increasingly grandiose, would not allow interpretations by "talking through them," became increasingly engrossed in the analyst's personal life, wished to see the analyst's apartment, and became arrogantly competitive with regard to understanding analytic interpretations and external events, as well as showing contempt for advice, interpretations, and interventions. A pseudostupidity about the meaning of his productions also began to make an appearance, together with beginning ideas of reference, paranoidal ideation, misidentifications, splitting processes, and severe resistance to therapy. I have frequently found arrogance in homosexual patients of paranoid disposition who, hating their homosexuality and unable to accept it, project this hate upon the analyst and feel he despises them for their psychosexual *disorder. A profound negative therapeutic reaction may then develop.*

Arrogance is an acute or chronic affective state characterized by undue attitudes of superiority toward others and manifested by an overbearing manner, presumptuousness, haughtiness, superciliousness, insolence, and even insulting behavior. It is a form of reactive behavior directed not only against instinctual impulses but also around conflicts of self-esteem. It is not difficult to detect that beneath most manifestly arrogant behavior there are deep feelings of inferiority, and, conversely, one frequently finds that beneath an attitude of outward self-depreciation there may be a deep-seated arrogant attitude. In the psychoanalytic therapy of narcissistic personality disorders, when a full exploration of the underlying conflicts is effected, one frequently sees an excessige rage and demandingness (Kernberg, 1975) and an arrogant, parasitic, and exploitative relationship to others (narcissistic arrogance).

In underscoring the seriousness, if not indeed the potential malignancy, of this affect, Bion observes that "where life instincts predominate, pride becomes self-respect; where death instincts predominate, pride becomes arrogance."

In this paper I propose to deal with the appearance, in the material of a certain class of patient, of references to curiosity, arrogance, and stupidity which are so dispersed and separated from each other that their relatedness may escape detection. I shall suggest that their appearance should be taken by the analyst as evidence that he is dealing with a psychological disaster. The meaning with which I wish to invest the term "arrogance" may be indicated by supposing that in the personality where life instincts predominate, pride becomes self-respect; where death instincts predominate, pride becomes arrogance.

Their separation from each other and the lack of evidence of any relatedness is evidence that a disaster has occurred. To make clear the connection between these references, I shall rehearse the Oedipus myth from a point of view which makes the sexual crime a peripheral element of a story in which the central crime is the arrogance of Oedipus in vowing to lay bare the truth at no matter what cost.

This shift of emphasis brings the following elements into the center of the story: the Sphinx, who asks a riddle and destroys herself when it is answered, the blind Teiresias, who possesses knowledge and deplores the resolve of the king to search for it, the oracle that provokes the search which the prophet deplores, and again the king who, his search concluded, suffers blindness and exile. This is the story of which the elements are discernible amongst the ruins of the psyche, to which the scattered references to curiosity, arrogance, and stupidity have pointed the way.

I said that these references are significant in a certain class of patient; the class to which I refer is one in which psychotic mechanisms are active and have to be analytically uncovered before a stable adjustment can be achieved. In practice, analysis of such a patient may seem to follow the patterns with which we are familiar in the treatment of the neuroses, but with the important difference that improvement in the patient's condition does not appear to be commensurate with the analytic work that is done. To recapitulate, the analyst who is treating an apparently neurotic patient must regard a negative therapeutic response, together with the appearance of scattered, unrelated references to curiosity, arrogance, and stupidity, as evidence that he is in the presence of a psychological catastrophe with which he will have to deal.

It is important that reference to any of these three qualities should be treated by the analyst as a significant event demanding investigation and provoking more than usually stubborn resistances. Unfortunately, the problem is complicated by a fact which must be already evident, and that is that the analytic procedure itself is precisely a manifestation of the curiosity which is felt to be an intrinsic component of the disaster. As a consequence, the very act of analyzing the patient makes the analyst an accessory in precipitating regression and turning the analysis itself into a piece of acting out. From the point of view of successful analysis, this is a development that should be avoided. Yet I have not been able to see how this can be done. The alternative course is to accept the acting out and regression as inevitable, and if possible to turn it to good account. This, I believe, can be done, but it involves detailed interpretation of events that are taking place in the session. These events are active displays of the mechanisms of splitting, projective identification, and the related subsidiary phenomena of confusional states, depersonalization, and hallucination, which have been described by Melanie Klein, Segal, and Rosenfeld as part of the analysis of psychotic patients.

In this phase of the analysis, the transference is peculiar in that, in addition to the features to which I have drawn attention in previous papers, it is to the analyst as analyst. Features of this are his appearance, and that of the patient in so far as he is identified with the analyst as, by turns, blind, stupid, suicidal, curious, and arrogant. I shall have more to say later about the qualities of arrogance. I must emphasize that at this stage the patient would appear to have no problems other than the existence of the analyst himself. Furthermore that the spectacle presented is one, to borrow Freud's analogy, similar to that of the archaeologist who discovers in his field work the evidences, not so much of a primitive civilization, as of a primitive catastrophe. In analytic terms the hope must be that the investigations which are being carried out will issue in the reconstruction of the ego. This aim is, however, obscured because this analytic procedure has become an acting out of destructive attacks launched against the ego, wherever it is discerned. That is to say, the ego whether it appears manifest in the patient or the analyst. These attacks closely resemble the description given by Melanie Klein of the infant's fantasied attacks on the breast.

If we turn now to consider what there is in reality that makes it so hateful to the patient that he must destroy the ego which brings him into contact with it, it would be natural to suppose that it is the sexually orientated Oedipus situation, and indeed I have found much to substantiate this view. When reconstitution of the ego has proceeded sufficiently to bring the Oedipus situation into sight, it is quite common to find that it precipitates further attacks on the ego. But there is evidence that some other element is playing an important part in provoking destructive attacks on the ego and its consequent disintegration. The key to this lies in the references to arrogance.

Briefly, it appears that overwhelming emotions are associated with the assumption by the patient or analyst of the qualities required to pursue the truth, and in particular a capacity to tolerate the stresses associated with the introjection of another person's projective identifications. Put into other terms, the implicit aim of psychoanalysis to pursue the truth at no matter what cost is felt to be synonymous with a claim to a capacity for containing the discarded, split-off aspects of other personalities while retaining a balanced outlook. This would appear to be the immediate signal for outbreaks of envy and hatred.

I propose now to devote the remainder of this paper to description of the clinical aspect of the material which I have so far approached theoretically. The patient in question did not at any time behave in a way which in my view would warrant a diagnosis of psychosis; he had, however, displayed the features I have mentioned, namely, scattered references to curiosity, arrogance, and stupidity, together with what I felt was an inadequate therapeutic response. At the period with which I deal, the significance of these features had become clear, and I had been able to give him some insight into their relatedness and the increasing frequency with which they appeared in the forefront of his material. He described his behavior in the sessions as mad or insane, and he showed anxiety at his inability to behave in a way which his experience of analysis had shown him to be helpful in furthering analytic progress. For my part, I was impressed by the fact that for several sessions at a time he seemed to be devoid of the insight and judgment which I knew from previous experience that he possessed. Furthermore, the material was almost entirely of the kind with which I was familiar in the analysis of psychotic patients. That is to say, projective identification was extremely active, and the patient's states of confusion and depersonalization easy to detect and frequently in evidence. For a matter of some months sessions were taken up entirely with psychotic mechanisms to an extent which made me wonder how it was that the patient was apparently continuing his extra-analytic life without, as far as I knew, any material change for the worse.

In its simplest form this material appeared in sessions when the patient's associations lacked coherence, and consisted of "sentences" which were remarkably deficient in one or another aspect of the grammar of conversational English. Thus, a significant object might be mentioned, but there would be no pronoun or verb, or a significant verbal form would appear such as "going skating," but there would be no mention of who was supposed to be doing this or where, and so on in an apparently inexhaustible number of variations. The establishment of an analytically potent relationship by means of verbal communication thus seemed to be impossible. Analyst and patient together formed a frustrated couple. This in itself was not new, and on one occasion, during a relatively lucid session, the patient himself observed that the method of communication was so mutilated that creative work was impossible, and he despaired of the possibility that any cure could come about. He was already quite familiar with the sexual anxiety inherent in such conduct, so it seemed reasonable to suppose that some progress would follow, and it was the more surprising that this did not in fact happen; the anxiety of the patient increased. I was eventually forced to assume, on theoretical grounds, that progress had taken place and that there was a change in his behavior which I was failing to observe. With this assumption in mind I attempted to cast about for some revealing clue which would indicate what this change might be. In the meantime the sessions continued much as before. I remained at a loss until one day, in a lucid moment, the patient said he wondered that I could stand it. This gave me a clue: at least I now knew that there was something I was able to stand which he apparently could not. He realized already that he felt he was being obstructed in his aim to establish a creative contact with me, and that this obstructive force was sometimes in him, sometimes in me, and sometimes occupied an unknown location. Furthermore, the obstruction was effected by some means other than mutilation of verbal communications. The patient had already made it clear that the obstructing force or object was out of his control.

The next step forward occurred when the patient said that I was the obstructing force, and that my outstanding characteristic was "that I could not stand it." I now worked on the assumption that the persecuting object that could not permit any creative relationship was one that "could not stand it," but I was still not clear what "it" was. It was tempting to assume that "it" was any creative relationship which was made intolerable to the persecuting object through envy and hate of the creative couple. Unfortunately this did not lead any further because it was an aspect of the material which had already been made clear without producing any advance. The problem of what "it" was still, therefore, awaited solution.

Before I discuss this problem further, I must mention a feature of the material which had led up to this point, because it contributes to an understanding of the next step. During the whole of this period which I have been describing, references to curiosity, arrogance, and stupidity became more frequent and more obviously related to each other. The stupidity was purposeful, and arrogance, not always called by that name, was sometimes an accusation, sometimes a temptation, and sometimes a crime. The cumulative effect of these references was to persuade me that their relatedness depended upon their association with the obstructive object. Curiosity and stupidity waxed or waned together: that is to say, if curiosity increased, so did the stupidity. I therefore felt some gain in knowledge of the character of the obstructive force. What it was that the object could not stand became clearer in some sessions where it appeared that in so far as I, as analyst, was insisting on verbal communication as a method of making the patient's problems explicit, I was felt to be directly attacking the patient's methods of communication. From this it became clear that when I was identified with the obstructive force, what I could not stand was the patient's methods of communication. In this phase my employment of verbal communication was felt by the patient to be a mutilating attack on his methods of communication. From this point onward, it was only a matter of time to demonstrate that the patient's link with me was his ability to employ the mechanism of projective identification. That is to say, his relationship with me and his ability to profit by the association lay in the opportunity to split off parts of his psyche and project them into me.

On this depended a variety of procedures which were felt to ensure emotionally rewarding experiences such as, to mention two, the ability to put bad feelings in me and leave them there long enough for them to be modified by their sojourn in my psyche, and the ability to put good parts of himself into me, thereby feeling that he was dealing with an ideal object as a result. Associated with these experiences was a sense of being in contact with me, which I am inclined to believe is a primitive form of communication that provides a foundation on which, ultimately, verbal communication depends. From his feelings about me when I was identified with the obstructive object, I was able to deduce that the obstructive object was curious about him, but could not stand being the receptacle for parts of his personality, and accordingly made destructive and mutilating attacks, largely through varieties of stupidity, upon his capacity for projective identification. I therefore concluded that the catastrophe stemmed from the mutiliating attacks made upon this extremely primitive species of link between the patient and analyst.

CONCLUSION

In some patients the denial to themselves of a normal employment of projective identification precipitates a disaster through the destruction of an important link. Inherent in this disaster is the establishment of a primitive superego which denies the use of projective identification.

The clue to this disaster is provided by the emergence of widely separated references to curiosity, arrogance, and stupidity.

THE PSYCHOLOGY OF BITTERNESS

JAMES ALEXANDER

(1960)

More than any other psychoanalyst in America, James Alexander of Chicago has devoted a great portion of his psychoanalytic career to investigating the affects. This passionate dedication has led to the publication of over a dozen papers on both the clinical and theoretical aspects of affects and their derivations. Four of these, "On the Affect of Horror" (1972), "On Gloating" (Whitman and Alexander, 1968), "The Psychology of Bitterness" (1960), and "Faith, Trust and Gullibility" (Isaacs, Alexander, and Haggard, 1963) are included in this volume. Others deal with foolishness (Alexander and Isaacs, 1968), seriousness (Alexander and Isaacs, 1963), surprise (1968), courage (1969), excitement (1971), and pathos (1973).

Alexander correctly observes that not only the psychiatric resident but even the experienced clinician is likely to take affects for granted. For example, a patient may be described as "bitter," but then we are likely not to have examined this character trait with the care and detail we give to such symptoms as acting out, fantasy, or dream material. Scientific work dedicated to penetrating the secrets locked within an affect can only increase our clarity of description of a particular patient, add to our knowledge of both his psychic health and psychopathology, and enrich our total understanding of him.

Bitterness, when present to an exceptional degree, can produce a chronic ego state, involving the whole personality. The embittered person considers himself the victim of justified grievances and usually does not enter therapy with any intention of modifying his state, for he does not consider his symptom morbid, but simply "an unpleasant feeling justified by external reality." His sense of injustice, however, is felt with deep sincerity. There is a querulous note in those who are bitter. The bitter person feels "reproachful, resentful over pain whose reason he cannot understand, which appears to him unnecessary . . . but deliberately inflicted by fate, in short, as a 'persecution.' " In psychotic depressions, the presence of bitterness augments destructive aggression against the self, and "bitter scorn" is heaped upon the self. The flavor of "victimization" which runs through bitterness places this feeling in the category Alexander terms the "paranoid affects," e.g., stage fright, vengeance.

All of Alexander's clinical material reveals that "weaning through trickery" (without actual refusal to give the breast), and only partial rejection, in contrast to total neglect and rejection, are common factors in the production of bitterness. He speculates that the first bitter taste may indeed come from regurgitated bile. The sour person, in contrast, feels more completely rejected than the bitter one. Sourness results from severe disturbances in mother-infant relationships such as severe maternal rejection. In my own clinical experience, the persistence of the affect of sourness in a paranoid type of patient presents an almost insurmountable therapeutic impasse.

Alexander contributes to a developmental theory of affects by placing them in certain phases of pre-oedipal and oedipal development. The structuralization of the psychic apparatus into the entities of id, ego, superego, and ego ideal must occur before the affect of bitterness is fully formed. An ego ideal has to exist before the ego can entertain concepts of justice and injustice and render judgments. His clinical material strikingly demonstrates that certain important psychic differentiations must take place before certain affects can develop.

This paper is restricted to an attempt to investigate psychoanalytically one specific affect, bitterness. I take it for granted as self-evident that bitterness is an affect, and I consider embitterment a chronic ego state involving the whole personality, induced by the ego's task of coping with the affect when it is present to an excessive degree.

Because of space limitations this will be primarily a theoretical paper with only brief clinical references. It is hoped that other psychoanalysts will be able to test my theoretical formulations against their own clinical material. I shall attempt to deal metapsychologically with the problem of bitterness, and then to make some brief attempts to apply the concepts herein presented to the realm of what is generally called applied psychoanalysis.

THE PHENOMENOLOGY OF BITTERNESS

From the phenomenological standpoint, bitterness is often encountered clinically, as well as in our general life experiences, but so far as my clinical experience goes, it has never been a major complaint like the symptoms and feelings which usually bring patients into treatment. Why is this? Bitterness appears to be experienced not as morbid, but rather as an unpleasant feeling justified by external reality, hence appropriate, and therefore not a sickness. Resentment is felt over what appear to the bitter person as justified grievances. This tends in the direction of making demands for the redress of the grievances. The feeling of bitterness, at least in a small degree, is a universal experience, except for those who die in early youth. It does not constitute a clinical or sociological problem unless the affect is quantitatively great. When intense, bitterness is always associated with a burning sense of unfairness or injustice, a protesting feeling of having been wronged without cause, or at least without sufficient cause. This sense of injustice is felt with deep sincerity by the embittered person.

I would like to relate here a clinical excerpt to illustrate this point. The patient was an elderly man, asthmatic, manic at times, often suicidally depressed, overtly homosexual, always obsessive-compulsive. His mother had been incredibly controlling, depreciating, castrating. He was extremely intimidated, inhibited, desperately afraid of his mother. One day during his late latency his mother decided it was time her son learned by play baseball, to which end she procured ball, bat, and glove. She exerted every effort to force him to learn, but with total lack of success. He just could not or would not learn to play baseball. He could do nothing right, he threw like a girl, etc. She finally desisted from the effort to teach him with the comment, "I did not raise my boy to be a girlie-boy."

This memory, which he called "The Baseball Incident," was a focal point in his analysis. He felt bitter toward his mother for her utter intimidation of him, but what made his cup run over with bitterness was his mother's disclaimer of any responsibility for forcing him into a passive, feminine identification, and then compounding these injustices by not allowing him to be what she had forced him to be.

To return to the phenomenology of bitterness, the affect of bitterness or the state of embitterment produces effects largely in the character structure, with few somatic manifestations, that is, alloplastically rather than autoplastically.

Physiological concomitants are minimal, unlike what occurs with such affects as anxiety, rage, or depression.

I do not work with children, but my general impression, derived from the analysis of adult patients, is that bitterness does not occur as a fully developed affect until the latency period, and is met with still more frequently during adolescence. Bitterness may not become manifest until adulthood, even late adulthood. Bitterness which becomes manifest only in adulthood usually follows some signal defeat—often involving treachery—in love or war or politics, etc. Everyone intuitively recognizes that a notable intrapsychic victory has been achieved when someone who has suffered a signal defeat or loss is not embittered. Observers rarely fail to comment approvingly when they find victims of grave defeats or losses who are not embittered.

Something will be said about sourness later in this paper. If it is true that bitterness is more common in men than in women, and sourness the reverse, I am not sure how to account for it except by speculating that it may be related to the fact that ours is a modified patriarchal form of social organization, which has tended to penalize women. Two other speculations may be relevant. One has to do with differences in psychosexual development, particularly in connection with the Oedipus conflict; the other with innate differences in the instinctual drives, particularly the aggressive drives.

Qualitatively, we can detect in bitterness a querulous note. The querulous person seems to be asking a question of the universe in general: Why? Why? Why? The reason for this is that the bitter querulent feels reproachful, resentful, over pain whose reason he cannot understand, which appears to him unnecessary, not inevitable, but deliberately inflicted by fate—in short, as a persecution. This clearly relates bitterness to the paranoid affects.

Bitterness may fail to protect the self in states of bitter remorse over sins and follies, real or imagined. In some severe psychotic depressions, bitter scorn and contumely are heaped upon the self. Still, as Freud has shown us, these self-reproaches are really levelled against the introjected object with which the self is identified. Despite these exceptions (which are an economic problem) in which bitterness fails to keep the destructive aggression externalized, it does tend to oppose the guilty, depressive tendency to desert the self. Thus bitterness has an adaptational value which tends to maintain life in its bitter struggle for existence.

The Genetic Aspect of Bitterness

In turning to the genetic aspect of bitterness, I would like to introduce this phase of our subject with two brief clinical references. The first is that of a woman patient, a sixth-grade teacher, who was reporting a classroom incident that had occurred earlier in the day. It concerned a twelve-year-old boy who often gave her trouble with his sullenness and outbursts of assaultive rage. Generally she had shown a good deal of tact and sympathetic understanding with this possibly psychotic boy. This particular day she said he had behaved like a mad dog, and then she exclaimed, "He is so bitter he spits bile!"

The second is the case of a man who, whenever he suffered a humiliating defeat, would fall to the floor writhing in an agony of bitterness. At these times he would experience an intense bitter taste in his mouth. Lack of time forbids my relating more details than that he learned from a much older half sister that during the latter part of his nursing experience his mother found out that the patient's father had an un-divorced wife in Europe, and that therefore she was not legally married. She drove this man from the home, but continued to nurse the patient a few months longer until she came down with tuberculosis.

I would now like to state my thesis as to the genesis of the affect of bitterness; namely, that this lies in the nursing phase of life, that the erotogenic zone involved is the mouth, and that the first bitter taste comes from regurgitated bile. These factors of time, anatomical locale, and quality of sensory experience have clinical significance only in a setting of mother-infant conflict. The tasting of bile is an experience common to all, and the reaction to this experience is the *anlage* of the affect of bitterness. Bitterness per se is not pathological. When its occurrence has pathological significance, this is due to traumatic fixations which result from severe mother-infant conflict, wherein the infant's alimentation was disturbed by colic, indigestion, and vomiting. These fixations, as usual, predispose to regression with later developmental conflicts. The nature of the mother-infant conflict which produces intense bitterness has a special quality. There does not seem to be outright rejection and neglect of the infant. These mothers give the breast, but the infant feels the milk is poisoned. This is due to the infant's perception of maternal rejection, its consequent reaction of hate for the mother along with its experience of colicky abdominal pain and the bitter taste in its mouth. The memory traces of these experiences are cathected by the affect quality we call bitterness. If this cathexis is intense enough the bitterness will be pathological. If not so intense, the bitterness will have adaptational value, but if too intense it predisposes the individual to regression during the anal-urethral and phallic-oedipal phases of development. Unmastered conflicts during these developmental phases are defeats which through regression link up with the *anlage* of bitterness. The defeats are felt as narcissistic injuries which cause regression to more primitive kinds of object relations, which really mean object loss. Bitterness is a protest against the object loss, and a goad to desperate efforts toward reinstatement of the lost object.

I would like at this point to appeal to further clinical evidence derived from the analyses of four quite bitter persons. Two patients of mine, plus a third one reported to me by Martin Grotjahn in a personal communication, were weaned by mothers who painted their breasts with quinine. They were given the breast as often as they wished until they no longer asked to nurse. A fourth instance was of a Southern man who had had a Negro mammy. His mother weaned him by painting her breast with lampblack and presenting it to her son with the question, "You don't want your mammy's breast, do you?" He shook his head and never asked for the breast again.

The clinical material just cited all has in common the nursing phase of life, weaning through trickery without actual refusal to give the breast, bitter taste, only partial rejection with absence of neglect.

Sourness

Let us turn to a related affect or affect state, that of sourness. The first sour taste comes from regurgitated hydrochloric acid. The neglected, starved infant has no milk in its stomach for the casein to absorb the hydrochloric acid. Its vomit thus tastes very sour. It seems that the sour person feels more completely rejected than the bitter person. The infant who is fed but feels poisoned by its mother's hate and its own hate for the mother seems to vomit contents more distinctively bitter than sour. These different physiological and psychological experiences produce different affects and different characterological effects. It appears that the *anlage* of sourness develops slightly earlier than the *anlage* of bitterness, though both appear during the nursing phase of life. The fully developed affect of sourness also appears earlier than the fully developed affect of bitterness, which so far as I can tell is not seen until latency. The cross, ill-tempered, disagreeable—in short, the sour—child is often seen among young children who have not reached the latency period. The embittered person is likely to be more verbal, more intellectually concerned with justice, defending his right to anger and to the demand for redress of injustices, whereas the sour person is likely to be less articulate, but just as hostile in an intransigent, uncompromising way. The sour person is not concerned with justice. The expression "sour old maid" is used of an elderly unmarried woman who has regressed under the impact of disappointment and blasted hopes to pregenital fixations, mainly at the oral level. The character structure is dominated by the affect of sourness, usually with some admixture of bitterness. Her attitude, then, to the external world is chronically unhappy, bitingly attacking. All sweetness is eaten away by the acidulous sourness.

Ezekiel 18:2 says: "The fathers have eaten sour grapes, and the children's teeth are set on edge." This suggests the importance of dentition in the development of the affect of sourness. Bitter substances have little effect upon the teeth. Though the taste of sourness is experienced very early, this sensory experience does not at once produce the affect of sourness. Everyone feels sour on occasion, but this fact has no clinical significance unless the sourness is quantitatively great, in which case it results from severe disturbances in the mother-infant relationship, such as severe maternal rejection. The affective response to this situation experienced along with the sour taste, particularly after dentition begins in the second half of the first year of life, generates the affect of sourness. The sour disposition predisposes to failures and disappointments, souring one further on life, in turn making satisfactions ever less likely.

The importance of the concept of justice/injustice in the genesis of the affect of bitterness indicates that a great deal of psychic differentiation has had to occur before bitterness can exist. Sourness can exist with less structural differentiation than bitterness. Structuralization of the psychic apparatus into the tripartite entities of ego, superego, and id has had to occur before bitterness can be felt. An ego ideal has to exist for the ego to entertain concepts such as justice/injustice, and to render judgments on this basis. Sourness is a more primitive affect than bitterness. Sourness requires no more in the way of differentiation of the undifferentiated psychic apparatus present at birth than the primitive ego and id.

COMPARISON OF BITTERNESS WITH DEPRESSION

Thus we see that bitterness is not a simple affect, if there be any such thing. However, it is a specific affect, a qualitative entity, not just a medley of other affects. I assume that some affects are simpler than others. Sourness appears to be a simpler affect then bitterness. Anger and rage are simple affects. Depression is not an affect, but a complicated ego state made up from the affective standpoint of a medley of affects such as sadness, hate, guilt, anxiety, and other affects. Rochlin (1959) has shown that the early reaction to loss is withdrawal. Depression can occur only later. Spitz (1950) and Engel (Engel and Reichsman, 1956; Engel, Reichsman, and Segal, 1956) have shown that anxiety cannot occur before about the eighth month. Before that, only the precursors of anxiety exist. These are: startle reaction, more or less global unpleasure, distress, restlessness. While the state of embitterment is an unhappy state, the self-accusing melancholy of depression is not present. In bitterness, defeat is not conceded as an intrapsychic event. In bitterness, final defeat may be conceded, but the defeat is wrought by external forces, usually treacherously. Bitterness tends to influence the ego to resort to the use of projection as a defense mechanism, thus reproaching the object rather than the self as in the depressions. Bitterness has a centrifugal rather than a centripetal effect. This is one of the main economic functions of bitterness in psychodynamics.

More extended comparisons of bitterness with depression cause one to note that depressions are poorly rationalized, whereas bitterness is well rationalized. There are agitated depressions, but, by and large, depression tends in the direction of passivity, while bitterness is a goad to action, often reckless action. Depression tends toward solitariness rather than toward group formation. Bitterness has a socially cohesive effect, though of a factional character. In depression, projection is not much resorted to because guilty submission to the punitive introjects occurs. Bitterness promotes the proclivity to resort to the use of projection. Object relatedness is reduced by depression. Bitterness tends to produce and maintain strong—maybe pathological, but certainly strong—object relationships. The projection in bitterness consists not only of the punitive introjects but also of the pain within the self. This pain is a native part of the self, but under the sway of the pleasure principle the ego would like to disown it. The projection of the punitive introjects means that the battle with the object world is on again. Thus bitterness is more likely to result in murder, whereas depression is more likely to cause suicide.

TYPICAL WAYS IN WHICH THE EGO HANDLES THE AFFECT OF BITTERNESS

It is time now to examine some of the typical ways in which the ego deals with the affect of bitterness. It seems that poets, philosophers, and religious writers agree with the common experience of mankind that life is bitter. Therefore, a good adjustment or adaptation to life would require that the ego deal adequately with this reality, the bitterness of life. Sometimes the ego of certain individuals never copes with this reality except by phobic avoidance. One such individual was a man who avoided arguments at all costs. He was peculiar in his dietary habits, never eating anything sour or bitter. He ate only sweet and salty foods. He got through life by constant placation and cajolery. He was alcoholic. He rarely admitted anger (and only when drinking) and never admitted bitterness, though he had experienced much he could have felt bitter about.

Another way some egos deal with bitterness is to use it to justify brutal aggression. Such persons assert that injustice and treachery have embittered them beyond endurance. This way of handling bitterness has important sociological implications.

Masochistic adaptations to bitterness are common. In one type bitter defeats are masochistically enjoyed openly. One such woman would make pessimistic predictions about the unsatisfactory outcome of something or other. Then she would unconsciously connive at bringing it to the predicted bad end. At such times, she would smile in a more or less pleased manner and say, "Now wouldn't you just know the damned thing would turn out that way!"

In another type the masochistic enjoyment of bitterness is vehemently denied. One man would unconsciously connive at his own bitter defeats and humiliations. When the defeat or humiliation was accomplished, he would on some occasions fall to the floor and writhe almost orgastically while experiencing an intensely bitter taste. This symptom seemed to be hallucinatory. The way this man's ego handled his intense bitterness was to enjoy it masochistically, but to deny the masochistic enjoyment. He spent much of his analysis denying that he contrived his own bitter defeats and that he enjoyed them.

Some Applications of the Theoretical Formulations on the Subject of Bitterness

I would now like to make some brief applications of the theoretical formulations about bitterness here presented to some areas of the realm generally called applied psychoanalysis. In the area of wit and humor the essence of sarcasm is bitterness. The sardonic is a variety of the sarcastic which is especially brutal, but at the same time the bitter aggression is somewhat masked by a veneer of suavity. Grisly humor is grim humor associated with the horrible and the horrifying, but it is without bitterness in any significant sense. There are always at least traces of bitterness in irony, but usually the bitter aggression is gentler than in sarcasm. Cynicism refuses to take anything seriously, and bitterness tends to produce seriousness. The cynical person is sour rather than bitter. Bitterness tends to produce irony, sarcasm, or the sardonic rather than the cynical.

Closing Formulations

Finally, it seems evident that dynamically, bitterness exerts a considerable, even a dominating, influence on how we love and hate. The pathological handling of excessive amounts of bitterness either sadistically or masochistically interferes with loving, making it precariously brittle or even impossible. Phobic avoidance of bitterness has grave effects upon the personality also. As a mordant fixes a dye in the fabric of a textile, so does bitterness fix hostile aggression; that is, bitterness changes anger into hate. The embittered person finds it hard to forgive when his sense of justice is offended. When the mordant is sourness the internal object representations are cathected hatefully without deterrence by scruples about justice. Economically, bitterness acts as a facilitator in the adjustment to the reality that life is bitter; that is, in the transition from the pleasure principle to the reality principle. Bitterness is a complex affect with equally complex vicissitudes in the ego's handling of it. If the ego does not phobically have to avoid bitterness or succumb to it sadomasochistically, it adds new and meaningful dimensions to the reality it perceives and experiences pleasantly. This is more or less parallel to the addition of the bitter taste as acceptable to the palate, thus avoiding insipidity and monotony.

The instinctual impulses by definition are innate. The aggressive energies can become destructive in intent if there is too much frustration or other varieties of pain. The affective accompaniment of the earliest mobilization of destructive aggression I will call rage. Even though we usually understand the word rage in the superlative sense, the affect I have in mind at this point still has degrees of intensity and is objectless. With a certain amount of ego development comes an awareness of objects, and the rage can become focused upon objects. If the rage cannot be abreacted, or the object forgiven, the object is then hated. This last sentence refers only to the deployment of hostile aggressive cathexes, that is, it deals with quantity and direction, but not with quality. The qualitative change that turns rage into hate is through the addition of bitterness or sourness, though the quality of the hate is different depending on whether the added affect is bitterness or sourness. Freud, in various writings such as the "Three Essays" (1905c), has mapped the vicissitudes of the libido. No nearly so adequate mapping of the aggressive cathexes exists. A partial check can be made on the correctness of the above contention through introspection when we recall that whenever we have hated we have felt bitterly toward the object.

I am told a greeting among Chinese peasants is "We eat bitterness." This seems admirably to sum up my thesis that the bitter taste and the affect of bitterness are closely related. Ego development makes more differentiated affects possible, and the affects in turn further ego differentiation. Bitterness can occur only after considerable ego development has occurred, and in turn plays a part in further ego development. Just as with other affects such as anxiety, bitterness has positive adaptational value if not too intense. If bitterness is quantitatively too great it causes ego distortions and attendant disturbances in loving and hating.

ON ENTHUSIASM

Ralph R. Greenson

(1962)

I first became acquainted with Greenson's paper "On Enthusiasm" when it was presented as the Presidential Plenary Address before the American Psychoanalytic Association in 1960. Delivered and received with enthusiasm, it lucidly presents the structural, dynamic, economic, and genetic findings on this affective state, as well as defining normal, mature, and pathological varieties of enthusiasm.

Greenson termed enthusiasm a mood state, not an emotion, inasmuch as the entire self and object world is changed and the total personality is transformed. Enthusiasm may be included in the compound affects or enduring feeling states, such as kindness, heartlessness, sympathy, love, or sadness. These phenomena are complex fusions of affect components.

To recapitulate Greenson's hypothesis: Pathological enthusiasm is often preceded by some deprivation, even of a mild variety. A change occurs in the self-image due to incorporation of and identification with an idealized external object. Predisposing factors are denial and contradiction of previously painful childhood experiences that have not been assimilated. The greater the idealization of the previous events, the more pathological the enthusiasm. There may be a concurrent sense of being united with or in possession of a wondrous object whose function is to deny an underlying deprivation.

Greenson makes abundantly clear that enthusiasm brings a partial regression, a regression in the service of the ego, in contrast to the all-inclusive regression seen in hypomanic states. Enthusiasm may act as a defensive operation against opposite feelings, such as depression and sadness. A crucial development in the childhood of those who become chronic enthusiasts is a history of overgratification during the early period of life, followed by unexpected and severe deprivations in later childhood.

Enthusiasm is a happy and joyous state of mind. It is a condition of high spirits—a special form of elation. Enthusiasm has some of the buoyancy of euphoria and the activity of mania, and it is obviously different from the blissful and peaceful elations. It is my aim to differentiate enthusiasm from other varieties of elation and to distinguish several types of enthusiasm. Then I shall attempt to formulate some of the metapsychological elements which make for the phenomenon of enthusiasm.

I

Enthusiasm is a passionate state of mind. It is exciting, active, and noisy—not quiet or passive like bliss. In this regard it resembles the hypomanias, only the activities are more realistic and adaptive. The more incongruous or bizarre the activities, the more likely that we are dealing with pathological enthusiasm or a hypomanic state.

There is an air of extravagance and expansiveness about enthusiasm—a readiness to use superlatives. The enthusiastic person does not merely feel good or even very good, but great—in fact, "the greatest!" There is a sense of exuberance, richness, an abundance of good fortune; yet with it all, there is some awareness that one is exaggerating; but it is enjoyable, and one is reluctant to give it up.

Enthusiasm has the quality of an infatuation, and indeed it is always present when there is infatuation. However, enthusiasm can occur without romance and without sex, and in regard to an inanimate object. But enthusiasm, too, contains a feeling of being captivated, an awareness of folly, a loss of one's reason. It is characteristic for both enthusiasm and infatuation to occur suddenly.

A person filled with enthusiasm is generous, and has an urge to share his richness with others. To be enthused means to feel full of goodness, as contrasted to the feeling full of badness in the melancholias, and feeling full of emptiness as in boredom (Greenson, 1953). The wish to share with others is urgent, even compelling. One cannot remain enthusiastic alone. Like laughter, one needs cohorts, accomplices. They have to be converted to enthusiasm, or else the enthusiasm is endangered.

For all its noisy busyness, enthusiasm is fragile and capricious. It can be punctured like a balloon. There is something inflated about enthusiasm which makes it so vulnerable. The lack of response from a "wet blanket" can easily smother its flame, and a bigger enthusiasm can shrivel it up. Normal enthusiasm is a temporary state of mind. When it is prolonged, it is likely to be neurotic or a hypomania. One can become repeatedly enthusiastic about the same thing, but the state of enthusiasm is a temporary one.

By and large, enthusiasm is contagious. It is easy to find cohorts. There seems to be a readiness in others to participate vicariously in enthusiasm, as with laughter. When that happens, there is the feeling of joining and being a member of a group—a feeling of belonging. But in those who do not share in the enthusiasm, one can frequently observe a response of enthusiasm envy. People who coldly watch another's enthusiasm often have a feeling of being left out, cheated—of not belonging. The enthusiastic human being has an air of possessing something valuable, and those without it, or without the opportunity to participate in it, feel like "have-nots." People who are prone to evoke enthusiasm often become leaders, and it is indeed one of the most valuable characteristics in determining leadership potential.

Enthusiasm transforms the total personality; it is a mood, and not an emotion. The entire self and object world is changed (Jacobson, 1957b). One finds qualitative alterations in feeling tone, behavior, thinking, attitudes, values, and expectations.

For all its fanciful quality, in normal enthusiasm there is always an awareness of reality, and perhaps a kind of tongue-in-cheek attitude, for the enthusiastic person is well oriented. Furthermore, enthusiasm lends itself frequently to adaptive, constructive, and even creative actions. Although it contains some element of play, enthusiasm can also be used for serious work.

This much is the more or less manifest picture of enthusiasm. I now propose to explore more carefully and deeply some of the structural, dynamic, economic, and genetic findings. Furthermore, I shall attempt to differentiate between the normal, mature and the pathological varieties of enthusiasm. The pioneer work in this field of affects and moods has already been done by Freud (1917, 1921), Abraham (1924a), Lewin (1950), and Jacobson (1953a, 1957b). Rado (1927b, 1933), Deutsch (1933), Bibring (1953), and many others have also made valuable contributions (Fenichel, 1945; Greenson, 1954; Klein, 1948). This presentation is derived from their findings, and is an attempt to extend them.

II

Let me begin by giving some typical examples of infantile enthusiasm.

1. A woman buys a hat and becomes enthused. She has bought many hats, many of which she liked, but this particular hat brings enthusiasm. Why? She says, "It does something for me, it's not just a hat." It does something? What does that mean? She does not merely look prettier in that hat. It changed her. Analysis revealed that it changed her self-image. The hat altered her picture of herself. Just prior to buying the hat, her analysis was concerned with her feelings of inferiority due to her exaggerated awareness of being penisless and therefore unattractive. The new hat changed this; it lent her some penis quality, it contradicted her feelings of inferiority. She was enthused, and rushed to her friends to share in and confirm her good fortune.

2. An adolescent girl is unexpectedly given a gift of a beautiful European sports car. She is enthusiastic. Her old car pleased her, but she never enthused. But this car was "for her." The other car was middle-aged and married-looking. This car was sleek and shiny and graceful. She gave it a name—a girl's name, and a European name— to suit its personality. She drove differently, masterfully. She lost weight and became sleek and shiny and accented the European features of her appearance. She became colorful instead of her usual retiring self. It was like an infatuation. She fell in love with the car and, as adolescents do, identified with it. Her self-image changed. She had found a new and a better identity. She was a "new person."

What can we learn from these examples? Apparently the hat and the car made some qualitative change in the self-image and in the object world of these people. The possession took on some highly valuable quality—it became idealized. The object seemed to possess precisely those qualities which represented a wish fulfillment in the individuals described. The possession turned out to be a projection of the ego ideal onto the object. The possession then represented an idealized aspect of the self. By possessing such an idealized object, a change occurs in the self-image. As one of my patients put it succinctly when she waxed enthusiastic over the purchase of a new house: "It is not just mine; it *is* me."

Apparently possessing such an idealized object brings with it a feeling of being joined with it, a feeling of incorporating it, identifying with it, and making it part of the self. The slang expression used currently in reference to an object evoking enthusiasm is "I eat it up." This puts it very well. When you feel you have eaten it, it is part of you, then you can become enthused. This feeling of being joined to some idealized object resembles the fusion of ego and superego which Freud (1917, 1921), Lewin (1950), and Jacobson (1953a) describe as typical for states of elation; but there is an important difference. In enthusiasm the feeling of being joined or joining is to an external object; it is temporary, and it is partial. In pathological states like the hypomanias, the fusion is with an internal object. In enthusiasm, external objects are needed in order to perpetuate the state, whereas the manias are relatively independent of external objects. Carnivals and holidays evoke enthusiasm. One needs the confirmation and approbation of others in order to maintain one's enthusiasm. The sense of fusion is temporary and limited, and extremely vulnerable to the influences of the external world and reality—yet enthusiasm seems to share with the hypomanias this feeling of being joined to some idealized object.

How typical is this for enthusiasm? The word enthusiasm is derived from the Greek word *entheos*, meaning to be inspired by God, or to be possessed by God or some superhuman power. The German word *Begeisterung* has the same meaning. The enthused human being feels as though he had breathed in, inspired, something divine and wondrous. And, like inspiration, enthusiasm leads to a creation—a creation of a modified self-image, which is richer and grander (Kris, 1952b). Now one has to share it or prove it; hence the running to friends and cohorts. In normal enthusiasm, there is little exaggeration and what there is, one is aware of. In mature enthusiasm, the objects which evoke it are more in accordance with one's conscious ideals; in infantile enthusiasm, the objects are derived from childhood values. In any case, enthusiasm denotes a temporary leave of absence from reality and the superego (Kris, 1952b). The changes which occur in the state of enthusiasm are a result of wish fulfillments and represent a triumph of the pleasure principle. The objects or situations which produce enthusiasm are "dreamy." American slang seems to confirm some of Lewin's ideas about sleep, the dream, and elation. Enthusiasm is a kind of dream state, enacted while awake.

III

But the pleasure gain which occurs in enthusiasm is not only derived from the union with an idealized object. Part of the joy comes from having successfully denied and contradicted something painful. The new hat denies the penisless state; it contradicts it by proclaiming the possession of something penislike. The new hat performs on a phallic level what the new car does on an adolescent level for the nineteen-year-old girl. A new and shiny identity denies and contradicts the previous drab identity.

Various methods of denial obviously play a great role in the production of elated states, as many authors have found

(Deutsch, 1933; A. Freud, 1936; Lewin, 1950; Jacobson, 1957a, 1957b; Greenson, 1958). In enthusiasm, too, denial may be necessary in order to achieve the idealization of the enthusiasm-producing object. One may need a selectivity of perception in order to hypercathect the good qualities and decathect the bad, so that the idealization can take place. The more one has to resort to denial to achieve idealization, the more pathological is the enthusiasm. Normal enthusiasm is induced by worthy objects, which do not have to be distorted. For example, one can become enthused by listening to a great musical performance. One does not have to deny the existence of a few wrong notes in order to be normally enthusiastic. If one does, then we are no longer dealing with normal enthusiasm, but with enthusiasm needed for some neurotic purpose. Normal enthusiasm is a bonus, not a need. It is true, however, that normal enthusiasm is a welcome change from the ordinary deprivations and disappointments of everyday civilized life. But it is evoked by worthy objects and situations; it is temporary and helps one to face reality after the detour of enthusiasm. Neurotic enthusiasm, on the other hand, is evoked by objects or situations which are inappropriate, and is prolonged to ward off some other painful, underlying state. Let me give an illustration.

A thirty-five-year-old male patient whose usual mood was dour and mistrustful had the following experience during his third year of analysis with me. In an hour, he felt my tone of voice to be critical. He reacted to this by whimpering, becoming petulant and tearful. In this hour I handled the situation by admitting that it was possible my tone might have been critical, but it did not seem to justify his childish reaction. His reaction must have come from something else. He mulled this over and then recalled, at first vaguely and then more clearly, some hitherto hidden memories of childhood, in which he had this whimpering reaction to his father. The patient left the hour in good spirits. Two hours later he phoned, something he had never done before in his analysis. He was enthusiastic; a rare mood for him. He could not work, he was impelled to call me, to tell me this was the greatest analytic hour he had ever had, and he had had several years of previous analysis, and I was the best analyst he had ever had. My technique was superb, I had handled him magnificently, he was so grateful that I had taken him as a patient, and on and on. I said nothing. Eventually, his ardor was spent and he closed by saying, "I want to thank you for everything, and I'll see you on Thursday." I replied: "All right, but your next hour is Wednesday." Silence on the other end of the phone.

The next hour, Wednesday, he reported grimly that my remark had killed his good mood. Then he bitterly complained of my sarcasm, my irritability, how disappointed he really was in me as an analyst, and how I really was like his father, and on and on.

In the course of the next several hours, I learned something about this patient's neurotic enthusiasm. During that hour of the childish whimpering, as I began to talk, before he actually grasped the meaning of my remarks, he was afraid I was going to punish him. When he realized my tone and my words were not punitive but compassionate, he felt relieved and grateful. He then eagerly sought to confirm my hypothesis that his reaction did indeed come from his past. He found some real memories which proved this, but gave them to me as a gift, to repay me for my gift to him. The hour ended with his feeling he was not a whimpering child caught in some infantile act; on the contrary, he was a hard-working patient. My intervention, which evoked this whole sequence of events, was selected and magnified into a wonderful interpretation, and then this was so generalized that I became a superb analyst. He participated in my greatness and was transformed into the lucky fellow who was fortunate in being able to join me in this intimate and wonderful relationship. Once we were joined in this way, he became enthusiastic. The entire experience hinged on his use of my intervention to ward off his underlying anger and disappointment. He confirmed my interpretation and avoided his hostility by escaping into his past reactions to his father. His enthusiasm was the result of this successful denial plus the feeling of union with me. It was a screen mood to hide, as a reaction formation, another, opposing mood (Greenson, 1958). The enthusiasm became a resistance, a temporary obstacle in the analytic work, as Lewin (1950) has pointed out in regard to the elations.

This patient called me to share in his good mood; but, more important, also to confirm and perpetuate his good mood. He sensed it was false and shaky, and he needed me to maintain the artificial good feeling. His remark, "I'll see you on Thursday," indicated the breaking through of his hidden anger and disappointment.

How does this situation compare to normal enthusiasm? Let us take the experience of listening to a great artistic performance. One goes with some positive expectation, but there are misgivings; the music is strange, there are a few wrong notes, but then the great artistry of the performer becomes strikingly apparent and one is enthused. It seems that here too one has to overcome something opposite to become enthused. The big difference is that one does not have to deny this or repress it in normal enthusiasm. One can admit one's previous misgivings or the lack of perfection and still be enthused.

The more pathological the enthusiasm the more it is created by and used for denial. Such enthusiasm requires cohorts and accomplices who will help maintain the denial, not just witnesses and sharers. It is a denial *a deux*—a happy phrase suggested by Hanna Fenichel in a personal communication to the author.

There is a wide range of enthusiasm, going from the normal through the neurotic to the hypomanic elations. In all there is the feeling of being joined to something wonderful. In enthusiasm, normal and neurotic, one feels one is fused to an external object and this is partial and temporary. One is aware of being in a special state of mind. These enthusiasms can be corrected and influenced by external reality factors. Hypomanic enthusiasm is tied up with an internal fusion, between ego and superego, and is not easily amended by reality. Normal enthusiasm requires little denial, only the overcoming of some slight discontent or misgiving. Pathological enthusiasm requires a good deal of denial in a variety of ways.

IV

Experiences which produce enthusiasm are those which simultaneously evoke the pleasurable feeling of possessing or being united with a wondrous object and also denying an underlying deprivation. As I have already indicated, certain possessions can do this. Enthusiasm can be elicited in relation to possession of objects on any and all phases of psychosexual development. There seem to be oral, anal, phallic, and adolescent enthusiasms. The hat and the car were examples of enthusiasm on a phallic and an adolescent level. Financial gain, the acquiring of a big pile of money, can give rise to an anal enthusiasm. The pleasurable eating experiences of a gourmet are obviously oral enthusiasms.

Achievements and success of certain kinds can also produce enthusiasm. Creative work, coming upon a new idea, making discoveries, are very apt to evoke enthusiasm.

Children, sweethearts, and pets are particularly suitable as enthusiasm producers. Participating as an audience in certain events can do the same. The sports fan reacts to his team as the music lover does to his favorite artists. The observer feels joined to the performer and participates in the latter's triumphs. The beauty of nature can also stimulate a reaction of enthusiasm, although this quickly becomes a more peaceful and blissful kind of elation. One gives oneself up to the beauty of nature rather than making it part of oneself. At any rate, in all the above instances, the feeling of being united and joined to a wonderful object, the temporary and partial sense of identification, makes it possible to deny the discontents of everyday life, and one is enthused.

V

Enthusiasm is a state of great activity. An enthused person seems suddenly to have acquired a great abundance of energy, and the world seems pliable and accessible. There is a plethora of enterprise, talk, gregariousness, and imagination. A question that now arises is: where does this new quantity of energy come from? Freud (1921), Jacobson (1957b), and others have noted the striking economic changes which occur in all joyous states. It is as though an abundance of psychic energy, which had been ordinarily consumed elsewhere, has now become free and available.

It has been hypothesized that the fusion of ego and superego in manic states is responsible for the liberation of this energy. The union with an idealized object does away with all tensions between ego and superego; the superego temporarily gives up its functions. Thus, the id is free from pressure and is permitted greater discharge.

There is another reason for the surplus of energy. The process operating in enthusiasm is similar to what we see in laughter. The joke makes the ego's defenses unnecessary, and so does enthusiasm. The energy which has been used for defense can now be utilized for enthusiasm. All the dangers from the id, superego, and the external world are denied, making other defenses unnecessary. It is a triumph of the pleasure principle, and the ego has the world as its oyster.

The activities which are indulged in, in enthusiasm, are often creative and worthwhile. Enthusiasm can serve an adaptive ego function, and, in fact, one may not only perform well, but extraordinarily well. The enthusiastic teacher is an apt example. The enthusiastic person feels as though he has borrowed strength from the object of his enthusiasm—he has been inspired. Actually, he has borrowed strength from himself. The increase in capability comes from his sense of fusion with the idealized object which he has created from unconscious sources within himself. It resembles the kind of feats of strength one can see in hypnosis. The activities of the enthusiastic person are different from the activities of the hypomanic; there one sees more agitation and less accomplishment.

The energy which is freed seems to be essentially instinctual and libidinal and not neutralized. Enthusiasm is a passionate state of mind. The activities which are pursued with enthusiasm are loved in some form or other. It is my clinical impression that enthusiasm frees and channelizes great quantities of energy, but the quality of the work which is accomplished lacks the evenness and steadiness that one sees when neutralized energies are utilized. It seems to me that here one is dealing with a deneutralization in the service of the ego. The instinctualized energies, however, seem to be predominantly libidinal. When enthusiasm acquires an important aggressive coloring, we are usually dealing with fanaticism and not enthusiasm.

The activity of enthusiasm distinguishes it from the blissful and serene states of elation. First, the enthusiast has to do something to maintain his pleasurable state of mind. The blissful person has achieved it. Second, the enthusiast has actively incorporated and taken into himself something wondrous, whereas in blissful ecstasy there is the feeling of having given oneself up to something bigger. The reactions to the beauty of nature seem to belong to this second category. There seems to be a different kind of identification in enthusiasm and in bliss (Lewin, 1950). Blissful ecstasy has an element of passive surrender, while enthusiasm is actively struggling.

VI

Enthusiasm brings with it, as do moods in general, a partial regression in the state of mind (Jacobson, 1957b). We can see it in the ego functioning with the tendency toward distortions in thinking, the denials, the generalizing, exaggerations, and flighty judgments. The superego manifests its regression by renouncing its critical functions, by the fusion, the externalization, and the idealization. In the object relationships we see predominantly transference reactions, object hunger, and identifications. From the standpoint of the id, the pregenital strivings seem to be in the foreground. And the activities seem to be performed with libidinal energies, deneutralized energies.

However, it is to be stressed that although all these regressions can be seen in enthusiasm, they are temporary and selective. They can be brought to a halt immediately, even though reluctantly, and despite the regressive features, much creative work and achievement can be accomplished. Work performed in enthusiasm is a true example of regression in the service of the ego (Kris, 1952b). This is in contrast to the more permanent and all-inclusive regressions which we see in the hypomanias.

VII

I should like to turn now to the enthusiast, for certain additional insights into the vicissitudes of enthusiasm. It is striking how differently people react when one describes someone as being enthusiastic and when one calls someone an enthusiast. Enthusiasm is not only reputable but enviable, whereas the enthusiast is in disrepute. Apparently, when enthusiastic reactions become a character trait, a habitual, chronic response, although they afford pleasure to the bearer and the audience, they also devaluate.

The enthusiast is a caricature of normal enthusiasm. First of all, he is not as selective, and the occasions which evoke enthusiasm are less worthy. The enthusiast is felt to be gullible, credulous, and somewhat of a charlatan, for he seduces you in his enthusiastic responses more than occurs in normal enthusiasm (Hoffer, 1954). Although his enthusiasm about a particular item is temporary, he is so frequently enthused. He has the zeal of a true believer, only he is fickle. He is like the fanatic, only less venomous (Hoffer, 1954). He resembles the Don Juans of achievement whom Fenichel (1945) describes, a relatively successful acting-out character, who restlessly goes from one triumph to another without ever achieving contentment. Diagnostically, the enthusiast belongs to the group of oral character disorders with a chronic optimistic attitude (Katan, 1934). The hunger for new objects and new experiences which Abraham (1924a) described in the manias is also characteristic for them, but the enthusiasts still retain their reality testing. Each single instance of enthusiasm is influenceable and changeable, but it is the constant search for new experiences which will evoke enthusiasm, and this factor gives them their driven character. In the enthusiast the emotional intensity serves an important defensive as well as expressive function, a point which has been described by several authors (Siegman, 1934; Weiss, 1959; Greenson, 1958). I believe they are characters in search of a screen; furthermore, Rado's (1933) ideas about drug addiction seem to be quite relevant in understanding some of the problems in the enthusiast.

I would like to describe some of the clinical findings in an enthusiast I analyzed some years ago in order to bring up some special points for discussion. The patient was an extremely successful man of fifty-five who came for treatment because of a sleep disturbance and a fear of becoming addicted to sleeping pills. The patient had reached the top of several professions and at the time of his analysis had reached the pinnacle of success in his third field. His propensity for enthusiasm was a vital factor in his success in each endeavor. He enjoyed his successes, but restlessly sought new worlds to conquer. He claimed to have had a happy marriage for thirty years, despite the fact that he had been constantly involved in different extramarital love affairs from the beginning of his marriage. The affairs were not merely sexual adventures, but were intense, romantic involvements where he fancied himself in love and loved, and he was exuberant and enthused. When these infatuations ended, and the patient ended them when "the magic" went out of them, the women remained his staunch admirers. His work was such that he could hide his absences from home behind the cloak of his profession. When he did spend time with his wife, he was easily able to be kind and considerate, and she felt herself fortunate to have such an attentive husband whose only weakness was his passion for his work. He was warm and devoted to his children whenever he did spend time with them, and they adored him. In his social groups, and there were many, since he was never able to be happily alone, he was beloved. In those sophisticated and jaded gatherings, he was the life of the party, where much liveliness was needed to cover the agitated boredom that prevailed. Every new venture, professional, sexual, or social, he undertook with optimism, responded with enthusiasm; and this was contagious.

The insomnia which brought him for treatment was of a particular kind. He could readily fall asleep, but could only stay asleep for a few hours. Once awake, he became restless and agitated. He felt impelled to get out of bed and eat or drink or talk to someone. If he fell asleep again, it was a bad sleep full of disturbing dreams. This was in contrast to the first sleep which was a good sleep and full of pleasant dreams or no dreams (blank dreams?). A "good" orgasm or a pill or a meal produced the good sleep. A partial orgasm, alcohol, or fatigue produced the bad sleep. He enjoyed naps. He slept well when he knew he only had a limited time for sleep. He slept poorly after being the life of the party. Physical pain helped him to sleep well. This pattern of sleep disturbance had existed all his adult life. He began taking sleeping pills some ten years before treatment, and although he increased the amounts, and they deepened his sleep, they did not appreciably lengthen his sleep. Further, he began to like the hangover sensation of the pills the next day. He felt pleasantly dreamy, somewhat gay. He described it as a feeling of something good having happened to him, a piece of good fortune, but he could not remember it. He felt as though he had eaten something delicious and the aftertaste lingered on the next morning in the pleasurable hangover. After the bad sleep, he awoke with a bad taste in his mouth and was irritable.

Analysis revealed that "good sleep" was possible only if he felt pleasantly full, satisfied, virtuous, and not alone. The prospect of sleeping for eight hours made him feel lonely. As I said before, he could always nap, because then he could "see" the beginning and ending of the stretch of time he was to sleep. He felt as though the two hours of the nap were boundaries and he could touch them, whereas to sleep for eight hours was to be all alone in a big bed with no boundaries to touch. He tried never to sleep alone, and hugged the pillow if there were no person available. His marital situation deteriorated with his success, for then his wife acquired twin beds, and eventually a separate bedroom. He usually slept about four hours with pills, as though this stretch of time were the greatest interval he could endure without being fed. This oral quality in his sleep activities was also pronounced in his sexual behavior.

In the course of the analysis, it became clear that this patient had an almost fetishistic attraction to the female breast. He always looked first at the breasts of every woman he met. If the breasts seemed voluptuous, he was interested. He had to be able to fantasy that the breasts were full, engorged, not withered or empty or even partly full. He needed to believe that the breast was on the verge of overflowing. Second, the woman had to appear cold and disdainful in some aspect of her behavior. What he loved above all was the delicious sense of surprise when an apparently cold woman gave him, and him alone, her overflowing breast. An important feature of his relationships was that the woman experience the same kind and quality of enthusiasm that he did. As soon as he detected some loss of enthusiasm in her, not even discontent, he was through. He could enjoy the affair only as long as it was completely mutual.

His sexual activities were revealed to be oral sucking activities to him, no matter what parts of the body or whatever actions were pursued. There was a great deal of cunnilingus and fellatio, which he perceived as giving and getting of a breast. He and the partner would alternate in the active and passive roles and both would have to take place. Intercourse proper was felt as a giving of his penis-breast into a vagina-mouth. In intercourse he did not take, he felt as though he were giving. He had his orgasm when he imagined his partner did, out of identification with her. In all sexual activities there was a big one and a little one, a mother and a child, and he loved to play both roles. He was the sucking child and the loving giver of the breast. More than that, he fantasied in his sexual activities that he created breasts. By exciting a woman, he imagined he gave her breasts full of milk. When he was excited, the woman made his little penis-breast into a big milk-containing penis-breast. He was offended if his semen was not considered delectable. All secretory products of his women were a delicacy to him. He particularly enjoyed all those positions of sexuality which obscured who was doing what to whom. He strove to achieve a feeling of oneness, a union. The quality and quantity of his orgasm depended on how well he achieved this sense of fusion.

Apparently, at first his partners enjoyed the patient's sexual virtuosity and seemed to respond in kind. Once they indicated that they had lost any of their enthusiasm, he became disenchanted; the spell was over, and he departed. Obviously he needed to feel that he, and he alone, was completely satisfying. He could not tolerate any semblance of a rival or any lessening of the mutuality, the oneness.

The history of the patient reveals some of the sources of this behavior. For a long time he maintained he was his mother's favorite, and he had many screen memories to "prove" it. He was the product of an unhappy marriage, and both parents openly acknowledged this. He was the younger of two boys and avowedly the favorite. But his entire behavior had a reactive quality. Already in the initial interviews this was demonstrated. When he was animated, his face seemed youthful and cheerful, but when he paused, he looked even older than his years, and sad. During these pauses, he frequently sighed. This was particularly true during his analytic hours.

But to return to the patient's history. He claimed to be the favorite, and he spent his whole life as though he were confirming this. However, a person who feels truly loved and favored does not have to continue to prove it. A person secure in his position is confident, trusting, and peaceful, not exuberant, overambitious, and restless. He had a memory of early childhood where his mother is bathing him and saying with pride, "My, what a big penis you have." This is obviously a screen memory, because he spent his life getting women to confirm this. If he had truly believed it, he would not have had to become promiscuous.

Behind the happy facade of screens, three important events came to light. He was breast fed for a long time, which abruptly stopped when his mother became pregnant. She later miscarried. When he was age six of seven, his mother had an affair which almost precipitated a divorce. When he was fourteen years old, the mother had another affair, and at this time the patient ran away from home, never to return except for occasional triumphant visits when he was much older. I believe it is this history of overgratification followed by unexpected and severe deprivations which makes for such an acting-out, oral, screen character (Greenson, 1958). But I would like to return to a consideration of the role of the breast in this man's chronic enthusiasm.

I have described some of his overt behavior and fantasies which indicate his need to feel that he was being given the overflowing breast by a loving woman. I can add that his dreams were full of symbolism referable to his mother's body and breasts. He dreamed of all kinds of fruits, persimmons, avocadoes, grapefruit, etc., which clearly referred to sizes, shapes, textures, and tastes of breasts. He frequently mentioned odors as well as temperature in his associations. In his nightmares, he was drowning or suffocating, or being smothered by substances which were warm, soft, moist, and had an odor. To be enveloped by such a substance could be immensely pleasurable or frightening. It seemed to depend on the aggression, or lack of it, in his superego, whether he could enjoy this envelopment or whether it terrified him in his dreams.

He considered himself lucky and "born with a breast in his mouth." This feeling threatened to leave him, however, and he had to search for experiences which would recreate the sensation of the overflowing breast within him; then he would become enthused. Once he achieved it, he had enough to share with the world, but if it left him, he was depressed and agitated. Rado (1933) and Lewin (1950) have described similar findings in drug addiction and elation.

The patient could attain this feeling from the sexual activity described above, from his professional successes, or from an admiring audience. They all evoked the feeling, "I've got it." Archimedes must have been enthusiastic when he shouted "Eureka—I have found it." The feeling of triumph seems also to be related to enthusiasm, although in triumph the emphasis is on victory over adversity rather than possession. (The feeling "I've got it" is also expressed as an attitude in poise.) To return to the patient, he did so much in his enthusiasm not merely to discharge the excitement, but to evoke it anew, to deny the underlying depression. The feeling of possessing the overflowing breast, or of remembering it, which was the trigger for producing his enthusiasm, had to be constantly sought for in the external world, because the memory of it in his past was a myth, i.e., some truth and much distortion.

VIII

The original model for this joyous feeling of enthusiasm seems derived from experiences at the mother's breast in nursing. Blissful ecstasy seems to portray the giving up of one's self to this bigger entity, the mother, after one has gained complete satisfaction at the breast (Lewin, 1950). This seems to be true of all the blissful elations, which entail a passive-submissive surrender to something bigger. One allows oneself to become incorporated, and in Lewin's terms, one allows oneself to be devoured and to sleep. Enthusiasm, on the other hand, seems to be modeled after some other pleasurable aspect of the nursing situation. It seems plausible to reconstruct the following situation: a child has been hungry and is now given the breast willingly or warmly. The child sucks eagerly. It is able to remember the anticipated pleasure of satiation. However, it is also able to remember the previous deprivation, the feeling of hunger. When the child recalls the memory of the hunger while it is still nursing, it begins to nurse with enthusiasm as long as the breast is available and is given warmly. He is still not completely satisfied while he is enthused. But he is aware of being on his way to satisfaction. The mutual enjoyment of the nursing mother is a necessary component since it makes for the necessary amount of security which enthusiasm requires. It is this combination of events which seems to be characteristic of enthusiasm.

If we scrutinize normal enthusiasm at a later date, we can find similar components. It is prefaced by some deprivation, no matter how mild; then some idealized object appears which offers the possibility for satisfaction. Possession of this object or mutuality in the object then brings about the feeling of enthusiasm. The enthusiastic person is still not completely satisfied, but he has tasted some satisfaction, expects more, and the memory of past deprivation is temporarily overcome by the feeling of enthusiasm. He then feeds others who feed him back in their mutual relationship. It is this feature which makes the enthusiast so dependent and the enthusiasm so vulnerable. The combination of partial satisfaction with the hope of more and the dim memory of past deprivation makes the enthusiast seek enthusiastic cohorts and accomplices.

In the patient described above, the repetitive search for enthusiasm-evoking objects was constant. The infatuations, being the life of the party, the nature of his sexuality, the short-lived good sleep, the screen of being the favorite, and the dim memory of his past unhappiness all seem to fit in with this formulation. In enthusiasm, the union which is sought for is really a reunion, an attempt to return to an older, unconscious, fuller satisfaction. People who lack all enthusiasm have abandoned hope of ever gaining even this partial and temporary gratification.

I am sure there is much to be added about the nature of enthusiasm. However, I do not feel equal to pursuing this task any further at this time. I can assure you, however, that what I have done, I have done with enthusiasm.

ON BEING EMPTY OF ONESELF

Enid Balint

(1963)

Enid Balint, a British psychoanalyst, describes a unique and immensely painful affective state occurring in a border-line or psychotic young woman. Whenever I read "On Being Empty of Oneself" I am struck by the sheer horror of Balint's patient's suffering and the apparent hopelessness of her prognosis: she was at first capable of making only the smallest degree of contact with the therapist for the shortest periods of time. Even the most experienced psychoanalyst cannot remain unmoved by the slow yet steady movement toward health as a result of psychoanalytic treatment, against formidable psychological odds and extra-analytic difficulties. Such moving descriptions of the psychoanalytic treatment of severely ill patients are particularly frequent in the writings of analysts of the British and Kleinian schools. One is moved in a similar fashion by the work of Searles (1960) and his co-workers in America and Mme. Sechehaye's (1951) description of Renée's schizophrenic psychosis and subsequent recovery in Symbolic Realization.

While the English phrase "He is full of himself" is an ordinary one in our language, its corollary, "He is empty of himself," does not exist. It is not to be confused with simply feeling "empty," a frequent complaint voiced in response to

335

disappointment or by those in a state of boredom. For Sarah, it meant that she felt "as if she could not have anything inside her because there was nothing to feel it with." She lived in a nightmare world in which she was "not recognized," "not seen." Associations and interpretations would have no meaning for her. She constantly tried to find out if the therapist knew when she was really frightened, in contrast to when she was only pretending. She lived with the conviction that a terrible void existed between her life, the analyst's, and everyone else's.

When events and activities did take place in her head, these events belonged to the nightmare world in which, for instance, "wolves constantly and ceaselessly chased around inside her head, or in which her head consisted of hundreds and hundreds of little bits like mosaic, each with the most elaborate picture on it." At each session she was astonished that the analyst recognized her and knew who she was. She was terrified of living in a void. As she improved in therapy, she began to feel her hands become alive and belong to her. Until then, they were often experienced "as if lifeless and made of steel."

According to Balint, these individuals characteristically do not like to be left alone and find it difficult to do anything for themselves or by themselves. "Shy in company and easily embarrassed," they dread human contact and resent being helped by others. Some withdraw from everyday life to such a degree that they begin to appear confused.

Balint concluded that in these patients the nucleus of self and body-ego formation was based not on feelings arising out of body-self sensations, reinforced and enriched by responses from the mother to them, but on early introjections (in the Kleinian sense) alive and threatening to swamp the self. "Healthy projective and introjective processes were stunted. The infant remained isolated from reality."

There is an English phrase, "He is full of himself," which means that the person in question is happy and proud, having accepted himself and his achievements. In other words, he is identified with himself, either permanently or, at any rate, for the moment. The opposite phrase—"He is empty of himself"—does not exist in the English language, but related ones such as "He doesn't look himself today" or "I don't feel myself today" are quite often heard. They always mean that there is something wrong with the person, and the last conveys in addition that a feeling of uneasiness is present. It is not clear whether the ego or the self is wrong, but what is clear is that one feels the other to be dystonic.

This paper brings some clinical material to bear on a very complex area of psychoanalytic theory, the relation between the ego, the body, and the self. Here highly uncertain boundaries separate the various concepts proposed. To mention a few: Freud in 1923 introduced the concept of the "body ego"; later Federn (1926) speaks of "ego experience" and "ego feeling"; Schilder (1923) of the "body schema" and later (1950) of the "body image," which was taken up by Scott (1948). Hartmann (1950, 1955) and others speak of the self and of the self-representations, and the relationship between them and the ego. Since I do not intend to start my paper with a number of intricate definitions, I shall use only the concepts of self and the development of the self, and will not either clearly delineate or even touch upon the parallel and possibly even sometimes identical processes that lead to the acquisition of a properly functioning ego and superego.

In our clinical work we quite often see people—either moderately or severely ill—for whom the description "he is empty of himself" might be helpful. The feeling of emptiness may be rather mild or very severe. To mention a few of their characteristic difficulties: these people do not like to be left alone, and they find it difficult to do anything for themselves by themselves; in spite of this, they often dread human contact and resent being helped by others. They may appear merely inhibited; they are perhaps shy in company, easily embarrassed, awkward with their hands. In some cases they can hide and even overcome to some extent their inadequacy and feelings of emptiness, and can be active and successful, though never satisfied with their activity. Under favorable circumstances they are also able to keep up a more or less normal social life, where they can be very popular.

At the other end of the scale, these people have to withdraw completely from everyday life, but this withdrawal, instead of helping, aggravates their state and may lead to a sort of confusion. If hospitalized at this point, the patient's confusion may be halted or even diminished, because he is cared for without any obligation to those caring for him, i.e., the patient is not alone—but not actively with anyone.

How can one understand the coexistence of these two apparently unrelated conditions: "being empty of himself" and the need to have somebody there, although this does not make him feel better or more "full of himself"? I wish to stress here that the presence of a real person may or may not improve the situation in mild cases. In severe cases, however, it never does.

I suggest that this disturbance in the relationship both to the self and to the environment originates in a fairly early phase of human development; perhaps in the area of the basic fault (Balint, 1958) or before or during the onset of the paranoid-schizoid position (Klein, 1946).

What I can add are some clinical observations on the possible psychogenesis of this feeling of emptiness. As will emerge in my discussion, this psychological condition is closely related both in its nature and in its chronology to the importance for the child of communication with his mother and her ability to provide for him a feeling of time for growth and development.

These observations might also contribute something to our knowledge of the special psychology of women. In my clinical experience, the feeling of being empty or of "being empty of herself" is more frequently found in women than in men, as already noted by Erikson (1950). Further, this disturbance may be linked with another, which in my experience is also encountered more frequently by women than by men; namely, that they are full of rubbish, which is valueless and lifeless, like sawdust in their teddy bears. Such women often say that they feel stuffed and uncomfortable, even after a small meal. From here various threads may lead to a theory of the symptomatology of anorexia.

Much help in understanding this condition can be found in the Kleinian literature, in their dynamic approach to the inability to take in and keep alive good objects inside the self, and in their ideas on the early onset of envy. These ideas, though valuable, seem insufficient, since the patient described in this paper was troubled more by the lack of self than of objects, good or bad, inside herself. True, she could not take in good objects. This could be connected with her oral attacks on her objects and, later on, her envy of them. In my opinion, however, the envy seemed to arise only after feelings of being empty of herself had been overcome (i.e., after the patient had acquired a feeling of self), and appeared to be connected with a more advanced stage in development than the one which I shall be describing.

The question arises here: have these patients ever felt that they were "full of themselves," that they are really living in their bodies and were the same people, whom other people would recognize if they saw them from day to day; that is, did something occur to them in their development that created the feeling that their essence had been taken away from them, although they had once had it?

My paper is based mainly on certain aspects of the developing transference of a patient, whom I shall call Sarah, who was twenty-four when she was referred to me for analysis. I shall attempt to show the ways in which I understood these aspects of the transference, and how I used them for therapeutic purposes. This selection cannot, of course, be taken to mean that other aspects of the transference were absent, or were not observed or used; only that I needed these in particular for my reconstructions and theoretical conclusions. I am stating this in order to avoid giving the impression that this analysis was one-sided or that it consisted mainly in the aspects which I shall be describing.

Sarah's parents were well-to-do professional people from abroad. Her father was described by both my patient and her mother, whom I saw when she came to England during the analysis, as a man with a violent temper who was never able to control himself. He was disappointed when his third child, my patient, was born a daughter, although his two elder children were sons. The mother seemed a depressed woman with precarious self-esteem, who relied on her children to take her side in her stormy marriage.

Sarah was breast fed and, according to her mother, there was always a plentiful supply of milk, and Sarah was a perfect baby. Very early she started to play with her brothers who were only a few years older than herself, climbing trees and competing successfully with them in every way. She did well at school and at games, was good at horse riding. Her mother showed me a photograph of Sarah aged seventeen, so that I could see what a beautiful and glamorous girl she had been until the breakdown, which occurred soon after she arrived in London and which brought her to analysis. Sarah's mother could not understand how her daughter could have changed so much, and stated emphatically there had been no trouble at all until perhaps a year before the breakdown. The breakdown was put down to the fact that at that time Sarah's father had been particularly violent, and this might have worried his daughter. Sarah's mother's pride was deeply hurt by her daughter's illness. She was sure that if Sarah was spoken to sensibly she would be quite all right again in a few weeks' time.

During analysis, it became clear that Sarah had in fact always been in difficulties. She described how at a very early age she lay awake terrified in bed, frightened to call out, listening with panic to her heartbeats in case they stopped. From transference reconstruction it also appeared that from still earlier times she would lie rigidly in anticipation of some object descending upon her from above, and crashing onto her head. This object was sometimes described as a rolling pin, sometimes a rock, and sometimes a cloud. I also have good evidence for believing, although I was very doubtful whether this was fantasy or a reality for much of the analysis, that when she was about six or seven years old, the younger of Sarah's two brothers had intercourse with her, and continued to do so until she was about twelve. Her mother's failure to recognize the trouble her daughter was in at that time, as well as at an earlier age, was worse for my patient than the experiences themselves. Sarah saw herself at best as scorned, but usually as not recognized, not seen. In fact, as I will show later, one of the main themes in her treatment was the difficulty one person must experience in recognizing another (see Laing, 1960). She could never understand how I should know who she was when I went to the waiting room to fetch her for her session.

Sarah came to England when she was twenty-four years old, in order to undertake some postgraduate training, but almost at once she became confused and acutely anxious and had to abandon her training. She managed to move to the house of some elderly relatives near London, and got herself referred to a psychiatrist. Once she broke down she was unwilling to work or to do anything except bring herself to analysis each day. She wore the same clothes all the time, winter and summer, and for most of the analysis did not take off a thick cardigan. She managed, however, to appear normal enough to travel on the train and underground. The relations with whom she lived tolerated her queer behavior, with some support from me and from the doctor who referred her for analysis.

After the first few months of treatment and during the first phase, which lasted for about one and a half years, Sarah covered herself up with a rug and turned away from me. There were long, strained silences, and sometimes some violent outbursts of feeling, but usually a rather flat atmosphere was maintained; feeling was mainly shown when Sarah had to cover the distance from the door to the couch, which she did with some difficulty. During this first phase, Sarah experimented with my ability to tolerate her confusion and withdrawal. Her transference reaction was to expect that anything that happened between us, either her associations or my interpretations, would have no meaning. She said, as some other patients do, that she was sure that I must repeat the same interpretations automatically at the same time in the analysis of every patient, and that perhaps I kept records of different sessions and played them over again in turn to each patient. But instead of being contemptuous and angry, as some patients are about this, she accepted as inevitable the fact that our relationship was meaningless. This material was interspersed with fairly coherent normal oedipal material, which demonstrated very strong penis envy, and also with accounts of many homosexual and heterosexual exploits. Her associations, though, were for the most part about, for instance, the wild animals which encroached on the city where she used to live, and how children were often swept into gutters and never seen again, and how frequently snakes were found and killed in the city. There was always a danger that termites might burrow under the foundations of houses and trees, and cause them to collapse. She was frightened of undermining me and of being undermined by me. I was seen as a whole separate person or animal, and she expected me to see her in the same way. She frequently said she would kill herself. At this stage she never looked at me except for brief moments, but she constantly tried to find out if I would know when she was really frightened and when she only pretended to be so and, on the other hand, whether I would force her back to work and, in so doing, into her mother's world which she experienced as a complete void. She dreaded the void more than anything else; much more than her own nightmare world. She was constantly strained and had difficulty in living—moving about—getting up—going to bed—everything caused strain and anxiety.

During this first phase of analysis, Sarah's mother came to England and tried to remove her daughter from treatment and turn her back into the normal girl she really was. I had hoped she would look after her daughter for a time, but this was clearly out of the question. Sarah, though, was determined to stay in analysis and managed to take matters in hand. She passively resisted all attempts to make her go to parties and buy new clothes, but agreed to be seen by a very undynamically oriented psychiatrist. She was clever with the consultant, appeared to outwit him, and led him to tell her mother that he could not take her daughter away from analysis for six months at least and that she should not be forced to work for that period.

Soon after her mother left England, Sarah's only intimate friend committed suicide. Sarah gave up attempting to look after herself, became confused, terrified, and withdrawn, and I had to refer her to a mental hospital. She stayed there for three months and I was able to visit her occasionally. On entering the hospital she was described as "depressed, inert, with marked volitional disturbances. No evidence of psychotic experiences." Her personality was said to be schizoid, mildly obsessional, suppressed aggression, intelligence superior.

Shortly before this period of hospitalization, after about one and a half years of analysis, the second phase of treatment started when one day Sarah noticed a piece of paper and a pencil on a table near my chair. She asked if she could take them and, when I agreed, she put the paper on a table near the couch where I kept an ash tray for her, and she began to draw. Her drawing was made up of little lines and dots, and although disconnected, gradually they filled up the whole sheet of paper. She then took another sheet and did the same thing again. This activity was not undertaken easily —as if giving pleasure or satisfaction—but with intensity and great effort.

After this, she spent part of each session drawing in this way. I interpreted this activity as an attempt to communicate with me and show me herself and her sensations and how scrappy they were, because she could find no words to describe them. It was not important if I did not then or later understand and interpret her drawings; but I had always to recognize them as communications, respect them and respond to them. On some days when I was perhaps less responsive, she would notice this and would withdraw, but say nothing. I did not notice this for some time, but later she told me about it and said that it was all right because she now knew that I would probably be more alive the next day, even if I seemed rather remote on that day. The rest of each session was spent in normal analysis; Sarah started to recollect her dreams and to associate to them.

I kept her drawings in a portfolio in my room. Later, when she brought me paintings, I also kept her paintings, and it gradually became understood between us that she was giving me bits of herself, of her body, and that I was collecting them and keeping them in one place in my room. As time went on, the paintings, which of course she did at home, became more integrated, but not until toward the end of the analysis, in the third phase, did they represent whole objects; in this, the second phase, they were often quite clearly distinguishable part objects, breasts, penises, ovaries, and other parts of the body. Sarah had studied biology and used some of her knowledge, but nothing was ever complete, and nothing ever joined up with anything else until the final phase.

It was only during the third and the fourth phases of analysis (i.e., from the fourth year to the sixth) that Sarah was able to *speak* about her body. Before that she spoke of events and activities in her head, but these events belonged to the nightmare world in which, for instance, wolves constantly and ceaselessly chased round inside her head, or in which her head consisted of hundreds and hundreds of little bits like mosaic, each with a most elaborate picture on it.

This period, the third phase of work, was characterized by violent changes of mood, which were repeated session after session. Many of the sessions seemed to fall into three periods; the first a violent one, during which Sarah hit the couch or the cushions, clenched her fists, flung cushions on the floor, tore up her drawings, and crouched away from me sobbing. After about ten minutes—when I had interpreted this behavior—the second period of the session started, and Sarah almost seemed to collapse onto the couch. She then started to suck her fingers or some part of her hands, or she left her mouth open making sucking movements. She became quiet and then only after a time she started to speak, and the third phase of the session started. Her associations were of this character: she said she wished that she were a bat so that she could come into my room and sit on the ceiling, or that she could be a monkey jumping from branch to branch. She described how at the beginning of analysis she used to sit up on the ceiling, or on a cupboard in the corner. I had not realized, she said, that on the couch was only a shell with an eye in it. Or she would talk about beautiful streams, which were clear and good on top but poisonous lower down. She expressed vehement fear of death, of killing, and in particular of being poisoned. In this period, as in the previous one, she repeatedly threatened to kill herself. More meaningful work could then be done on her fear of her oral impulses and on the danger of projecting them into me and into her environment. At one point during these associations Sarah often turned round so that she could see me. She began to speak about her need for me always to be the same and about her astonishment that I could recognize her day after day. She was still terrified of living in a void and of not being recognized.

By this time, I was beginning to understand something of the meaning to her of this void. During the third phase of treatment, toward the end of the session, Sarah sometimes turned away from me in a withdrawn way, looking frightened, angry, and pale. I came to realize that this behavior related to my impatience of her continued illness, or occurred when I appeared to think that she was exaggerating or pretending to be more ill than she really was, or the reverse, when I took her condition more seriously than was actually warranted. By the material which followed these episodes I learned that she felt deserted by me, and felt that if she did not withdraw and go back to her own nightmare world at these times, she would once more have to live in a void. *The void in fact was caused by my presence when I did not understand her*, because that meant that I saw only the external shape of her body, so to speak, but not what really matttered—herself. We were strangers: I became alien to her. I will discuss this topic more thoroughly later. It gradually transpired that she felt in a void and/or empty of herself in the presence of people who were, so to speak, in another world but did not recognize this fact, or failed to recognize that she was in another world.

In the period of her withdrawal what was libidinal satisfaction for me had ceased to be libidinal satisfaction for Sarah. Similar behavior occurred if I was ever carried away by my "understanding" of some material which at that time was quite irrelevant to Sarah's real communication.

At about this time in the treatment, during the fifth year, Sarah recalled a dream which she had first told me about a year before. In the dream a dog came out of the sea and bit her and then disappeared. This reminded her of a previous dream in which a bird swooped down, gashed her on the head, and disappeared. In this earlier dream she said that what had hurt her most was that the bird never turned back; it was quite unconcerned, indifferent. She then went back to the dog dream and said that when the dog bit her he took away her uterus, but now she had got it back again and could feel it inside her.

At about the same time she began to feel her hands as alive and belonging to her, which, until then, were often experienced as if lifeless and made out of steel. The common denominator of these two and many other similar experiences is that she could not have anything inside her because there was nothing to feel it with.

The theoretical question arises here, was this loss of feeling a secondary defensive mechanism against an earlier paranoid persecutory position and her own destructive urges? My impression is that it was not so, but on the contrary, it perhaps prevented the development of one. Admittedly, the patient's statement that her hands were of steel is a possible indication that the syndrome described in this paper was a secondary defensive development arising out of an earlier disturbance suffered at the time of the prevalence of the schizoid-paranoid position, and not a precursor or a mechanism to avoid its onset.

However, I would like to point out here that before this rediscovery of her own uterus in her body, Sarah showed only a manageable amount of hostility or resentment in the transference, nor was she often unbearably afraid of me or of her hostility toward me. One might almost say that as soon as she rediscovered herself, i.e., filled herself up, she became terrified of her own hostility to me and, of course, parallel with it, of mine to her. Her projective processes began to operate, and this part of her analysis was accompanied by the emergence of intense paranoid projective fantasies. Before this discovery, in contrast, her relationship to me and her expectation of me was of an empty and lifeless person. Her anger was despairing and aimless.

A week after the reanalysis of the dog dream, she reported another dream, in which she was asleep and awoke to find that the light on the ceiling in her bedroom was on fire. She rushed to her parents' room to call for help. Her parents did not come, but her brother came instead and, as he was tall, he could reach the fire and put it out. When he left her he warned her never to touch the bulb again or to turn on the light. I knew enough at that time to enable me to interpret her fear that she had now turned on the light again and had got the bulb, globe, uterus, back inside herself and was in danger of catching fire. In response she told me other dreams in which it appeared that if she was empty she and presumably her objects were safe; if she was full with feelings, urges, desires, she felt she might catch fire, and although a man might come and put out the fire, he would later ignore and leave her, taking away what she had inside her, and she would be empty of feeling once more. She became very disturbed here, and this material was repeated again and again in different forms and could be worked through in spite of great strain. Her fear that if she had any feeling it would be "put out" and she would be deserted could be tolerated so long as she knew that I saw her distress but did not try to change her, to "extinguish" her feelings. Although at this time—in the fifth year—Sarah knew she could have only about a year's more analysis, any movement from me that could be interpreted as a wish to make her well or get her back to work and so-called normal life, heralded a period when she was withdrawn, lifeless, and hostile.

Returning now to the case history, this working-through period was brought to an end when Sarah recalled one day going into her parents' bedroom in great trouble. She thought that she must have been about six, and it must have been the first time that her brother had had intercourse with her. Her parents had noticed nothing and she had said nothing. They had treated her just as usual; this had made her feel utterly alone and empty. To begin with, she had accepted this loneliness, but in time it had become a terrible struggle even to get up each morning, and almost impossible to go into a shop and ask for anything, because she did not expect to be seen, recognized, or understood.

The principal fantasies about the loss of feelings and about being empty were expressed by Sarah in genital terms, that is, by the loss of her uterus. The connection between these fantasies and aphanisis (Jones, 1929c) is obvious. In spite of this, I have the impression that the expression in genital symbols is a secondary phenomenon. A possible theoretical explanation for the use of genital symbols may be that the basic disturbance happened at such a early stage and was so traumatic that a long time had to elapse before the patient could allow it to emerge into consciousness; by that time the language of genital symbolism had been established. Sarah's associations and behavior in the transference give support to this theoretical construction. Her behavior for most of the analysis was highly primitive, and can only be described as pregenital: for instance her intense urge to suck, which itself could only be reached after a long period of analysis. Only after these critical periods had been worked through did the patient begin to have feelings inside her body, which, remarkably, were soon expressed in genital terms. Prior to this, she had clearly shown me her desire for the breast and her wish to get it inside herself, and her attacks on it, which prevented her doing so, but I had not understood her wish to get her feelings of herself back inside her body. When she began to speak about her uterus, however, it did, clearly, at that time, symbolize her whole self, but she began to talk about it only when she felt that I would understand this. At this time, she brought a very small pear-shaped pebble to show me, which she had found on the beach before she came to England. It came, in fact, from the beach where the dog came at her in her dream. She was able to show me the pebble when she knew I would recognize it as a symbol of her uterus and of herself.

Before summing up, I wish to report very briefly on the end phase of the analysis and on a follow-up of more than two years. During the last, the sixth year of her treatment, as I have said, Sarah experienced violent aggressive-paranoid feelings, but was able to contain them in the analytic situation. Normal analytic work continued, centering particularly on Sarah's relationship to her father and brothers. She tried to get a job but failed, probably partly because she interviewed badly. She finally decided to take a secretarial course, so that she could at least earn money in case, as she hoped, she could return to England. Her mother visited London again at that time; I saw her and she expressed pleasure at her daughter's improvement. During the sessions at this time and though only for brief periods, Sarah was very angry, disturbed, and withdrawn. We did a considerable amount of work on her anger at being forced to go home, at being deserted by me, on her intense fear that she might lose herself again, that is to say, have "herself" taken away by someone; and also on its meaning in terms of projection, and chiefly her fear that her impulses were too disturbing to be projected into the external world.

When she left we agreed that she would write to me from time to time, which she did. To begin with she lived at home and was unable to settle in a job. In a letter written about a year after the termination of her analysis she reported a dream which was an obvious continuation of the "dog dream" and which I was therefore able to interpret in terms of her fear of loss of self and body contents.

In answer, she wrote that my interpretation was right. She had now reached the decision to move to another town and live with a woman friend; the following week she started a job, using her University qualification for the first time, which she has kept ever since (about one and a half years). Two months later I received from her mother, who had visited her, a letter in which she said: "Her first few months here imposed a strain on her, but I was delighted at the self-control she was able to command." And another passage added: "To me she seems perfectly relaxed and is entering more and more into everyday affairs of life. I do feel now that the long years have not been in vain."

I have also had letters from the friend with whom Sarah lives—a University Professor—in which she expresses appreciation for the work of analysis. She has asked me whether analysis always achieves such good results.

Summary

A. RECONSTRUCTION OF PREANALYTIC DEVELOPMENTS

1. Sarah's mother did not notice, or ignored, or could not respond to, her daughter. She could therefore not provide the proper feedback or echo which was needed. This faulty relationship continued during Sarah's childhood and throughout her whole life.

2. Because of this lack of feedback Sarah felt that she was unrecognized, that she was empty of herself, that she had to live in a void.

3. If she was empty of herself, no one could recognize her; she was ignored, alone, and relatively safe.

4. To have something, Sarah created a nightmare world which she felt was located in her head. This also served as an outlet for her aggressive impulses.

5. In order to try to satisfy her parents, Sarah did well until she was about seventeen, although constantly suffering from strain and feelings of impending catastrophe, which went unnoticed.

6. Finally the feeling of unreality became unbearable, and when she arrived in London (where she knew analysis was available) she broke down.

B. DEVELOPMENTS DURING ANALYSIS

1. During analysis she became aware of her feelings of being empty of herself, expressed often as seeing herself outside her body. She felt that on the couch she was a shell with an eye in it. Inside she was full of dead people and objects.

2. She then began to experiment with putting bits of herself into me (and my room) and getting my response to them. She gave me drawings, representing sensations, movements, and parts of her body which were collected in my room, as

were her associations, she felt, inside me as I demonstrated when I remembered them.

3. Sarah began to have body feelings—i.e., felt herself to be inside her body—and parallel with that the external void began to fill up.

4. This led to fear of losing herself again and to a phase of paranoid anxiety.

C. THEORETICAL CONCLUSIONS

1. It is well known that the ego and the self develop in certain respects spontaneously or autonomously by what is called maturation. In other respects, however, their development depends on a proper interaction between the growing individual and its environment.

2. In this paper I have tried to describe one mechanism of the interaction which I have called an echo or feedback. The infant, by his behavior, stimulates the environment, and foremost his mother, to various reactions. Echo and feedback can be described as what the mother contributes to the stimulus and reactions out of her self.

3. The infant then gets to know what he is like in terms of someone else's—the mother's—experience, the mother lending her ego to integrate and reflect back the child's communications. The infant therefore gets to know himself, and his mother at the same time, by how she reacts to him. If the mother's reactions do not make sense to the child because, for instance, she is too preoccupied with her own ideas or feelings, then it is not a proper feedback. On the other hand, good mothering, or proper feedback, is what makes sense to the child.

4. There is no possiblity of the development of a healthy self when there is no proper feedback at acceptable intervals. My idea is that these need not be at fixed moments or periods. A few may be enough— and each can be valuable

and start a development. (Possibly even a rejection or a reproof may be experienced as a feedback if it makes sense to the child.)

5. These ideas lead to interesting problems regarding technique, such as the difference between interpretations and feedback, and the different treatment necessary for withdrawal or secondary narcissism.

To end my paper, I would like to say that in general, if the interaction between the growing individual and the environment leads to severe disappointment, two reactions can be observed:

a. The increase of aggressiveness and hatred in the individual.

b. Deficiency symptoms in his development. Sarah's analysis enabled me to isolate (more or less completely) this deficiency reaction, and led me to the theoretical conclusions which I have just summarized.

FAITH, TRUST, AND GULLIBILITY

Kenneth S. Isaacs, James Alexander, and Ernest A. Haggard

(1963)

This paper is largely concerned with trust, with faith and gullibility at opposite ends of the "trust spectrum," studied in contrast. That trust, usually considered a character trait, is also an affective state, is readily apparent in (1) the sense of confidence and reliance exuded by those who trust, (2) the feeling state and sense of commitment which is imparted to object relations, and (3) the presence of tender and sympathetic feelings toward others.

The concept of "key" affects was first introduced in this paper to underscore the observation that some affective states, like trust, have a more crucial position in the psyche than others, in that upon their development depend the later emergence of other affects. The authors contend that if, within certain epochal periods, certain affects do not make their appearance, it is difficult if not impossible for them to appear at a later stage of development.

A similar idea was suggested by Spitz (1959) in another context, namely, his concept of the cause and prevention of psychiatric disorders. In order for normal development to occur there must be a synchronicity between physical and psychological maturation. A similar "timetable" would seem to exist for the healthy development of affects. The two, "maturational compliance" and its counterpart "develop-

355

mental (psychological) compliance," have to occur simultaneously to ensure the development of the healthy personality.

INTRODUCTION: IMPORTANCE, DEFINITIONS, KEY AFFECTS, OVERVIEW

The centrality of affects in personality theory is endorsed by many writers since Freud: Brierley (1951), Fenichel (1945), Rapaport (1942), etc. It has become apparent that some affects seem to have crucial positions in the psyche (e.g., greed, love, hate, envy, jealousy, bitterness) and thereby serve as nuclei for character subformations in what we term affect clusters. Descriptions of these affects appear in the literature. Some of these and other affects have positions of such importance that they collectively determine the over-all basis for both degree and quality of perception of, and orientation to, the world. That is, the presence of one of these affects makes the experienced world a vastly different place for the individual from what it is without that affect, and this difference goes will beyond the specific affective experience.

The writers categorize "trust" as one of such important affects. This paper will attempt to outline some of the ramifications of the presence or absence of this affect, the process of its development, and special problems related to trust. Alexander (1960) has already remarked that affects may be placed in developmental series, that one affect may be a prerequisite to the development of other affects, and likewise these later affects form the basis for development of still other affects. Alexander and Isaacs (1963) have discussed affective attitudes and their influence. These preconscious affective attitudes are thought of as forming in relation to affect clusters and in turn serving in the determination of deployment of cathexes.

In affective development certain key affects eventuate as

an aspect of an epochal event. Six epochs of affective differentiation have been suggested elsewhere (Isaacs, 1956). These may be described as: (1) the points of self-nonself distinction, (2) the development of part-object relationships, (3) the shift from part-object to whole-object relationships, (4) the development of resolved whole-object relationships, (5) the shift from two-object to three-object relationships, and (6) development of complex multiple "interreactions." With each level of development, new affective experience becomes possible and the complexity of the perceived world increases.

The ego differentiation which occurs does so in a stepwise series, and occurs at each of these phases in rather dramatic simultaneous advances in several aspects of the personality. At each epoch simultaneous affective, interpersonal, cognitive, conceptual, and other changes take place —in other words, broad lines of ego development are found. The ego capacities before and after such epochal events are vastly different. If the epochal event does not take place at the appropriate age, such shifts become increasingly difficult in proportion to the amount of delay. Thus it is exceedingly difficult to influence shifts many years after the appropriate age.

With the development of these stage-by-stage series of differentiations, the individual with these broad lines of ego development becomes capable of new distinctions. He can, at each stage, discern the psychological content appropriate for that specific stage, and can also comprehend the psychological content at whatever previous stage he has passed through. Some problems are involved in this for the immature person. Since at each stage psychological factors of that stage and of the previous stages are comprehensible to the individual, those differentiations still to be attained can be perceived only in terms of a grossness or a haziness, or else, more commonly, are blithely subsumed under the psychological knowledge of his current stage. Thus, for instance, the person who has not developed to the stage of trust does not perceive the distinction between faith and trust, or he will perceive the distinction as insignificant in itself or in its consequences. From the point of view of such primitive characters, the distinctions that the more mature persons make are seen as being unreal, as without consequence, as perhaps a play on words, as a kind of naïveté, or as a preoccupation with trivia.

Psychoanalytic literature describes a number of aspects of personality related to ego development. The best-known and most widely described aspect is that having to do with psychosexual levels in combination with the oedipal development. The series of levels of development which we are describing here is not in conflict with those aspects of ego development described in terms of psychosexual levels but, we think, is complementary to it in the same sense that Erikson's series (1950) is complementary. We are considering that the individual develops in terms of a number of series of developmental aspects.

The present paper deals with some elements at one of these epochal events, without attempting to describe the pervasive changes at other such points in the individual's life.

The fact of trusting or not trusting determines by itself large aspects of the subjective world of the individual. Expectancies, anticipations, and hopes are influenced by it. Perceptions and conceptions of self and others, and the interpersonal possibilities, are vastly different for the trusting and the nontrusting. Thus the trusting and nontrusting live in different worlds. Economic, social, political, and religious philosophies are each to some extent dependent on the sense of trust, and the realistic awareness that not all people are trustworthy, and that not all people trust. The rules and regulations of our society are set up to deal with various kinds of failures in trustworthiness (e.g., both criminal and commercial law). It may be said that in this way trust forms such an important part of the basis of the current social structure that without trust and trustworthiness we could not have our form of society.

In psychotherapy, and especially in psychoanalysis, the presence of trust is of such importance that the therapy will inevitably founder if some kind of trustfulness is not felt by the patient. If a patient does not trust, he does not impart; if he does not impart with minimal reservation, psychoanalysis cannot be an effective alliance for mutual working out of the intimate problems of inner life.

Theories and Literature

Despite its importance, we know very little about this affect. The literature includes Erikson's (1950) description of *basic trust*, which is a renaming of Benedek's (1938) *confidence*, and which we consider as a part of the basis of both faith and what we term trust. The development of a trusting relation to an adult is described in passing by Susan Isaacs (1949) as the first development of trust.

The absence of trust may occur in various ways, and its absence, whether with faith, mistrust, or distrust, is thought by us to be attributable variously to psychological immaturity, malformation, or current unadaptability. Since this is not a case study, only brief mention of case material will be made for exemplification. This is not a formal research study, and only suggestions for tests of hypothesis will be made, plus reference to some completed but as yet unpublished studies of ego development.

Let us consider what trust means to us and how it is different from some other affects. It connotes an affective attitude primarily directed outward, involving a sense of comfort, confidence, and reliance that certain acts and behavior will or will not occur. So far this does not distinguish it from a family of affects including confidence, faith, certainty, assurance, etc. Faith is commonly used in a religious sense as a generic term subsuming both what we distinguish as blind faith and as trust. These latter two affects, as we think of them, have connotations which suggest to us that the religious generic term "faith" could stand some differential study by theologians along the line of the distinction we shall describe below. But we will not pursue the religious connotations here, and only briefly a little later.

Faith is an undoubting, unconditional belief in which data for proof or refutation are ignored. There is an unswerving adherence to a person or principle, without need for proof, and with a steadfastness even in the face of proof to the contrary. Such adherence is not due to either present or past proof. We will use the term "trust" to denote the state of undoubting belief in which questions have been raised in the past, but having been resolved, are unlikely to be raised again, and are certainly not active now. Trust we think of in the sense of making predictions in terms of reality testing. Faith we think of in the sense of wishful predictions in absence or ignorance of reality factors. Faith therefore often uses "untestables" as a meaningful component, which cannot be proved or disproved. Trust we see as more personalized, as more differentiated than faith.

By the term "distrust" we intend to connote an absence of assurance and reliance, with the special quality of a certainty of the absence of trustworthiness in the other person. By the term "mistrust" we intend to connote its older sense of a doubtful, sceptical, uncertain wariness about trusting another person; that is, a tendency toward distrust. By the term "gullibility" we intend to connote a readiness to believe that what is wished for, often unconsciously, is to come true, despite reasonable unlikelihood. It is thereby a readiness or desire to be deceived.

Ontogenesis—Normal and Abnormal Development

The above series of kinds of certainties and uncertainties may occur in the same person at different times or circumstances, or any one of these may be a characterological aspect of an individual. In the earliest infantile period of life we assume the presence of a sense of omnipotence. This sense of omnipotence is later disrupted as a result of the persistent impingement by the reality of the infant's relative impotence and integration of that reality by the infant, following which the omnipotence is projected onto others. The result is that expectations of satisfaction come to be mediated through others, who, through projection, come to be perceived as omnipotent. From here on we can begin to see the interrelation of the terms just defined, and why we wish to distinguish one from the other. Faith has to do with the sense that the omnipotent other can and will do whatever is desired. In contrast, trust that the *real* other will do this implies a sound reliance on a specified other person after questions have been raised—about him, about expectations of him, and doubts satisfied. The infant in blind assurance of the omnipotence of the parent awaits—perhaps impatiently, but nevertheless confidently—the satisfaction of his wishes. Faith is a comparatively unsophisticated affect, which occurs with little differentiation in the perception of the other person involved, since it is partially a result of the projection of the fantasied omnipotent self. The ramifications of this in a person's life are many. Some effects will be described later.

It is only when there is a later development of the interpersonal attitude of assurance arising out of actual interaction of the child with his parents, rather than through projected fantasy, that the more differentiated relationship which we term "trust" can develop. Trust is an affect, a feeling. Trusting is an intrapsychic *act* in which the affect of trust is felt in relation to a particular object; that is, trusting imparts a particular quality to an object relationship. This can only come about through, first, some capacity in the child to differentiate the inner from the outer reality; that is, the wished-for reliance and the actual experience of being able to rely. Faith is thought of as a nursing-stage development. Faith has originally to do only with the mother, trust with both father and mother. Those persons with only faith differ from those who can also trust—in their fantasy, in object relations, and in the psychoanalytic process.

Since empirical observation, the inductive method, and experimentation are slow and tedious, coupled with the fact that human life is short, and, as Hobbes (1651) says, in many ways brutish, reality-testing or opportunity for proof is very limited. Existence does not allow us to put everything to the test, and therefore we learn experimentally the trustworthiness of but a limited number of things. Thus even those of us capable of trust have to take many things on faith.

We have already pointed out the roots of trust in the confluence of infantile "confidence" with the projection of omnipotence leading through faith to trust. At present, we can merely point out what we believe to be some major threads in the development of trust, but which we believe to be a step forward in the definition of this key affect. Trust may be a keystone affect—prerequisite to the development of a host of other psychic advances—or it may be merely an easily discerned concomitant of these other advances. Understanding of which it is must await further research. Regardless of the outcome of such investigation, trust is at least a harbinger of many changes in the individual.

Let us first mention some of these changes briefly, and then describe some more fully. The advent of trust appears to coincide with the resolution of conflict among introjects, and through this—improved whole-object relations—adoption of clear roles and definition of ego boundaries. There is also the appearance of new bases for tender feelings; that is, sympathy supplanting pity, tenderness supplanting scorn and contempt, cooperativeness supplanting the "law of the jungle," and time-binding supplanting biding of time. There is an increasing endurance of object relations, further superego development, and a new quality of introjects.

We consider the definition of ego boundaries to be a developmental task. When definition of ego boundaries is still partial and therefore not certain, much ego cathexis is allocated to defining and securing the boundaries to prevent encroachment. Persons who are thus engaged must necessarily be wary of others, if not actively distrusting. The perception of others interpersonally and in terms of object relations is distorted by concerns related to boundaries. Others are perceived as acting upon the self, or the self as acting upon others, not in terms of mutuality.

Trustworthiness is intimately related to trust. It connotes a serious commitment which stems from ego ideal, from quality of introjects, and from capacity to perceive the sensibilities of others. Trustworthiness is, in turn, perceptible to others as a characteristic distinctly different from the uncommitted, perfidious, and transient qualities in the relationships of untrustworthy persons.

Development of trustworthiness occurs with the formation of appropriately responsible attitudes toward obligations, considerateness for others, stability of involvement, etc. It is our impression that trust develops through both identification and validating experiences with trustworthy persons (Peck and Havighurst, 1960). It does so in a social matrix providing regularities and certainties of structure of interactions. The infant learns the reliability and repeatability of care and consideration by the parent. He learns the consistency of parental behavior. He learns the seriousness with which the parent regards his wants and needs. In such a relationship, over time, responsibility can develop, ego boundaries are defined, and concern about encroachment of ego boundaries therefore subsides. We do not take a stand on whether the development of trust secures the ego boundaries or whether the definition of ego boundaries allows trust to form. It seems probable that some precursor interaction occurs prior to the stepwise change. This is an important point which deserves research.

It is the forthrightness of parents in their dealings with the child which we think of as determining the fate of the child's developing sense of trust. The parents' serious involvement in the child as a worthy individual, and the moral qualities of the parents, are both adopted by the child through the process of identification, and thus trust, and especially trustworthiness, are related to superego formation. Schlesinger's paper (1961) has connotations for this process.

In a situation where a parent is not trustworthy, whether in large or small ways, a defect in the child's development of trustworthiness is likely to occur. Infantile faith, it seems to us, must be an almost universal phenomenon, developing as a consequence of early expectations of gratification, even where actual gratification is minimal. Faith develops, therefore, mainly from fantasy events. When a parent misuses the faith and the developing trust of a child, a disillusionment occurs which is a great blow to the psyche. If the child has a strong enough ego, he will integrate the fact as a determinant of limitations and restrictions on the trustworthiness of parents and others. If he has a somewhat weaker ego, the disappointment may connote a loss of the illusion of ideal parents and thereby mean a resulting bereavement, loneliness, and depression. In such circumstances —anger over the loss of the illusion, and guilt over the anger —the distrust may be repressed and leave the child unprepared to discriminate between trustworthy and untrustworthy persons. He has thereby become gullible, for he can only indiscriminately trust. Gullibility has to do with a persistent need to be deceived. The fact of being repeatedly deceived may serve additionally as a reassurance that the parents are actually no less trustworthy than anyone else.

There is what may be termed a gullibility or credulousness of innocence or ignorance, but most typically, gullibility is pathologically misplaced trust, the misplaced trust being the direct consequence of guilt. Guilt makes one deny knowledge which one really has. A notorious confidence man, Yellow Kid Weill (Weill, 1948), is quoted as having said that all the victims mulcted were mulcted through their cupidity. The victims denied their guilt, so that it operated unconsciously and made them victims, when their conscious wish was to victimize others.

Following definition of ego boundaries and development of trust, consideration for others and sympathy for others appear. The perception of others through sympathy involves an identification with the other in a holistic sense. This, however, is not the same as the more differentiated empathic sensitivity. The latter point appears to be why trust can only be a necessary but not sufficient precondition to an analytic relationship. Integrative observation requires more than trust.

The differences between those persons who trust and those who do not trust is evident in their perceiving and experiencing of the realm of possibilities, for the realm of freedom is vastly enlarged for the assured (i.e., trusting and even faith-filled) person in comparison with the unconfident, untrusting. A further difference exists between the perceived and subjective worlds of those who merely have faith and those who also trust. The factors which are weighed by each in decision-making are different. The unconfident, unassured person is always in danger, always threatened, lonely, fearful, and isolated. If one cannot judge who is and who is not trustworthy, he must choose among a few alternatives: for example, timid isolation, aggressive blustering attack to avoid surprise attack (thus retaliating in advance), or formation of transitory alliances which are uneasily maintained and which frequently and suddenly shift. He has to maintain a constant alertness because there are, for him, no cues as to from whom or when an attack will issue.

The trustful person has less anxiety about inner or outer dangers; this thereby facilitates new experiences. He lives in a world which includes friendly, cooperative persons. He anticipates acceptance by reliable and trustworthy persons. He experiences sympathy and compassion within himself and within others.

The nontrusting person has expectations of harm. He is always at least a little wary. The common affective experience is fright, for the world is perceived as a dangerous place. The gullible person perceives the world through unrealistic hopes for safety and comfort, for pleasure and gratification. The realistically trusting person is able to know when to be wary, but can discriminatingly relax in safety and confidence. In this sense, trusting and nontrusting persons are worlds apart.

The perdurant refractoriness of lack of trust is illustrated by a patient who had been seen twice a week for three years. She had not felt close to anyone since the beginning of the oedipal phase, and had no memory of fully trusting anyone since that early period. Needless to say, she had no more trust for her therapist than for anyone else. Her distrust, which interfered with treatment in many ways, was discussed in therapy many times. In one such interchange she said, "Why should I trust you?" The therapist replied, "Why shouldn't you trust me?" To this the patient responded, "I don't know you. If I trust you, and I am mistaken, I may be hurt by you." The reply of the therapist was, "You have seen me many times, but you are still afraid to trust me on the basis of those experiences?" The patient's reply was, "That's not the point. Even though you have not harmed me in the past, how do I know that you won't in the future?" That question, by which the patient meant, "How can I feel trust when I do not?," is not a question we can answer. But we can suggest the process by which trust can develop. Nontrusting persons have, in angry despair, been convinced (have reached conviction in which no open-mindedness remains) that no one is trustworthy. They will no longer apply the inductive method. They no longer doubt. They have reached a negative certainty. This certainty about there being no trustworthiness to be found anywhere in the world is denied, while consciously they think they are willing to give others the benefit of the doubt. But certainty precludes further testing.

Trusting involves perception and judgment. It involves reality testing for the presence or absence of trustworthiness. If trustworthiness is found, there follows the intrapsychic act of trusting, which involves the willingness and the ability to make a commitment to an object deemed trustworthy.

For the person who does not trust, the fact of experience of safety in a relationship, even when repeated hundreds of times, does not result in learning; the inference he makes is that he has been safe only because of his alertness. He does not infer that he is with a trustworthy person. There is a duplication of this in the international scene, and it is at this point that the dangers in international relations are awesome. Proponents of unilateral withdrawals as a means of teaching nontrusting cold-war opponents that we are trustworthy, do not realize this last fact. With an attitude of distrust, learning of safety does not occur. Conditioning experiments are not necessarily applicable to all human learning, nor does it seem likely that international conflicts can be solved in this way, for it is not a matter of simple conditioning where some learning occurs with every trial. Gullibility is a dangerous risk internationally, just as it is interpersonally.

The patient referred to had been loved and well treated until the age of four. At that time two events occurred which proved traumatic. There was the birth of a sibling and rejection by a prudish father when she turned to him erotically for comfort. Nevertheless, the fact of her early trusting formed a bedrock to which the therapy could return. Although with exceeding slowness, the therapy progressed, and with recovered trust the patient was finally able to enter analysis.

In contrast, a patient who grew up from infancy in a situation which was fraught with uncertainties, inconsistent loving acceptance alternating with open rejection, could not trust. She was seen weekly for two years. She appeared for treatment as a lonely, suspicious young woman, with many hysterical symptoms, each of which appeared for varying lengths of time, disappeared, or was displaced by others. She had undergone many medical and surgical treatments which were costly, time-consuming, and ineffective. Bitterness about those and other experiences, as well as toward her parents, was intense.

She had experienced so few relationships with trustworthy persons that she could not discern whom to trust and whom not to trust. She was therefore nontrusting. Her guilt over her rage at her untrustworthy parents forced her to deny her distrust. She was unconsciously determined to prove everyone untrustworthy. If they were, she would gullibly fall a victim to them. If they were trustworthy, she then had to prove delusionally that they, too, were untrustworthy. Because of this, she repeatedly put herself into positions which could not but end in disappointment, if not harm to herself.

She had never in her life developed what we consider a trusting relationship. Instead she had a blind faith, and a strong need to believe and rely on others. It is perhaps a tribute to the human race that she was not gulled constantly, for she was always ready to believe on first acquaintance, and always quickly disappointed. She rarely distrusted before and always distrusted after involvement. At base, she could not trust others, although she gave the appearance of trusting. That is to say, she was always suspicious and distrustful, but by denial of her distrust became gullible. The treatment was foredoomed to failure.

A third patient, a man of twenty-one when he started treatment, was seen for one and a half years, then, following a two-year interval, was seen for one year, and, following another two-year interval, was seen for three years. At the beginning of the first course of treatment he appeared to be a young man heading either for "skid row" as a drunkard, or to a penitentiary for his criminal activities. He had never held a job for longer than one day, drank liquor to the point of blackout, and had a history of various antisocial acts. He obviously did not trust, considered that everyone was out for himself, as he himself was, and could not perceive kindliness or trustworthiness in others. He was bitter, resentful toward society and toward his parents for their inability to cope. His infancy, despite economic impoverishment, was filled with acceptance from his mother. His father was a brutelike but not unkindly man who worked hard and regularly on a menial laboring job each day and drank himself to a stupor each night. The patient's capacity to have resentment about the differences between his life and the lives of some about whom he could read, plus his fears for his future as he saw his childhood companions become derelict alcoholics, inmates of penitentiaries, and some undergo capital punishment, created an urge in him to rise above his apparent prospects, and a motivation to seek help.

But he could not trust. Even though many changes occurred, for years his psychotherapy was marked by a wariness and a limitation on his frankness. Although trust had been a subject for discussion several times, only seven and a half years after he had initially started treatment did the following interchange occur. Therapist: "You don't trust anyone, do you?" Patient: "No one" (pause)—and here added something which he had never before stated to anyone: "Except you (pause) a little." He then appeared surprised and frightened about what he had imparted.

From this point he rapidly and dramatically changed in many aspects of his life. He adjusted to his work better, started planning to join a fraternal organization, controlled his wife-beating tendencies, expressed wishes to do kindly, helpful, and cooperative things for those around him, attempted to induce his wife to join a church for the sake of the more enduring relationships possible there, and abruptly stopped his lifelong petty thieving. He had simultaneously developed both trust and trustworthiness, as well as sympathy and compassion.

The fact of allowing himself to trust enabled him to perceive the world differently. He knew that the fraternal organization comprised primarily trustworthy persons, and he also knew that many of the persons whom he had known from the past were not trustworthy. The treatment continues under the beneficence of trust, and there seems to be some likelihood that he will continue to progress. He seems certainly secure in the role of a useful and constructive citizen.

The above illustrations may serve to indicate the function of trust in therapeutic activity. It is our impression that trust may rarely develop in the therapeutic situation but forms an absolute prerequisite to integrative psychoanalytic activity. Thus, childhood trust forms a basis for treatment trust. In contrast, infantile faith forms a basis for magical, sometimes silent, demands on the analyst.

When the patient distrusts (as with the typical paranoid patient), psychoanalysis, insofar as it requires a mutual participation with the patient freely imparting, cannot occur. When the distrust is in the nature of the less malignant but still pathological immature distrust, there are the restrictions of wariness and guarding which stand in the way of the analytic process.

One of the common forms of absence of trust in psychoanalysis is the transitory mistrust which occurs on the basis of projected abhorrence against the emerging unconscious material. So long as the feeling is *mistrust*, the analysis may remain on sound grounding. If the absence of trust takes the form of *distrust*, the analysis is likely to falter if not terminate. The mistrusting patient diminishes his credulity and thus his capacity to take seriously what the analyst says. The distrusting patient carefully fends off the analyst, and the analysis.

When a patient's affective attitude toward his analyst is faith-filled, there is a tendency to have complete belief in the analyst with an unquestioning expectation of (magical) results. The blind and unquestioning faith leads to a degree of credulousness which blocks perception. Such a person will undauntedly try or accept any comment, interpretation, or suggestion of the analyst. He will try strikingly different reformulations without question. Faith quells anxiety and forestalls close examination of a situation.

When the patient bases his expectation of analysis on a faith affect cluster, there is usually a blind and hidden grandiose expectation of gratification. Such a patient believes that change will occur regardless of the kind or amount of his participation, and there is the expectation of magic or miraculous change brought about through an omnipotent analyst who is expected to perform miracles to enable the patient to be comfortable, content, happy, satisfied, gratified, relieved, and pleased, regardless of the circumstances in which he might find himself; and he expects that this will be achieved without his having to take any active part or having any responsibility for the process. The patient with faith is a poor prospect for psychotherapy, and a highly improbable risk for psychoanalysis.

In contrast, the trusting patient has the belief that the analyst understands something of people, of a treatment process and technique, and that if the patient participates in the process there is a reasonable likelihood of cure. The trust in the latter case has to do with a real person with real qualifications and real limitations, and there is an interpersonal object relation which is quite different from the fantasy component in the attitude of the faith-filled patient.

Religious Conversion Experience

We would like to make brief mention of trust and religious experience. The religious experience of the trusting differs from that of the faith-filled. For instance, the religious conversion experience may occur as either an upsurge of blind faith or as a result of a surge of trust. If the basis of the conversion experience is partly that of the projected omnipotence, as occurs, we believe, in many revivalist meeting experiences, we expect that the endurance of the conversion is likely to be brief. If the basis of the conversion is actually that of development of trust through the process of identification and slower testing of doubts, then the tenure may be enduring. Thus, the conversion experiences are quite different in quality, even though, superficially, they may appear much alike.

Trust and Whole versus Part Object

Trusting another person requires that the other person be seen as a whole object. Prior to whole-object perception, trust cannot occur. That is to say, the notion of trusting another when the other does not exist as an identifiable and definable whole object is a contradiction, for one cannot trust knowingly a part of a person.

Paranoid suspiciousness is of special interest in relation to trust, because it is in the paranoid states that some of the most marked pathology of trust is to be seen. The suspicious distrustfulness of the paranoid is notorious. Hate, spite, vengefulness, and jealousy are also paranoid affects and appear in the absence of realistic justification of these feelings.

We would like to make a distinction between the suspicious distrust of the paranoid and the "normal" distrust that everyone feels from time to time. Time considerations prevent a full elaboration of this matter, which must therefore be left for another paper. We would, however, like to suggest that the paranoid's suspicion is related to his projecting outward certain feelings and impulses which his morality will not allow him to admit as being a part of himself. He thereby, to some extent, reduces or fractionates his self and, willy-nilly, others. In a sense, therefore, he has reverted to part-object relationships and the pretrust stage; and in another sense he has shifted to a peculiar fractionation of object relations which is *unlike* infantile part-object relations.

Another aspect of paranoid development has to do with the fact that the superstructure of paranoia is erected upon a base which has its origin in that stage of psychosexual development which Freud (1911a) called the "pleasure ego." In this stage of development the older infant or small child looks upon any pain as originating from without. All the good, that is, the pleasant, it attributes to the self, and all the bad, that is, the painful, it attributes to the external world. Everything painful is thus seen as persecutory. The child who is loved, made secure, cherished, comforted, allowed nonetheless to be free, will be spared excessive pain, and so spared excessive persecutory feelings. However, the pregenitally traumatized child will enter the oedipal phase under a handicap of poorly resolved conflicts. These excessive conflicts will make it likely that the child will not traverse the oedipal phase of psychosexual development successfully.

We do not regard the fact that everyone has some suspiciousness as due to the failure or even partial failure of the positive Oedipus or triumph. Those minimal paranoid traces we think of as due to the continuing effect of the universal experiences and reactions in that part of the preoedipal period called the stage of the pleasure ego. Thus an ultimate theory of paranoia we think of as requiring distinctions among normal traces of suspiciousness, healthy and appropriate distrust, and paranoid suspiciousness.

Summary

The concept of trust is complex. We have had to use words such as faith, trust, and gullibility, although the precise meanings and differences among these words are often clouded by common usage. What is most important is the sets of relationships surrounding each of these concepts. The amount of receptivity to and cognizance of reality, the differentiated or undifferentiated response to reality, what goes into individual predictions, what for each individual constitutes verification, and how the individual relates his past experiences to his present and his future—these are ways in which the subjective worlds of individuals vary. Trust is one of the important determinants of the subjective world. Trust has roots in the earliest experiences of the child; has necessary preconditions for development; has an orderly developmental sequence. In any individual there may be appropriate development, limitation of development, maldevelopment, or defense against use of the capacity to trust, and pathologies in relation to trust. The functional uses of trust in psychoanalysis and psychotherapy are discussed. Trust and social structure is mentioned.

ON THE NATURE OF
CRYING AND WEEPING

Robert L. Sadoff

(1966)

Crying and weeping, perhaps even more than anxiety, are commonplace in the consultation room. The therapist sometimes responds with a countertransference reaction, rather than in an investigative manner, simply offering help, sympathy, and solace, or consciously and/or unconsciously wanting the weeping to stop so that he can "get on with the therapy." Crying and weeping are the modes of expression, the vehicles, by which affects are released, expressed, and communicated.

Crying consists of two basic components: vocalization and weeping. Vocalization includes calling, shouting, screaming, groaning, whining, wailing. Weeping is the "shedding of tears from an emotional stimulus" and is an exclusively human phenomenon not present in lower animals. The initial cry at birth is a reflex act, which becomes in turn increasingly purposeful. The infant expects a response from the environment, and the cry is an attempt to attract attention from a distance.

The culturally accepted expression of grief involves the integration of the two components of crying—weeping and vocalization. The feelings expressed are primarily anger and sorrow; their communication may be of a "hostile, dependent nature invoked from a position of weakness and hopelessness."

Weeping is both phylogenetically and ontogenetically a later development than crying. In weeping itself, one is attempting to rid oneself of some annoyance, of some emotional pain. Tears "help to wash away the pain of separation" or rid oneself of a disagreeable tension in the body. This latter function, the washing away of painful affects, may be expressed in bodily terms and can be observed clinically in psychosomatic disturbances. The skin has been referred to as the "outer rind of the ego," and psychogenetic dermatological conditions are often an expression of weeping.

Sadoff believes that, whereas one is tempted to relate a theory of expression of affect to the symbolic association of body fluids, whether lacrimal, urethral, vaginal, urinary (Greenacre, 1945a, 1965), it is more reasonable at this stage of psychoanalytic research to state that, as in the case of crying, lacrimal secretion is only one aspect of a general body reaction in which the whole glandular system is stimulated, causing the secretion of fluid. In part it is a generalized response to a stress situation (Wolff, 1953).

Why do we cry? We cry because we feel helpless, in a position of weakness; this is more likely to occur when we are fatigued. Underlying these feelings is a wish to be reunited with a nurturing, succoring, comforting mother figure. This complex affective medley also contains elements of sorrow and anger; sorrow for loss of the love object, and anger at being deprived of it. Contrary to the frequent presence of fear and/or anxiety, whether in its pure or alloyed form in many affects, fear is not the principal affect expressed in crying and weeping. Characteristically, when fear is terminated relief is experienced and crying may occur. In order to comprehend the meaning of crying, one must analyze the meaning and content of the anxiety state preceding it.

Sadoff suggests that the development of tears may be related to the development of differentiation of self and nonself, i.e., "may be linked to the development of object relations in the infant and thereby becomes involved in separation anxiety and grief reactions." Tears communicate silent distress, imploring others' aid. A masochistic female patient in analysis with me wept only from one eye, the eye closer to the vision of the analyst. Sadoff also thinks that the ability to weep may be of great psychic significance to an individual because it means he is able to expel pain and affects from the body or expel bad internalized objects. It remains for future investigators to determine if "the prevention or excessive stimulation of the flow of tears or the vocal outcry either consciously or unconsciously leads to difficulties in expression of affect through other channels." In this connection, Searl is of the opinion that excessive screaming or its damming up can produce serious consequences in later life.

Indeed, Franz Alexander's successful psychoanalytic therapy of children suffering from bronchial asthma revealed the significance of suppressed and/or repressed crying as a key psychodynamic issue in the development of this serious physical disorder (Alexander, French, et al., 1941).

INTRODUCTION

The subject of crying covers a vast area of study and has many ramifications. This paper will review the physiological, psychological, psychoanalytic, and sociocultural literature on crying and weeping and will discuss the subject in relation to the expression of emotion.

Crying seems to be a universal phenomenon in man and appears in some form in most of the higher animals (Darwin, 1873). It is seen from the study of languages and primitive thinking that crying is a general reaction that consists of two basic components—vocalization and weeping. Vocalization includes calling, shouting, screaming, groaning, whining, wailing, bawling, and moaning; weeping is defined here as the shedding of tears from an emotional stimulus. The vocal component of crying is seen in both animals and man, but weeping seems to be exclusively human.

The differentiation of crying into its two components is important in understanding the meaning of crying in both adults and children. Perhaps this distinction is seen best in the crying of infants. The newborn may cry with gusto but not with tears. The lacrimal apparatus is fully developed at birth and capable of secreting tears on corneal irritation but not by crying during the first two to three months.

The initial cry at birth is purely a reflex act since the neonate is incapable of voluntary activity. This cry is life-saving; it serves a valuable physiological function by expanding pulmonary capacity. Crying soon after birth seems to be a response to physiological needs such as hunger, cold, or pain. As these demands are met, the conditioning element is added, and the cry becomes more and more purposeful. The infant "expects" a response from the environment and cries for the mother to relieve his discomfort. The nature of this cry is necessarily vocal, to attract attention from a distance. If the purpose of crying in infancy is to summon aid during distress and the vocal component of crying serves this purpose, what then is the function of tears? How has weeping evolved in conjunction with vocalization as a part of the crying reaction?

DEVELOPMENT OF WEEPING

Weeping is both phylogenetically and ontogenetically late in development. Darwin (1873) says that weeping has been acquired since the period when man branched off from the common progenitor of the genus Homo and of the nonweeping anthropomorphic apes.

In the culturally accepted expression of grief there is an integration of the two components of crying—weeping and vocalization (the latter including wailing and singing). The feelings expressed include primarily anger and sorrow, and the communication appears to be one of a hostile dependent nature evoked from a position of weakness and helplessness.

There is yet another significance to weeping as it relates to mourning. According to Jackson (1957), a person who weeps in mourning is resorting to a technique developed in childhood for ridding one's self of annoyance. If a foreign object is lodged in the eye, tears will work to wash it away. If the pain is located somewhere else in the body, a flow of tears may work as a form of emotional relief. In mourning, tears may help to wash away the pain of separation. Searl (1933) suggests that the aim of weeping is to scream the disagreeable tension out of the body. To quote Ovid: "It is a relief to weep; grief is satisfied and carried off by tears."

Thus, weeping seems to have the function of washing away pain and painful affects from the body. We behave toward pain as though it were something removable from our bodies, and to bring this removal about we mobilize the whole bodily apparatus. The organism makes efforts to expel the painful affects through all apertures and from all mucous membranes (Peto, 1946).

The phenomenon of washing away or exteriorizing pain or painful affects seems significant in the relationship of weeping to general body secretions (Heilbrunn, 1955).

SYMBOLIC REPRESENTATION OF WEEPING

It is not surprising, then, to see reports in the psychoanalytic literature equating symbolically the various fluid secretions of patients. Saul (1938) presents the case of a girl who unconsciously associated weeping, urinating, vaginal leucorrhea, and nasal catarrh—all related to unsatisfied receptive demands. He found a similar relationship of weeping to chronic catarrhal conjunctivitis, vaginitis, and nasopharyngitis. Fenichel (1945) feels that hysterical crying spells frequently correspond to a displacement upward of conflicts around sexualized urination. Greenacre (1945a, 1945b) describes two types of neurotic feminine weeping, both associated with urination. Freud (1900) supports this relationship by indicating that secretions of the human body can replace one another in dreams. A fifteen-year-old male patient of the present author, who first appeared with urinary inhibition, has recurrent dreams of urinating and awakens to find he has had a seminal emission.

Many expressions have come down through the years to indicate a symbolic association of the body fluids. "Bloody tears," seen in hysterics; the expression, "sweating blood"; Churchill's famous "Blood, toil, tears, and sweat"; and the old Jewish expression *"Pischen fun dee aygehn"* (Peeing from the eyes), are examples. Shakespeare said: "The blood weeps from my heart."

How does the vocal component of crying fit into this general scheme? Can vocal productions be viewed in a similar manner as the production of tears? People commonly speak of a "flow of words," "fluent speech," "outpouring of words," or the "stream of speech." Hence, vocal productions seem conceptually to have a fluid quality similar to that of tears.

Fenichel (1945) discusses the urethral eroticism of speech, and equates in the unconscious the flow of speech to the flow of urine. M. Katan (1953) considers the speech of manic patients and concludes that it has a urethral meaning by a displacement from the urethral zone to the mental processes. The combination of a fear of wetting one's self with urine with the involuntary retention of urine is known as "stuttering urination" or "stammering bladder" (Van der Heide, 1941), thus relating speech and urethral functions. In his summary equation of body-phallus Lewin (1933) equates symbolically tears, saliva, voice, speech, and screams to semen and urine.

It is tempting to try to relate a theory of expression of affect to the symbolic associations of the body fluids, but such an approach does not seem valid at this stage in our knowledge. Rather, it seems more reasonable to view lacrimal secretion as only one aspect of a general body reaction in which the whole glandular system is stimulated, causing the secretion of fluids. This is supported by Wolff (1953), who says responses to stress include nonspecific organ reactions which are always the same in all organs— swelling, hyperemia, hypersecretion, and hypermotility.

Physiological Aspects of Crying

In the general reaction of crying there are many associated somatic manifestations, such as vocalization, sobbing, and lump in the throat. There are physiological changes, such as gross alterations in body posture and behavioral reactions. Changes in respiration include sudden jerky inspiratory movements with prolonged expirations and some degree of glottic spasm. Darwin (1873) describes accurately the facial motions of crying, including involvement of facial muscles, tongue, and lips. He suggests that the eyes close to prevent congestion caused by the increased pressure on the eye during crying. He concludes erroneously that tears are secreted primarily because of the contraction of the muscles around the eye.

Tears are secreted by the lacrimal gland and the accessory lacrimal glands. The hypothalamus is considered the center for psychogenic stimulation of tears, but many place the psychogenic crying center in the limbic lobe. The fifth cranial nerve carries the afferent fibers to the lacrimal gland and the seventh nerve the efferent fibers by way of the greater superficial petrosal nerve and the sphenopalatine ganglion. Paralysis of the cervical sympathetic nerves causes an increase in tears whereas paralysis of the facial nerve, which carries the parasympathetic fibers, causes a suppression of tears, indicating a parasympathetic stimulation to lacrimation. Increased thyroid secretion produces a low threshold for tears, whereas atrophy of the thyroid gland, as in cretinism, is characterized by an absence of tears. This relationship of thyroid secretion to the production of tears suggests a general association of weeping to certain forms of somatic illness. An examination of the role of crying and weeping in respiratory and dermatological disturbances sheds additional light on this relationship.

Perhaps the most significant contribution was made by Kepecs et al. (1951a) when they showed the relationship between crying and exudation into the skin. Using cantharides blisters under hypnosis they demonstrated that inhibition of weeping is followed by a drop in the rate of exudation and later by a rise as the inhibition was continued. This is interpreted by the authors as indicating a tendency to break through the inhibition at the skin level, and they postulate that weeping is a function not only of the lacrimal glands but also of the skin.

In another study, Kepecs et al. (1951b) noted that in some patients under hypnosis weeping occurred only when a dermatitis was present; no weeping occurred when the skin was clear. They describe a patient in a post-partum psychosis who did much wailing and bawling but shed no tears during the study. There were no significant fluctuations in the blister fluid level. This suggests, they say, that a very deep repression of weeping, as in profound depression, will also operate at the blister level.

The physiological mechanism of urticaria is complex and not entirely known. It is essentially parasympathetic in mediation being relieved by adrenalin. Saul and Bernstein (1941) report the case of a woman with urticaria and its reciprocal relationship to weeping. When the patient wept she did not have urticaria, and the attacks usually terminated with weeping. Conversely, when she suppressed her weeping she developed urticaria.

Saul and Bernstein (1941) state that the weeping in urticaria is that of an angry cry, expressing dependent, aggressive conflicts. They feel that the psychodynamics of urticaria are related to those of asthma, in which an inhibited angry cry of frustrated dependency has also been postulated. Alexander and French (1941) point out that the purpose of crying is to retain the love of the mother and that its suppression leads to difficulties in respiration. Fenichel (1945) regarded the attack of asthma as the cry of longing for mother. Many have postulated that the asthma attack is a maladaptive form of the cry which was suppressed in childhood by negative reactions and punishment by the parents. The child then "chose" to express his pain in the abnormal response of the asthma attack. It is an important clinical observation that many asthma attacks terminate when crying begins (French, 1939).

Affects Expressed by Crying

What are the principal affects expressed during crying and weeping? It has been postulated that tears most easily result when fear, grief, and joy are brought into action. Among the Samoans the causes of crying that are mentioned are grief, pain, anger, and fear. The Samoan woman, how-

ever, cries principally from anger. Borquist (1906) says that
it seems likely that all painful states of mind, when the
intensity is great enough, normally express themselves in
crying.

The primary stimulus in crying in asthma and urticaria
seems to be the desire—expressed from a position of weakness, helplessness, and fatigue—to be reunited with a nurturing, succoring, comforting mother figure. This suggests that
the principal affects involved are sorrow and anger, sorrow
at loss of the love object and anger at being deprived of it.

What of the fear of not being reunited with the mother
figure? Except in children, fear alone does not seem to be a
principal affect expressed in crying. Adults, however, may
scream with fear, and this vocalization may be a carry-over
from the childhood cry in fear. Tears are usually not shed
during a fear state, but one often notes vomiting and incon-
tinence of urine and feces during intense fear reactions.
Weeping may follow termination of the fear, as relief is
experienced.

Is joy an important feeling expressed in crying or
weeping? According to Freycinet, tears are recognized
among the Sandwich Islanders as a sign of happiness
(Darwin, 1873). In the Kalevala we read of how the great
Finnish hero, Wainamoinen, who enchanted beasts, birds,
and fish, shed tears of gratitude following his wonderful
harp music (Jobes, 1961). Weiss (1952), however, feels that
the cry of joy at the happy ending is really a cry of sadness in
recognition of the former absence of happiness and that
joy per se is never the primary feeling expressed in crying.
This cry at the happy ending might also be viewed as a
cry of anger for past deprivation of joy, or a cry of sadness in recognition of previous joy that is long gone.
Tennyson beautifully expresses this interpretation of weeping:

Tears from the depths of some divine despair—
Rise to the heart and gather to the eyes
In gazing on the happy autumn fields—
In thinking of the days that are no more.

In the reaction of grief, the feelings expressed are primarily sorrow and anger. Mourning songs and lamentations, as already noted, express these same two affects. Elizabeth Barrett Browning says: "Tears are the silent language of grief." The role of crying in grief reactions is discussed by Bowlby (1960a, 1960b, 1961), who describes the reaction of a healthy child over six months when removed from its mother. Initially there is a phase of protest, with loud cries and violent behavior. This is replaced by the phase of despair, characterized by intermittent and monotonous wailing indicating a state of misery. He believes sorrow and anger to be nearly always present in mourning as a means of recovery of the lost love object. This dual reaction persists even into adult life, according to Bowlby. Weeping is a regressive phenomenon, recapturing the feelings of weakness and helplessness of the child as it calls out for aid and support.

Vocal productions such as talking, praying, and screaming are found to be effective devices in preventing the flow of tears. On the other hand, tears rarely prevent vocal expressions; rather, they often precede wailing, sobbing, and other vocalizations noted in the crying reaction. It seems, then, that tears are more often defended against than vocal expressions, indicating a difference in feeling about the two components, with perhaps a more negative attitude about weeping.

Perhaps this differentiation is related in some way to the function of crying as a communication of distress to others, imploring their aid. Grinker (1953) addresses himself to this problem by relating the aridity of the depressive to the crying but nonweeping infant, and contrasting them to the wetness of the psychosomatic patient. He concludes that the development of tears is related to the development of a differentiation of self and not-self. He postulates an intrinsic difference between the depressive and the psychosomatic patient in the meaning of crying and weeping.

DISCUSSION

Weeping is considered a regressive phenomenon, recapturing the feelings of helplessness and dependency experienced by the infant calling for mother to relieve his distress. The development of tears may be a link between the original reflex cry of the infant, conditioned to purposive behavior as a call for help, and the development of object relations leading to separation anxiety and grief reactions.

The ability to weep, then, might be related to the ability to conceptualize objects internally. Animals cannot conceptualize nor do they weep. If weeping functions to expel painful affects from the body, it might function also to expel the bad internalized object. Weeping may also be interpreted as a reaction to the loss of the object that was magically expelled by the individual's expression of anger. Weeping, being more expulsive and repelling than attracting, would be more likely to function as a call for help from within, and vocalization as a call for aid and support from without.

Utilizing the various avenues of approach, one may consider the nature of crying as follows. The lacrimal secretion in weeping may be viewed as only one aspect of a general body reaction in which the whole glandular system is stimulated, causing the secretion of fluids. This would be consistent with the Kepecs findings. What, then, is specific about lacrimal secretion? Why is it the principal secretion associated with crying? One explanation is that the body ego resides primarily in the face, and expression of affect is most appropriate in the facial area. Darwin's description of the involvement of the facial musculature in crying is pertinent here. It might be speculated that disorders in affectual expression find outlet in other areas of secretion, such as the skin or the respiratory tract.

Considering the discussion of the symbolic relationship of the body fluids and vocal productions may lead to the following kinds of questions. Of what significance is the inhibition or excessive stimulation of weeping in abnormal forms of expression such as "weeping dermatitis," urticaria, or enuresis? How important is the inhibition or stimulation of the vocal component of crying in such illnesses as asthma or speech disorders? In summary, does the prevention or excessive stimulation of the flow of tears or the vocal outcry, either consciously or unconsciously, lead to difficulties in expression of affect through other channels? These are important considerations in understanding the dynamics involved in the expression of affect in psychosomatic and emotional illness.

It would be of significant research value to study further the physiological correlates of weeping as well as the various ramifications of this universal reaction in terms of unconscious symbolization and concept formation. A thorough examination of "normal crying" is also indicated, as is a further study of the relationship of crying to the development of speech.

ON SARCASM

Joseph W. Slap

(1966)

There are people who employ sarcasm so habitually that they are referred to as chronically sarcastic. Sarcasm may occur in short verbal bursts or repetitive attacks or be a chronic mood state in which there is a definite "sarcastic" coloration to the entire personality.

What type of experiences induce this condition to play a part in an individual's life, and what are the mental processes underlying the state of sarcasm?

Sarcasm is a bitter, caustic, or stinging rebuke expressing contempt. It may be an inverted or ironical statement provoked by some offense or shortcoming, imagined or real, on the part of another person. Its intent is the destruction of the prestige and self-esteem of the object.

Slap's thesis is that sarcasm appears in those whose unconscious psychodynamics would make them prone to depressive illness. "It represents an oral-aggressive attack either on the frustrating object who witholds narcissistic supplies or on an envied rival who appears orally satiated."

The nuclear problem in these individuals arises from a failure of early gratification and satiation at the breast. Injury to self-esteem is equated with deprivation at the breast. When the depression-prone suffer an injury to their self-esteem or are otherwise frustrated in their need for external supplies, they react with oral rage. This rage is at times discharged as sarcasm. The oral rage, in turn, punishes *the disappointing object or deprives the envied rival of the good object through verbal assaults upon it.*

The author gives two clinical examples, one from a psychotic patient, the other from a neurotic patient in analysis. The neurotic patient suffered intensely because he was the youngest of three children born to parents who desired a female child. Unwanted by his mother, his early care was relegated to a nurse, in contrast to the favored parental care given to the other children. Against this backdrop of childhood rejection by his mother, he later continually interpreted his wife's actions and verbal comments as if they were both sarcastic and demeaning. His retaliatory rage was expressed covertly in dreams of oral aggression and more openly, in sarcastic replies, both in fantasy and reality.

Slap comments on the interesting relationship between sarcasm and satire. Satire is aggression much modified by ego activity, in contrast to sarcasm, which involves poorly neutralized primitive aggressive impulses.

Patients who are liable to depressive moods growing out of experiences of rejection often use sarcasm to express their anger toward those who have hurt them. Most of us have indulged in sarcasm on occasion and to a degree are sensitive to it. Yet it is the depression-prone who employ sarcasm so habitually as to be called sarcastic, and they are often the ones most vulnerable to it. Webster's *New International Dictionary* reveals that the word sarcasm is derived from the Greek *sarkazein*, meaning to tear flesh like dogs. It defines the word as "a keen or bitter taunt; a cutting gibe or rebuke"; as "the use of bitter, caustic, or stinging remarks expressing contempt, often by inverted or ironical statement, on the occasion of some offense of shortcoming, with intent to wound the feelings." Two elements stand out: first, the oral aggression, largely unconscious, but revealed in the derivation and in the use of the terms bitter, cutting, and contempt; and second, the intent to damage the self-esteem of the target or to lower his prestige in the eyes of others.

It is my thesis that the sarcastic trait appears in persons who have a tendency to become depressed. It represents an oral-aggressive attack either on the frustrating object who withholds narcissistic supplies or on an envied rival who appears orally satiated.

For example, an internist suggested to an analyst that he name his newly acquired sailboat the "Couch"; later he apologized for his sarcasm. He himself had been considering the purchase of a boat but had not done so. He envied the analyst, who seemed quite happy with his new possession. The aim of the gibe was to make fun of the article in which the analyst had made a narcissistic investment and to change the self-view of the analyst from that of a sporty yachtsman to a laughable stereotype. A colleague offered as an example of sarcasm an anecdote in which Lady Astor said if Winston Churchill were her husband, she would poison him. Churchill replied that if he were her husband, he would take poison. Churchill's remark changed the image of Lady Astor from that of a haughty aristocrat to one of an unbearable scold.

It is regularly observed that persons subject to depression have a fragile self-esteem which is dependent on the narcissistic supplies afforded by objects. According to Rado (1927b), "they have not attained to the level of independence where self-esteem has its foundation in the subject's own achievements and critical judgment. They have a sense of security and comfort only when they feel themselves loved, esteemed, supported and encouraged" (p. 422). As explained by Fenichel (1945),

The primitive methods of the regulation of self-esteem arise from the fact that the first longing for objects has the character of a longing for the removal of disturbing displeasure, and that the satisfaction by the object removes the object itself and revives the narcissistic state. The longing for the return of omnipotence and the longing for the removal of instinctual tension are not yet differentiated from each other. If one succeeds in getting rid of an unpleasant stimulus, one's self-esteem is again restored. The first supply of satisfaction from the external world, the supply of nourishment, is simultaneously the first regulator of self-esteem [p. 40].

Thus self-esteem and prestige are derivatives of the infantile experience of satiety at the breast, and in the unconscious they have the meaning of possession of the breast or its nourishing product. Injury to self-esteem is equated with deprivation of the breast. When the depression-prone suffer an injury to their self-esteem or are otherwise frustrated in their need for external supplies, they react with oral rage. This rage is at times discharged as sarcasm. The sarcastic attack is an attempt to punish the disappointing object (as in the Churchill anecdote) or is aimed at making the envied rival feel deprived of the good object (as in the sailboat example). In the unconscious this attack takes the form of a cannibalistic onslaught.

I shall offer two clinical fragments from patients in whom depression has been a feature. One is taken from a single interview with a psychotic patient and the other from an analysis. In each the patient, suffering from fragile self-esteem growing out of the maternal relationship which was experienced as being rejecting, reacted with, and had conflicts over, cannibalistic impulses directed to the mother.

A twenty-six-year-old married woman, diagnosed as schizoaffective schizophrenia, was interviewed before a small group of residents. She first asked for some coffee from a machine in the corridor, specifying it be black. Prior to this episode she had taken her coffee "loaded with cream and sugar." She also requested a cigarette which she smoked with protruded lips, evidently to keep it from touching her teeth. She was an only child. When she was three years old, her mother suffered a heart attack. The child felt the mother had become sick because the child was bad. She dreamed: Her mother was dead and she asked the mother to come back. The mother said, "Maybe, if you are good."

She had never forgotten the dream and it had troubled her all her life. She bitterly described her mother as over-critical, impossible to please, and the ruler over her father. An indication on the chart that there was some religious preoccupation prompted me to ask her about this. She said she had no problem with religion save that God expected perfection and that she, being only human, could not hope to satisfy Him. She then turned to her resident and asked for the return of her ground privileges. (She had been put in seclusion after attacking a nurse.) She unjustly characterized the resident as being cruel and punitive. When she was challenged on this and the question of her own responsibility was raised, she insisted it was up to the doctors who knew so much about mental illness and who had the power to cure their patients. These remarks were made with a straight face; and while I sensed discomfort at this overestimation of our powers, it did not occur to me that she was being sarcastic until Katan's (1959) elucidation of Schreber's sarcasm came to my mind.

I then asked her if I detected a note of sarcasm in her remarks. She smiled and said, "No, not sarcasm—gentle satire. As a child I once won a prize in an English contest for my light and gentle humor. Sarcasm is sick humor." I asked for an example of sick humor. She told us that when she was a teen-ager, late one Friday night, "when everyone could eat meat," there had been a torso murder in the neighborhood.

With a group of friends she had gone to see the body which had not yet been removed. Satisfied in its curiosity, the group retired to a hamburger place. When the food came, a boy "who has since died of cancer" said, "Goody, torso burgers!" The patient immediately ran to the ladies' room and threw up. She went on to tell how upset she was by the state's attempts to have the murderer executed. After all, he was crazy.

In this interview the patient brought out her conflicts with oral aggression. She made oral demands for the cigarette and coffee, which were unusual in this kind of interview, but in both instances there were manifestations of defense: the cigarette was not allowed to touch her teeth and the coffee was purged of its resemblance to mother's milk by removing the cream and sugar. She felt her mother was begrudging of love, warmth, and approval. Though she would sarcastically attack maternal and other authority figures, she specifically denied the use of sarcasm which she equated with cannibalistic attack. That she participated in such fantasy, however, is indicated by her vomiting and her identification with the torso murderer.

As shown in her dream, the patient dreaded the power of her destructive impulses as they might destroy the person on whom she depended. In truth she was not always able to control them, as witness her attack on the nurse. She used aggressive humor as a means of innocuous discharge, but made the distinction between sarcasm and satire; the former she treated as the naked instinctual urge, the latter as a considerably tamed derivative.

The second case involves a more mature personality. His problems with his mother involved phallic as well as oral drive development with considerable condensation of the derivatives. As a result of the defensive activity of the ego, the manifestations of his troublesome urges are more subtle.

A thirty-four-year-old accountant came into analysis because of a general sense of constriction and an anhedonia despite good health, financial security, an interesting position in which he won steady promotion, and a family consisting of an attractive, educated wife and two fine sons. He was the third of three sons and was born to his parents in their forties. The oldest son, sixteen years the patient's senior, was an exceptional student, first in his class in every school including medical school, and his mother's favorite. The second son, seven years older than the patient, was a fine athlete and a popular personality. When the mother's unplanned pregnancy was discovered, her physicians suggested a therapeutic abortion because of her age and physical condition. But she decided to have the child in the hope it would be a girl. She recovered from the delivery slowly while the child was handed into the care of a nurse who remained with the family until the patient was old enough to go to school. In his early years the patient suffered with eczema, asthma, hay fever, and mastoiditis, which often kept him indoors or in bed. He was also quite short. When he was five, he was sent to Florida with the nurse because of his respiratory troubles. He interpreted this as a further rejection by his mother and a deliberate move to keep him weak by separating him from his father and the athletic brother.

A prominent theme of his analysis was his anger at mother, who preferred "her son the doctor" and "her son the athlete." In the patient's mind she was antagonistic to his ambitions, which he expressed in Walter Mitty fantasies. In his adulthood this was played out with his wife and immediate superior at work in the roles of mother and scholar-brother. He would often interpret neutral remarks by his wife as being quite demeaning; until well into the analysis it was impossible for him to be assertive with her for fear of losing her love. If he felt rejected by her, he would develop separation anxiety and brooding, depressive moods. When disputes arose among relatives, he acted in such a way as to please the others without regard to his own convictions or convenience. In the analytic hours he was often witty in a satirical vein, but he could not use aggressive humor at home. While on the outside he appeared mild and compliant, his oral-aggressive impulses were manifested by his wit, nail-biting, and voracious style of eating. When he felt demeaned by his wife, he had a recurrent hypnagogic fantasy of gouging her with a huge "tusklike" penis. His affectionate name for his younger son, with whom he identified in his aggressive moods, was "tough tooth, the tiger." In sexual play he was disgusted by handling or sucking the breast. He had a similar aversion to juice-filled fruits, particularly tomatoes. He disliked the experience of biting through the firm skin and having the juice run into his mouth. He had the habit of picking his nose and ingesting the products.

His oral aggression also expressed itself in dreams. One evening the patient invited an out-of-town business consultant to his home for dinner. Both men were tired at the end of a long day. When the guest left, the patient's wife asked him what it was in their work that so took the life out of them. He experienced a momentary feeling of resentment, as though her question was intended to demean him, to imply he was a weakling. However, he gave her a highly logical and intellectual answer, taking into account the nature of the work, financial pressures, and office relationships. The sarcastic reply he was tempted to give was in the manifest content of the dream he had that night: "I was an elevator operator. There was a lot of debris around. A little girl was peering into an ashcan. I was explaining to her that this was the burnt debris of people and that we had a special conveyor for removing this debris. I was laughing at this evil joke."

He associated the Nazi extermination ovens to the burnt debris. To his wife's question, what took the life out of them at work, he would have liked to say, "Oh, we have ovens in which we cook our employees and a conveyor belt by which we remove them." In the dream he restores his self-esteem by representing himself as the adult in control and his wife-mother as a naïve child. While he had no associations to elevators at this time, they represented a penis in previous dreams. In life, when riding elevators, he compares his size with that of the other passengers.

The fantasy of cooking people and putting the ashes out with the trash is expressive of the patient's relationship with his mother. At the time of her terminal illness and death, which occurred during his analysis, he showed neither sorrow nor mourning, whereas he is a sentimental person and shed tears when he learned of the death of his childhood nurse. It was as if he had disposed of his mother a long time ago. A year later the patient arranged to go out to dinner with some friends the night prior to the unveiling of his mother's gravestone. He felt guilty over this pleasurable eating when he reflected that on the morrow the official mourning period would be over and "that would be the end of her." Afterwards he spoke of the ceremony as being "quick and dirty." This handling of the maternal introject is an instance of what Abraham (1924a) described in manic-depressives as psychosexual metabolism.

DISCUSSION

The psychotic patient called attention to a relationship between sarcasm and satire while the neurotic was often satirical in an amusing way. The terms have overlapping dictionary definitions but they are clearly not synonymous. Rather there seems to be a continuum, with sarcasm as an expression of unmodified oral-aggressive fantasies at one pole and satire as aggression much modified by ego activity at the other.

Sarcasm involves primitive aggressive impulses arising in a person who feels injured, deprived, or abased, and it seeks vengeance on those who are responsible. The sarcastic person is still needy, involved, and dependent on his objects. Satire differs from sarcasm in at least two respects: first, satire is a muffled attack and a display of cleverness. There is emphasis on the defensive activity and the talent of the ego at the expense of raw aggression. Second, satire gives the impression of a more or less independent attitude on the part of its user toward his object. One has the feeling that the satirical person has in the past suffered a traumatic disappointment but has at least partially overcome it and attained independence, albeit retaining an angry, rueful, or critical attitude toward his object. He seems to polish his target off as if he no longer requires it or has good expectations of it, and would not mind if it disappeared or if he lost its love forever. It may be pertinent that satire is derived from the Latin *satur*, meaning filled with food, sated.

Kris (1952a) has emphasized mastery as a precondition to the enjoyment of the comic. There are two forms of mastery which help account for our ability to enjoy satire. One is the mastery over the aggressive drives, the comfort one feels with instinctual pressures which are well within control. In this connection Greenacre (1955) writes of Lewis Carroll's struggles with oral rage: "In those individuals in whom these early months and years are particularly tormented ones, the vulnerability is greater and the work of restraint more intense. It is Carroll's supreme art that he furnishes an unconscious outlet through humor for exactly these primary destructive pressures without a provocation to action" (p. 257). However, she notes that not everyone can enjoy the Alice stories; for some they are disturbing.

The second form of mastery is over the object or at least over the dependency on the object. In the enjoyment of satire we re-experience the triumph over the object whom we need no longer. One less readily identifies with the sarcastic person because to do so requires regression to the point of feeling defective, deprived, and dependent.

The social phenomenology of sarcasm can perhaps now be more readily understood. Persons with problems over oral deprivation are most apt to use sarcasm; at the same time they are frequently most sensitive to it. Persons with humility tend to be insensitive to sarcasm although they can recognize and may resent the hostile intent. Arlow (1957) has written that smugness represents oral satiety with incorporation of the good object, and that smug people arouse considerable hostility in those who feel orally deprived. My observation is that this hostility is frequently discharged as sarcasm. The overbearing authority figure who gives little in the way of praise or other reward may arouse sarcasm, although because of his position the remarks are more likely to be made about him than to him.

Individuals with fragile self-esteem often mistake sincere praise for sarcasm (Levin, 1965), because they feel unworthy of good opinion or because they project their own aggressive impulses. Sarcasm is a tool of the weak because it is indirect and can sometimes pass for playfulness. At times the victim is taken in while others understand. The artful practitioner may leave his target in doubt as to whether the remarks are sincere or sarcastic.

Summary

Sarcasm when used so consistently as to constitute a trait appears in depression-prone individuals as an expression of oral rage directed at a frustrating object or an envied

rival who appears orally satiated. In the unconscious, sarcasm has the meaning of a cannibalistic attack. This is borne
out by the derivation of the word, its frequent characterization as bitter, biting and cutting, and by clinical examples.

ON VENGEANCE:
THE DESIRE TO "GET EVEN"

CHARLES W. SOCARIDES

(1966)

The conscious aim of vengeance is retribution, punishment, and a longed-for state of peace. The unconscious aim is to overcome and hide a disastrous damage to the ego, one that was experienced during the earliest years of life and revived in adulthood.

The aim of vengeful impulses is to destroy a formerly idealized internalized object who, once affording strength and pleasure, has now become persecutory. The successful projection of hate onto the external object makes it a target for destruction. In these individuals a superego figure onto whom strong envy has been projected is the most likely choice to become particularly persecutory and is experienced in the unconscious as one who interferes with thought processes of the patient and with every productive activity in which he engages, ultimately even with the sense of well-being and pleasure in living. This may well be the motivational force behind the enigmatic assassination of nationally loved and/or envied figures (e.g., the Kennedys). "The aim of vengeance is to destroy the envied superego figure conceived of in the unconscious as a depriving and persecutory force."

Of additional interest are contributions regarding the relationship between sexual passivity and vengeance, and

403

the observation that while the vengeful individual does not consciously experience guilt, unconsciously he suffers intense guilt feelings which remain in repression, or a severe depression would ensue. To differentiate paranoid individuals from those who are dominated by vengeful feelings is of crucial importance; the diagnosis will determine the prognosis, the likelihood of psychotic breakdown, and the potential for acting out of murderous impulses.

This paper presents various theoretical and clinical data concerning the affect of vengeance in order to develop further the psychoanalytic theory of affects. This study, beginning with genetic considerations, will be presented from the point of view of superego, ego, and id manifestations. It should be understood that superego, ego, and id expressions of this affect are in continual interplay, now one, now another, dominating the clinical picture and giving it a particular configuration.

Many vengeful patients suffer from a profound oral deprivation. Some patients, however, in direct contrast, speak of their earliest childhood with fondness and pleasure, though their happy, if not nearly idyllic, childhood memories concerning orality were only rarely borne out during analysis. Perhaps these two observations are not unrelated in their etiological significance. The originally deprived patient can no longer tolerate further deprivation; the originally satisfied (satiated) one is intolerant of any severe deprivation in adulthood. These two factors have also been alluded to by Fenichel (1945).

Curiously enough, vengeance—one of the most persistent and powerful emotions of man—has had little attention from scientific investigators. Much attention, however, has been given this state by poets, playwrights, and other artists.

Vengeance is a complex emotional state apparently derived from pain and rage secondary to loss. The usual response to suffering due to loss of a love object is sadness, grief, or depression. These feelings might also tend to provoke aggression, but sadness and depression do not primarily involve an aggressive conflict, either with external reality or endopsychically. Clinical observations suggest, according to Jacobson (1957b), that sadness predominates in depression only as long as the libidinal investment in the object world can be maintained by the veering away of aggression to the self. Angry or vengeful moods can be provoked by feelings other than hurt or disappointment. They may be precipitated by narcissistic conflicts, that is, from guilt conflicts or experiences of failure or faults, with resultant feelings of loss, where the self-directed aggression is secondarily turned toward the object world.

Surface manifestations of vengeance achieve almost a classic, unvarying pattern. The person is grudging, unforgiving, remorseless, ruthless, heartless, implacable, and inflexible. He lives for revenge with a single-mindedness of purpose. Passionately he moves toward punitive or retaliatory action—above all other desires is the one to "get even" (in effect, to get more than "even"). Whether he feels and acts from the conviction that he is engaged in "just retribution" or "malicious retaliation," the clinical picture is identical.

The pseudocourageous nature of those in a state of vengeance is strikingly evident in their seeking revenge against all odds and no matter the cost. Such an individual will not let the wrong done him go unpunished. Querulously he complains that he is no inferior to suffer the abuse of others. Transiently, the vengeful person may become aware of the irrationality and inappropriateness of his feelings and aims, but this awareness is quickly obscured by the overriding strength of the affect. He does not experience guilt. He shows no concern about the possible moral and social consequences of his act.

Vengeance is usually a private matter; exceptions are the vengeful acts of groups, e.g., vendettas, feuds, lynchings, retaliatory political or military acts solely for the sake of national pride. In group vengeance the affect may often persist beyond the span of a lifetime and be passed on to others (death pact).

At deeper psychological levels the self and the object world are changed, producing alterations in behavior, thinking, attitudes, values, expectations, and feeling tones. If the object of the avenger's wrath is not within his surveyance, an increase in the tension state may occur. He may imagine that new wrongs are being perpetrated against him. A similarity to the sensitive phases of paranoid development is obvious, although a paranoid condition may not occur. As in other intense affective states and moods, there is little possibility for an alteration of the environmental conditions with a resultant decrease in tension because the patient screens out all stimuli which contradict his emotional state. Vengeance is continually fed through imaginings and fantasies of the previous injuries dealt him. He then may unconsciously or consciously provoke acts inimical to his well-being, thereby proceeding to a state of "justified" vengeance. The avenger, furthermore, offers as undeniable proof of the wrong he has suffered his loneliness and the absence of all former pleasures. This is a consequence of his choosing to absent himself from congenial society until his aim of vengeance is achieved.

He is suffused with large amounts of instinctual energy predominantly aggressive in nature. In this respect there is a striking comparison between enthusiasm and vengeance. In the former the instinctual energies are primarily libidinal in nature (Greenson, 1962).

The conscious aim of vengeance is retribution, punishment, and a longed-for state of peace. One finds routinely, however, that the act itself is highly overdetermined. Unconsciously the aim of the vengeful individual is to hide a more disastrous damage to the ego, a damage experienced during the earliest years of life and underlying the specific injuries of which he complains. In this sense the act of revenge is a defense mechanism whose function is to conceal the deepest traumata of childhood. In psychoanalytic therapy, once the revenge motif is worked through, these primitive conflicts are revealed.

No introduction to the concept of vengeance could be made without citing a most revered reference from the Bible: "Vengeance is mine; I will repay, saith the Lord." This injunction, which appears in the New Testament, progressively developed from a harsh pre-Judaeo-Christian code—the *Lex Talionis* (An Eye for An Eye). Later we find in Chaucer, "Vengeance is not cured by another vengeance, nor wrong by another wrong"; from Bacon: "A man that studieth revenge keeps his own wounds green, which otherwise would heal and do well . . . as vindictive persons live the life of witches, who as they are mischievous, so end they unfortunate."

Genetic Considerations

Inasmuch as painful stimuli are ubiquitous in the early months and years of infancy, elucidation of specific factors producing the later-to-be avenger is precarious, difficult, and often problematical. Affective states and mood predispositions are determined by many factors, including the child's inherent drive potential, the depth and intensity of his object cathexes, and his inherent tendency to respond to frustration, or deprivation, with lesser or greater, rapidly passing, or more enduring ambivalence. The earliest libidinal or

aggressive reactions to specific objects may later be transferred from these experiences to all objects and experiences.
This produces a special coloration of the object world for the
child.

The genesis of vengeance is intimately related to the
origins of love and hate. "Love is derived from the capacity
of the ego to satisfy some of its instinctual impulses autoerotically by obtaining organ-pleasure. It is originally narcissistic, then passes over on to objects, which have been
incorporated into the extended ego, and expresses the motor
efforts of the ego towards these objects as sources of pleasure" (Freud, 1915a, p. 138).

Following this lead, the opposite condition applies to
rage, hate, and vengeance. These originate in the ego's
inability to satisfy the instincts autoerotically. The ego
therefore incorporates hateful internal objects. In love the
mode of striving of the ego is toward these objects as a
source of pleasure; in vengeance the striving of the ego is
against these objects as a source of pain, to insure their
destruction.

Freud (1915a) believed that love "becomes intimately
linked with the activity of the later sexual instincts and,
when these have been completely synthesized, coincides with
the sexual impulsion as a whole" (p. 138). The preliminary
stages of love reveal themselves as temporary sexual aims,
while the instincts are passing through their complicated
development. These aims are severely interfered with if there
is an admixture of rage and hate. Freud furthermore saw love
progressing through various phases of change in development; first, the phase of incorporation or devouring in which
love is compatible with the abolition of any separate existence on the part of the object and which he designated as
ambivalence. "At the higher stage of the pregenital sadistic-
anal organization, the striving for the object appears in the

form of an urge for mastery, to which injury or annihilation of the object is a matter of indifference" (Freud, 1915a, pp. 138-139). This preliminary stage of love was hardly to be distinguished from hate in its behavior toward the object and "not until the genital organization is established does love become the opposite of hate" (Freud, 1915a, p. 139). In effect, Freud felt that the relation of hate to objects was older than that of love and was derived from the primordial repudiation by the narcissistic ego of the external world whence flows the stream of stimuli. "As an expression of the reaction of unpleasure evoked by objects, it always remains in an intimate relation with the self-preservative instincts; so that sexual and ego-instincts can readily develop an antithesis which repeats that of love and hate" (Freud, 1915a, p. 139). When the sexual function is governed by the ego instincts, at the stage of the sadistic-anal organization, they impart a quality of hate to the instincts' aim as well.

The admixture of love and hate from which springs vengeance is to be traced to the "preliminary stages of loving which have not been wholly surmounted; it is also in part based on reactions of repudiation by the ego-instincts, which, in view of the frequent conflicts between the interests of the ego and those of love, can find grounds in real and contemporary motives" (Freud, 1915a, p. 139). In both cases, therefore, the admixture of hate may be traced to the source of self-preservative instinct. Furthermore, hate acquires an erotic character, and the continuity of the love relationship remains. In effect, ontogenetically, hate may be of earlier origin than love; the earliest conflicts of life are between the interests of the ego and loving objects outside of oneself.

The vengeful person unconsciously still desires to recapture the love object. Both love and vengeance are characterized by the tendency toward activity: in love, to secure the love object once again for pleasure; in vengeance, to secure the love object for the expression of hatred. The vengeful person, like the person in love, cannot rest without expressing this motoric aspect of his powerful affect.

In reconstructions from adult analyses vengeance was seen to originate in the survival of the retaliation wishes of the infant toward the mother for deprivation during the oral period, later reinforced by deprivations during the pre-oedipal and oedipal periods. The penis envy of women and the castration anxiety of men, including their retaliatory phallic passivity, had at their roots the earliest relationship to the mother and the destructive feelings allied with her. All phallic conflicts in these vengeful patients were based in the initial disturbance in the earliest object relationships.

In the earliest years of life the relationship of maternal goodness, patience, generosity, satisfaction, and the fantasies which accompany these early primitive conceptualizations enrich the child and become the foundation for hope, trust, belief in goodness and the future. Conversely, the aim of the vengeful, greedy, envious, jealous impulses is destructive introjection—not only to rob but to put bad parts of the self onto the hated object in order to spoil and destroy it. This has been previously described as the destructive aspect of projective identification starting from the beginning of life (Klein, 1932). (I doubt, however, that these complex *conceptual* psychic processes as described by M. Klein can exist at such an early age, i.e., three months.) Damaged fundamentally in the capacity to love, the vengeful person is unable to withstand future states of deprivation, and attacks individuals in the environment as if they were representations of the depriving breast, frustrating mother, absent father, lost penis.

It is well known that the introjection of the good mother becomes a source for the satisfactory construction of the good ego and later ego integration and object synthesis. If this is satisfactory, a strong ego is developed and the individual is able to identify with specific objects. Indiscriminate identification is characteristic of a weak ego and leads to confusion between self and object and a grave disturbance in object relations. This shifting from idealization to hatred due to the weakness of the ego aids in changing the formerly idealized person into that of a persecutor and in projecting onto him envy, greed, hostility, anger, and vengeful attitudes. He then becomes the despoiler of the avenger from whom the latter must exact revenge.

Individuals who are likely to become vengeful are often found to have defensively idealized their childhood. The underlying envy, greed, and tendency toward vengeance are split off but remain operative and are liable to disturb relationships in the future. These partial identifications allow the avenger to abstain from hateful actions and temporarily simulate good object relationships. Very often powerful and creative figures are identified with but are also envied. A superego figure onto whom strong envy has been projected is the most likely choice to become particularly persecutory and is experienced in the unconscious as one who interferes with thought processes of the patient and with every productive activity in which he engages, ultimately even with his sense of well-being and pleasure in living. This may be the motivational force behind the enigmatic assassination of nationally loved and envied figures whom the assassin did not know personally and against whom he had no actual grudge. The aim of vengeance is to destroy the envied superego figure conceived of in the unconscious as a depriving and persecutory force. The essence of the vengeful state of mind is to rob the loved object of what it possesses and spoil it. These possessions may be beauty, reputation, accomplishments, or even the object's very life (murder) or the assassin's life (suicide) if by so doing pain and harm could be inflicted.

Ordinarily during the oedipal period feelings of guilt and mourning are experienced and resolved. Whether this can be achieved depends largely on the emotions the child once felt toward his lost love object. Normally the gaining of new objects such as the father, siblings, and other compensations lessens the degree of hate and vengefulness toward the mother. The oedipal stage has a profound effect upon whether vengefulness or envy is to be reinforced or attenuated. During the oedipal period and the genital phase the change from all other desires to genital ones often decreases the importance of the mother as the source of all satisfaction. Hate may then be displaced onto the father or siblings. The girl may identify with the mother and the boy with the father, in which case a range of sublimations becomes possible and decreases the intensity of the affect of vengefulness.

Vengeance as an Expression of Id Drives

Crimes far in excess of any possible injury suffered by the criminal are commonplace. One need only turn to the pages of the daily press to find reports of violent acts carried out by those who consider themselves rising in justified retaliation to "get even." Most murders are termed "crimes of passion"—clinically, they represent an overwhelming breakthrough of id impulses and their vengeful expression. In a recent study nearly one third of psychiatrically hospitalized murderers were found to have suddenly expressed vengeance in a murderous act as the result of intolerable vengeful feelings secondary to ideas of morbid jealousy and infidelity (Lanzkron, 1963). It has been reported that twenty-nine percent of all homicides in the United States (of which there were over seven thousand in 1962) are directed against immediate family members, and nineteen percent of murders outside the family were identified as lovers' quarrels. This constitutes a total of forty-eight percent (Uniform Crime Reports, 1962).

Murder by groups is exemplified in the sacking of cities and even in organized society's demand for the death penalty in crimes where there has been no destruction of life. Sexual molestation of children is punishable by death or life imprisonment in more than half of the states in this country. Sadistic or sadomasochistic practices, whether sexual or nonsexual, carried out by groups or singly, contain unconsciously the affect of vengeance.

Often vengefulness undergoes displacement. For example, Don Juan, deserted by his mother in childhood, spent his entire life getting women to fall in love with him and then rejecting them. This was a simultaneous satisfaction of both aggressive and libidinal drives. Don Juan was afraid of being rejected; the women's love served as a reassuring counterphobic measure.

There are women who take revenge on men due to their infantile sadistic conception of sex and continually pay back ("get even") an old grudge against the male ("vengeance masked by love" [Menninger, 1959]). Many women so envy (often quite unconsciously) the man's possession of the penis that they may make every effort to make him unhappy in life.

In clinical practice one frequently sees a relationship between sexual passivity and vengeance. The vengeful person seeks to restore his identity and attempts to undo the damage done to his phallic integrity.

Patient A, after feeling rejected because of his girl-friend's critical attitude, dreamed: "I take a piece of wood out of my leg, throw it on the ground and stamp on it." This was an act of vengeance to deprive his lover of his penis since by often demeaning him she had forced him into the role of sexual passivity. In order to get even with her he punished her by punishing himself. At the same time he asserted himself actively by withholding and destroying his penis. As one might expect, he developed a severe potency disturbance.

In the above example three fundamental characteristics of vengeance are demonstrated: (1) a desperate attempt to forestall threats of castration and a loss of a sense of identity; (2) an attempt to ward off depression over loss or disappointment in love (or other severe disappointment); (3) a joining of superego and ego where the id is free and permits discharge of its drives into aggression. (The patient no longer passively endures his castration but actively induces it—simultaneously punishing his girlfriend—albeit in a self-defeating fashion.)

Myths, legends, and tales of vengeance usually involve the threatened castration of the later-to-be avenger. In Dumas' *The Count of Monte Cristo*, in addition to the hero's, Edmond's, incarceration, one of his persecutors seduced and married his betrothed. Edmond spent much of the later years of his life wreaking vengeance on all those who had attempted to destroy and castrate him. In the legend of Helen of Troy, Helen was stolen from the Greeks by the Trojans. Quite possibly the Greeks felt this was a national "castration"—the result of her abduction was a protracted war.

The affect of vengeance, however, does not require heroic themes. The most common precipitating situation is that of rejection or abandonment in a love relationship. The disappointed one may at first become depressed, masochistic, or suicidal. He may make frantic attempts to become resigned to the loss of the loved one and begin to undergo the

normal process of loss and mourning. However, complications may occur. In some instances, he may still proclaim
his "love" and turn against others whom he imagines to have
robbed him of his love object. At other times, his aggression
may be directed toward her and he will begin to seek vengeance against her. This condition leads to a spiraling
downhill development. Although the revenger does not
acknowledge it, in actuality he no longer can regain the lost
love object and his previous relationship with her; he is
dominated by his wish to reform and regain her through
punishment. His own suffering increases with each attempt
at vengeance.

In addition to investigating the origins of love and hate,
Freud devoted considerable attention to the problem of the
transformation of love into hate. I have found only one
reference to vengeance or revenge in Freud's writings, although hate, aggression, and sadism are frequently mentioned. This reference is in connection with the development
of depression. A study of his ideas on depression and
revenge sheds further light on the problem: "In both disorders [depression and obsessional neuroses] the patients
usually still succeed, by the circuitous path of self-punishment, in taking *revenge* on the original object and in tormenting their loved one through their illness, having
resorted to it in order to avoid the need to express their
hostility to him openly" (Freud, 1917, p. 251; my italics).

In "The Ego and the Id" Freud (1923) stated that clinical
observation showed that love is very often accompanied by
hate, that hate is frequently a forerunner of love, and that in
many circumstances hate changes into love and love into
hate. Of course, someone may first love and then hate the
same person without extracting vengeance. Other individuals, however, may be changed into persecutors and
express aggressive and often dangerous impulses toward the

formerly loved object. In the latter condition Freud assumes that there is no alteration in the behavior of the object which plays a part in this, but there is, on the other hand, an "ambivalent attitude . . . from the outset and the transformation is effected by means of a reactive displacement of cathexis, energy being withdrawn from the erotic impulse and added to the hostile one" (Freud, 1923, pp. 43-44). This is a displaceable energy which is in itself neutral but is able to join forces either with an erotic or with a destructive impulse.

Freud, through his analysis of the obsessional neurosis, indirectly supplied us with a significant insight into a mechanism in vengeance. In obsessional neuroses, "what guarantees the safety of the ego is the fact that the object has been retained. . . . through a regression to the pre-genital organization . . . the love-impulses . . . transform themselves into impulses of aggression against the object" (Freud, 1923, p. 53). In contrast, in depression, the object has been lost and the destructive component has entrenched itself in the superego and turned against the ego: ". . . the love for the object— . . . which cannot be given up though the object itself is given up—takes refuge in narcissistic identification, then the hate comes into operation on this substitutive object, abusing it, debasing it, making it suffer and deriving sadistic satisfaction from its suffering" (Freud, 1917, p. 251). There has been a turning around upon the self.

The development of vengeful feelings from an antecedent love relationship is dependent on the following factors: (1) an ambivalent attitude from the outset—a mixture of love and hate; (2) withdrawal of energy from erotic impulses which is then used to supplement the hostile energies of the avenger; (3) a regression to pregenital organization; (4) an insuring of the safety of the ego in that the love object is retained.

Above all, in vengeance an attempt is made to: (1) provide for the safety of the ego; the self is not blamed as commonly seen in depression; (2); the superego is not invaded by destructive components which would rage against the ego; (3) in place of the latter, love impulses are transformed into impulses of aggression directed against the object secondary to the regression which the patient has undergone.

A vivid example of the transformation of love into hate and vengeful violence was presented in a recent news story concerning a former Hungarian Freedom Fighter, later a physician in the United States. Upon learning of the infidelities of his wife, he poured acid over her body, especially her face, to exact vengeance and because he "loved her" and wanted to "save her" from doing harm to herself by future infidelities.

VENGEANCE AND EGO OPERATIONS

In the act of revenge the wish is for acknowledgment of one's power, superiority, rights, and judgment. The avenger hopes thereby to regain strength and his former sense of identity. Also, through the bond of hate and vengeance a replacement of the previous libidinal bond has occurred. The patient may then succeed in avoiding anxiety, which would otherwise have resulted from the complete loss of any bond with the love object.

In addition, the avenger prefers to experience rage and hate rather than fear. This is commonly seen in those who once felt forced into sexual passivity; in the unconscious this was tantamount to a self-castration. In attempting to reduce castration anxiety these individuals may be driven to destroy the love object.

The avenger often has considered himself to be a male without any phallic deficiency in adult life. In certain circumstances he may suddenly be threatened by loss of this self-image, loss of the love object, financial distress, etc. Resorting to vengefulness is a startling proof, however, of his unconscious infantile fears, his castration anxiety, his feelings of inferiority and smallness. In adult life, the initial infantile aggression becomes manifest instead of the deeper underlying castration fear. Typically, such persons have developed a defensive screening out of their fear and have imagined themselves to be the proud possessors of a large phallus, the favorite child, loved and admired. This response to the adult frustration contradicts these earlier infantile convictions. This mechanism, which consists essentially of attempting to deny the wrong that was done to him in childhood, does not sustain him for long. It is a form of temporary denial which may involve depressive and repressive mechanisms, during which time he may feel that he has not been truly injured or harmed by the neglect and lack of love in his family. However, he may suddenly find that he reverts to overt expression of rage and vengeance through displacement and reaction formations. Vengeance may then be expressed through a vivid acting out.

Patient B, a successful young attorney, had been severely neglected by his mother and left to the care of nursemaids. Consciously, he never complained of his mother's complete indifference to him as a child. When his girlfriend begged him to marry her, he rejected her because she was of a different faith. Her response was to turn her back and to close the door. A few hours later the patient presented himself at the door, bleeding from self-inflicted razor wounds and smeared with dirt. He thereby demonstrated to his girlfriend (mother) her bad treatment of him when he was a child.

The ego may disguise vengeance as (1) moral masochism; (2) pathological jealousy; (3) acts of "justified" aggression (either toward the actual victim or toward others); (4) reaction formations such as excessive pity, sympathy, benevolence.

An identification with the one who has damaged him may take place. The threatened loss of his identity forces the avenger to behave as he believes the other one behaved toward him. For example, the avenger may engage in promiscuity, lying, or deceitfulness "in response" to the lying, deceitfulness, or promiscuity of the person who wronged him. This identification with the aggressor increases the feeling of loss of self but at the same time allows for aggressive discharge. The avenger's search for self-esteem and identity is doomed to failure even if he carries his aims to completion since the difficulty lies within himself.

Vengeance may flourish in the soil of masochism. The great lengths a person may go to in order to wreak vengeance may be masochistic in themselves, and he may become depleted morally, socially, and financially.

Patient C, a twenty-six-year-old homosexual man, separated from his wife, of definite aesthetic and artistic talent, was destructive in his work, sexual, and social relationships whenever anyone began to be "nice" to him, thoughtful, considerate, or favor him. When a business partnership began to become successful, it would lead to his turning his "vitriol" on his partner and finally estranging him. He did not "trust" the friendship, which meant that he would not expose himself to the possibility of deep disappointment and hurt, the loss of ego and identity, which he had experienced at the hands of his mother in early childhood. His father had been forced to leave the family due to his mother's acrimonious attacks when the patient was only one year of age. The patient had "vowed" vengeance against the submission of his ego to the mother's domination. In summary, the loss of his father and the presence of his tyrannical, nonloving, depriving, "crushing" mother led to a loss of ego identity, a loss of his penis, and intense feelings of smallness. In his late teens this developed into a wish to gain love and affection and a penis through the identification during sexual intercourse with his partner's penis. He also experienced vengeful homicidal impulses toward both male and female. He often told the analyst: "Out of the blue I have the thought I'd like to kill you."

To control his homosexual impulses and his aggressive drives he adopted a masochistic position which kept him bereft of power, success, and satisfaction. This masochistic position warded off murderous impulses—the choice of the lesser evil. However, in his masochism one could easily discern an expression of vengeance and his frantic attempts to control it. At the same time that he assumed the role of the helpless, suffering, weak individual, he said: "I shall not cooperate with you; I am stronger and bigger than all of you; I don't need my 'nothing' job; I do not have to rely on my wife, need no friends, I am invincible."

It became clear during the analysis that he could wreak vengeance on his mother, who constantly told him how good she was to him despite his father's desertion, through demonstrating to her his complete failure in life. He would take vengeance on the analyst by walking out during sessions and by not getting well.

The affect of vengeance was unconscious for many months in this patient. When the vengeance motif was interpreted, he finally discovered that "I have been so consumed with revenge—makes an awful lot of sense to me. It keeps popping up in my mind. For example, I feel so vengeful toward my wife. I hope her new play fails, that she never remarries and that she never has the children she wants so much. It's like 'Take that—and that—ha ha!' It's so childish. It's not clear hate. It's like when you think, 'I hope you don't have a baby, ha ha!' It's the kind of hate children feel. If I succeed in vengeance, it's a pathetic aloneness I feel, all love is just dead. It makes me feel a little bit like a baby, like I want to cry, ask forgiveness, a hollow triumph. It destroys me—I've done it to you, mother, wife, and I feel a murderous elation, but then I feel a loss of all love and the bottom falls out. I give nothing, I get nothing, I go nowhere, I might as well kill myself, might as well. . . . My complete revenge would lead to a hollow triumph—yes, then I wouldn't want to go to bed with my wife after that. I'd just want to shake. Even if I killed her, what good does it do me to kill her?

"Sometimes I feel like killing my mother and now like killing my wife. I'll kill her, kill her, and then I'll kill myself. I'll zip all the skin off her. But I can't kill her even though I don't like anyone. My mother indirectly made me lose my father and when I see that scene from my childhood with his ripping her hair, she seems to me to be the bad one and I feel guilty for that feeling. She's the horror. When he's ripping her hair, I feel that if I were older and I let out what I really felt when I was three, I would have cheered him on. You remember the time I attacked her and was sent to Bellvue—I stopped and the bottom dropped out. I felt completely destroyed. This way I would like to punish my wife, too. But if I did, I would get nothing but my vengeance. I go nowhere, I might as well kill myself. I think I want to show them both how I have been mistreated, first as a child and now by her. When I become masochistic, not only do I prevent myself from being destructive toward them but I have found out that I can even sustain stronger hate the more masochistic I stay. It keeps the hate good and strong, it feeds it."

Very often the hero—the one exalted in life and in literature—may represent a reaction formation to feelings of vengefulness due to childhood fears and inferiorities.

Through counterphobic measures the hero performs unnecessary and dangerous feats which will ensure him against
castration. He thereby denies his fear of castration and
attempts to compensate for it. If never defeated, he may,
indeed, remain a hero. The avenger, in contrast, denies the
fact that he has *already* been castrated; he must therefore
force his castrators to reinvest him with power and strength
and return his lost phallus. Revenge, however, is never
completely satisfying. No matter the punishment meted out
to his enemies, the unconscious castration, the loss of
identity, persists and cannot be erased from memory. Patient
C voices the futility of wreaking complete vengeance on his
rejecting mother and wife.

Vengeance as an Expression of Superego Conflict

In the vengeful act the apparent absence of the restraining mechanism of conscience and the conscious absence of guilt is a striking phenomenon. The most violent
crimes may be committed and sadistic practices carried out;
instead of a reduction in the feeling of moral pride there very
well may be an increase in the sense of self-esteem. The
avenger attempts to masquerade as his victim's superego.

Punishing the victim may also be due to the displacement of guilt and finding a scapegoat, as Loewenstein (1951)
described in *Christians and Jews*. In the latter connection,
mass vengeance, whether against the Jew, black, or other
minority, may allow for the temporary lowering of superego
barriers in order to fulfill the oedipal wishes against the
father in the presence of the group (sharing the guilt mechanism). Such acts upon a helpless minority may provoke
retaliation, which is then used by the avengers to justify their
own course. In this fashion one also escapes superego guilt.
In vengeance, conscious superego guilt is absent and in-

stinctual aims, especially those of aggression, are paramount. This is in contrast to states of boredom (Greenson,
1953) in which instinctual aims and objects are repressed
because of guilt. In the final analysis, one gains the distinct
impression that the demands of the superego are partially
met through the punishment of someone else—the imagined
offender. This might be termed a hypocritical distortion of
the superego (de Forest, 1950). Unconsciously, however, the
vengeful person suffers intense guilt feelings which must stay
in repression or a severe depression ensues. In effect, he
protests: "It is not I who has destroyed the good breast
(mother)—it is she." Nonetheless, there remains the deeply
repressed conviction that this childhood happening is the
result of one's own bitterly resentful and destructive impulses toward good objects (satisfactions) (Klein, 1957). The
resultant guilt induces a need for self-punishment usually
expressed as a decreased evaluation of self and a renewed
projection of blame.

Although a seeming overvaluation of the self frequently
characterizes the avenger, the underlying diminution of self-
esteem leads to his withdrawal, both physical and mental,
from all former pursuits. A middle-aged storekeeper, cheated
out of his business by a partner, instead of expressing his
murderous vengefulness and attacking his former associate,
became depressed and extremely self-depreciatory.

Vengeance bears certain similarities to paranoid conditions. Like vengeance, in paranoia there is a superego
regression (Hesselbach, 1962) and guilt projection. In both,
the projection of guilt onto others is to create a superego for
the other supposedly guilty party and to mete out punishment. Vengeance, therefore, as well as paranoia, sets up an
alter superego against which the unconscious superego of the
patient may wage its tyranny.

The diagnostic difference reveals itself in the following

factors. (1) In the paranoiac there is a psychotic elaboration of the injuries perpetrated against the patient; the vengeful patient shows no such dereistic thinking, although he bitterly complains of damage done him. (2) Whereas the vengeful patient may suddenly erupt in violent action, upon its consummation he is almost always aware of its inappropriateness, although he both lacked this awareness before the act and was unable to inhibit his action; the paranoiac continues in his unreal thinking. (3) A study of the premorbid personality is of crucial significance diagnostically. (4) In the paranoiac there is a denial of reality: "I don't hate him; he hates me." The aim of the vengeful act is not only to punish his victim but to elicit from him the admission: "I'm sorry I did it to you; you are superior, more powerful, and I bow to your judgment and decision."

Viewing superego functioning in its broadest conceptualization, not only is vengefulness to be eschewed but its opposite, forgiveness, cultivated. Forgiveness *releases* the individual from superego bondage. It is the only relief from the burden of contriving and acting out multiple painful intrapsychic mechanisms which the condition imposes. Freed from this painful affect, new love relationships may be possible and the individual's instinctual energies are again made available for useful and constructive aims. A true victory lies not in vengeance but in overcoming the infantile damage done to the ego and constructing a more stable and mature ego based on reality and able to endure its disappointments.

One cannot, of course, expect a vengeful patient to divest himself readily of so meaningful an affect which has so overwhelmingly pervaded his psyche. To make this change the patient must perceive the true nature of both vengeance (including its infantile origin) and forgiveness—and the privation or enrichment which, respectively, inevitably follow. The primitiveness of the affect of vengeance severely blocks the total ego development of the individual and deprives him of any pleasurable adaptation.

Summary

The genetic forerunners of vengeance are found in the earliest object relationships. Initial disturbances due to oral frustrations result in the ego's inability to satisfy the instincts autoerotically and in an incorporation of hateful internal objects.

In contrast to love, in which the mode of striving of the ego is toward objects as a source of pleasure, in vengeance the striving of the ego is against these objects as a source of pain to ensure their destruction.

The aim of vengeful impulses is not only destructive introjection, but to put hated parts of the self onto the hated object in order to spoil and destroy it. Even spoiling of the self may be resorted to in the hope that it will result in the object's pain and suffering. Envied superego figures, e.g., national leaders, conceived of in the unconscious as depriving and persecutory, often become the target for vengeful individuals.

Severely damaged in the capacity to love, the vengeful person reacts to life's losses and disappointments as if they were representatives of the depriving breast and mother. Infantile retaliatory impulses are reinforced by later deprivations of the preoedipal and oedipal periods. Superego, ego, and id manifestations of vengeance are described along with the underlying psychic mechanisms.

Vengefulness consistitutes an effort to express and forcibly secure instinctual needs, to assuage guilt, to relieve fear and aggression. With the infantile origin of vengeance exposed, the ego is strengthened to deal more effectively with reality pursuits.

ON GLOATING

ROY WHITMAN AND JAMES ALEXANDER

(1968)

In a biographical note to this editor, Dr. Whitman remarks that this joint study was in part an outgrowth of his long-standing interest in sports and the psychology of sports. Gloating is one of the "difficult feelings that winners have to deal with," for gloaters are "sore winners" in contrast to the usual "sore losers." Whitman has also written on humiliation and chagrin, feelings that accompany the experience of losing in its widest sense.

Gloating is an affective expression of the satisfaction of vengeful feelings, a sadistic enjoyment of someone else's discomfort, injury, and defeat. There is an intense oral savoring of the hated object, of the envied object's suffering. This savoring experienced by the gloater as a well-deserved self-vindication simultaneously functions as a self-enhancement. Descriptively, the diametric opposite of gloating is sympathy.

Fleeting periods or low intensities of certain affective experiences might be considered normal. Gloating, a transitory experience, becomes pathological when it occurs chronically and/or produces changes in character structure or character traits. For example, gloating produces two effects on behavior. The less frequent is that of an "obviously courteous, seemingly polite but in fact suavely mocking" person. The second, more common type, is an

427

individual in whom one perceives a look of smiling scorn, of malignant satisfaction—"an orallike drinking in with the eyes the suffering of the defeated object." In chronic "gloaters" one may analytically discover superego defects which are responsible for the failure of the ego to neutralize aggressive drives. The authors use the term "superego bribery," meaning that a person may consciously and/or unconsciously devise situations wherein he is subjected to humiliating or shameful experiences at the hands of others so that he can later engage in gloating retaliation free from the restraints of conscience and of guilt. In most people, the desire to gloat may produce such intense conflict that the wish may be completely unconscious, revealing its presence only in dreams.

In all four of the clinical examples given, the authors' patients had experienced envious relationships with younger siblings who had in fact been far more successful in later life. Preliminary to this, however, they had all suffered from oedipal conflicts in which a rival parent enjoyed the child's defeat. In other words, the parent gloated. This led to bitterness in the child, a wish to avenge himself on the parent and "revel in it." Ultimately, gloating was displaced onto other rivals or became a strong emotional contaminant in relations with the opposite sex.

The feeling of gloating is an affect that has not, to our knowledge, previously been studied psychoanalytically. Like many other affects, gloating is particularly closely related to the oral-erotogenic zone. Envy, greed, bitterness (Alexander, 1960), and smugness are examples of affects intimately related to the mouth. Gloating is an affective expression of the satisfaction of vengeful feelings. It is the sadistic enjoyment of someone else's discomfiture, their injury, defeat, and being discredited. Gloating is the opposite of sympathy.

The German term for gloating would be *Schadenfreude.* There is an intense oral savoring of the hated, envied object's suffering which is felt by the gloater as well-deserved self-vindication and self-enhancement.

BEHAVIORAL ASPECTS

Gloating has two characteristic effects on behavior. The less frequent of the two common behavioral patterns is one of an obviously courteous, seeming politeness, but, in fact, suavely mocking. The more common pattern is undisguisedly visual, an orallike drinking in with the eyes the suffering of the defeated object. If in this pattern of gloating the gloater speaks, his voice will be charged with an excitement of almost orgastic proportions. The voice will be charged with intonations of malicious satisfaction in which there are strong undertones of gleeful exultation.

More transient states of gloating known to all of us may be fleetingly expressed by the flicker of a smile which is immediately quelled. The tripping and falling of even the closest friend often produces a rapid smile which is even more rapidly covered up. The essential comforting wish seems to be, "I'm glad it is he and not me." Gloating has the implication of a longer-lasting feeling state as implied by the words "gaze" and "dwell," in the dictionary definition. Nevertheless, the widespread nature of impulses to gloat suggest that it is closely related to survival mechanisms. In fact, the confusion between being glad that it was another soldier, not oneself, with the subsequent overwhelming guilt at such pleasure, is often a basic dynamic of war neuroses.

DYNAMIC AND STRUCTURAL ASPECTS

From the structural point of view, since gloating is an amalgam of libidinal and aggressive drives, it may be called sadistic. The erotic side of the sadism predominates. The overt expression of this sadism is dependent upon a dynamic interplay of the drives with the superego and ego ideal as mediated by the ego. The superego is either previously gratified or held in abeyance and does not forbid being unsportsmanlike in the cruel enjoyment of the defeat of an opponent. The ego ideal is involved too, in that the ideals of forgiveness, tenderness, compassion, etc., are insufficiently cathected. In this regard it is to be expected that certain cultures do not have such ideals and therefore that gloating is a socially sanctioned form of behaving.

The relative weakness of the superego and ego ideal permit the ego to enjoy the id demands for vengeance, in the fullest enjoyment thereof, in gloating. Some guilt feelings may also exist in the gloater, but bitter feelings over wounded pride and overweening envy are stronger than the guilt feelings and so, psychoeconomically, the gloating tendency prevails over compassionate tendencies. In persons with a chronic tendency to gloat, there are transient or permanent defects in the superego which have failed to help the ego with neutralization of aggressive drive energies.

But it is an infrequent thing to see a chronically gloating person. Rather, previous gratification of superego demands permit the gloating tendencies to emerge. In this respect, one would also expect that group phenomena, because of the superego-relieving effect of the group on the individual, might often lead to gloating situations. Such is often true, whether it is the victory of one college over another in football, or the victory of one country over another in war. In this regard, the relative restraint of Israel in engaging in a gloating response over the defeated Arab countries has been cause for much wonderment by the world. Possible explanations certainly include intense identifications with victimized people as well as the ego ideals of compassion and generosity in victory. Finally, there is the realistic wish to avoid retaliatory vengeance, since gloating and vengeance are often in a circular relationship between individuals and between groups.

Since superego lessening is a condition of gloating, there is the clear possibility of superego bribery taking place. Thus, if one has suffered, e.g., the psychology of the exception, he may enjoy revenge, and gloat without great inhibition. Shameful situations as well as painful ones may lessen positive, ego-ideal pressure by a similar mechanism. Sports again provide a useful behavioral-science laboratory. Severe defeat or humiliating setbacks may permit gloating following victory. The person may even set up situations where he is shamed or humiliated so that he can indulge in vengeance and gloating. The triumphant return to one's home town permits gloating as a compensation for the previous injuries received to one's narcissism.

Suicide fantasies permit gloating because they imply self-destruction and self-suffering first. Such suicidal fantasies are dominated affectively by gloating over the dismay, guilt, consternation, horror, grief, and shock the suicidal person expects his suicidal death to evoke in the survivors. Not only does the suicidal person gloat in anticipation of the pain the survivors will experience, but he fantasies that he will not be annihilated, but will continue to hover around in ghostly fashion to observe and savor gloatingly at how appalled the survivors are. Encountering such fantasies in some deeply depressed patients is probably an experience common to all analysts.

Finally, as we shall see in a later clinical example of the analyst's daughter, humbling of one person by another permits gloating because one was, after all, only an innocent bystander.

Often the superego and the ego ideal are only secon-

darily activated. Thus expression of gloating may secondarily produce remorse, which is an affect occurring after the
deed, as contrasted with guilt (Freud, 1930), which occurs
before or during the deed. Or it may produce secondary
shame and ensuing dissatisfaction with the self. A gloating
patient will typically say, "I could not resist rubbing it in:
now I wish I had." Sometimes the secondary shame is so
great that the person feels humiliation because of the naked
expression of his sadism and moves into the position of his
behavior becoming totally ego alien as described by the
negative ego ideal (Kaplan and Whitman, 1965). He has
become a despised person not only because of his inadequate response of compassion, but because he has indulged
in an inadmissible feeling. Again we must emphasize that
whenever there is a precondition to certain feelings and
behavior, this always contains the possibility of being
brought on more or less consciously by the person to permit
an emergence of the otherwise forbidden feeling. Thus the
competitor may fall way behind so that he then permits
himself to gloat over his "comeback" whether he is victorious or not. "I really came from behind to beat you!" he
may exult.

Another interesting dynamic seen clinically is the use of
masochistic identification as a denial of gloating. Thus the
person, in order to explain his smile of glee at another
person's misfortune, may claim that he suffered like the
other person because of his guilt over that person's pain. But
the smile is usually sadistic (and gloating) as well, and this is
usually less easily owned up to.

From a topographic point of view, there can be both
conscious and unconscious gloating. The examples of gloating in the dream described below, in terms of discomfiting
the analyst in the ward situation, was unconscious until the
meaning of the dream was worked out.

One aspect of the audience's laughter at the comic who falls about is the permissible gloating that may take place in this situation of clumsiness and failure. A pie-in-the-face type of clowning is the humiliation of another person (similar to excreta in the face and mouth) which is controlled and done purposefully with mitigated anger, and thus permits acceptable gloating in the perceiver.

GENETICS

Abraham (1924) described envy as an oral trait. In contrast to Klein (1957), who ascribed envy to the very first relationship of the infant to the breast, Abraham felt that the second, or oral-sadistic, stage of libidinal development lay behind envious hostility. Abraham also described generosity as an oral feature; and generosity and its corollary, magnanimity, can be seen as the antithesis of gloating.

Though they are often used interchangeably, there is some advantage in distinguishing between envy and jealousy. Envy is the hostile feeling that another is enjoying superiority, advantages, or success, that one would like to have oneself. The envious impulse is to take it away or spoil it. Klein emphasizes that envy implies the person's relationship with one person only, and goes back to the exclusive relationship with the mother and the mother's breasts in particular. Jealousy is based on envy, but implies a relation to at least two other people; love has been taken away from the subject by another person, love which was his due. In this respect, though both envy and jealousy may lead to vengeance and gloating, gloating is almost always a two-body situation wherein the presence of a third uninvolved person leads to shame and inhibition. Thus a jealous response may regress to an envious one and lead to vengeance and gloating.

A significant reference to pointing out the very primitive roots of jealousy is contained in Othello:

> But jealous souls will not be answer'd so;
> They are not ever jealous for the cause,
> But jealous for they are jealous; 'tis a monster
> Begot upon itself, born on itself.

The very envious person is insatiable because his envy stems from within and, therefore, always finds an object to focus on. Shakespeare uses jealousy interchangeably with envy and uses an oral metaphor to describe its effect:

> Oh beware my Lord of jealousy;
> It is the green-eyed monster which doth mock
> The meat it feeds on ...

Klein points out the similarity to the expression, "To bite the hand which feeds one," which she points out is synonymous with attacking the breast.

For purposes of our discussion on the genetics of gloating, this early insatiable envy leads to an insatiable desire for revenge. The source of this insatiable envy may not only be that the initial experiences with the mother and the mother's breast were frustrating, but the fantasy that another person experienced the relationship with the mother in a highly satisfactory way. In this situation both envy and jealousy are activated. These early factors give rise to the sources of envy in the oedipal situation as well as ongoing sibling rivalry and the conflict between the sexes.

In the positive oedipal conflict of the boy, he wishes to kill or castrate the envied, jealously hated father. In the positive oedipal conflict of the girl, she wishes to kill, humiliate, and displace the feared, hated, and envied mother. Not everyone ends up in his development especially prone to gloat, so some other ingredient in the oedipal conflict has to be present to produce the outcome of the gloating tendency. One oedipal complication which produces this result is the rival parent's too-intense enjoyment of the child's oedipal defeat, a parental gloating response which produces a narcissistic injury to the child. This produces bitterness in the child too great to become reconciled to the oedipal defeat. So the child continues to wish to revenge himself upon the rival parent and to feel like reveling in exacting vengeance upon the rival parent. This may subsequently be displaced upon any rival, though usually of the same sex.

In sibling rivalry, the child wishes to punish the envied sibling because of parental favoritism, real or imagined, toward the sibling, and to extract a savage gloating joy in punishing the hated, rival sibling. Anal-sadistic impulses to the rival, particularly by torturing him in withholding certain possessions, become prominent.

The conflict between the sexes provides many opportunities for gloating. Some women with never-quelled penis envy, and who as a consequence are filled with malice and castrative vengefulness toward men, gloat with immense satisfaction over the weaknesses and failures of men. Men who fear and despise women for being penisless gloat triumphantly over them for wanting a penis and being totally unable to get one.

Object Relations and Transference Aspects

The effect of gloating upon the object relationships of the gloater is of a damaging character. Gloating offends and repels. Gloating, being so completely inhumane, tends to evoke vengeful feelings in the object being gloated over, even in those with no very great tendency toward vengefulness. The truth in the saying that vengeance is sweet may be due to the experiencing of the affect of gloating. In vengeful fantasies, there are often found pregenital excretory elements, such as torturing the hated object with indignities like urinating upon it, forcing it to eat feces, etc. The importance of the oral aspects of gloating is exemplified by the expression "rubbing his face in it," or "rubbing one's nose in it." Some of the masochistic reverberations of these sadistic impulses can be found in the expression, a "shit-eating grin." Here the gloating is indicated by the grin, but the fantasied punishment visited on the hated rival is portrayed as taking place on the self. We have particularly been impressed by the anal-excremental attacks involved in gloating fantasies which are second in importance only to the oral components and are combined in the phrase "shit-eating."

As Socarides (1966) and Searles (1956) both emphasize in their papers on vengeance and vengefulness, there is a maintenance of an object relationship through these affects. In the process of gazing maliciously there is an ongoing object relationship, so that the affects of vengeance and gloating may serve to prevent the loss of the object and even regain it for further relationship. Furthermore, as Searles (1956) stressed, vengeance may be a method of defending against the affect of grief, which is then only experienced as the desire for revenge. Gloating also hides usually infantile painful narcissistic wounds where the gloater was once gloated over with consequent grief and humiliation.

One of the commonest considerations that inhibit women from gratifying their sexual wishes is the fear that the man will consider that he has made a fool of her, will laugh at her, will despise her, will, in fact, gloat over her. The basic elements of excretory control are relevant inasmuch as the woman feels that the man will mock her for losing control in a sexual way which has infantile sphincter references. Such an outcome of a sexual experience would be so humiliating that it understandably inhibits her. If it in fact happens, the narcissistic wound is so painful that she becomes very vengeful, and keenly desires an opportunity to avenge herself and then gloat over the offending male.

In relationship with the analyst, the patient may gloat over any of his failures, even if they lead to a masochistic triumph. Interpretations that miss the mark, slips of the tongue by the analyst, ability to momentarily jar the analyst from his analytic stance, etc., are all gloated over by these envious patients. An important aspect of this envious triumph is that it contributes to a negative therapeutic reaction. Failing to achieve any other triumph over the analyst, the patient may resort to getting sicker to discomfit and discredit the analyst, and then gloat over the analyst's inability to get him well.

A patient who seldom dreamt was being treated for a stubborn problem of impotence. He reported a dream after 355 hours of analysis:

CLINICAL EXAMPLE I

A ward doctor was helping me sit up in bed in a hospital ward. Everybody around was admiring the doctor for this. I suddenly realized that he was getting all the credit and I abruptly decided to slump back down again. I felt a malicious smile of satisfaction cross my face as I observed the doctor's bewilderment when he realized he could not cope with this turn of events.

FORMULATION

The strength of the patient's need to defeat the analyst and gloat over this defeat was unrecognized by the patient until the meaning of this dream was worked out.

COUNTERTRANSFERENCE

There is no question that gloating tends to produce a counterreaction of irritation, annoyance, and retaliation. Only by the analyst's being aware of his counterhostility to this affect can he prevent himself from responding in kind. Apparently something is touched off within the analyst that he finds distasteful and is completely opposed to his analytic stance of compassion. Despite such insight, however, we have found ourselves having quite negative feelings toward those of our patients who indulge in gloating.

The main countertransference response we have noted is a withholding. Thus, the patient who gloats is responded to by silence. More mature responses consist of a disarming openness. Thus, one patient gloated that the analyst has made a particularly revealing slip of the tongue. The analyst quietly remarked that he also had an unconscious and why was the patient so surprised to see it show itself? This undercut the patient's gloating, because for the gloating response to continue it must feed on the continuing discomfort of the object, whether that is real or fantasied. The analyst's response prevented the patient from indulging this fantasy further.

CLINICAL EXAMPLE II

An extremely competitive woman graduate student got great pleasure in seeing the analyst at a drugstore trying unsuccessfully to get his small daughter to leave with him. She felt enormously pleased at his discomfiture and silently cheered the little girl on in her defiance. In the following analytic session she verbalized these feelings and described how much she had savored them in the hours following the episode.

FORMULATION

This was related in the interview to her own anal stubbornness in relation to her parents. She had been given frequent enemas by her mother to release her "constipation." The analyst's little daughter did what she would have liked to do but only occasionally had dared. Also very pertinent in understanding this episode was the patient's competitive relationship with a younger brother who had been very defiant to the mother. She had both envied and depreciated his willfulness and "pushiness." Her enjoyment of seeing a male (the analyst) thwarted in getting his way was related to her retaliatory envious wishes that the brother get his "comeuppance."

CLINICAL EXAMPLE III

A young female patient had heard that the analyst was going to present a paper on tennis at the American Psychiatric Association meeting and had the following dream: Dr. R ran lightly to the stage across the seats of the auditorium, tripped, and fell flat on his face. She had an obvious feeling of delight in the dream.

FORMULATION

The patient related her envy of her brother and some of his success. She chose this particular form of failure because of the humorous outcome of a tennis winner were he to jump the net, trip, and fall. On a deep level, however, the smashing of the other person's face was highly significant, and related to her intense oral (later phallic) envy of her brother and her observation of his breast feeding.

This had clearly become a character trait in relationship to men when they became rivals of hers. She was highly gratified over their failure. This character trait had also become generalized to females, particularly those who were "favorites."

CLINICAL EXAMPLE IV

A thirty-three-year-old internist in private practice felt chronically envious of all his colleagues who were in academic medicine, or who published productively in medical journals. In the early part of his analysis he confessed that he .read the newspapers and particularly the obituary columns in order to find items about some of his many rivals which suggested failure or chronicled their deaths.

His total outlook toward people was so governed by his envy that, for example, in dining-room situations were somebody to spill some food on himself the patient would gain a malicious satisfaction from the former's discomfiture. One particularly striking example he gave was in a duplicate bridge tournament when he and his partner had doubled their opponents' contract and had set them seven tricks; he broke into an uncontrollable broad smile verging on laughter which he could not quell, and his symptom of gloating became highly uncomfortable to him as players from neighboring tables looked at him curiously.

FORMULATION

He had a younger brother who was far more successful than he and had been so from birth. Some of his earlier memories concerned his envy at his brother's breast feeding.

In the transference he constantly depreciated the analyst and dreamt of him as a younger brother figure. His life history was marred by repeated failures, which he brooded over and which exaggerated the narcissistic injuries he felt at the hands of younger, more successful men. It is also clear from this example that gloating, like many affects, can overwhelm the individual and produce a state that clinically looks almost hypomanic. Hitler dancing a jig upon the capture of Paris is a vivid illustration of this. Triumph may shade into gloating. Ezra Pound, after Churchill lost an election, wrote, "Oh, to be in England, now that Churchill's out!"

DISCUSSION

In all four of the clinical examples, the patients had experiences and envious relationships with a younger sibling who had, in fact, been more successful in many ways than they. This initial oral envy led to competitive feelings which were so intense that there was invariably malicious satisfaction at any failure by their rivals.

This gloating response led to secondary shame and remorse and occasional ensuing self-punishing behavior, which, however, was never sufficient to impede the gloating response. Gloating was inhibited only when the psychoanalytic process unearthed the roots of envy of the younger sibling. Eventually some of this envy could even be traced back to the original disappointment and frustration with the mother prior to the advent of the sibling and which made the sibling the source of the intense envy and jealousy.

Though we have not specifically discussed gloating under the heading of the economic factors, essentially it is a psychoeconomic problem. The desire for revenge and victory over the hated rival gets out of hand. In this regard this paper has a wider application than merely the description and elucidation of the dynamics and genetics of an emotion, important as the emotion may be. This importance derives from the unique failure of the human species to limit intraspecies aggression.

In his book *On Aggression*, Lorenz (1966) describes the various forms that members of the animal kingdom use to inhibit aggression. There is the well-known example of the wolf who turns his head away from his foe, offering him the vulnerable underside of the throat. The jackdaw holds the unprotected base of the skull under the beak of his aggressor, which is the very spot where an attack would be lethal. Lorenz comments that at first it looked to him as if the sole constituent of this submissive attitude was the presentation of the most vulnerable part. He later realized that this would be suicidal because of the fact that an animal at the height of its aggressiveness only gradually dissipates its aggression. He concludes, therefore, that the immediacy of the inhibition suggests a built-in mechanism of immediate effectiveness.

The human being has no such built-in mechanism for preventing the carrying through of a destructive act. This is one way of describing the serious threat of nuclear warfare to mankind, since a victor in a traditional way may not feel bound to inhibit the total destruction of his enemies.

Gloating, then, derived from excessive envy due to early deprivation experiences and not inhibited by the erection of superego and ego-ideal inhibitions, becomes a significant affect to examine. When the malevolence of the victor's pleasure is acted out rather than experienced, there is the opportunity for complete destruction of the enemy. Conversely, as we have described above, gloating is so damaging to the opponent's self-esteem that he may consequently nurse desires for total revenge in the future.

We come to several conclusions similar to those of Lorenz. Sublimating activities such as sports and/or a global activity such as the Olympics serve to dissipate aggressive envious behavior. In addition, gloating is specifically interdicted in sports, and it serves to vindicate further the ego ideal of magnanimity and generosity in victory as well as in defeat.

Summary

We have examined in some detail the affective state described as gloating. We have pointed out its oral roots in envy, which result in an erotized aggression and vengeance toward the vanquished enemy. We have described its role in psychoanalysis, in which it may lead to a negative therapeutic reaction and, finally, we have made some generalizations about the importance of such affects in the coping with aggression by all human beings.

PATHOLOGICAL JEALOUSY

PING-NIE PAO

(1969)

Pao's paper represents a high point of our psycho-analytic understanding of jealousy. During the course of the six-year analysis lucidly presented in this paper, the patient recovered completely from this torturous condition.

Although jealousy is a universal experience, the difference between normal and pathological jealousy may be likened to that between grief and melancholia. When pathological, it is a persistent ego state emerging from a variety of conflicts. Jealousy may be projected; it may be delusional; it may be pathological; and it may be normal (but by no means rational).

Pao's important contribution here is his delineation of the nature and meaning of the narcissistic predisposition (a narcissistic dependency combined with frustrated oral needs) which sets the stage for the later development of jealousy. When Pao's patient was avenged by the return of his wife who had previously been unfaithful, he developed striking fears of sexual diminution, jealousy, and regressive symptoms. What the patient feared above all was to be "second best," an experience he had undergone in early childhood. The mechanism of projection of his own infidelity upon the heterosexual partner played a relatively minor role compared to other important dynamic findings. Similarly, the role of unconscious homosexual impulses was of only minor significance.

That jealous patients suffer from a severe degree of psychic masochism is self-evident. Loewenstein (1957) noted that: "where jealousy of a younger brother ... played an essential role in the genesis of the patient's masochism, the masochistic desires would overwhelm the patient as soon as he began to imagine that his sexual partner preferred another man. He traced his masochistic wishes to a screen memory in which his mother took care of the preferred, one-year-old brother while he himself was lying very tightly swaddled in a crib, simultaneously enjoying this situation and suffering from it ..." (p. 203).

Jealousy, while ordinarily not delusional, may undergo psychotic elaboration. One of my patients, an involutional, melancholic male suffering from intense jealousy, continually searched for evidence of his wife's infidelity by examining her urinary products in the toilet bowl. Particular variations in smell and color were reacted to with delusional convictions that she had been with her lover only a few hours before. These intense emotional experiences often aroused this patient to sexual excitement. This extreme example highlights the common observation that jealousy may indeed function as the masochist's aphrodisiac.

Jealousy, according to Melanie Klein (1957), is greed stimulated by fear. She further comments that jealousy means that someone else has taken over or been given the good breast, which by right belongs to the individual: "Jealousy fears to lose what it has; envy is pain at seeing another have that which it wants for itself..." (p. 78). There is a close connection between jealousy, greed, and envy. The envious person is insatiable: "The envious man sickens at the height of enjoyment. He is easy only in the misery of *others. All endeavors to satisfy the envious man are thereby fruitless"* (Klein, 1957, pp. 7-8).

During an analysis of over six years' duration, it was possible to study in considerable detail the symptom of pathological jealousy, which at times assumed delusional proportions, in a man who otherwise showed no impairment of major ego functions, was able to carry on productive work without interruption, and who could undertake classical analysis without the use of parameters. This rare combination of an intact ego and the isolated but persistent symptom of pathological jealousy is unlike many cases reported in the literature in which the patients were either psychotic, or briefly studied, or the pathological jealousy was a transient symptom. In the analysis of this case, the original trauma that left an oral cast on his future personality development and that paved the way for the formation of his pathological jealousy could be reconstructed. It was therefore possible not only to confirm Riviere's (1932) and Fenichel's (1935) observations that oral fixations are important in the development of pathological jealousy, but also to augment the historical details about the origin of the fixation.

Freud first formulated the mechanism of pathological jealousy on the basis of Schreber's case in "Psycho-Analytic Notes on an Autobiographical Account of a Case of Paranoia" (1911b), and later elaborated on it in "Some Neurotic Mechanisms in Jealousy, Paranoia and Homosexuality" (1922). He distinguished between the projected and the delusional jealousies: "... *projected* jealousy is derived in both men and women either from their own actual unfaithfulness in real life or from impulses towards it which have succumbed to repression.... [The delusional jealousy] too has its origin in repressed impulses towards unfaithfulness;

but the object in these cases is of the same sex as the subject" (1922, pp. 224-225). He also made these penetrating observations: normal jealousy, although by no means rational, "is compounded of grief . . . and of the narcissistic wound, . . . further, of feelings of enmity against the successful rival, and of a greater or lesser amount of self-criticism which tries to hold the subject's own ego accountable for his loss. . . . [Jealousy] is a continuation of the earliest stirrings of a child's affective life, and it originates in the Oedipus or brother-and-sister complex of the first sexual period" (1922, p. 223).

Jones (1929b) agreed with Freud on projection and homosexuality. In the elaboration of Freud's thesis that jealousy is compounded of grief, hatred, and narcissistic wound, he made valuable contributions to the elucidation of the narcissistic dependency in the person predisposed to pathological jealousy. In Jones's view, narcissistic dependency results from guilt in oedipal situations; guilt leads to fear of the father and inversion; inversion leads to fear of the woman, from which flight and infidelity arise; the latter is projected in jealousy.

Brunswick (1929) described in detail her two-and-a-half-months' analysis of a case of delusional jealousy which supported her conclusions that the unconscious homosexuality was the cause of the illness of the woman patient, the homosexuality having its basis in the accidental attachment of the normal passivity of the small child to an object which happens to be feminine (though phallic), the striking point in this case being the entire absence of the Oedipus complex. The patient was fixed at a preoedipal level. It is obvious that Brunswick's work was handicapped by the fact that the patient was psychotic and the analytic work brief.

Riviere (1932) described the analysis of a transitory symptom of morbid jealousy which occurred during the course of her analysis of a woman patient. She noted that the patient's jealousy was associated with an unconscious fantasy which consisted of the impulse to seize and obtain from some other person something she greatly desired, thus robbing and despoiling him or her. The triangular situation included the patient and two other objects: the first was the object of her desire, whose possession meant her gratification; the other object was the person who suffered the robbery and spoilation. Riviere observed that the general explanation of the patient's jealousy as a projection of her infidelity was clearly insufficient, and she therefore offered the following interpretation for the relationship between flirtation and jealousy: in the jealousy mood, others were robbing the patient of everything, whereas in flirtation she was doing the same to all around her. Riviere was of the strong opinion that the origin of the fantasy was in the oral-erotic and oral-sadistic phase of development.

Fenichel's (1935) contribution can be viewed as a direct extension of Freud's and Jones's works. Elaborating also on narcissistic dependency as Jones did before him, Fenichel observed, however, that the narcissistic fixation, or a fixation on a primitive mechanism of regulation of self-regard, coincides with an oral fixation. Fenichel's conclusion is parallel to Riviere's, as he had also noted (despite their different theoretical orientations in regard to the concept of defense, the concept of superego, etc.).

Similarly, Chatterji (1948) concluded from his clinical material that the pathological jealousy is not one of a genital oedipal level but is of purely oral origin. However, Barag's (1949) report on her analytic work of less than a year with a case of pathological jealousy seemed to deviate from the above trend of investigation. Barag characterized her patient (a man) as remaining narcissistically fixated on the phallus: "He loves his wife narcissistically as he loves his penis. To the extent that she becomes, for him, his penis, he has a partial feminine identifcation. This phase [penis-mother identification] would be the transition in the development of the increasing hetero- or homosexual object choice" (Barag, 1949, pp. 10-11). At one point she spoke of the patient's "thieving" from mother but gave the impression that this "thievery" was in no way related to oral-sadistic drives. It is most unfortunate that Barag did not mention Riviere's or Fenichel's work. As a consequence, we are left to wonder if the oral material abounding in the presentation played any role in the symptoms of pathological jealousy.

Seidenberg (1952), like Barag, viewed the jealousy as a precipitate of oedipal struggle. Using as evidence the plots of two dramas as well as two clinical cases, Seidenberg stated that the castration fear implied in this wish must be responsible for the suffering and anxiety of the jealousy.

Clinical Material

R was referred for psychoanalysis because of his acute anxiety and depression, which were increasing and interfering with his work. An efficient corporation executive in his mid-thirties, he had been married for over ten years and had four children. About two months before beginning his psychoanalysis, his wife had informed him that she was in love with another man who happened to be his best friend. This took the patient completely by surprise; he had thought that their marriage was a good one, even though he never felt satisfied with his wife. The most upsetting aspect was that his best friend should do this to him. As the wife walked out of their home and bade him good-bye, the patient felt betrayed, humiliated, and bitter; he wanted to "tear down the pillars of the temple, to kill all the Philistines as Samson did." He must get revenge, he told himself again and again.

He decided on two courses of action: to make his friend cuckold, and to woo back his wife and then "dump" her as she did him. Step by step he carried out his plans. But when his wife returned home his desire for revenge had disappeared.

Following their sexual reunion, the patient became very self-conscious about the size of his penis and began to probe his wife about her experiences with her lover. Listening to her description he felt overwhelmingly jealous. Now he thought about his wife all the time. At work (he attended to his work perfunctorily) his thoughts would dwell on her eyes, her smiles, etc., which to him became perfect creations of nature, and he felt he could not wait to go home to embrace her. As soon as he got home he was troubled by the thought that she had a lover who was once his best friend. In order to assure himself that he meant more to her than her lover did, he pressed her to tell him all the details, without any omissions, of how she and her lover spent time together. If she refused to cooperate, he decided that she had secrets to hide from him and his jealousy was heightened. If she did cooperate, he would weigh carefully whether or not he was better than his wife's lover and whether or not she was more giving to him than to her lover; as a rule he could always find reasons to feel self-loathing and jealousy. On nights when his wife went to community functions he felt lost and compelled to spy on her to make sure that she was not meeting with her lover. He made mysterious phone calls to be sure she was at the destined place. When she returned he felt that she did not greet him warmly and seemed indifferent to the suffering he had just gone through. He felt jealous and suspicious. He would study the creases in her dress, stealthily examine her purse, the car, etc., to be sure there was no evidence of her meeting with her lover. To dispel his doubts he would then ask devious questions to get to the smallest detail about what she did and to whom she talked. His energy seemed indefatigable. When she felt exhausted, he decided that she was evasive.

Soon he hit upon an idea: "If she loves me, I need not be jealous. So let her prove to me she loves me." Thereafter he designed task after task for her to perform. Because of the nature of these tasks she could rarely have passed his test; for instance, he would suddenly issue an order forbidding her to do a chore which she had to attend to; he would ask her to undress when and where he wanted her to, disregarding the fact that she would then be exposing herself to their children; he would ask her to perform perverse acts which he knew she would not do. Even on those occasions when she did pass his test he was not satisfied, he would muse, "This task was too easy. I must try her with another one which is a bit more difficult." Thus he was compelled to design task after task and to ask her to perform them again and again.

At times, when feeling very tired and agonized by his own activities, he entertained the idea of getting far, far away. He thought: "My wife was the cause of the trouble. If only I get away from her I'll be all right." He would drive away, drink solitarily at different bars, feel lonely, and fantasy more satisfactory relations with girlfriends he had had in the distant past. As he turned his thoughts, as he invariably did, to recollections of unflattering experiences with them, he became disgusted with himself, wished that he was dead, and contemplated suicide. When he found himself dwelling on suicidal thoughts he became scornful of himself for being a coward and would then turn his thoughts toward his wife. Then he would worry that his wife might again turn to her lover. He had to rush home to "stop all the nonsense." Essentially he knew what he was doing was ridiculous, but he felt unable to stop. As time went on and he felt his misery getting more and more intolerable, he decided to seek relief through treatment.

The patient was in good contact with reality. Despite his current internal struggle, which resulted in increased use of alcohol, poor sleep, and generally depressed mood and appearance, he was working full time. "When I got into the swing of things I could do a good job." Being a voracious reader he was familiar with psychoanalysis.

His parents were living and well. His father was a self-made man, but despite his success in his business was hypochondriacal at home and always in the background of his excitable, suspicious, and demanding wife. R was the second of three brothers; the older brother was five years his senior (the mother had no pregnancies in these five years) and the other brother, thirteen months younger. Both brothers, as well as their families, were described as being free from neurotic problems.

R perceived himself as a complacent person. From the age of nine he enjoyed solitary reading more than anything else. Merely to prove that he "could too," he entered competition at times, especially when feeling challenged by the younger brother. He had won high academic degrees in his graduate and postgraduate work, and recognition in high school sports. During puberty he was acutely aware that he "did not belong," even though he always had friends; he was an intellectual, a highbrow, who had little in common with others. His experience with girls was satisfactory but he felt he never had enough of his share with the type of girls he coveted, those who were beautiful and popular.

Following graduation from college he married; his wife was beautiful but not very popular: "In fact, she was sort of alienated like myself." He admitted his ambivalence toward the marriage and gave the following reason: "I did not quite want to get married but I did not want to let go of her either. I didn't propose; she did." He described his ten years of marital life as being good, for his wife never complained, even though he did not feel satisfied with her. When she made a suicide attempt and subsequently asked to leave him, he was so shocked that he thought of treatment for her as well as for himself. Now he seemed to have "forgotten" the impact of these events. He said he loved his children but admitted that he had not been spending much time with them for the last three to four years, although he could not give any reason for his change of attitude.

At work, he felt "insignificant" even though he was actually highly respected for his knowledge of his own and the related fields. He was close to only a few of his colleagues with whom he could engage in intense intellectual arguments, which he would win. He related to his "best" friend, involved in the present crisis, in an entirely different fashion. They shared a common interest in ham radio, took trips together, and rarely argued competitively. Their relationship was an altogether congenial one. Above all, R admired this friend for his self-assurance, virility, and chivalrous ways with women. This friendship, which had begun about four years before, was not limited to the two men; their wives were also congenial.

Following the brief review of his background, the content of the hours in the next four months consisted essentially of his description of his feelings. When it was pointed out to him that his jealousy seemed to weld his wife, his friend, and himself together, he began to speak of his sadness for having lost his "good" woman, and for having lost his best friend. Some time later he began to experience anger. At first the anger was directed at himself for not watching his wife, not treating her better, etc., but later it was directed toward his wife, which she took without uttering a complaint. During these four months, although the patient seemed to put concerted effort into delimiting his conscious thoughts to a description of his various feelings and his recent interactions with his wife (including assignment of tasks, etc.) to substantiate his grief, his jealousy, or his rage, he freely associated and had many dreams. These free associations and dream associations revealed his preoccupation with the size of his genitalia, castration fears, maternal identification, and fear of this identification. Clearly the preoccupation earmarked the appearance of hitherto repressed oedipal fantasies.

At about the time the patient began his analysis, his wife also started analysis. In the fourth month of her analysis she decided she would not respond to her husband's incessant questioning about her relationship with her lover; in short, she struggled to discontinue the sadomasochistic relationship which had been established between them. This change on her part resulted in the patient's repeatedly dreaming of being murdered and subsequently in a brief paranoid reaction for which there was no need to introduce any parameter of treatment. He reported that he was being "investigated" at his work, and he was visibly panic-stricken. In reality, this investigation was an annual affair to which he had been subjected several times in previous years. Yet such knowledge did not allay his anxiety, for he felt there was something different this time. "The investigators were looking for something special," and therefore he had to look out. Thus when meeting with the investigators he was evasive and argumentative. This attitude of his had puzzled them and aroused their suspicions, resulting in an unnecessarily thorough and prolonged check. Interpretation of the "loss" of his wife dispelled the paranoid symptom. Instantly, however, he returned to various themes of jealousy. In the beginning, he had "controlled" the hours in such a way that he rarely allowed his analyst to complete a sentence. Despite interpretation of the defense, his "control" persisted. As a result the analyst's activity was, for a time, limited to saying "jealousy again."

R's associations can be exemplified by the following excerpt: "Last night we had blueberries for dessert. I asked my wife why she didn't serve blackberries; we had plenty of blackberries in the garden. I told her so many times that the grocery bill was exorbitant, that she was always exceeding the budget, and that she could save by serving the black-berries, cabbage, string beans, etc., which I planted in the garden. She said she would, but she bought the blueberries; she said the kids wanted blueberries. Maybe they did, but she should have carried out her promise to me. I don't know why I asked her to come home. Now I have a new problem, to send her away, to divorce her. I do not love her now. . . . I don't love my mother; I guess I never loved anyone." At this point he cleared his throat and went on. "It is not true. I loved my wife and I must still love her. This morning she said that tonight when I came home she would not be home, she would be downtown shopping and would come home later. I asked her if I could meet her somewhere. She said, 'It is not necessary.' I felt then that she was to meet some man . . . she could be stepping out on me again." From the association it was obvious that the thought of his offer to meet her downtown, which was to him an indication of his love for her, was used to obscure his fear that he was incapable of love. When his extreme effort to obscure whether he could or could not love was finally explained to him, he relaxed his "controlling."

In the subsequent months it was possible to note that jealousy consisted of two components: "I love her," and "Let her prove to me she loves me too." At first, he perceived that the component "I love her" was *ipso facto* one which no one, the patient himself least, should question: therefore, his primary concern was "Let her prove her love to me." It took some time for him to realize that "Let her prove to me" was merely a projection of his own feeling of incapacity for loving. He seemed to be saying, "It is not I who cannot love; it is you who does not love." When he did realize the purpose of the projection, he stopped "testing" his wife's love for him by assigning her tasks to perform.

Although he continued to function well at his work and did, in fact, receive promotions, his behavior in the sessions now became more regressive. Earlier in his accounts of the triangular situations, his wife was identified as the mother and the third person (her lover or her analyst) as the father. While included in the triangle, the patient found himself "standing outside looking in . . . to discern their interaction . . . to find out their secret." Now his wife was still identified as the mother, whereas the third person was the younger sibling. Thus, casting the analyst in the mother's role, he watched closely to see if the analyst was more attentive to him than to his other patients. Arriving for his hour early, and leaving late, he scanned other patients' emotional states when they left the analyst's office. One day when he observed a patient leaving the office laughing, he became very distressed, for he felt the analyst had never treated him so well as to make him feel so happy. On another day, when he left the office he encountered a new patient, a woman, and the complained bitterly in the next hour: "I can accept those I saw before; they must have started treatment before me. This face was new; she must be a new patient. I can't stand the thought of you having a new patient."

Subsequent associations and enactments in the transference led to clarification of the infantile composition of the triangle by the mother, R, and his younger brother. At the age of sixteen months, three months after the birth of his younger brother, he had measles and was "isolated" for a time. After recovering he became a poor eater, and his mother's obsession about "feeding people right" made her begin to force food upon him. This eventually resulted in setting up a pattern of interaction between the mother and the son: he was indifferent to food; she would urge him to "have another bite"; there was a tug of war between the two of them; the mother felt frustrated and would then say, "Nobody loves me, I'm going out and eat worms." She would go away, pouting, and he would feel guilty about not having given in to his mother's wishes. This interaction must have served him well in "winning" his mother to himself; but, needless to say, this way of winning the mother was not at the expense of his younger brother. As R became mother-tied, the younger brother was free to leave the mother. For instance, while the younger brother learned how to roller-skate with children in the neighborhood, R, now feeling challenged, had to learn the same thing in his mother's kitchen. Perhaps because of this close mother-son tie, with increased proximity which facilitated identification between the mother and the son (or was it because of the massive introjection of the lost mother at thirteen to sixteen months of age?), his personality and his mother's showed a great resemblance. Both were sensitive, easily hurt, ready to make others (who were considered offenders) feel guilty, and both were jealous and suspicious (mother always fussed at others, believing they had secrets which were kept from her).

After working through the triangular relationship, the analysis entered another phase. Now the analyst was seen essentially as the patient's older brother, whom he adored, and his father, whom he despised. Since the patient was five or six, this brother, five years his senior, was his hero. The older brother was acclaimed everywhere he went and was a successful professional man. Despite his brother's various merits, the patient's aggrandized view of his brother was, he felt, engendered and reinforced by his mother, who went out of her way to extol her older son's success among her relatives and friends. In contrast, the mother never spoke of the husband in this manner. Whenever she did mention the father to her children she assigned him a punitive role: "Wait until I tell your father when he comes home." That the father indiscriminately carried out his wife's wishes had been one of the reasons for R's disrespect for his father, the other reason being the father's assumption of "a child's role" through his hypochondriacal complaints and other acts that minimized his own importance in the presence of his wife.

Casting the analyst in the role of the older brother and father, the patient saw him either as a socially successful professional man or as a helpless Milquetoast, led by his wife. It was only many months later that he could recall his walks with his father, in the woods and alongside the river bank near his father's summer home. He recalled how amazed he was to discover his father was on boxing and basketball teams in college, that his father was shrewd in his business dealings. It was then that he began to respect his father and then that the split paternal imagos became united. Speaking of his father's sexual potency, the patient recalled with intense fear a screen memory in which he (at age six to eight) and his younger brother were riding pillows in the bed, a game they often played at bedtime. Suddenly, responding to his brother's statement, "A stick, jumping up and down," R was panic-stricken. He screamed and screamed until his father rushed to his aid and showed him that there was no stick in the room. This screen memory led to associations of witnessing the primal scene. (Both the patient and his younger brother slept in the parents' bedroom until R was six.) There followed a series of anxiety dreams of plane crashes, of being given injections and

enemas. He recalled that during Army service he had fears
that he would be approached homosexually. He recalled no
conscious thoughts of this kind during the rest of his developmental years, including the years with his best friend.
These thoughts about homosexuality led to associations
related to passivity and maternal identification.

The patient now wanted to be a man. Enacting the
oedipal situation, he had a "compulsion to steal" a married
woman. His effort was rewarded. When the woman began to
speak of marrying, he at first became elated, but soon
became terrified and terminated the affair; he felt that if they
were married the woman would soon find out his incapacity
to love. At this juncture he became jealous of his wife again.
At the sight of his wife he was reminded of her lover, even
though this man had not been coming near her for the past
three years. He perceived his wife not as his own but as
"some man's wife" who was desirable but who was forbidden to him. He was greatly distraught and he again
needed to design tasks for his wife to perform. This recrudes-
cence of his jealousy was brief; it passed away when its
defensive use was noticed. It was then clarified that, in the
content of the oedipal situation, the meanings of the two
components of jealousy were: "I love you" equates "I love
you, Mother," and "Let *her* prove she loves *me*" was addressed to the father in order to shift responsibility, so as to
allay R's own castration fear and guilt.

As his feelngs of fear and guilt were worked through the
patient began to feel that his wife was now his own. They
bought a house; previously he had resisted his wife's desire
to own a house because of his fear of transience. At this
juncture his wife was planning to discontinue her analysis,
and he spoke of terminating his analysis so that he might
finish before she did. Thoughts of termination of analysis
produced anxiety dreams and fantasies that he would never

amount to anything unless he could enact the Bible story in which David killed Goliath. He felt that he had to choose between kill-and-replace and remain-in-the-background. Now it became understandable that he could argue (or compete) with and win over those for whom he held no respect; he had to avoid those whom he did respect for they stirred up conflict in him. Following this phase of analysis he felt more at ease with his competitiveness and undertook to write a book, to fulfill a long-cherished but suppressed wish to outdo others. It was not obvious at first that writing a book was an acting out of maternal transference. Soon, however, it became evident that the completion of his wife's analysis had reopened the narcissistic wound of his lagging behind his brothers' successes in the past as well as in the present. Now, while in analysis, he had to seek concrete success by himself through the book, just as he had to learn a to roller-skate in his mother's kitchen.

In the process of writing this book there was a re-experiencing of anal material (withholding, difficulty in expelling, need for milk of magnesia, or an enema) as well as oral (compulsion to read and take in from books). But of utmost interest during this phase was his repeated demonstration of narcissistic absorption in his undertaking and of ignoring the existence of the analyst. During the hours, after perfunctory reports of current events, often devoid of emotion, R began to "write" his book or to turn his thoughts to the book. This behavior persisted, despite interpretations which he validated, until the first draft of the book was completed.

In retrospect, he noted that his behavior in analysis during the writing of the book was also reflected in his daily living with his family, i.e., he "ignored" them and he "disappeared" from them. By "ignoring" he meant willfully paying no attention to them in order to establish the fact that they should attend to his needs but not he to theirs. By "disappearing" he meant an automatic, unwilled turning of his mind, in the midst of conversation, to something else, a passage in a book he had just read, a scientific subject, etc. He said he had to ignore his wife; otherwise he could be reminded of her act of infidelity which had established the fact that he was second best and that he had wed a second-best wife. He had to ignore the analyst while writing the book, for he would likewise be reminded of his wife's analysis being finished first. "Thinking of myself as second best, and as one qualified to get only second best, makes me angry." He also became aware of his hate for his mother as the one whose behavior made him feel "I could not be anybody or get anything but second best."

In analysis he now enacted the "ignoring" and the "disappearing." He fell silent when he "disappeared." When the silence was punctured, he would engage in a brief argument and would fall silent again. He said he felt depressed, that "fighting with you is better than feeling depressed . . . but I don't even feel like fighting." During R's silent hours the analyst felt a general malaise, lacked concrete thoughts, lacked energy to formulate his thoughts, and often felt an urge not so much to end the silence as to end his own unpleasant feelings. As the cycle of the patient's falling silent, the analyst's effort to break the silence, the ensuing protest on R's part was repeated again and again, it gradually became clear that this must simulate the feeding struggle that was set up between the mother and the son when he was about sixteen months old. As he accepted the interpretation that his "disappearing" served the function of getting the analyst, his wife, or others to arouse him as once it served to get his mother to coax him to eat, he described his belief that to love is to possess; for instance, if his wife loved him she must possess him or claim him from "disappearing." He further elaborated that his disappearing protected his "secrets." This was related to the Bible stories of David and Goliath and the destructive rage of Samson who, after being betrayed by a woman, tore down the pillars of the temple.

But R revealed secrets other than destructiveness; he had always felt that he was second best, would only get second best, and he had therefore decided not to love others or to respect others' needs. He had been quite aware, since adolescence, that there existed a "gulf" between him and others that made him feel alienated and not belonging. Vaguely he felt that this "gulf" was his fault but decided "What the hell! Why bother to get something second best that I didn't want anyway?" He secretly entertained the idea that he was a great lover, but did not want to waste his great love on anyone who did not deserve it. When he first met his wife he had hopes of realizing his dreams of being a great lover, but he soon "discovered" his wife was a disappointment. She had many drawbacks (e.g., she was not popular; she did not give in enough, and therefore she did not love him enough) and she was, at best, a second best. When he was about to get married, he decided to be generous and to make her over but, in the ensuing years of marriage, he realized that he was mistaken to want to turn a disappointment into something different. Then he began to ignore her or disappear from her, although he did not consciously experience rage or hatred toward her. He turned more and more to books, having first become an avid reader at the age of nine. "Books are greater than human beings. One can take in or reject whatever one wants to without feeling guilty. Such simplicity of life one cannot expect from his fellow human beings."

Following much working through of his "disappearing" or narcissistic engrossment, R was subsequently able to consider terminating the analysis, which had lasted six years.

NARCISSISTIC FIXATION AND NARCISSISTIC OBJECT RELATION

R was five years younger than his older brother. It was unclear how his mother felt about becoming pregnant, or about having a baby after not having an infant in the house for over five years, or how this lapse of five years made her care of R different from the way she cared for her other two children. Also, there was no information in regard to R's special sensitivity or his behavior as a newborn infant. Although the early mother-infant interaction is unknown, it might be assumed that he was reared in an average expectable environment (Hartmann, 1939) or in a good enough holding environment (Winnicott, 1958a), and that the mother served reasonably well as the protective shield (Khan, 1963).

At the height of R's late oral and early anal phases of development, the mother's pregnancy (her reaction toward it is also unknown) with R's younger brother became evident. His reaction to the pregnancy and to the events associated with the birth of the younger brother was not traceable. It is conceivable, however, that after having been subjected to these events—especially the birth of the younger brother when R was thirteen months old—that aggression and loss were linked together. When he was sixteen months old, a critical age of becoming assertive, demanding, and locomotively active (Gesell and Ilg, 1943) and of acquiring awareness of self (Spitz, 1965), he contracted measles; the timing of this event might consequently stir fear of self-assertion or of aggression. And the experience of separation from the mother at this stage might reinforce the linkage between aggression and loss. When the mother and the son were reunited, R declined feeding, resulting in the development of a unique interaction between the two of them; namely, R's refusal of food, mother's urging him to take another bite, and the ensuing struggle until one (usually the child) succumbed to the other's will. It is possible that, at an earlier stage of the struggle, R was not "refusing" but was simply anorexic, that his lack of appetite was symptomatic of a reaction to the loss of the mother (Spitz, 1946). The repeated forcing of food by the mother who misread the cues could, however, serve as cumulative traumata, as Khan (1963) puts it, which led eventually to the formation of what Greenacre (1959) has termed "focal symbiosis" with the mother, to the precipitation of an oral cast to his future character development, to the narcissistic fixation with the tendency of self-engrossment and grandiosity, and to the need on R's part to mold himself into behaving passively in order to free himself from the responsibility of being an initiator of the loss.

In his object relations, following the traumatic experience, R was most at ease if he actively set up the above-mentioned interaction and could behave passively in it. Or he would simply not relate to others, either by becoming self-engrossed or by engaging them, without a real consideration of their existence, in a struggle to win. To him, to love was to possess. For instance, he loved his wife, therefore he possessed or owned her. Because he desired to be loved by her he expected her to possess him and therefore to claim him from his self-engrossment. In general, he was never content, for he never did find himself in total possession of others, nor others of him. In preadolescence he discovered a special value in reading; namely, from the books he could take or reject without guilty feelings. Henceforth, hiding behind the bookstacks became an effective way to nurse his narcissistic wound. But the more he found satisfaction in books, the more his relations with humans suffered.

Notwithstanding the traumata and the resultant fixation, R did develop adequate ego strength and adaptive skill to sail through various developmental crises and become a husband and father and assume a responsible job. But however successful he was in the eyes of society, he could not be unaware of his internal strife or the existence of the "gulf" between himself and others. Obviously feeling helpless to deal with his inner conflict alone (and his narcissistic grandiosity could not allow him to seek help from others), he simply tried to be more self-engrossed and, in a sense, more regressed. His withdrawal led to the deterioration of the marital relation, the wife's suicide attempt, his increasing distance from his children, his need to form the friendship with the man who became his best friend, and, eventually, to the crisis which brought him to analysis.

Jealousy is a universal experience. The difference between "normal" and pathological jealousy is, as Fenichel puts it, similar to that between grief and melancholia. Unlike envy, the experience of jealousy involves three persons instead of two. Because three persons act as the "stars" of the jealousy drama, it may be intimated that jealousy must be first experienced at a time when the developing and maturing child acquires the ability clearly to distinguish persons around him. At such times, he must have already been able to distinguish self from others, to establish a certain degree of object constancy, and to formulate a rudimentary set of self-representations and object representations. It is not the intention here even to speculate which of the two emotional experiences—jealousy or envy—could possibly be first experienced by a human child. Three-person or two-person dramas are mere descriptions of the phenomena, with no implication of sequences of developmental phases.

The intrusion on the dyad relation between the mother and the child by a third person, such as the father, sibling, or others, is inevitable. Therefore, every child knows jealousy feelings as soon as his ego equipment permits him to conceptualize them. But to formulate the self-representations and the object representations in order to stage or restage the jealousy drama requires something special. In R's case, as much as he might have had fleeting experiences of jealousy toward his father and his older brother, it was not until his traumatic experience at the age of thirteen to sixteen months, causing grief and fear of aggression, that he began to boost the importance of his younger brother as the star of the jealousy drama of the self-representation and the object representation, and to enact it. The replaying of the drama could have various repercussions; for instance, the creation of an ego state of jealousy which could be reactivated by the experience of grief or aggression, or both; the exploitation of such primitive defenses as projection, denial, etc., in order to avoid the experience of grief and aggression and to maintain a homeostatic or tension-free state; the reinforcement of the experience of the ego state of jealousy, which paved the way for the symptom formation of pathological jealousy at a later date.

THE MECHANISM OF PATHOLOGICAL JEALOUSY

The symptom of pathological jealousy in R's case appeared after he was reunited with his wife. When he lost his wife to his best friend, he was sad, angry, and revengeful. When he got even with his friend, he concentrated his vengeful feelings on his wife. He wanted to "dump" her as she did him. But, upon reunion and following their sexual relations, he was seized by jealousy, became concerned with the size of his penis, and questioned his wife persistently about her relations with her lover. The sequence of the occurrence of the events would seem to confirm the generally accepted view of union of penises and of homosexuality and thereby the theory that pathological jealousy is the result of the projected homosexual impulses. However fitting the theory appeared, one is nevertheless puzzled as to why the symptom did not occur at the time R made his friend a cuckold. Did not the penises unite then too? When one studies the symptom of pathological jealousy during the course of this analysis, one finds with astonishment that the rise and fall of the symptom did not coincide with the homosexual impulses but with a concern over narcissistic self-engrossment. Saddled with the two inconsistencies listed above, one proposes to turn to the consideration that jealousy is an ego state that can be reinstated by various conflicts, like those over homosexual impulses, oral-sadistic impulses, etc. In R's case, the onset of the symptom was not precipitated by homosexual impulses alone but was also compounded by oral-sadistic impulses. And later in the analysis the symptom seemed to be brought to the fore by conflicts over aggression and narcissism.

It seems that by conceiving pathological jealousy as a persistent ego state which can be reinstated by various conflicts, Riviere's and Fenichel's studies are rendered more consistent with Freud's. It must be emphasized that the concept of jealousy as an ego state was implied in Freud's definition of jealousy which, when condensed by Jones, is: jealousy is compounded of grief, hatred, and narcissism. To wit, in this definition, jealousy is a complex ego state involving all components of the psychic structure—id, ego, and superego.

HOMOSEXUALITY AND PROJECTION

R's best friend fits into the description of what Sandler et al. (1963) called the "part-ideal self" and of what Blos (1962) described as the "idealized self-image." In his best friend, R could find those traits required in a "successful" object relation. Perhaps a desire on his part to imitate or identify with this friend determined their congenial and unrestrained relationship devoid of the "gulf" which existed in the patient's relations with other human beings of either sex at that time. In this narcissistic homosexual relationship various disturbing thoughts could occur. For instance, there might be momentary existence of the "gulf," there might be experience of homosexual impulses. Although such disturbing thoughts were not confirmed by R, their existence could safely be speculated, as they could be documented in the transference manifestations in the analytic work. Perhaps it is due to such disturbing thoughts that men feel it necessary to bring their wives onto the scene. Although one must take into account the mental state of both R's wife and his best friend at the time to understand the eventual outcome of the whole affair, one could agree with Riviere, Chatterji, Barag, and Seidenberg that "the patient plays an active role . . ., actually or imaginatively bringing together his spouse and her lover." However, the purpose of bringing the two together, in R's association, did not quite substantiate the generally accepted view of "union of penises in the woman" (at least in the concrete sense) nor Barag's view of union of the wife—who was identified as one's own penis—with her lover's penis, nor Chatterji's view of removing the danger inside the wife by means of her lover's penis. It fitted better Seidenberg's view, the revival of the oedipal conflict with the third person, a part-ideal self, playing the role of the son in the oedipal triangle.

Lagache (1950) studied pathological jealousy in overt homosexuals. He found it necessary to distinguish active and passive homosexuality and concluded that pathological jealousy was only related to passive homosexuality, whereas overt, active homosexuality was only a form of acting out. In the analysis of my patient, however, the connection between jealousy symptoms and passive homosexuality was not always traceable. Projection of infidelity impulses, both homosexual and heterosexual, was considered as the basis for pathological jealousy, although Riviere takes exception to this view. While projection was very much used by R as a defensive mechanism, causal links between infidelity and projection were not obvious. At one point, when he had an extramarital affair, he developed jealousy feelings toward his wife. In this instance, jealousy certainly appeared to be a reprojection of his own infidelity, but closer scrutiny revealed that, even there, his concern over narcissistic unrelatedness was interpolated between the jealousy and the infidelity impulses. In short, in the study of the associations in R's case, the data about homosexuality, passivity, and projection were abundant, but they did not seem to be direct, causative factors of the symptom formation of pathological jealousy. Rather, they all existed in parallel.

SUMMARY

From the detailed study of a patient, pathological jealousy could best be understood as a persistent ego state, capable of being instituted by conflicts over homosexual and oral-sadistic impulses, and by other conflicts as well, including those surrounding grief and narcissism. From this point of view, divergent explanations of pathological jealousy, as expressed in the literature, became complementary.

ON NOSTALGIA

Jack Kleiner

(1970)

Nostalgia is better known to psychoanalysts and lay-men alike through familiarity with Proust's masterpiece, Remembrance of Things Past, *than through psychoanalytic studies. Only two psychoanalytic papers have been written on nostalgia, one by Martin (1954) and the one offered here. (Another, by Werman [1977], is about to be published.) A definitive psychoanalytic study of the life of Marcel Proust by Milton Miller was published in 1956, aptly entitled* Nostalgia: A Psychoanalytic Study of Marcel Proust. *Scientific neglect may stem from a lack of appreciation of the painfulness of the "bittersweet affect," its frequent occurrence in the form of mild, short-lived episodes experienced by many who do not suffer from any serious psychic disorder, and because it is erroneously considered to be merely a mild variant of depression. It differs significantly, however, from temporary depressive feelings, disillusionment (Socarides, 1971), disappointment, homesickness (Sterba, 1940), simple loss reactions and other feeling states with which it is often confused. When severe, it may even be deemed a clinical condition in its own right. Chronic nostalgia may be profoundly damaging to all areas of functioning.*

Apparently random thoughts may precipitate nostalgic memories varying in intensity from "What has happened to

471

all these years? Where have they gone? What a waste!" to
"The past is lost. The future can never be realized. All is
empty. All is lost." "The nostalgic is destined to remain with
a bittersweet feeling of hopelessness," for the past can never
be recaptured in reality—only in fantasy. When severe, the
nostalgic wishes to rid himself of nostalgia as if it were an
irritant, a foreign body within himself, which in some way
he might be able to expel. Expiatory processes that can be so
effective in guilt are usually of no avail in ridding oneself of
nostalgia. Those in a true depression or period of sadness
may experience a bout of nostalgia.

Etiological factors include oral problems over weaning
or the rivalry of siblings, loss of siblings through death, and
loss of mother-child relation because of hospitalization or
loss of a parent. Nostalgic feelings occurring in childhood
must be successfully overcome if they are not to have pronounced effects on later phases of development.

In general, nostalgia follows upon traumatic events with
a damming up of libido, which the ego cannot discharge.
The trauma occurs when the ego is very immature and
consists of the loss of an object or a part of an object, leaving
the ego in a painful state because it could neither master the
trauma nor undertake the work of mourning. Instead, the
ego attempts to deal with object loss by denying its occurrence. It attempts to incorporate the lost object, but of
crucial importance is the fact that the aggression aroused by
the loss of object produces alterations in the ego through
reaction formations, especially idealization. It is important
to note that the fixation upon the past and the wish for
unification with objects (primarily through incorporation
with the preoedipal mother) do not arise solely from oral
fixations but from the ego's unsuccessful attempts to deal
with its later conflicts.

Nostalgics are characterized by an insatiable yearning

for lost objects and an unwillingness to undertake the work of mourning. This is dramatically demonstrated by the presence of nostalgia in later life, characterized by a tendency to postpone mourning or to mourn incompletely. There is thus an interference with the normal development of an important function of the ego.

Nostalgia is common to human experience. Its essence is a wish to return to an idealized past. Nostalgics long for some aspects of the past, but strangely, its recollection brings a bittersweet pleasure. They seem to realize, however dimly, that the past can never be recaptured. Nostalgics yearn particularly for their childhood; memories of home and family insistently intrude into their awareness.

Nostalgia has been recorded by and, in turn, has influenced the most treasured heritage of any culture or age. It may have changed the awareness of its own history and literature. History describes the Jews, vanquished in battle by the Babylonians and exiled by the victorious king, Nebuchadnezzar, as languishing and waxing nostalgic for their homeland:

> By the waters of Babylon
> There we sat down; yea, we wept
> When we remembered Zion [Psalm 137:1].

That succeeding generations can elaborate and embellish a poetic utterance to the point of creating a myth of nostalgia is suggested by a contemporary historian (Diamont, 1962). He casts doubt upon the long-held view of the exiled Jews and their yearnings:

> Many Jewish history books draw a picture of sorrow and desolation when writing of the Jewish captivity in Babylon. Fortunately, this is an inaccurate picture. In

the sixth century Babylonia was ruled by a series of enlightened kings who treated their captives with tolerance. These Jews who "wept by the rivers of Babylon" were but a handful of zealots; the rest of the Jews fell in love with the country, prospered, and became cultured [p. 54].

The ancient Greeks lived with illusory memories and beliefs brought about by a too strict immersion in the noble Homeric legends, later clinging to them when the fabric of their society became threatened by the philosophic doctrines of Skepticism and Cynicism. Similar attitudes appeared during the Middle Ages. John Huizinga (1954), historian of that period, wrote of the attempt made to overcome the prevalent pessimism of the times by envisioning an "ideal past." According to him, the content of the ideal was a wish to return to the perfection of an imaginary past. All effort to raise life to that level, whether in actual life or in poetry, was an imitation of it. Thus chivalry was an imitation of the ideal hero. Of all the illusions of the time, the strongest and most persistent was the desire to return to nature and its innocent charm by an imitation of the shepherd's life. (He adds that in much the same way that Jewish history may have been inaccurately portrayed, the chroniclers during the Middle Ages tell more of the cruelty, rapacity, and self-interest of the knights than of their dedication to an enlightened ideal. As with all nostalgics, the past becomes glorified.) Later, the philosophers of the Enlightenment of the eighteenth century looked to classical antiquity for inspiration and sustenance, and one of its members, Rousseau, promulgated a return to nature as the happiest condition of man.

The desire to return to an ideal state—a state characterized by simplicity and goodness, in short, by freedom from conflict—finds its ultimate hope for realization in a reunion with nature. This theme pervades literature (although ration-

alized in many ways, from the vantage point of psychoanalysis its determinants are unconscious and are derived
from infantile longings). Theocritus, a Greek poet, was
perhaps the first to write poetically of the beauties of the
countryside. The attachment to nature, the longing for its
idealized virtues, contributed decisively (if it did not actually
originate) a new literary form, the pastoral poem (Durant,
1939). Theocritus had emigrated to Alexandria from his
homeland, and it is precisely in the emigre that one would
most likely find the nostalgic. He perfected the idyl, the
eidyllion, or little picture, with its connotation of a rustic
tale. In more modern times, the nineteenth-century romantic
poets, reacting to the demands of the scientific and economic
materialism of their day, found refuge and release in fond
contemplation of nature.

The themes of growing old and yearning for one's lost
youth and friends as well as for one's lost loves have created
some of the most nostalgic reflections in poetry; for example,
the following lines from the sonnet by Shakespeare which
later inspired the title of Marcel Proust's great novel of
nostalgia, *Remembrance of Things Past*:

> When to the sessions of sweet silent thought
> I summon up remembrance of things past,
> I sigh the lack of many a thing I sought,
> And with old woe new wail my dear time's waste:
> Then can I drown an eye, unused to flow,
> For precious friends hid in death's dateless night. . . .

Or consider the "Sonnet" by Edna St. Vincent Millay:

> What lips my lips have kissed, and where, and why,
> I have forgotten, and what arms have lain
> Under my head till morning; but the rain
> Is full of ghosts tonight, that tap and sigh
> Upon the glass and listen for a reply,

And in my heart there stirs a quiet pain,
For unremembered lads that not again
Will turn to me at midnight with a cry.
Thus in the winter stands the lonely tree,
Now knows what birds have vanished one by one,
Yet knows its boughs more silent than before:
I cannot say what loves have come and gone,
I only know that summer sang in me
A little while, that in me sings no more.

Among novelists, Thomas Wolfe shows clearly the influence of nostalgic feelings. The titles of two of his books, *Look Homeward, Angel* and *You Can't Go Home Again*, quickly hint at preoccupation with the past. Wolfe was always the stranger in a foreign land. Forever the adolescent in an adult world, he could neither achieve maturity nor recapture the secure childhood of fantasy. His past enveloped him like an airless room. That Wolfe appealed to literate, sensitive adolescents is easily understood, when one remembers the adolescent's closeness to his own childhood and his struggle to emancipate himself from it. Perhaps all writing in its final essence and purpose is autobiographical.

It is indeed surprising that little attention has been given to the subject of nostalgia in English-language psychoanalytic literature. Perhaps it is because it has been regarded as a variant of depression or, more likely, because it seldom becomes a clinical problem in itself. Nonanalytic literature, although having little to add to an understanding of the condition, nevertheless has made some interesting observations and commentaries.

An extensive review was made years ago by W. H. McCann (1941). According to him, a description of the subject begins with J. Hofer in 1678:

Hofer described two cases of a sickness which he had observed to be quite similar to a condition called

> "schweizerkrankheit" by the Germans, "mal du pays" by the French, and "malatia del pais" by the Spaniards. Hofer was the first to describe the condition as an illness and to call it 'nostalgie," a term which, like its English equivalent "nostalgia," comes from the Greek word "nostros," meaning return, and "algos," meaning pain [p. 165].

Hofer thought of it as a disease originating in the inner parts of the brain, where there occurred a migration of animal spirits causing a thickening of the blood. Almost every known symptom, in Hofer's opinion, has been interpreted as nostalgia, from cessation of the menstrual flow, foul breath, and diarrhea to severe fever, convulsions, and stupor. Since Hofer, several authors, the first of whom was Jaspers, attempted to correlate nostalgia (more precisely, homesickness) with criminal behavior. In 1795, Jaspers described a terribly homesick servant girl who set on fire the home of her employer. Others also connected it with pyromania and even murder.

There is a tendency in nonanalytic literature to equate nostalgia with homesickness. In fact, Webster's *Unabridged Dictionary* defines nostalgia merely as homesickness. It would seem more appropriate to think of homesickness as an acute affect associated with separation from one's familiar surroundings, though of course the feeling may become chronic. One thinks, as good examples, of the child at summer camp, longing to return home, or of the soldier away in a foreign land counting the days until his term of duty ends. Both conditions are relieved when the sufferers are reunited with their homes.

It is normal for anyone removed from his usual surroundings to experience, to some degree, sadness, emptiness, and reduction of interest in the external world. It becomes pathological if the reaction is excessive, as, for example, the child who becomes terrified and inconsolable when he is merely to sleep overnight at the home of a friend. Anna Freud (1965) notes the inappropriate application of the term "separation anxiety" to many diverse clinical entities, including homesickness, and states that the latter condition indicates an excessive ambivalence toward mother, parents, or home when a separation occurs.

> The conflict between love and hate of the parents can be tolerated by the child only in their reassuring presence. In their absence, the hostile side of the ambivalence assumes frightening proportions, and the ambivalently loved figures of the parents are clung to so as to save them from the child's own death wishes, aggressive fantasies, etc. In contrast to the separation distress of the infant, which is relieved by reunion with the parent, in ambivalence conflicts reunion with the parents acts merely as a palliative; here only analytic insight into the conflict of feelings will cure the symptom [p. 113].

In this connection, it is interesting that homesick children at times become sad when they leave the hated camp to return home; suddenly the *separation* from camp becomes painful, illustrating very well the influence of ambivalence.

It is true that any individual will become despondent if he thinks he will never be able to return to his home and loved ones because of external forces which cannot be controlled or modified. It is to be expected that the resultant pain and suffering will be intense, but even after a substantial period of time has elapsed, reminiscences about what has been lost will never have the bittersweet taste of nostalgia but instead will be accompanied by pure pain. Anyone who has sustained the real loss of an object in the external world will become depressed, even if the object is not a narcissistic object choice nor invested with unconscious fantasies aggravated by ambivalence, and even if the object still remains in the external world. The more the ego realizes its helplessness in recapturing the object, the more desperate is the situation. Should the person, by some change in fortune, be reunited with the lost object, the symptoms would be expected to disappear. This would not be typical of nostalgia. One thinks, as an example, of the middle-aged college graduate who reminisces with a mixture of sadness and pleasure about his college days. When he returns for a class reunion, nothing is relieved; in fact, the nostalgia may become intensified, for the past can never be recaptured in actuality for the nostalgic, but only in fantasy. Furthermore, he seems well aware he can never satisfy his longings; that he is destined to remain with a bittersweet feeling of hopelessness.

It is not correct either to think of the nostalgic person as being merely sentimental. The sentimentalist exhibits an excess of emotion, overreacts to charged situations, and in general gives the impression of being simply immature; his emotions are short-lived, inappropriate, often shallow, and coincide with the immediate situation. The longing and yearning are absent. The romantic, on the other hand, lives in fantasy, satisfying his wishes in a make-believe world of romance, falsifying the present, idealizing the past, and glorifying the future. Thus neither the homesick person nor the sentimentalist nor the romantic show the peculiar combination of sadness and pleasant reminiscing. Nor do they exhibit another peculiarity in the patient to be described: a wish to get rid of the nostalgia itself, as if it existed as an irritant, a foreign body within; as if by expelling something else, the nostalgia itself would disappear.

In the English-language psychoanalytic literature Editha Sterba (1940) described a five-year-old girl who, after being forced to leave her native land, developed what Sterba considered to be extreme nostalgic reactions: complaints of what had been left behind, visible grief, silence, and refusal to eat. The child had been weaned at six and a half months, after which she insisted upon taking a so-called "dribbling" cloth with her to bed. The birth of a sibling at four apparently reactivated the weaning trauma. The child became exceptionally interested in visiting her grandmother's home, where she had the opportunity to milk cows. Sterba felt this interest represented an oral substitute for the lost breast. Eventually, the loss of her country was experienced as identical with the trauma of weaning. This child was not in treatment, and interpretations were made to her by her mother, who was obviously familiar with psychoanalytic thinking. It is questionable whether this child was truly nostalgic or was simply in a state of bereavement.

Fodor (1950) wrote of the search for a prenatal state, the desire to return to the mother's womb, as the wish motivating nostalgic yearnings. This wish also produces fantasies in some of having been of royal birth, as well as explaining why some individuals experience ecstasy when floating in water. "The outstanding motive behind the desire to return into the womb is the attainment of happiness in the only perfect form we have known" (p. 35).

Martin (1954) preferred to think of a "true" and a pathological nostalgia. True nostalgia is a biological inclination to return home as a source of strength and is "an active urge to keep in touch with our roots," in contrast to its pathological counterpart, which expresses morbid anxiety. Biological nostalgia is conceived as a rhythmic, evolutionary growth process similar to the "homing instinct" found in fish, birds, and animals. It is a healthy surrender to the biological inclination to return to the past, to childhood, to sleep, and to the unconscious. Pathological nostalgia, or nostomania, may result when an individual is forced into an awareness of his total involvement in internal conflict and reacts to this new awareness with an intensification of "compulsive conflicting attitudes toward authority, i.e. by over-reactive movements toward and against the home, literally and/or figuratively" (p. 101). Present-day culture, with its emphasis on independence and its overvaluation of the intellect at the expense of emotional expression, makes difficult the acceptance of the true utility value of nostalgia.

Fenichel (1945) explains nostalgia as a wish to return to the preoedipal mother. Freedman (1956) described an artist who suffered from severe anxiety and periods of nostalgia. Here, too, the nostalgia was related to a striving for the preoedipal mother, but it was also found that the affect served to repress destructive wishes toward the patient's father and that certain locales became associated with these wishes. The nostalgia served as a counterphobic mechanism, and once the repressive aspect of the nostalgia began to fail, phobic reactions to those very locales actually developed.

All authors agree on the importance of the preoedipal mother in the emotional development of nostalgics, but since this is true of many neurotics, one must look for specific factors in their life histories. Sterba (1940) attempts to show the influence of oral factors, but we do not have the opportunity to see their influence upon the girl's later childhood and adulthood. While we are given a graphic account of Freedman's patient as an adult, his earliest memories begin at five and there is little preoedipal history. In the patient to be described, there is an abundance of early material, especially that concerned with orality, and it is possible to see the marked effect that this and other specific events had upon the development of later nostalgic feelings.

The patient, Mrs. F, a housewife in her early forties, became involved in treatment in a manner that reflected her difficulties. She sent her twelve-year-old son for help, presumably because of school difficulties. The boy merely needed some counseling, after which Mrs. F hesitatingly asked for treatment for herself. For a long time, she said, she had been suffering from depression, which, upon investigation, turned out to be feelings of inadequacy to which she reacted with depression. She experienced periods of sadness and crying over which she had poor control and which, in turn, injured her self-regard. All in all, her self-esteem was at a low level in spite of being well liked by others, for she had many friends. Knowing she was a good homemaker and mother was also of little use in raising her spirits.

It became evident that in her sadness she was being overcome by nostalgia. In such a mood, there were these recurrent thoughts: "What has happened to all the years? Where have they gone? What a waste!" Then would follow childhood memories—memories of moments of quiet intimacies with her parents, romping with playmates, a lazy summer afternoon, or a cozy, snug, and protected feeling on a winter evening at home. Even a friendly glance or kind word from a stranger remained with her to be cherished for many years. A chance remark in casual conversation could stimulate the memories. At times during her hours, when she seemed to be in good spirits, a random thought would suddenly precipitate nostalgic memories, and the patient would become angry at the memories for being there and with herself for having become upset. She looked upon them as foreign bodies that were within her but which she could not eject. This was in contrast to the moments when she treasured her memories. The theme throughout was of something lost—something once hoped for but now never to be recaptured, as well as something once hoped for but now never to be realized. The past is lost, the future can never be realized, all is empty, all is lost.

Prominent as a source of disappointment was her marriage. Mrs F was a very voluble woman, but such an interesting storyteller that she was constantly sought out by others. She was very concerned with social matters and could always be counted upon to contribute generously to any charity which aroused her sympathy. Few failed to do so. She had strongly protective feelings for the underdog. She enjoyed art and music and longed to own objects of art and to attend concerts. There seemed little that did not interest her, that could not arouse her curiosity and wonder and excite her sense of participation. She surrounded herself with experiences and impressions as if they were precious jewels to exhibit to others and to be fondled by her in solitude.

Unfortunately, her husband, an obese and phlegmatic man, would have none of this. A hard-working owner of a small factory, his only interests, according to her, were food, sleep, and sex. If she could drag him to a concert, he would fall asleep; objects of art were considered by him to be investments and not for esthetic delight. He ridiculed her many activities, and whenever she was uninterested in sex, he blamed it on her being tired from overinvolvement in her social and charitable organizations.

For a long time she tried to use her treatment to change him, rather than to realize that he was content with himself and that her only choice was to accept him as he was. She had to acknowledge the painful reality of having made a poor marriage. This intensified the "what a waste of years" feeling. On further analysis, it evolved that she unconsciously cherished an idealized image of her father, and her husband fell far short of it. Her father, who died when the patient was in her twenties, was a robust and active man whose curiosity had no limits. He was intensely interested in all aspects of life, had an enormous number of friends, and was somewhat of an adventurer and wanderer. The patient was born in Kentucky during the Depression, and uncertain economic conditions caused the family (the parents, the patient, and a year-older brother) to move, first at six months from her birthplace to another area in Kentucky, and then to New York City at one year of age. It was on the trip to New York that a fateful incident occurred for the patient and the development of her nostalgia—the death of her brother in an automobile collision.

The family remained in New York until she was six. The father's desire to travel took them to Europe for a year. Upon their return, business conditions again became bad, and the family returned to Kentucky, where the father conceived the idea of working an abandoned mine. This venture failed, leaving the family in desperate straits. Eventually, her father became involved in the used-car business. Conditions improved and he became an important member of the community. He became well known for his generosity, the legend that survived him being that he never turned down a request for a loan or handout. To those at home, he seemed less charitable. He used any excuse to go wandering on so-called business trips. The patient never entertained the thought that he might be using these trips for sexual purposes. Being deeply attached to him, she could not permit herself such ideas. Her guilt over her fixation led her to marry someone very different from her father while unconsciously not relinquishing her father. The failure of her husband to fulfill her unconscious wishes concerning her father, and the further realization that she could never have anyone like him, evoked the desperate conclusion that she could never be satisfied and all was lost. The unconscious longing for the ideal father turned her affects and thoughts to the past, to memories associated with him, and thus contributed to her nostalgia. She maintained her libidinal tie with her father through an identification with him: she showed his exuberance, excitement, curiosity, collecting of friends, charitable interests, etc.

The patient had allowed herself only one love affair before marriage—a prolonged relationship with an older man, an army officer, during World War II when she worked as a secretary on an army base. This man was a notorious *bon vivant* who quickly attempted to seduce her. She was strongly tempted to yield, but countered the temptation by trying to make him become virtuous. She refused to marry him, telling herself he would be unfaithful to her and that they had incompatible personalities. For many years thereafter she mourned this lost relationship, had many fantasies about how it might have been had she gone through with the marriage, and often speculated what she would do if she were to meet the man again. It was clear that she could not marry him because he too closely resembled her father, and her object choice had to be someone vastly different.

She became drawn to her husband by the need to succor the weak and helpless. His leg had been badly injured on the African front by a mine explosion. She became acquainted with him while he was recuperating at a nearby Army hospital and immediately felt the need to take care of him. He appeared to her as a woebegone and pitiful person, and in this relationship appeared the mother-child tie that was one of the basic determinants of her nostalgia. The need to change him—he was taciturn and appeared to her to be withdrawn—surfaced as it had with her previous lover. She was strongly attracted to him also because of his need for close family ties, a need she felt herself. In one way, he strongly resembled her father: periods of apparent softness and weakness alternated with a stubborn will.

The painful realization of loss in connection with the

father led to analysis of the tie with the mother. The material amply confirms the thesis; nostalgic wishes represent a wish for reunion with the mother, with particular emphasis upon the oral phase of libidinal development. The patient often thought of herself, even in adult life, as being at one with the mother. She described her mother as being not just a mother but also a true and close friend, almost as if they were twins. When, during the treatment, her mother died, it was as if a part of her had also died.

As mentioned, when Mrs. F was one year old her older brother was killed. Her mother, she was later told, went into a deep depression. The patient was also told she herself lost her appetite sometime thereafter. She was being breast fed, and her mother was advised by her physician to continue breast feeding to overcome her depression. It would appear that the mother had discontinued the breast feeding because of her depression. Subsequently, breast feeding continued until she was eighteen months old, certainly a long time in our culture. The brother at the time of his death was still being nursed. When the family moved to New York, they lived briefly with an aunt who was sickly and had a newborn infant. The mother proceeded to suckle this child also.

A male sibling, B, was born when the patient was two and a half, and he, too, was suckled for eighteen months. Another boy, P, was born when she was ten, and he was suckled for ten months. The patient reacted to B's birth with marked aggression. Once, while he was being nursed, she struck him so severely with a hairbrush that he had to be hospitalized. For this, she was dealt with very sternly. She resolved to be a good little girl to gain her mother's love. This alternated with periods of naughtiness, when she found being good did not sufficiently withdraw her mother's attention from her brother. Later in life, she and B became very close, in contrast to her relationship with P.

It seemed that the loss of the breast during her mother's depression and then being reunited with it for a long period, as well as the loss of the mother (which must have occurred because of her depression), produced an intensified libidinal fixation on her. The birth of B undoubtedly furthered this development. Many things appeared throughout the patient's life to attest to this in terms of a wish to be reunited with the preoedipal mother, while other phenomena indicated conflict over strong oral drives. For example, although in constant motion and seemingly unable to relax, Mrs. F could float for hours in water. She loved water and felt encapsulated in it, secure and serene, away from life's demands. She compared this to how a baby must feel in the womb. Also, when troubled, she could sit for hours by the ocean and feel at one with it. At such times, she would "take in the ocean" and would feel she had "come home." The unconscious equation of water with mother and return to the womb is, of course, well known.

Mrs. F frequently complained of being unfulfilled and of having felt so all her life. There were times, however, when she described herself as feeling at one with the universe: in and by water, listening to music, or observing beautiful scenery. But usually she was searching for something to fill herself with to overcome the unfulfilled feeling. "All my life I've been searching for something. Maybe I'll find it here or there. I thought going to school would bring it, or getting a job, or traveling, or marriage; but nothing, I'm always disappointed. I don't know what I want." It seemed quite clear that she was unconsciously searching for the lost breast and mother.

The desire for reunion led to an almost mystical longing to go to Israel. For as long as she could remember, she had had a passionate devotion to the country. It was her "homeland," the land of "her people," of her origins, etc. The wish became a compulsive urge. Although she had never been there, she cried at the thought of a coming visit. There she could be at one with everyone. She had a similar mystical approach to gardening. Spring found her impatient to be on hands and knees, grubbing in the soil, serene with her close contact with "mother earth," as she invariably described it.

A dream illustrates her oral orientation: "I went back home to Kentucky. The house was now a nursing home. There were several additions on it." Her immediate thoughts prior to recalling the dream had been: "Why am I eating so much? Cake and bread. Food has suddenly begun to have meaning for me for the first time in my life." The day of the dream she had put new numbers on her house. The numbers reminded her of her house number in Kentucky. "Kentucky makes me think of home. I got an invitation from a friend there for her son's Bar Mitzvah. Nursing home—my parents —taking care of them." When food and nursing were connected, that a nursing home is where one is nursed as well as where one does nursing, she responded: "You mean I want to be a child again? Yes. To avoid responsibilities. Yesterday, I had such trouble asking my husband to get new lighting fixtures. (Tears.) The day before, I felt so wonderful, enveloped by a warm glow, because I felt for the first time in my life I amounted to somebody, that what I was doing in life was worthwhile." When asked for associations to being "enveloped in a warm glow": "I've come home safe, secure." (Tears.) Feeling worthwhile, she is now allowed to eat and have children (the additions to the house).

The patient had much conflict over oral drives. Both she and B, breast fed for eighteen months, developed a strong aversion to milk. As a child, she abhorred sweets, never ate ice cream or candy, and instead developed a taste for sour and tart foods (the younger brother liked milk and sweets). In her adult life, she could not tolerate anyone who indulged

in anything to excess, particularly food. It made her nause-
ated to watch anyone overeat. Yet, she enjoyed cooking for
others and gained quite a reputation as a gourmet cook. Her
husband stuffed himself, and she battled with him to control
his weight (she had the proverbial thinness of a rail). But she
continued to stock the kitchen with all the foods he enjoyed.
Obviously, she gratified her repressed wishes through his
gluttony, by her constant talking, by collecting experiences
and friends, as if storing them up against the threat of future
loss. When her husband wanted to suck her nipples in
foreplay, she felt revulsion and accused him, to herself, of
being a baby wanting to suckle at the breast. On rare occasions, when she could permit herself to be uninhibited, she
allowed him to and experienced an overwhelming excitement, followed later by shame. Objects were treated as food
to be incorporated. The love of her parents for her was so
real she could touch it, and when her mother died, "It was
like I lost part of my diet." She identified strongly with those
in need. At six, it was too painful for her to watch a Charlie
Chaplin movie—he seemed so "woebegone, lonely, forlorn,
and hungry." She played both mother and child in her
relationships.

Before her treatment, she rarely thought of her brother's
death. Now it frequently intruded into her awareness,
although she had no recollection of the event itself. For a
year after the accident (she was told by her mother), whenever she saw any blond boy from behind, she asked if he was
her brother. She was told she had wandered forlornly about
the house and yard looking for him, calling his name in a
questioning voice. As these thoughts came to consciousness
she constantly asked herself if his death could be why she
mourned so deeply for the past and explained life's seeming
such a waste. Did it explain also her feelings of imperma-
nence—that anything good is lost or taken away?

The loss of breast, mother, and brother so early in life left its imprint on later phases of development. The patient was told she was quickly toilet trained at about one year, apparently just before the fatal accident with its disastrous effects upon her mother. Throughout her life, Mrs. F. was reluctant to part with things. For example, she had a wardrobe of clothes with many out of style, but she could not bear to get rid of them. "I fondle them as if they are old friends. I can't throw anything out. I've never been able to part with anything since I can recall—clothes, souvenirs, old friends, memories, even the dead. I can't let it just lie there. I want to wrap it all around me, for security, as if I can't stand alone." All objects, animate and inanimate, were strongly cathected and had to be retained for fear any relinquishment of an object would be experienced as a painful loss. As a child, she usually held in her urine, hopping about on one foot, rushing to the bathroom at the last possible moment. She frequently had accidents.

Her phallic phase was heavily influenced. When she was two and a half, she recalled carefully examining her brother's toes. After this, she was very curious about how things worked and always compared herself unfavorably with boys. She despised being a girl and desperately wanted to be a boy. A tomboy in latency, she became the leader of a gang of boys. Horrified and angry the day of her first menses, for it meant she could no longer go swimming with the boys at any time, she asked her doctor to do something to change her into a boy. Her brother was highly valued by her parents, and she tried to emulate his achievements. One snowy morning she drove to her appointment when the roads were virtually impassable. She thought I would admire her courage and strength; and, if men patients were able to come, she could also. She was very small-breasted, and this was a painful injury to her self-regard; but earlier she had welcomed her delayed breast development, for then she could carry on the fantasy of being a boy. Her son was little more than an extension of herself. She gloried in his achievements but showed less interest in her daughter's successes. She had always felt degraded and different, with the thought that something about her had not turned out right; something had not developed, or if it had, had been lost. Her castration complex had been severely aggravated by her prior sense of loss as well as by the unfortunate comparison with B.

The emotional tone investing her oedipal conflict indicated a wish to guard against loss. She professed to love both parents equally, and it was indeed very difficult to elicit hostility to either. She wanted to hold onto them and imagined she was surrounded by their love. The hostility she could express was usually based on something realistic either parent had done, but rarely because her libidinal strivings had been frustrated. The libidinal fixation on her father was intense, but she never developed strong hostility to her mother, because her attachment to her precluded the development of marked overt aggression for fear of losing her. The threat of losing an object rather than the object's love, and with it the loss of the need-satisfying function of the object, perhaps stifles the development of aggression and ambivalence toward the object and stimulates what Bowlby (1960b) has described from a biological approach as attachment behavior.

Her first adult love object was a man who had many characteristics of her father. The affair was entered into halfheartedly, as if it were a game in which she knew she would be the loser. The patient knew at the outset the relationship was destined to fail. It seemed to be an abortive, one-shot attempt to recapture the lost and idealized father. Thereafter she was very careful in her contacts with men, shunning any sexual involvement, and finally entering into marriage with a man with whom unconsciously she could act out a mother-child relationship. In spite of his stubbornness and seeming indifference to her needs, he was quite dependent on her at times, and she could play mother to him. In so doing, she avoided the threat of loss. At the same time, the relationship developed a masochistic flavor; she could complain and carry on that he did not satisfy her needs. With her need-oriented behavior, she never complained that her husband did not love her; it was more that he left her empty, unfulfilled, and hungry. She found much to admire in him at the outset because he had exceptionally strong family ties, particularly with his mother. This was overwhelmingly attractive, as it appealed to her primitive need to be one with the object. She was neither borderline nor psychotic, however, for the object always remained in the external world.

There was a noticeable longing for the freedom of pleasure in instinctual functions. The patient aptly characterized this as "the good old times." The following dream is instructive: "I am driving a car from the rear. Then I have an accident. Then I go barefoot to a store. I am wrapped in a fur coat. Everybody is catering to me. Then I go to an old-fashioned store, the kind with bushels of coffee on the floor. That reminds me of when I was a kid and I'd go to the store and put my arms up to my elbows in coffee barrels. In the dream, a man is part of the store. He says, 'Give her what she wants.'"

Before relating the dream, the patient had said people were nice to her when she shopped in stores, but was that because she had money? What if she had none; would they still treat her so? She wondered if I would like her if she did not pay for her treatment. 1 should be like the man in the store who gave her whatever she wanted. To drive the car from the rear was to do everything backwards. She could urinate (have an accident), go naked (the reverse of wearing a fur coat), not pay for her bills, and still be loved. The dream had a sense of urgency which she associated with urinating. It indicated a strong desire to have instinctual freedom. At this point in her treatment, resistance had become strong and she had fleeting thoughts of discontinuing. She was feeling better about herself, less inhibited and guilty. She rationalized by saying she now wanted to see how well she could do, but what she wanted was to indulge in infantile pleasures on her own without the arousal of guilt and shame. The treatment acted also as a temptation to regress, which was threatening to her.

Mrs. F had many dreams of wetting the bed, luxuriating in the feeling of being swept away by water, and several times during treatment actually did wet the bed. Once during latency, after wetting the bed, she experienced a sensation of marked warmth and a floating-in-air feeling. When her amniotic sac burst during delivery, there was a great momentary sense of freedom before "civilized feelings set in and I had to control myself."

Just as the nostalgia expressed the wish for instinctual freedom, so at the same time it satisfied superego demands. If she could but return to the days before the development of her aggression to her brother and whatever aggression she allowed herself to have in her positive oedipal strivings, then she could be loved and accepted by her superego. To feel worthwhile, to be enveloped by the "warm glow," was to feel acceptance by her superego.

Concerned as this woman was with life and the past, it was to be expected that there would be a corresponding preoccupation with the future and, ultimately, with death. The desire to return to childhood served as a strong defense against fear of death. When she was fifteen, she could not imagine she would live until twenty-five; when she did, she could scarcely believe it. Death would intervene to frustrate her infantile longings and, at the same time, serve as punishment for having them. All her urgent collecting of memories was to get all she could out of life because death was imminent. "Gather ye rosebuds while ye may." She often thought of death when speaking of the dead brother: "I, too, will not live long." She had had overt death wishes toward B, and she would be punished for them by what had happened to the dead brother.

Concern with death is, in part, a concern with time, and the patient had peculiar experiences in this regard. It appeared that she could foretell certain aspects of the future, particularly as it involved B. As noted, both had been breast fed for eighteen months, and they shared a bedroom until late in their teens. In spite of her earlier hostility to him, a very close relationship developed as they grew older. During her adult life, he made his home in the South, and she sorely missed him. They spoke frequently on the phone. The patient could predict almost to the hour when he would call. Diligent investigation never revealed a pre-existing pattern of telephoning which could have unconsciously influenced her. Sometimes she would call her brother on impulse after just having spoken to him, only to have him answer quietly: "I was expecting your call." Again, nothing had been prearranged. One is reminded here of Freud's comment on thought transference and telepathy in his paper, "Dreams and Occultism" (1933a):

> We are once again left with a *non liquet* [not proven]; but I must confess that I have a feeling that here too the scales weigh in favour of thought-transference.... No doubt you would like me to hold fast to a moderate theism and show myself relentless in my rejection of everything occult. But I am incapable of currying favour and I must urge you to have kindlier thoughts on

the objective possibility of thought-transference and at the same time of telepathy as well [p. 54].

Time, incidentally, seemed to have conspired with her not to show its presence. She looked ten years younger than her age and was so regarded by her friends. In fact, she kept her true age a secret from them. The younger one appeared, the longer one lived. Wishes, unfortunately, are victimized by reality.

It would appear that nostalgic tendencies are associated with an inability to mourn. According to Anna Freud (1960), mourning indicates an effort to accept a fact in the external world (the loss of the cathected object) and to effect changes in the internal world (the withdrawal of libido from the lost object and identification with it). This presupposes certain capacities of the mental apparatus: reality testing, acceptance of the reality principle, and partial control of id tendencies by the ego. These capacities are underdeveloped in the infant. "Before the mental apparatus has matured and before, on the libidinal side, the stage of object constancy has been reached, the child's reactions to loss seem to us to be governed by the more primitive and direct dictates of the pleasure-pain principle" (p. 180).

When the patient lost her brother (aggravated by the temporary loss of her mother), her reality testing was not sufficiently developed to accept the fact that the object no longer existed. The loss was a traumatic event; consequently, she was filled with accumulated libido. The inability to discharge the libido left her in pain, and she was driven thereafter in attempts to discharge it. She continued for some time to search for the lost object. Frustrated finally in this, one can speculate, an incomplete incorporation of the object followed. He existed partly within her, but partly in the external world, for she began to search for the "something missing." Although the refusal to eat after the brother's death may have been an identification with the depressed mother, it is possible that it also represented a realization that total incorporation would have meant the complete destruction of the object, as well as being an effort to reunite with him. Undeniably frustrated by being unable to find her brother, a great deal of oral aggression must have been mobilized, and she defended against this by refusal to eat.

At some later time, as a further effort to defend lost objects against her own aggression, she began to idealize them. This idealization spread to her entire past. She idealized her parents, for to have felt otherwise would have meant their destruction. Without idealization, the unleashed aggression probably would have resulted in deep depression. Because the object had not been completely incorporated, there remained hope of finding it once again. Unlike the severely depressed person who has taken the object into the ego and, therefore, feels hopeless, this particular nostalgic, unconsciously believing that the object still existed in the external world, was thereby able to go on hoping for a reunification with it.

It seems that the partially incorporated object remained as a noxious element within the ego, troubling it and interfering with its need for unity. Even when she felt well, as noted, a chance remark might stir up an association to the past, and she would respond with sadness and tears, but also with anger. There was something almost physical within her that would not allow her to be at rest. She would speak angrily of "a thing" that tormented her and how relieved she would be if it could be ejected. In fact, what she sought essentially was a completely untroubled state, the ideal ego. In her nostalgia, she longed for this. The yearning, therefore, was not only for the lost object, but to return to the time before the object was lost.

From this particular patient, it appears that nostalgia

followed upon a traumatic event with a damming up of libido which the ego could not discharge. The ego was then left in a painful state because it could not master the trauma. Because of its immaturity, it could not undertake the work of mourning. It attempted to deal with the object loss by denying its occurrence, by attempts at incorporation, and by idealization of the missing object. As these attempted solutions failed, the ego sought to lessen its pain by fantasies of reuniting with the preoedipal mother. The aggression aroused by the loss or threat of object loss produced alterations in the ego via reaction formations. The ego guarded its objects against its own aggression by idealizing them. Eventually, all phases of libidinal development were influenced by the threat of loss. The patient unconsciously yearned for return of her infantile instinctual freedoms. This, too, could be realized if she were one with the prohibiting object and, later, with the superego. The fixation upon the past and wish for unification with objects, primarily the preoedipal mother, did not follow solely from oral fixations evolving during the oral phase, but also from the ego's unsuccessful attempts to deal with its later conflicts.

What was most striking was the insatiable yearning for lost objects. A traumatic loss of an object by an ego unable to mourn may lead in later life to an unwillingness to undertake the work of mourning. Whereas insufficient reality testing in early life may preclude successful mourning, an unwillingness in later life to mourn, to postpone it, or to do it incompletely, may interfere with the normal development of this important function of the ego. Only after the patient accepted the fact that her infantile objects could not be regained was she able to accept substitutes in a meaningful way. As long as the search continued, the past intruded into the present, and the ego was governed as much by the pleasure principle as by reality.

Summary

Nostalgic yearnings, quite evident in literature and throughout history, have received little attention in psychoanalytic literature. A case of a severe nostalgic is presented in and an attempt is made to document the importance of pregenital, predominantly oral factors in the genesis of nostalgia. It is shown that, because of later conflicts, the nostalgic regresses to wishes for reunification with a pre-oedipal mother. Reactions to and defenses against threats of loss of objects are seen as coloring all developmental phases. Specific traumata in the nostalgic's early life history provide nostalgia with its peculiar bittersweet flavor. Nostalgic tendencies are seen as associated with an inability to mourn in early life, and later, an unwillingness to do so. Only after the search for reunification with infantile objects is given up is the nostalgic able to accept meaningful substitutes.

PSYCHOANALYTIC OBSERVATIONS ON THE CAPACITY TO LOVE

Martin S. Bergmann

(1971)

The most sought-after of all affects and one of the most difficult to define psychoanalytically is the affect of love. The best nonanalytic definition given by an author was that proposed by Balzac in Père Goriot *when he remarked: "Love ... the warmth of gratitude that all generous souls feel for the source of their pleasures."*

Bergmann reminds us that before Freud, love was the domain of philosophers and poets and, of course, those "in love." "They could not, however, discern how one form of love could be related to another, nor could they gain insight into the psychic forces that promote or retard the development of the capacity to love. Freud approached the mystery of love through another path, the path of infantile sexuality."

Bergmann presents a historical survey of Freud's concepts of love. The concept of narcissism was the essential element which enabled him to differentiate two sources of love: one, the narcissistic model, and the other, the anaclitic model. In 1914 Freud wrote that real happy love corresponds to the original condition in which object libido and ego libido cannot be distinguished (Freud, 1914a). In the same paper he contrasted erotic cathexis with the state of being in

499

love and offered observations on one of the puzzling features of love, namely, idealization.

Freud viewed difficulties in loving as stemming from a failure to resolve the Oedipus complex and he brilliantly defined the requirements for adult love: love becomes possible after puberty by the fusion of the two kinds of libido, the affective, tender emotions and the sensual.

While the affect of love is central to our theoretical concepts and our therapeutic work, little new ground has been broken in our theoretical understanding of this affective state until recently. There was a panel on "The Theory of Genital Primacy in the Light of Ego Psychology" (Panel, 1969) and there have been a number of clinical papers over the past few decades on various aspects of the psychopathology of love (A. Reich, 1953; Kernberg, 1974a, 1974b, 1977; Altman, 1977; Benedek, 1977). Perhaps the reason for this apparent scientific neglect lies in the observation that Freud himself had written such a masterpiece (1912) on this subject.

Bergmann is of the opinion that the anlage or roots of the capacity to love originate in the preoedipal phase. He emphasizes that his tentative conclusions are derived mainly from Mahler's work (1967) on the separation-individuation phase and require further validations. Bergmann speculates that the successful resolution of the symbiotic phase makes it possible for some individuals to exaggerate the difference between one human being and another and "hence enables them to love."

The relevance of object constancy to the capacity to love has not always been appreciated in psychoanalytic theory. The successful traversing of the last subphase of the separation-individuation process brings about a security that plays an important role in the attainment of object constancy. Those who cannot love need entertainment and socialization, and prefer short sexual encounters. They often dread the time when they will be left alone with their partners. Psychoanalysis of such people shows that their mothers were either excessively intrusive or so detached that they could not maintain contact with the child and let him be on his own, alone or in their presence.

In adult love relationships an object is often lost and an individual must then "refind" an original object. Individuals who have difficulty in forming love relationships suffer from "counterrefinding" problems—a term introduced by Bergmann—experience a lack of ardor in new relationships, and even a sense of estrangement. Psychoanalysis can be of value in these instances by revealing the nature of the original detachment and allowing mourning for the lost original object to take place. Bergmann warns, however, that when "the mother-child relationship has been pathological, the urge to refind a similar pathological relationship and then to attempt to reform the partner" dominates the individual's pursuit of the type of love object. If the mother was severely ambivalent, hating, or experienced special difficulty in loving the child during the early phase, the child may grow up believing he is indeed unlovable; assurances to the contrary are of no avail. Love relationships of these children in adulthood are often marked by a masochistic quality. As a further development of the latter theme, women who were hated by their mothers and loved by their fathers can love, according to Bergmann, but do not believe that they are lovable.

It still remains a serious question for research, however, whether an individual who has proceeded without traumatic interruption through the separation-individuation phase has a guarantee of his capacity to love or whether this is only a necessary preliminary or precondition in the appropriate direction.

From the Greek tragedians and the Roman poets the Western world has inherited the idea that love is an overwhelming and dangerous emotion that reduces the mind to a state of inconstancy and childishness. The destructive power of love is described with particular force by Euripides in *Hippolytus*. That play, it will be recalled, records the gradual disintegration of Queen Phaedra's superego and ego under the impact of her love for her stepson. Euripides lets the nurse say to Phaedra, "The love queen's onset in her might is more than man can bear," and the chorus implores Aphrodite: "O never in evil mood appear to me, nor out of time and tune approach" (Coleridge translation). Sophocles lets the chorus in *Antigone* sing:

> Love, unconquered in the fight, Love, who makest havoc of wealth, who keepest thy vigil on the soft cheek of a maiden; thou roamest over the sea, and among the homes of dwellers in the wilds; no immortal can escape thee, nor any among men whose life is for a day; and he to whom thou hast come is mad.
> The just themselves have their minds warped by thee to wrong, for their ruin ... [Oates and O'Neil, 1938, p. 445].

In a similar vein, Menander treats love as a sickness, and Plutarch as a form of madness. With the notable exception of Ovid, the poets of antiquity feared love because it induced regression, and were dimly aware of a relationship between love and infancy.

By contrast, Shakespeare's dominant attitude toward love is ambivalence: "The bitter-sweet character of the food of love is emphasised by Shakespeare as by no one else. It is luscious and bitter, sweet and sour, delicious and loathsome, 'a choking gall and a preserving sweet'" (Spurgeon, 1958, p. 147).

The metaphors with which Shakespeare expresses love are strikingly oral: "Love surfeit not. Lust like a glutton dies." And of Cleopatra it is said, "other women cloy the appetites they feed, but she makes hungry." And Juliet, the heroine that embodies love as few of his heroines do, declares, "My bounty is as boundless as the sea. My love as deep." Plato expressed the ambivalent feelings toward love by a myth. Eros is described in the *Symposium* (203) as the Son of Plenty (Poros) and Poverty (Penia). From his father he has inherited the sense of plenty that accompanies love, and from his mother, the distress that lovers feel.

Finally, there is a third group of poets and philosophers who affirm love without reservation. Russell (1930) quotes an anonymous poet:

> Oh Love! they wrong thee much
> That say thy sweet is bitter,
> When thy rich fruit is such
> As nothing can be sweeter.

And he himself adds: "... not only is love a source of delight, but its absence is a source of pain ... it enhances all the best pleasures, such as music, and sunrise in mountains, and the sea under the full moon. A man who has never enjoyed beautiful things in the company of a woman whom he loved has not experienced to the full the magic power of which such things are capable" (p. 40).

The three basic attitudes have in common the conviction that love is an overwhelming emotion which fundamentally affects the mental stability and the outlook on life of the person who is "in love." We intuitively recognize that a relationship is not love when a radical change in mood has not taken place or when the beloved is painlessly exchanged for another.

We speak of selecting a mate as we speak of choosing an

occupation, and we know that both decisions are the result of a complex interaction between conscious reality-oriented considerations and unconscious wishes. However, when the mate is chosen on the basis of realistic considerations, we suspect prudence rather than love. We speak of "falling in love," and earlier writers spoke of being smitten by love, and evoked the mythological image of the blindfolded Amor. Other languages maintain a similar distinction, as the German distinction between *lieben* and *sich verlieben*. In the vocabulary that Federn developed, we may say that love can be experienced with active or passive ego feelings (Bergmann, 1963). Thus, Robert Browning:

> How say you? Let us, O my dove,
> Let us be unashamed of soul,
> As earth lies bare to heaven above!
> How is it under our control
> To love or not to love? [*Two in the Campagna*].

In keeping with these passive feelings, lovers are prone to stress the accidental and unpremeditated nature of their meeting. Love, however, cannot simply be equated with a selection of a mate based on unconscious rather than utilitarian reasons. Psychoanalytic experience demonstrates that it is possible to have a relationship which is monogamous and tenaciously adhered to and yet devoid of the experience of love. Such mates often stand for parental figures that were more hated than loved, or for repudiated aspects of themselves.

Before Freud, love was the domain of philosophers and poets. Freud drew heavily upon this Western tradition, but these philosophers and poets did not have a genetic psychology at their disposal. They therefore could not discern how one form of love could be related to another, nor could they gain insight into the psychic forces that promote or retard the development of the capacity to love. By contrast, Freud approached the mystery of love through a path that had never been tried before—infantile sexuality. From this vantage point, psychoanalysis could make its unique contribution to the understanding of the origin of the capacity to love. I hope to show that today we can go further than Freud did in this understanding, since we have at our disposal not only his insights but also the findings of Mahler and her co-workers, observations that I believe have special relevance to the genesis of the capacity to love.

On the subject of love, classical thought from Hesiod to Lucretius remained firmly rooted in the mythopoetic point of view. Hesiod saw Eros not only as the god of sensuous love, but also as the power that binds the separate elements of the world. This view was taken over by the pre-Socratic philosophers. To Parmenides (fragment 13), love was the force that made men live and thrive. To Democritus (fragment 78), it was the desire for all beautiful things (Bowra, 1957, p. 196).

Freud (1937) acknowledged his indebtedness to one of the pre-Socratic philosophers, Empedocles, when he said: "... I can never be certain, in view of the wide extent of my reading in early years, whether what I took for a new creation might not be an effect of cryptomnesia" (p. 245). Freud (1925) acknowledged his indebtedness to Plato, at least indirectly, when he said: "... what psycho-analysis called sexuality was by no means identical with the impulsion towards a union of the two sexes or towards producing a pleasurable sensation in the genitals; it had far more resemblance to the all-inclusive and all-preserving Eros of Plato's *Symposium*" (p. 218).

Freud may also have been influenced by other Greek philosophers, since we know (Eissler, 1951) that Comperz's *Greek Thinkers* was one of Freud's ten favorite books.

In keeping with the mythopoetic view, love and hate were to Empedocles quasi-natural and quasi-mythological forces.

> When the elements combine to form animals or plants, men say these are born, and when they scatter again men call it death.... Never will boundless time be emptied of these two [fragment 16].
> In Anger all are diverse and sundered, but in Love they come together and are desired of each other. For out of these are born whatever was and is and will be— trees, men, women, beasts, birds and water-feeding fishes, yea and long-lived gods highest in honours [fragment 21].

To Empedocles, Aphrodite was not only a goddess residing on Olympus, but she literally entered men: "... she it is who is acknowledged to be implanted in the limbs of mortals, whereby they think kindly thoughts and do peaceful works, calling her Joy by name and Aphrodite" (fragment 17) (Guthrie, 1962).

I have quoted the Greek philosophers at some length because I wish to stress that the Greek concept of love was indeed a broad one, and Freud's idea of sublimation is at least implicit in their writings. It becomes explicit in the writings of Plato, who believed that all arts and sciences sprang from some longing or desire and therefore had their origin in Eros. "Touched by love, every one becomes a poet even though he had no music in him before." Not only the "melody of the muses," but also "the arts of medicine," the "metallurgy of Hephaestus," and the "weaving of Athena" are inspired by Eros (*Symposium*, 197). I have shown elsewhere (Bergmann, 1966) that Plato also anticipated Freud's topographic division when he described the emergence of oedipal wishes in dreams, "when the mild and rational soul is asleep." To Eros, Plato assigned the task of bringing together the two natures of man, the divine self and the tethered beast in him (Dodds, 1957).

Aristotle quoted with approval Euripides' statement, "Parched earth loves the rain and stately heaven, when filled with rain, yearns on the earth to fall" (*The Nichomachean Ethics*, Book 8). Browning, in the poem quoted earlier, used the same language, but to him the embrace of heaven and earth was a poetic metaphor, while to Aristotle it was a scientific explanation that illuminated the deeper origins of love.

This mythopoetic view of love as a cosmic force is beautifully expressed by Lucretius in his evocation of Venus (*Lucretius de Rerum Natura*, English translation, W. H. D. Rouse, Book 1, verse 1-50).

> O goddess, from thee, the winds flee away, the clouds of heaven from thee and thy coming; for thee the wonder-working earth puts forth sweet flowers, for thee the wide stretches of ocean laugh, and heaven grown peaceful glows with outpoured light.
>
> ... the herds go wild and dance over the rich pastures and swim across rapid rivers, so greedily does each one follow thee, held captive by thy charm....
>
> For thou alone canst delight mortals with quiet peace, since Mars mighty in battle rules the savage works of war, who often casts himself upon thy lap wholly vanquished by the ever-living wound of love.

Unlike the man of antiquity, modern man knows that waves do not laugh, winds to not flee, and herds obey instincts rather than goddesses. But poets are still permitted to relax the border between animate and inanimate, provided they speak in metaphors. Lovers and poets, according to Plato, had much in common. To lovers, too, is given the permission to relax the border between the animate and the inanimate, and this seems to be the reason why Russell (1930) can say that the ocean and the moon can be experienced in love with a magic they otherwise do not have.

The image evoked by Lucretius became popular in the Renaissance in the many paintings depicting Venus as holding the sleeping Mars in her arms and thus assuring peace. Freud's idea of taming aggression by fusion with libido therefore leans upon a long mythopoetic tradition. Greek philosophers also raised a number of the questions which Freud (1914a) dealt with in his study of narcissism. They wondered whether love arose from the need for an unlike complement or whether like was attracted by like. Aristotle even asked whether it was possible for a man to "feel friendship for himself." He went on to add, "devoted attachment to someone else comes to resemble love for oneself" (*The Nichomachean Ethics*, Book 9, Chapter 4).

In the context of this essay, it is of interest to note that Aristotle defined love as an intensification of friendship, "an emotion of such high intensity that it can be felt only for one person at a time" (*The Nichomachean Ethics*, Book 9; also see Hazo, 1967). Freud (1930) derived aim-inhibited love from sensual love (p. 103). Aristotle also recognized their affinity but, unlike Freud, derived love from friendship. Here I will be concerned only with love as defined by Aristotle and leave aside the manifestations of aim-inhibited libido.

Plato intuitively comprehended an aspect of love that psychoanalysis learned to appreciate only after Mahler illuminated the significance of the symbiotic phase in human development.

In the well-known myth told in the *Symposium*, man was originally a double. As punishment for his rebellion against the gods, he was cut in half, and the two halves forever yearn to be reunited.

For the intense yearning which each of them has towards the other does not appear to be the desire of lover's intercourse, but of something else which the soul of either evidently desires and cannot tell, and of which she has only a dark and doubtful presentiment. Suppose Hephaestus, with his instruments, to come to the pair who are lying side by side . . . and said to them . . . "do you desire to be wholly one: always day and night to be in one another's company? for if this is what you desire, I am ready to melt you into one and let you grow together. . ." there is not a man of them who when he heard the proposal would deny that this meeting and melting into one another, this becoming one instead of two, was the very expression of his ancient need [*Symposium*, 192, Jowett translation].

Two and a half millennia have passed since these lines were written, but only our recently gained knowledge of the intensity of the mother-infant relationship enables us to understand fully what Plato meant by the term "ancient need."

Freud's interest in this myth is worth noting. He knew of its existence at least as early as 1905, when he referred to it (1905c, p. 136) without mentioning Plato by name, calling it a poetic fable. He returned to it fifteen years later (1920, pp. 57, 58). He was then interested enough in this myth to ask Gomperz about its origin, and learned that it went back to the Upanishads, and even further back to Babylonian times. Freud was intrigued by this myth because it supported his hypothesis that the drives have "a need to restore an earlier state of things" (p. 57).

Mahler's discovery of the symbiotic phase offers a more plausible explanation and enables us to substantiate a demonstrable psychological phase for a biological speculation that even Freud accepted with reservations. He (1930) made the pertinent observation that, "At the height of being in love the boundary between ego and object threatens to melt away. Against all the evidence of his senses, a man who is in love declares 'I' and 'you' are one, and is prepared to behave as if it were a fact" (p. 66).

In the Bible, too, we find an awareness of the significance of symbiotic elements in love: "Therefore shall a man leave his father and his mother and shall cleave unto his wife: and they shall be one flesh" (Genesis 2:24).

In a fascinating study, Panofsky (1939) traced the motif of the blind cupid. We are so accustomed to the portrayal of the god of love as blindfolded that it comes as a surprise that Greek and Roman art never portrayed him a such. He appears blindfolded for the first time in the fourteenth century. "Blind cupid," says Panofsky, "started his career in a rather terrifying company. He belonged to night, synagogue, infidelity and death" (p. 112). The allegorical interpretation was most unflattering. "Cupid is nude and blind because he deprives men of their garments, their possessions, their good sense, and their wisdom" (p. 107).

Freud reversed the blind cupid metaphor. It is not Eros who is blind, but we who do not dare look at him. There were at least two reasons why Freud could look at love in a way it had never been looked at before. I have already mentioned that he looked for its origin in the formerly unsuspected area of infantile sexuality. Another reason was that love entered unbidden into his consultation room in the form of transference. It is fascinating to follow Freud's struggle against the acceptance of transference as a legitimate therapeutic tool. Breuer and Freud (1893-1895) referred to transference as a *mésalliance*, and called it "an external obstacle arising from a false connection" (pp. 301-304). After the turn of the century, Freud's understanding of transference had deepened: "What are the transferences? They are new editions or facsimiles of the impulses and fantasies which are aroused and made conscious during the progress of analysis; but they have this peculiarity, which is characteristic for their species, that they replace some earlier person by the person of the physician" (Freud, 1905a, p. 116).

For the next ten years, Freud maintained a line of demarcation between transference and love. However, in 1915, speaking of transference love, Freud (1915b) concluded:

> It is true that the love consists of new editions of old traits and that it repeats infantile reactions. But this is the essential character of every state of being in love. There is no such state which does not reproduce infantile prototypes. It is precisely from this infantile determination that it receives its compulsive character, verging as it does on the pathological. Transference-love has perhaps a degree less of freedom than the love which appears in ordinary life and is called normal; it displays its dependence on the infantile pattern more clearly and is less adaptable and capable of modification; but that is all, and not what is essential ... [p. 168].

Fromm (1956) accused Freud of failing to understand the nature of mature love. This I regard as a misunderstanding. A careful reading of the quotation above shows that, even in 1915, Freud was aware of the role of the ego in transforming or moderating the power of the infantile prototypes and adapting their demands to reality. However, in the context in which Freud was writing, this process was of secondary consequence, for the significant discovery was that love derives its power from the reawakening and the refinding of early relationships. It was this insight that enabled Freud to throw new light on the nature of love.

Apart from transference, references to love appear in

Freud's writings as early as 1894, when he communicated to Fliess: "Quite particularly often melancholics have been anaesthetic. They have no need for coitus. But they have a great longing for love in its psychical form ..." (Freud, 1892-1899, p. 192).

Although this early analysis of melancholia was still crude, if we compare it to Freud's (1917) paper on "Mourning and Melancholia," we find that he had already made the significant observation, amply confirmed in subsequent psychoanalytic literature, that depressives have a particularly strong need to be loved.

Freud made two contributions to the understanding of love at two different periods of his life. The first extends from 1905 to 1912; the second has its origin in the discovery of narcissism and extends from 1914 to 1921. The basic discoveries of the first period can be summarized by two statements: "Every state of being in love reproduces infantile prototypes," and, "The finding of an object is in fact a refinding" (Freud, 1905c, p. 222). This formulation echoes Plato's famous dictum, "All cognition is recognition." However, Plato believed that we recognize what we knew before birth, while Freud stressed that we refind what we once experienced as infants. At times, the resemblance to the infantile prototype may be no more than a similarity in facial features, bodily build, character traits, or even name. At other times, the whole state of being in love reproduces an infantile mode of feeling or an early ego state.

Freud had now formed an outline for a theory of adult love: love becomes possible after puberty by the fusion of "two currents of libido." The first, "affective current," goes back to infancy and to the parental prototypes, while the second, the "sensual current," has its origin in puberty. A failure to fuse the two currents into one can result in neurosis (Freud, 1912, p. 180).

The inclusion of the infantile prototype in adult love does not by itself lead to neurosis. It is conducive to a neurosis only under specific conditions. Freud (1910a, 1912) described the neurotic nature of certain infantile prototypes in detail, calling them "necessary conditions for loving."

> In normal love only a few characteristics survive which reveal unmistakably the maternal prototype of the object-choice, as, for instance, the preference shown by young men for maturer women; the detachment of libido from the mother has been effected relatively swiftly. In our type, on the other hand, the libido has remained attached to the mother for so long, even after the onset of puberty, that the maternal characteristics remain stamped on the love-objects that are chosen later, and all these turn into easily recognizable mother-surrogates [Freud, 1910a, p. 169].

Examples of such conditions or preconditions for loving may be found in the compulsive need of some men to fall in love with women who belong to other men, with promiscuous women, or with women who are or appear to be in need of rescue. Freud demonstrated that all these preconditions are techniques by which the primary process converts the woman into a mother substitute. They are "consequences of the fixation on the mother."

Neurotic women may suffer from similar preconditions. They are frigid in marital relationships and lose their frigidity only when love is secret or forbidden. Freud (1912) commented: "Where they love, they do not desire, and where they desire, they cannot love. They seek objects which they do not love in order to keep their sensuality away from the object they love" (p. 183).

This was written before Freud established the role of aggression in mental development, and fixations are described only in libidinal terms. Today, we know that hostility toward the original object is more important in the maintenance of such a fixation than the magnitude of infantile love.

Freud's papers on love were written only a decade or so after the discovery of the Oedipus complex as the nucleus of neurosis. During this period, he saw all difficulties in loving as stemming from an arrest caused by the Oedipus complex. That the inability to love may reach further back into pre-oedipal periods was yet unknown. It should be noted also that these papers deal more with psychic impotence than with the inability to love.

In 1905, Freud (1905c) saw impotence as an infrequent problem. Later, he became more critical of civilization (Freud, 1912): ". . . I shall put forward the view that psychical impotence is much more widespread than is supposed, and that a certain amount of this behavior does in fact characterize the love of civilized man" (p. 184). Freud (1912) came close to advocating psychoanalysis as the only remedy for a nearly universal psychic impotence: ". . . yet it must nevertheless be said that anyone who is to be really free and happy in love must have surmounted his respect for women and have come to terms with the idea of incest with his mother or sister" (p. 186).

It is possible to surmount what Freud called "respect for women" even without psychoanalysis, but it is difficult to imagine that anybody can, by his own efforts, overcome the horror of incest.

The discovery of narcissism opened the second period of Freud's insight into the nature of love. The concept of narcissism enabled him to differentiate two sources of love. According to the narcissistic model, a person may love what he himself is, what he was, what he would like to be, or someone who was once part of himself. According to the anaclitic model, a person may love the woman who feeds or the man who protects (Freud, 1914a, pp. 88-101). Both forms of love will pose difficulties in the course of development. Narcissistic love is unstable. Any disappointment in the perfection of the love object endangers it, and it is easily withdrawn back to the self. Anaclitic love is passive in its orientation. When it predominates, the active phallic wishes in a man and the corresponding wishes in woman to share the burden of life with her mate remain underdeveloped.

It is not unusual to find that patients seek analysis after the collapse of a love relationship. Here, important differences can be seen. When love is primarily based on object libido, the disappointment leads to mourning, but if the love relationship is primarily narcissistic, the desertion takes on the characteristic of a depressive constellation in the sense in which Bibring (1953) described it. It is then usually associated with rage, humiliation, and the collapse of self-esteem.

The concept of narcissism enabled Freud to gain a new understanding of the sense of bliss associated with loving: "Real happy love corresponds to the original condition in which object libido and ego libido cannot be distinguished" (Freud, 1914a, p. 100). When large quantities of libido are withdrawn from the self to the object, there often can arise a feeling of impoverishment. This is the metapsychological reason why so many lovers feel humble and only when their love is returned is the narcissistic balance restored (p. 98). The feeling of impoverishment associated with love that Freud speaks of is reminiscent of Plato's myth that Eros is the son of Poverty. In one of his later papers Freud (1927a) added, "The difference between an ordinary erotic object cathexis and the state of being in love is that in the latter, incomparably more cathexis passes over to the object and the ego empties itself as it were in favor of the object" (pp. 164-165). But why must man love at all? The question was answered by Freud (1914a) in quantitative terms: "A strong egoism is a protection against falling ill, but in the last resort we must begin to love in order not to fall ill, and we are bound to fall ill if, in consequence of frustration, we are unable to love" (p. 85).

Narcissism also enabled Freud (1921) to understand one of the puzzling features of love, namely idealization:

> The tendency which falsifies judgment in this respect is that of *idealization*.... We see that the object is being treated in the same way as our own ego, so that when we are in love a considerable amount of narcissistic libido overflows on to the object. It is even obvious, in many forms of love-choice, that the object serves as a substitute for some unattained ego ideal of our own. We love it on account of the perfections which we have striven to reach for our own ego, and which we should now like to procure in this roundabout way as a means of satisfying our narcissism ... [p. 113].

Freud's belief in the close connection between love and idealization is supported by Goethe's famous, posthumously published love poem (Eissler, 1963, p. 181). There, Goethe mournfully complains that only he and his beloved had been denied the eternal bliss of loving without knowing each other, that is, without seeing in the other what he never was.

Among psychoanalytic writers, Reik (1944) was particularly influenced by this view of Freud, and made it into the cornerstone of his own theory of love. Reik believed that a person who is about to fall in love suffers from a sense of discomfort and feels acutely aware that he has fallen short of his own ego ideal. Love offers an escape from this inner discontent. Reik quotes a statement by Goethe in *Wilhelm Meister*: "There are no means of safety against superior

qualities of another person but to love him." This view of
love also goes back to Plato's *Symposium*, when Socrates
traps Agathos, who has just delivered a hymn in the praise of
love, into admitting that love is inferior because it wants
what it does not possess.

Reik abandoned the hard-won connection between love
and infantile sexuality. Like so many pre-Freudian philosophers, he draws an absolute distinction between lust and
love. Lust is selfish, biological, and lacks constancy. Love is
artificially fostered by culture and only one person can be
loved at a time.

Freud's observation that love represents the projection
of the ego ideal also influenced Bergler and Jekels (1949).
While Freud stressed the similarity between transference and
love, Bergler and Jekels emphasized a crucial difference.
Love tends to follow a rigid pattern of choice. (We are
familiar with such statements as "This person is my type.")
Transference, psychoanalytic experience has shown, develops regardless of personality or appearance; it can even
disregard the sex of the analyst. Bergler and Jekels believed
that the difference is due to the fact that in love only the ego
ideal is projected, while in transference both ego ideal and
what they called the daemon (the punitive aspects of the
superego) are projected. The distinction is an interesting one.
But it also is not absolute. For many lovers, too, fear that
they are falling short of the requirements that they have
projected on their partners.

Idealization, as Freud had observed, constitutes an
essential component of the capacity to love. Those who can
idealize can establish a positive transference. However, I
have often observed that the transformation of such a proneness for idealization into a real capacity to love can be an
exceedingly difficult psychoanalytic task.

A. Reich (1953) described women who live in a subservient relationship with men whom they consider admirable and without whom they believe they cannot exist. The partner, Reich suggests, "represents the personification of a very early phallic ego-ideal. These phallic features overshadow the individual traits of the father" (p. 27). These women exemplify Freud's statement quoted earlier that "the object has taken the place of the ego-ideal."

Following Freud's formulations (1921), Reich emphasizes that these women suffer from an intolerable conflict between ego and ego ideal which has remained megalomanic. Failure to desexualize the paternal phallus is the main reason why the real characteristics of the father are unimportant in the selection of the mate. In other spheres of their lives, such women have a well-integrated personality and maintain a critical self-evaluation and good reality testing. Unlike the typical borderline and psychotic, whose ego functions as well as libidinal relationships undergo regression, these women illustrate that ego functions can be maintained on a high level, but the selection of the love object is in the service of a reliving of an early ego state.

Jacobson (1967) described a homosexual relationship almost opposite to that described by Reich. In her case, the lover retained for himself the prerogatives of the ego ideal and the rescuer, while he projected his id wishes on the partner. When these efforts to reform and rescue the love object failed, not only the relationship but the inner stability of the patient was endangered.

That projective mechanisms can be important in the selection of a mate without involving the ego ideal was demonstrated by a case reported by Ritvo (1966). A young man who was phobic as a child and compulsive as an adult, married, in the middle of his analysis, a phobic woman who, like him, had suffered from separation anxiety as a child. The marriage to a phobic woman enabled the patient to become the reassuring object. The marriage could also be used as a defense against the danger of regression to a phobic state.

In the cases described by Reich, Jacobson, and Ritvo, we can speak of the selection of a mate based on unconscious needs, but the question remains whether the emotion of love is experienced in such relationships.

While the writings of Balint (1948), Hitschmann (1952), and more recently Eissler (1963), show that psychoanalysts have never lost their interest in the subject of love, one must also admit that little new ground has been broken since Freud's contributions. Examination of the psychoanalytic literature reveals that very few contributions have been made specifically on the subject of love. I believe that this decline in interest goes back to Abraham, who equated love with genitality. In his classical table (Abraham, 1924a, p. 496), he divided the libidinal stages of organization into six, beginning with the early oral stage and ending with the final genital stage. Corresponding to the stages of libidinal organization were six stages of object love beginning with autoeroticism and ending with object love. In the course of this development, object relationships were said to develop from preambivalent to ambivalent and postambivalent. The genital stage was conceptualized as postambivalent. Although this classification was made in 1924, it was not yet based on the dual instinct theory. Derivatives of the aggressive drive are treated as belonging to the pregenital stages. Therefore, the genital stage could be conceptualized as devoid of aggression and hence synonymous with love (Abraham, 1924b). Freud's demands (1931) were less exacting:

> We cannot go so far as to assert that the ambivalence of emotional cathexes is a universally valid law, and that it

is absolutely impossible to feel great love for a person without its being accompanied by a hatred that is perhaps equally great, or vice versa. Normal adults do undoubtedly succeed in separating those two attitudes from each other, and do not find themselves obliged to hate their love-objects and to love their enemy as well as hate him. But this seems to be the result of later developments. In the first phases of erotic life, ambivalence is evidently the rule. Many people retain this archaic trait all through their lives [p. 235].

Abraham's table was incorporated without modification by Fenichel's (1945), and it served until recently as the basis for psychoanalytic nosology. Fenichel's formulations can be taken as representing the psychoanalytic view up to the end of World War II. "... children frequently are in love with themselves (secondary narcissism). They are capable of distinguishing objects and of loving objects as long as the objects procure satisfaction ..." (p. 84).

It is evident that Fenichel believed that children do not pass beyond the stage of need gratification. That children are capable of reaching the stage of object constancy is knowledge which has been acquired only after World War II. Fenichel went on to say: "One can speak of love only when consideration of the object goes so far that one's own satisfaction is impossible without satisfying the object, too ... in love, it must be a kind of partial and temporary identification for empathic purposes which either exists alongside the object relationship or alternates with it in short intervals. We know nothing about the specific nature of this identification" (p. 84).

Under the influence of Wilhelm Reich, Fenichel added: "Persons in whom the genital primacy is lacking, that is, orgastically impotent persons, are also incapable of love" (pp. 84-85).

What matters most for our purposes is Abraham's and Fenichel's seemingly self-evident equation of genitality with a postambivalent attitude and hence with love.

Anna Freud's (1963) concept of developmental lines has modified and in many ways replaced Abraham's classical table in current psychoanalytic thinking. She does not speak of a capacity to love, but only of "genital supremacy with libidinal cathexis transferred to objects of the opposite sex outside the family" (p. 248).

This historical survey has led me to conclude that psychoanalytic theory in its classical phase, that is, up to the end of World War II, had not developed a coherent theory on the subject of love. It did, however, formulate three basic ideas: (1) love becomes possible by the rediscovery in a new person of some aspects of the early love object; (2) love represents the transformation of narcissistic libido into object libido and a concomitant projection of the ego ideal on the beloved; (3) love becomes possible only when the genital phase has been reached. These ideas cannot easily be amalgamated into a coherent theory of love, for the first links love to a genetic sequence of events, the second conceptualizes love as a quantitative flow of libido from self to object, while the third sees love as an automatic byproduct of the last psychosexual phase of development.

Eissler (1963), in his biography of Goethe, further expanded the second, that is, the economic point of view on love. He noted that lovers never tire of repeating their vows of love. They behave in a way reminiscent of mourning: "But while the mourner is at a loss as to where to put his libido, the lover cannot obtain enough libido. Any libido that becomes disposable finds a set of images ready to be invested. The more he loves, the more he regrets that he does not have more libido to bestow" (Vol. 1, p. 660).

Furthermore, Eissler noticed that in a state of love, the

flow of libido is not diminished by sexual gratification. These observations tally well with the quotations of Shakespeare which I have presented at the opening of this paper. Eissler is of the opinion that these repetitious declarations of love are attempts not only to overcome ambivalence, but also to facilitate the withdrawal of libido from the infantile objects. Thus, Goethe could love only when he developed an inhibition against writing to his sister.

In Eissler's analysis, love does not come after the resolution of the oedipal and other incestual ties, but is itself the process in which these ties are resolved. Whether this is true for love in general, or only for the love of Goethe, is a matter that would require further investigation. Like Freud, Eissler sees the roots of the ability to love in the oedipal and other incestuous relationships. I believe that, owing to the contributions of Mahler and her co-workers, it is now possible to go further and seek the roots of the capacity to love in an earlier period of life.

According to Mahler's findings, after a brief, normal autistic phase, the infant enters into the symbiotic phase. Mahler (1967) writes: "The essential feature of symbiosis is hallucinatory or delusional, somatopsychic, omnipotent fusion with the representation of the mother and, in particular, delusion of a common boundary of the two actually and physically separate individuals . . ." (p. 742).

I have earlier quoted Freud (1914a, 1930) to the effect that love breaks down the barrier between self and object, and between narcissistic and object libido. We may conclude therefore that love revives, if not direct memories, then feelings and archaic ego states that were once active in the symbiotic phase.

In the great love stories, *Tristan und Isolde* or *Romeo and Juliet*, the *Liebestod* is chosen in preference to separation. It represents a poetic rendering of the emotions that belong to the symbiotic phase where separation means death. In real life, as Plato so beautifully described in the *Symposium*, lovers also use such a language, but fortunately they speak in metaphors. When this feeling is experienced as an entirely real one, we are no longer dealing with mature love but with a dangerous regression to the symbiotic phase. Because love revives emotions that once belonged to the symbiotic phase, then it becomes easier to understand why so many poets, notably Shakespeare, speak of love in terms of food. It is also more understandable why those who fear love so often employ the vocabulary of the oral triad (Lewin, 1950) and express the fear of being devoured by the love object.

To quote Mahler (1967) once more: "The specific smiling response at the peak of the symbiotic phase predicates that the infant is responding to the symbiotic partner in a manner different from that in which he responds to other human beings. In the second half of the first year, the symbiotic partner is no longer interchangeable . . ." (p. 745).

Robert Browning, in *My Last Duchess*, has given us a poetic description of the innocence of a woman who had not yet reached the stage of object constancy and therefore could not love:

> She had
> A heart—how shall I say?—too soon made glad,
> Too easily impressed; she liked whate'er
> She looked on, and her looks went everywhere.
>
> .   .   .   .
>
> She smiled, no doubt,
> Whene'er I passed her; but who passed without
> Much the same smile?

Although the partner is no longer interchangeable in the symbiotic phase, it is only in the fourth subphase of separation-individuation (Mahler, 1966) that a degree of object constancy is attained that makes the representation of the mother intrapsychically available to the child even in her absence.

In the sixth *Sonnet from the Portuguese*, Elizabeth Browning drew upon emotions that had their origin in the symbiotic phase together with the security that comes from the attainment of object constancy.

> Go from me. Yet I feel that I shall stand
> Henceforward in thy shadow. Nevermore
> Alone upon the threshold of my door
> Of individual life . . .
> The widest land
> Doom takes to part us, leaves thy heart in mine
> With pulses that beat double. What I do
> And what I dream include thee, as the wine
> Must taste of its own grapes. And when I sue
> God for myself, He hears that name of thine,
> And sees within my eyes the tears of two.

The separation-individuation phase has its contribution to make to the capacity for love. It is during this phase that the child first learns to be separate in the presence of the mother. Winnicott (1958c) calls this capacity ego-relatedness, but he contrasts this ability to be alone in the presence of another object with love which he calls an id relationship. My own observations have led me to different conclusions. Those who cannot love also cannot be alone with the love object. They need entertainment and socialization and prefer short sexual encounters. They often dread the time when they will be alone with their partners. Analysis shows that the mothers of such people were either excessively intrusive or so detached that they could not maintain contact with the child and yet let him be on his own or allow the child to be alone in their presence. In transference, this state may manifest itself in a wish to be with the analyst but not be forced to talk. Such patients experience intensely a seemingly paradoxical wish that the analyst remain available to them but refrain from intruding. This wish can easily be mistaken for a form of resistance, but it represents a new kind of relating and may be the forerunner of the capacity to love.

The relevance of object constancy to the capacity to love was not always appreciated in the psychoanalytic literature. For example, Hitschmann (1952) wrote: "I once knew a man . . . who used to fall in love with every young mother he met who held a child in her arms. He was motivated by the repressed memory of his mother with his younger brother in her arms" (p. 423).

Hitschmann, who here made full use of Freud's concept of the prototype, did not explain why this repressed memory evoked love when we would expect it to evoke jealousy or anger. One could argue, of course, that this falling in love represented a reaction formation against the aggressive wishes evoked by the sight of the young mother holding a child. However, I do not believe that it is desirable to speak of love when it is evoked by a category of women rather than by one woman. If Hitschmann's patient were neurotic, he could have fallen in love with one woman because he saw her holding a child. But this link to infancy would have undergone repression and would not be transferable to every woman holding a child. If the wish remains conscious, we are dealing with a special type of Don Juanism, that is, with a compulsive need to possess every woman with a young child, but not with love.

George Bernard Shaw is quoted by Hitschmann (1952) as having said, "Being in love means greatly exaggerating the difference between one woman and another." Following Mahler, we can say that it is the symbiotic phase and its successful resolution in the individuation-separation phase which makes it possible for some to exaggerate the difference between one human being and another, and hence enables them to love.

Shaw's remarks can be contrasted with Russell's (1951) dedication in his autobiography. It is a poem of an old man oriented toward death rather than that of a man seeking a life partner. Nevertheless, or perhaps even because it is a poem of old age, it has captured an essential feature of love.

> Now, old & near my end,
>   I have known you,
> And, knowing you,
> I have found both ecstasy & peace
>   I know rest
> After so many lonely years,
>   I know what life & love may be
> Now, if I sleep
>   I shall sleep fulfilled.

Russell asks for the difficult combination of ecstasy and peace, and love has to transform for him the fear of death into the fulfilled sleep of the satiated infant (Lewin, 1950). Many men have experienced genital pleasure including regard, tenderness, and empathy for their partner, and yet they have not known the experience Russell has described.

I would like now to add a number of probabilistic statements which I regard as likely to be true, but which will require further study before they can be definitely confirmed.

If we agree that the term "love" should be confined to the feeling that one person, and that person alone, can assure happiness, then those children who were reared by a series of rapidly changing nurses, or in institutions that did not permit a strong relationship to develop toward one person during the symbiotic phase, should, like Shaw, be unable to exaggerate the difference between one person and another and therefore be incapable of loving. Children whose parents were divorced and remarried before a stable object representation was established will have difficulty in loving. We often learn from patients that they had two fathers or two mothers, that maternal functions were divided between the mother and an older sibling, the mother and grandmother, or mother and nurse, and even mother and father. In the absence of one significant person during infancy, the integrative functions of the ego have a difficult task to perform. When such a child grows up, in order to love he must find in another person characteristics taken from many objects and integrate them into one. He often fails in this task and, as a result, every relationship represents for him only one aspect of an early significant love object. Sometimes the best that can be attained in such a case is a rotation of objects or the finding of an object that satisfies only one aspect of the unconscious need.

Particular difficulties are encountered when the father assumed maternal functions early in the infant's life, that is, when he bathed, fed, and otherwise cared for the infant. The difficulty is augmented when the father showed more tenderness than the mother.

When the original object was disappointing, the selection of the new object is based not on finding but on a compulsive avoidance of the original object. On the model of counteridentification, I would like to call such a selection "counterrefinding." Such relationships can at times be stable and may lead to important corrective emotional experiences, but they lack the ardor of the relationships which are based on the refinding of the original object. In some cases, I have noticed that the selection on such a basis leaves a sense of estrangement, that is, the person cannot understand why he selected his partner. Genitality may have been reached, but something crucial is missing. In such cases, psychoanalytic therapy can be helpful. When the attachment to the original object is made conscious and the patient realizes that the selection was made on the basis of counterrefinding, mourning for the lost original object can take place. When the libido is detached from the unsatisfactory object, new capacities for love become available. However, it must be admitted that when the mother-child relationship has been pathological, the urge to refind a similar pathological relationship and then to attempt to reform the partner is often overwhelming.

Children whose relationship to the mother had reached adequate intensity, but where the mother was either ambivalent or hating, also experience a special difficulty in loving. They can establish stable relationships and can even love, but since they themselves do not believe that they are lovable, assurances to the contrary are to no avail. They tend to provoke their mates to demonstrate that they are not loved. This is the pattern which Berliner (1958) has found to be typical of masochistic relationships. I have observed that women who were hated by their mothers and loved by their fathers can love, but do not believe that they are lovable.

Abandonment by the mother or her substitute during infancy or early childhood severely impairs the capacity to love. Nevertheless, some find unique ways of reliving the trauma in a restorative way, as the following case will illustrate.

Until his third year of life, Mr. A was reared exclusively by a nurse, who with the advent of the war had to flee the country without even saying good-bye to him. The nurse seems to have been a cold, demanding, and meticulous person. She dressed the child carefully, kept him clean, quiet, and away from the company of other children. When the patient came to treatment, he was meticulously dressed and made a scrubbed impression. To himself, as well as to his family, he was a puzzle. He was devoid of ambition, he seldom worked, he had cronies but no friends. There was nothing that he could tell one person that he could not, just as easily, communicate to another. He lacked any capacity for intimacy. Sexuality was limited to compulsive masturbation, and he had to prove to himself time and again that he was not injured by this masturbation. As one would expect, his relationship to the therapist was positive, but lacked any discernible intensity. He enjoyed coming and talking, but claimed that the analysis only helped him to fill empty hours. During summer vacations, he insisted that he never missed the analyst or gave the analysis any thought. His character structure and behavior in the analysis fitted well into the category that Gitelson (1958) described as ego defects.

During the third year of treatment, a nephew was born. Almost immediately, the patient identified with this nephew, and the relationship to the baby was the first in which I could discern any warmth. He displayed an unusual interest in the baby's welfare. He baby-sat, played with him, and even invented stories for him. When the boy reached the age at which the patient's nurse had left him, he fell in love with that boy's nurse, and thus established the first heterosexual relationship.

Perhaps because the disturbance was so great, the refinding process in this case had to take an almost uncanny concrete form. It also seems probable that a period of identification with the infant had to precede the renewal of the capacity to refind the lost object. It is not easy to determine whether treatment here facilitated this refinding, or whether the great similarity between the infantile and adult situation would by itself have created the preconditions for loving.

If the line of reasoning here pursued should prove to be correct, then the capacity to love presupposes a symbiotic experience which was allowed to proceed without traumatic interruption, and an individuation-separation phase in which the mother did not attempt to rebind the child to herself. The question still remains open whether the successful passage of these two phases by itself guarantees the capacity to love, or whether it is only a necessary, but not necessarily sufficient, condition for it. Clinical experience has shown that some lovers have successfully transferred character traits from the original oedipal parent to the new love object only to discover that they were repeating the unhappy relationship they had experienced as children. Such patients have reached the oedipal phase and have been successful in the displacement of their oedipal wishes upon new objects; yet this refinding was not conducive to happiness, but merely recapitulated the infantile situation. We must, therefore, assume that in order to be able to love, the early object representations must be benign and cathected more with libido than with aggression to make a happy displacement possible.

As I indicated at the beginning of this essay, love is experienced subjectively as an utterly unexpected event and often as a miracle. Why should it be so? It is suggested that the sense of the miraculous results from a dim presentiment that many psychic events have taken place simultaneously, quickly, and without conscious awareness. Furthermore, the psychopathology of love teaches us that love can take place only if every psychic event does not exceed a certain limit.

Let me enumerate some of these events: Freud had stressed that every finding must be a refinding, but this refinding must take place without reawakening the incest taboo. Later, Freud assumed that narcissistic libido must be transformed into object libido, but that this transformation must take place without impoverishing the self. I have stressed further that feelings belonging to the symbiotic phase of development must be awakened but without bringing with them a dangerous ego regression. It should be added that certain ego functions must be temporarily suspended, for example, reality testing must be given up if the necessary idealization is to take place, and yet, paradoxically, this very ego function must simultaneously make possible the selection of a good mate.

That so much can take place in a short time and end well in spite of the many pitfalls constitutes the unending fascination of love. As a result of these interactions, love presents us with a paradox. On the one hand, it is experienced as a unique, unexpected, and even unbelievable event. Lovers often express astonishment that they are capable of such bliss and such a wealth of emotions. On the other hand, the examination of love relationships often reveals that they represent, unconsciously, the resumption of significant relationships that were interrupted long ago. It would not be correct to assert that all lovers experience the emotions which we assume to be active in the symbiotic phase, but frequently love revives such feelings. We are thus led to the conclusion that when the symbiotic phase gives way to further development, it leaves as a residue a longing which remains ungratified until love comes.

THE PSYCHOANALYSIS OF SHAME

Sidney Levin

(1971)

"Whereas guilt is generated whenever a boundary (set up by the superego) is touched or transgressed, shame occurs when a goal (presented by the ego ideal) is not being reached. It thus indicates a real shortcoming. Guilt anxiety accompanies transgression; shame, failure" (Piers and Singer, 1953).

Since the publication of Piers and Singer's monograph, Levin has devoted considerable psychoanalytic attention to the elucidation, dynamics, and treatment of shame, the less familiar of these two affects. In this article he presents in clinical vignettes the external factors most significant in the arousal of shame, such as criticism, ridicule, scorn, or abandonment. The resultant shame is painful, and the ego presses into service the defense measures of limiting of self-exposure, repression, withdrawal of libidinal cathexis, and the discharge of aggression.

Unlike guilt, shame cannot be observed during the preoedipal period, nor does it apparently have archaic precursors as in guilt. It is also of interest that pride, the apparent opposite of shame, can be seen in the earliest years of life. Shame begins in early childhood and undergoes major reinforcements, transformations, and changes of emphasis during both the oedipal phase and the latency period. Those who consciously and/or unconsciously feel shame tend to engage in excessive preoccupation with certain

533

parts of their bodies, employ obsessional thinking, and displace the affect and feeling of shame onto others, especially parents.

A valuable avenue of research is suggested by Levin's observation that there are apparent constitutional limitations in the schizophrenic ego's ability to avoid shame through normal and defensive measures. Furthermore, he differentiates primary from secondary shame. Clinical examples demonstrate that shame frequently underlies fearful, depressed, even paranoid or severely inhibited symptom pictures—designed to avoid the conscious awareness of these intense feelings.

In my own clinical experience, one of the most difficult resistances in the therapy of borderline individuals is the removal of feelings of shame. This is also very common among overt homosexuals of paranoid disposition who, ashamed of their perverse acts and violently opposed to them, engage in a wholesale projection of shame onto the analyst, producing long silences, a paucity of fantasies, dreams and associated material, and, in some cases, a flight from therapy.

In contrast to guilty patients, who are likely to cry out and wish to investigate their source of distress, those who feel shame engage in a masochistic negative therapeutic reaction. Elucidation of shame mechanisms responsible for such blocks then leads to an unblocking and the consequent expression of deeper unconscious sexual fantasies, depressive feelings, castration anxiety, severe aggressive conflicts, and even to the expression of feelings of affection which once were reacted to by shame in the face of early parental harshness and rejection.

The fear of experiencing shame, for which Levin has coined the phrase "shame anxiety," is a type of anxiety deserving of most careful psychoanalytic attention.

I

When psychoanalysis is successful, it results, among other things, in a progressive alleviation of shame. In order to achieve this result to an optimum degree, it is necessary to analyze carefully the numerous reactions in which shame is involved. In an attempt to accent the importance of these analytic efforts, which are often overlooked or inadequately executed, the present article will focus upon this aspect of psychoanalysis to the exclusion of other aspects of psychoanalysis.

In a previous article (Levin, 1967a), I discussed the function of shame as a basic internal barrier to the libido, a notion originally proposed by Freud (1905c). I also pointed out that the external factors which are most significant in the arousal of shame are criticism, ridicule, scorn, or abandonment by others. Since strong feelings of shame are unpleasant, the ego, in accordance with the pleasure principle, attempts to avoid such feelings. During the process of development, these attempts precipitate out in the form of various defenses, some of the most typical of which are the following:

1. *The limiting of self-exposure.* In order to protect oneself from being shamed by others, each individual learns to avoid exposing certain thoughts, feelings, and impulses.

2. *Regression.* As the personality develops and shaming becomes internalized, certain thoughts, feelings, and impulses will evoke shame in the absence of self-exposure. As a consequence, in order to protect against shame, repression of many of these thoughts, feelings, and impulses may be necessary.

3. *The development of the ego ideal.* The numerous aspirations which are set up within the ego ideal reflect,

among other things, the wish to perform in such a manner as to protect oneself from being shamed by others.

4. *The limiting of libidinal investment.* By reducing the amount of libido invested in a person, one can become less vulnerable to his criticism or rejection and therefore less readily shamed by him.

5. *The discharge of aggression.* People often defend against shame by blaming someone else for their failures. They may also use more direct forms of aggression as a defense (Grinker, 1955). For example, it is not uncommon for a man who is ashamed of his deficient masculinity to behave in a sadistic manner toward others in order to prove his masculinity or to direct the attention of others toward his aggressive behavior and away from his sexual behavior, upon which shame tends to concentrate. In fact, there are those who actually become "criminals from a sense of shame" just as there are those who, as Freud (1916a) pointed out, become "criminals from a sense of guilt."

A variety of other defenses may also be instituted. If one reviews the list of major defenses tabulated by Valenstein (1961), it is apparent that many of them serve the purpose, among other things, of avoiding shame. The following are a few examples, taken from this list: altruistic surrender, asceticism, blocking, clinging to objects, clowning, mocking and scoffing, counterphobia, denial, desexualization, displacement, falling ill, intellectualization, isolation, projection, restriction of ego functions, sublimation, undoing, whistling in the dark, and withdrawal. The use of these defenses as a means of avoiding shame is a complex topic, which it is not possible to consider in a few pages. In the present article, therefore, I will not deal with all of these defenses but will discuss some general issues concerning the analysis of shame and will introduce a few examples for purposes of illustration.

II

The intensity of shame which a person experiences is determined by both constitutional and environmental factors. Although shame is not present at birth, it begins to appear in early childhood and may undergo major reinforcement or accentuation during the oedipal phase or latency (French, 1958, pp. 460-461). As development proceeds shame tends to concentrate upon aspects of the self which are exposed to others and may therefore be manifested through obsessive preoccupations with certain parts of the body. A common example is an obsessive concern with the size or shape of the nose. Although this type of symptom may at times be relieved by eradicating the apparent "defect" through plastic surgery, in many instances it remains after surgery since the underlying shame tends to persist. An eighteen-year-old girl believed that her nose was too large and persuaded her parents to permit her to have a nasal plastic operation even though they did not believe it was necessary. Surgery was successful from a cosmetic point of view, but within a few weeks the patient went to a psychiatrist in the hope that he might persuade the surgeon to reconstruct her nose in its original form, since she was now embarrassed about its shape. In other cases, following surgery the shame shifts to other parts of the body. A twenty-year-old girl initially had a plastic operation on her nose because she believed it was too large. A few months later she became preoccupied with her breasts and underwent a plastic operation in order to reduce their size. Her intense shame was not relieved by these procedures, but was again displaced; she now sought a plastic operation on her legs, which she described as "too heavy." At this point the family called a halt to surgery and sent her for psychotherapy.

The obsessions to which shame gives rise may readily

undergo displacement. For example, a young male college student manifested obsessive cleanliness as one of his symptoms. In analysis it was determined that in early adolescence he was ashamed of being Jewish and was obsessively preoccupied with this issue. For several years thereafter he hid his Jewish identity and was temporarily relieved of his shame. However, in late adolescence he felt guilty about his behavior and began to admit that he was Jewish. This change reactivated his shame and gave rise to a new symptom in the form of obsessive cleanliness, which arose largely as a displacement of the previous obsession, since it was based to a considerable degree upon the unconscious fear that others might consider him a "dirty Jew."

In many instances the focus of intense shame is displaced from the self onto external objects—one's relatives, one's friends, etc. For example, it is not uncommon for an adolescent to be intensely ashamed of his parents and therefore to avoid being seen with them.

III

There are many highly sensitive people who react to criticism or rejection with intense shame from early life onward. They are often quite secretive and may be incorrectly perceived by others to be snobbish. These highly sensitive people often develop perfectionistic aspirations, in the hope of reaching an unassailable state. They may also pay careful attention to the attitudes of others and may modify their behavior in extreme ways in order to avoid criticism. Although they may have a strong wish to be the center of attention, they may not act upon this wish, owing to an equally strong fear of being criticized or rejected.

Schizophrenic patients are usually quite sensitive to criticism and readily experience intense shame. Because of this sensitivity they often become very shy (Jacobson, 1964, pp. 197-205). It is my opinion that many of these patients start off in life with a constitutional limitation in the ego's ability to avoid shame through normal defensive measures. Superimposed upon this basic limitation may be the effects of excessive shaming during childhood, which may force the patient to use much of his free ego energy for suppressing or repressing shameful thoughts, feelings, and impulses. The resulting depletion of ego energy may then add to the basic weakness of the ego, making it more susceptible to psychotic developments. It is worth noting that when such a patient becomes psychotic, he often develops symptoms which reflect his intense shame, such as delusions of being watched, of having his mind read, etc.

IV

Those sensitive people who have strong primary shame reactions often experience, in addition, a secondary shame, which can be described as "feeling ashamed of reacting strongly with shame." This secondary shame often concentrates upon the person's underlying sensitivity to being shamed by others or upon the inhibitions which result from such sensitivity.

It is common for patients to attempt to counteract their secondary shame by denying their sensitivity. For example, the man who experiences intense shame when his sexual overtures to his wife are at times rejected may deny that he is reacting sensitively or even that he is reacting with shame. And when the anger to which his shame gives rise comes to the surface, he may attribute it to severe sexual frustration. In order to make this explanation appear logical, however, he may have to exaggerate the frequency of his wife's rejections (Levin, 1969).

It is also common for patients to attempt to counteract their secondary shame by denying their inhibitions. For example, the male college student whose intense primary shame results in heterosexual inhibitions may develop secondary shame in front of his peers concerning these inhibitions. He may then attempt to counteract the secondary shame by denying that he is inhibited, and in order to support this denial he may have to use various rationalizations. For example, he might claim that academic demands prevent him from going out on dates, or that he is opposed to permarital sexual relations on the basis of "moral principles."

V

Several years ago I was called to the emergency ward of a general hospital one evening to see a man who was trembling all over, as though he were reacting to some terrifying event. When I tried to find out what might have happened that day to arouse his fear, he answered in a cryptic manner that nothing unusual had happened; he merely went to work in the morning and returned home at the usual time. I found it difficult to elicit any details, but with some encouragement he described the routine events of the day. When I then asked what had happened on the way home from work, he answered in an unemotional tone that as he walked through the park near his home he was held up by a man with a gun, but since he had no money the man left and did not bother him any more. I commented that he must have been frightened by the gun and the possibility of being shot. He then replied in a highly indignant tone: "I've never been frightened by anything in my whole life!" This reply indicated that the experience of fear was intensely shameful for this man and was being repressed and denied. If such a patient were to undergo therapy, analytic efforts would have to be exerted to make him conscious of his shame and of the projections associated with it, namely, the expectation that others would ridicule him if they found out that he was frightened. If such analytic efforts were successful, the patient's shame concerning his fear would diminish and the fear itself would become conscious. He would also be freer to expose the fear to others. He might then find it possible to take a safe route home from work rather than have to walk through the park, which was a well-known hangout for thieves, in order to prove that he was fearless.

When intense shame envelops a person's normal affective responses, interpersonal relationships may suffer. In a previous article (Levin, 1969) I pointed out that when marital partners have had a fight with one another, their mutual expressions of guilt may facilitate a reconciliation. In other words, it is often through the expression of guilt that the libido, which has temporarily withdrawn to a narcissistic position, can return to an object-libidinal position. But if the partners are not conscious of guilt or cannot communicate it, owing to intense shame concerning it, a cold war atmosphere may prevail. When such people enter therapy, it is essential to analyze the shame, so that the underlying guilt can be liberated and expressed to one another.

In an earlier publication (Levin, 1967b) I pointed out that the first-year college student who becomes emotionally upset due to separation from his (or her) parents may feel intense unconscious shame about still being dependent upon the parents. Because of this shame, he may deny to himself and to others that separation from home is difficult, and he may offer various rationalizations to explain his emotional upset at school. Unfortunately, when a return home or a transfer to a college closer to home is indicated, the student's unconscious shame may make him resistant to such a step. In fact, he might even prefer to return home as an academic failure or as a disciplinary problem rather than as one who might be considered too immature to tolerate separation from his parents. Therapy for such a student will obviously require considerable analysis of the underlying shame.

VI

Although the alleviation of shame during psychoanalysis depends mainly upon the acquisition of insight, some degree of alleviation results merely from the patient's efforts to communicate to the analyst. When a patient brings up a new topic in the face of shameful feelings, the very act of verbalizing tends to mitigate the shame. The analyst's neutrality plays an important role in this change, since he does not express intolerant attitudes toward the patient nor does he react with intense shame himself and therefore avoid discussing topics which arouse the patient's shame. In fact, the analyst adopts a serious, shame-diluting attitude and is ready to hear more.

When a patient's primary shame gives rise to severe blocking during psychoanalysis, he may develop intense secondary shame concerning the blocking itself and may feel that he is failing in the analysis. As a consequence, he may manifest a depressive response to treatment, often with increasing reluctance to come to the sessions. If the secondary shame is then clarified, the patient usually becomes more tolerant of the blocking and the depressive response to treatment disappears.

As the analysis proceeds, the blocks themselves will tend to disappear. This change depends to a considerable degree upon the analyst's clarification of the primary shame responsible for the blocks. Such clarification is facilitated by the use of such terms as "self-consciousness," "embarrassment," "shame," and "humiliation" at appropriate times, thereby giving the patient useful labels to apply to his underlying feelings and reactions.

Sometimes the analyst intentionally reinforces secondary shame as a means of counteracting the patient's withholding tendencies. For example, the analyst may tell the patient that, in order for the analysis to be successful, the patient has to make repeated efforts to express his thoughts and fantasies. Such a remark can shame a patient into complying, since it suggests that the analyst will be disappointed if the patient does not continue to face his resistances. Furthermore, whether it is made explicit or not, the analyst's expectation that the patient will be utterly truthful contains a threat of disapproval if the patient is found to be using dishonesty as a defense.

In many instances the analyst has to stimulate further self-exposure by repeatedly urging the patient to communicate in detail. Sometimes an "exploratory guess" will help to overcome the shame barrier (Ferenczi, 1911; Levin, 1965). A single woman of thirty-five with a moderately deep depression talked repetitively, like a broken record, about her fear that she would never be able to marry because men invariably dropped her after a brief relationship. The therapist guessed that by talking only about heterosexual issues she was avoiding the topic of homosexuality, and he communicated this guess to her. She immediately confessed her homosexual affairs and it was then possible to analyze her intense shame concerning them. It is worth noting that this patient had gone to a previous therapist for over a year without revealing her homosexuality to him.

Patients who manifest severe blocking in analysis are often labeled with a diagnosis of hysteria. Such blocking can be thought of as phobic in nature, since it is based upon a high level of fear (i.e., the fear of experiencing intense shame). Patients with such fear usually have an inability to defend successfully against shame by expressing their sexual fantasies as derivatives that are removed from deeper shameful content (Levin, 1964).

Many patients experience intense shame in relation to feelings of affection. Several years ago I undertook the treatment of an unmarried middle-aged woman who complained of long-standing depression. After a few weeks of therapy she made a major confession, to the effect that for a period of two years in her early twenties she had been the "mistress" of a married man. When she first discussed this affair, her remorse focused mainly upon the illicit nature of the relationship. With further analysis, however, it became clear that she had been deeply in love with this man, but was ashamed to admit it. After this shame was clarified, it diminished considerably; and the intensity of her love broke through into consciousness. She was then able to grieve about losing this man. Following this phase of treatment, her depression diminished and she was freer in her relationships with men in general.

Much of the analysis of shame must focus upon the "fear of experiencing shame," which I have labeled "shame anxiety" (Levin, 1967a). This type of anxiety, which is as basic as castration anxiety, is felt largely as a combination of self-consciousness and the fear of being shamed by others. During the process of development, as successful techniques for avoiding shame are acquired, shame anxiety is transformed more and more into a form of signal anxiety (Fenichel, 1945, pp. 139-140).

When shame anxiety is subjected to careful scrutiny, it is found to consist of a number of specific fears, which are largely unconscious and which tend to become part of the transference. The contents of these fears include such factors as the specific aspects of the self for which one expects to be shamed, the circumstances under which one expects to be shamed, the individuals who might do the shaming, etc. It is apparent that much of this content is derived from past experience. However, some of the content is also derived from current reality, which always contains many realistic possibilities of being shamed. In assessing these possibilities the ego functions like a computer, since it continuously processes experiential data in order to determine what qualities in oneself are most likely to evoke the shaming responses of others, and, as a corollary, what qualities in oneself are most likely to elicit the esteem of others. These determinations involve complex integrations of past and current experience and take place largely on an unconscious level. In fact, much of the current reality which is thus integrated is perceived unconsciously. These unconscious processes, which enable the ego to set up its defenses against shame, can often be brought to consciousness and subjected to careful analysis.

Much of the analysis of shame is conducted in relation to the transference, and if this aspect of analysis is omitted, the patient's shame may actually become reinforced. A young male graduate student started an analytic hour by describing several incidents in childhood when he felt resentful toward his parents for going away on trips. He then expressed similar resentment toward his analyst for having taken a recent vacation. In interpreting these reactions, the analyst focused upon the patient's strong dependency needs (which were originally directed toward his parents and which were now being directed toward the analyst) and pointed out that when these needs were frustrated the patient became very angry at the frustrating object. The patient reacted to this interpretation as though it were a criticism, and following it he showed increased suppression of his dependency needs and increased efforts to hide the anger which arose when these needs were frustrated. On exploring the genetic basis for this response, it was learned that during childhood, when the patient reacted strongly to separation, his father would often shame him by calling him a "big baby." It was now apparent that the patient had experienced the analyst's comments as a repetition and reinforcement of these childhood experiences. After this issue was clarified and the patient's excessive shame concerning dependency was carefully delineated, the shame became mitigated and an increased tolerance for dependency needs evolved.

It is not uncommon for a patient to enter psychoanalysis with an unconscious hope of achieving a relatively shame-free state. This type of patient often grossly underestimates the shame reactions of others and may have intense envy of people who appear to be well poised. He may also incorrectly perceive the analyst to be essentially free of shame. This type of distortion usually serves a special purpose; it enables the patient to retain the unrealistic expectation of eradicating his own shame by becoming like an idealized other person. When the analyst also has unrealistic expectations of eradicating the patient's shame, the hope of achieving a relatively shame-free state may be reinforced.

Shame is often mitigated when a patient comes to the full realization that other people experience feelings of shame similar to his own. For example, after a period of analysis a student might remark: "Before I entered analysis, I realized that some people were afraid to speak up in class, but I didn't realize that everyone had such fear and that so many people had a great deal of it, even the teachers." Such a patient may now see others as fellow sufferers rather than as envied rivals, and he may now speak more realistically about people in general, without exaggerating their differences.

Counterphobic patients may behave in a manner which might be characterized as "countershame." Some of these patients appear to have deficient shame and may at times behave inappropriately with little apparent embarrassment and little apparent sensitivity to criticism. With careful analysis, however, one may find that the patient's shame is actually being repressed and that, as an auxiliary defense, the critical attitudes of others are being denied. When these defenses are successfully analyzed, more normal shame responses may evolve and the inappropriate behavior may then diminish or disappear.

The patient who has strong countershame may also have a strong need to shock others. It is not uncommon for this need to be unconscious and for the patient to be unaware of the shocking effects of his actions. And, surprisingly enough, when people avoid having contact with him, he may not understand why they behave this way. Considerable analysis may be necessary before he realizes that they avoid him largely to protect themselves from embarrassment. This realization is usually accompanied by greater awareness of the need to shock others and by greater effort to exert control over this need. As a consequence, the patient is usually better able to analyze the shame which he had isolated previously.

Sometimes a patient who behaves in an indiscreet manner does not isolate his shame but experiences it as a painful symptom which he hopes to eradicate through psychoanalysis. In other words, he wishes to be "cured" of his shame so that he may continue to indulge in his indiscreet behavior in an ego-syntonic manner. This wish is unrealistic, and the patient must be helped to realize that in order to protect himself from excessive shame he will have to control his indiscreet actions. Even if it were possible to build up his defenses against shame so that he might continue his indiscreet behavior in an ego-syntonic manner, his relationships with others would still be unsatisfactory.

The childhood "wish for perfection," which is often an

important motivation for treatment (Tartakoff, 1966), also has to be carefully analyzed in terms of underlying feelings of shame. When the analyst first indicates that the wish for perfection represents a wish to avoid shame by making oneself invulnerable to criticism, the patient may show strong resistance to this idea. And when the analyst first points out some of the patient's specific shame reactions, the patient may complain somewhat as follows: "What good is it to point out my shame? I want to get rid of it. I must therefore revive those early childhood experiences which gave rise to it." This attitude is often associated with the conviction that intense shame is based entirely upon early traumatic experiences, which only have to be brought to consciousness in order for the shame to be eliminated. A patient with such a conviction may therefore concentrate upon reviving early childhood memories. Although these efforts may foster the genetic analysis of shame, they may also serve as a major resistance to the analysis of current shame reactions. When these resistances are overcome and a more thorough analysis of shame is achieved, the wish for perfection tends to diminish. As a consequence, the original need for a "perfect" analyst, a "perfect" wife, a "perfect job performance," etc., gives way to greater readiness to accept compromises. Furthermore, since reality sense improves, the patient realizes not only that feelings of shame are universal but also that, at normal levels of intensity, they are essential mediators of normal interpersonal relationships (Levin, 1967a).

It is not uncommon for young people to enter into sexual relations in the face of intense shame which seriously interferes with satisfaction. By repeating the sexual activity, some alleviation of the shame may result. But in many people these effects do not occur, since the shame is unconscious. If treatment is undertaken and the underlying shameful thoughts, feelings, and impulses are brought to consciousness, relief of shame may occur; the sexual activity may then bring the satisfaction which the patient had originally anticipated.

Experiences of being teased by others, which are common in adolescence, tend to diminish considerably when adult life is reached. However, when a person who is highly shame-ridden reaches adult life, he may unrealistically continue to anticipate being teased by his peers and may continue to manifest defensive withdrawal or defensive teasing. Analysis can help such a patient to realize that his anticipations of being teased by others are unrealistic and are based upon persistence of adolescent shame reactions. As this realization is acquired, the patient's defensiveness may disappear, and he may begin to communicate with others in a more serious manner.

When analytic therapy is successful and shame is mitigated, many thoughts, feelings, and impulses which have been repressed owing to shame are made conscious. If the patient can then give up some of his characteristic secretiveness and expose to others in an appropriate manner more of his thoughts, feelings, and impulses, a further mitigation of shame may occur, since the previously anticipated rejection by others will not be forthcoming. This aspect of the therapeutic process is a form of working through.

The process of working through involves a gradual facing of new experiences and may also require a step-by-step expansion of sexual activity. A twenty-one-year-old female college student came to analysis with what appeared to be a "marriage phobia." She had been dating a young man for about a year and knew that she wanted to marry him but was unable to do so. On exploring her sexual behavior it was found that she was avoiding all types of sexual stimulation except for hugging and kissing, and that this avoidance was due largely to excessive shame. The genetic basis for these inhibitions could then be determined, especially the numerous shaming experiences to which she had been subjected in childhood, primarily by her prudish mother. Following this phase of analysis she permitted her boy friend to touch her breasts for the first time, and she was surprised to find that she actually enjoyed this experience, even though it was still accompanied by self-consciousness and embarrassment. With further analysis, she participated in and enjoyed additional forms of sexual stimulation, but only after she consciously faced the shame barrier at each step of the way. As a result of these new experiences, the alleviation of shame gradually increased and the fear of marriage dissolved.

When a patient is ready to face new experiences with the intention of mastering his shame, he has to proceed slowly in order to avoid experiencing overwhelming levels of shame which might lead him to recoil. In deciding upon a new course of action, therefore, he has to take into account his probable emotional reaction. For example, if he has a low tolerance for speaking before audiences, it may be wise for him to avoid undertaking a large number of such engagements. Or if he has a low tolerance for socializing, it may be wise for him to limit such experiences until further analysis raises his level of tolerance.

Although much of the analysis of shame falls into the category of ego analysis, a great deal of it falls into the category of ego-ideal analysis, since it involves the exploration of numerous "positive" and "negative" ego-ideal attitudes (Kaplan and Whitman, 1965). Furthermore, shame has to be analyzed at each phase of treatment since it represents one of the major motives for defense. For example, when a young man enters analysis his fear of being hurt by the analyst may be largely repressed due to shame. Therefore the shame may have to be analyzed *first*, before the repression can be released and the fear of the analyst brought to consciousness. As the analysis proceeds, one may find that the patient's anger at the analyst is also repressed due to shame; and the shame may have to be analyzed *first*, before the anger can be brought to consciousness. Some time later, it may become apparent that the patient's sexual feelings for the analyst are repressed due to shame, and in order to bring these feelings to consciousness one may again have to analyze the patient's shame. Each one of these steps may include not only careful ego and superego analysis but also careful genetic analysis.

Summary

In conducting a psychoanalysis, the efforts of the analyst must be directed, among other things, to a careful analysis of reactions involving shame. When such efforts are successful, a progressive alleviation of shame will result. The present paper focuses upon this aspect of psychoanalysis to the exclusion of other aspects of psychoanalysis.

ON DISILLUSIONMENT:
THE DESIRE TO REMAIN
DISAPPOINTED

CHARLES W. SOCARIDES

(1971)

DISCUSSION OF C. W. SOCARIDES' PAPER "ON DISILLUSIONMENT"
BY ARTHUR A. SCHMALE, JR.

*Dr. Socarides' interesting paper raises three distinct but
related issues. What is an affect; is disillusionment as he is
using the term most appropriately considered an affect; and
what is the relationship of disillusionment to depression?*

*Dr. Socarides speaks of affects and chronic ego states as
constituting severe blocks to our therapeutic endeavors
which must be treated as strong resistances in order to
uncover the infantile material. He also, when referring to his
concept of disillusionment, indicates that there are normal
and pathological forms of the affect. Socarides' conceptualization of affects as resistance or as serving an adaptive or
nonadaptive function goes beyond what is usually referred
to as the ego theory of affects. Affects are a reaction to
situations of danger—actual and anticipated. More broadly,
they indicate the ego's awareness of its capacity to integrate
id, superego, and external-world pressures at any point in*

This paper was formally discussed before the American Psychoanalytic Association in 1968 by Dr. Schmale of the University of Rochester. Dr. Schmale graciously
made his remarks available to me for this commentary.

time and space. It is thus not the affect itself that is to be seen as normal or pathological, but rather the ego's capacity to adjust to intrapsychic pressures, which is then reflected in a particular affect or a change in affect. In Socarides' paper, disillusionment represents more than an affective reaction of disappointment to an actual or anticipated danger in that there is included a desire to remain disappointed, which implies that an adaptation of sorts has taken place.

I propose that Socarides' disillusionment, which began as an ego awareness of a loss of gratification for which there was no replacement, became transformed into a symptom as a means of trying to terminate or overcome the conflict that gave rise to the affect in the first place. In other words, the ego may actively pursue what it has passively experienced as the trauma of object loss as a last means of achieving some kind of control. Thus, disillusionment, which is first experienced passively as disappointment, is turned into an active pursuit of the experience. As Freud expressed it in "Beyond the Pleasure Principle" (1920), the child has turned the traumatic experience into a game in order to master the situation. The game, which is repeated over and over, involves the active pursuit of activities in which some instinctual gratification will be achieved through the guise of the symptom. As expressed by Rapaport (1961), the process of turning passivity into activity successfully masters anxiety by setting up counterphobic defenses.

The desire to remain disappointed in the case of disillusionment and the desire to remain worthless in the case of melancholia indicate the masochistic turning of rage onto the self as a means of actively defending against the underlying affects of helplessness or hopelessness, respectively.

Psychoanalysis, in penetrating the intricacies of ego psychology, has turned increasingly to the study of affects.

These involve the whole personality, resulting in chronic ego states, thereby inducing the ego to cope not only with underlying conflicts but also with the initiating affect. Affects constitute severe blocks to our therapeutic endeavors and must be treated as strong resistances in order to uncover the infantile material. They loom prominently in the working-through process of successful psychoanalytic therapy.

This paper presents various theoretical and clinical data concerning the affect of disillusionment in order to develop further the psychoanalytic theory of affects. It presents illustrative clinical material and surveys the literature on the subject, welding into a coherent whole the psychoanalytic observations on this important aspect of behavior. It describes the affect of disillusionment; differentiates between pathological disillusionment and disillusionment as a normal psychic process; and demonstrates the adaptive and non-adaptive use of disillusionment.

Disillusionment varies in intensity from that which is adaptive to catastrophic disillusionment. Genetic considerations are presented as to origin. As with other affects, the id, ego and superego expressions in disillusionment are in continual interplay, now one, now another dominating the clinical picture.

Curiously enough, the state of disillusionment often alluded to by patients has received little psychoanalytic attention. But an immensely rich literature challenges us when we explore the contributions of poets, dramatists, novelists and those engaged in philosophical dissertation. It is thrust upon us that man's happiness or unhappiness is intimately related to the illusions he lives by, the reality around him, and his condition of disillusionment. Psychoanalysis can only profit from heeding some of these creative utterances on the nature of human vulnerability.

C. Giltman, in his poem "Disillusionment," emphasizes the self-protective and defensive measures necessary in relationship to others in order to avoid the pain of catastrophic disillusionment:

> Let me keep my eyes on yours;
> I dare not look away
> Fearing again to see your feet
> Cloven and of clay.

St. Bernard, in *De Consideratione*, bluntly asserts: "It is a misery to be born, a pain to live, a trouble to die." Robert Burns, in his poem "Despondency," exclaims: "O Life! thou art a galling load,/Along a rough, a weary road." Samuel Johnson in his novel *Rasselas* concluded that "Human life is everywhere a state in which much is to be endured and little to be enjoyed." Rousseau observed that "Man's frantic activity arises from a fear of quiet, the fear that if he is not careful he will glimpse some dimension of reality about himself and then fall into deep despair."

An unidentified author writes: "Dying's not the worst. It's living without a dream—or let us be less dramatic— without any real reason except that the body still functions— that's what I dread."

Bellow (1966) cautions contemporary society to divest itself of the vogue to be illusionless: "I am speaking of educated and indeed super-civilized people who believe that a correct position makes one illusionless, that to be illusionless is more important than anything else, and that it is enlightened to expose, to disenchant, to hate and to experience disgust ..."

Eugene O'Neill "was haunted by a central theme throughout his life which appeared in most of his plays ... Man cannot live without illusions; he must cling to his pipedreams, even knowing they are pipedreams, in order to survive" (Gelb, 1964). In *Don Quixote* Cervantes produced a masterpiece on the subject of illusions and their function.

T. S. Eliot, the poet of disillusion and despair, captured and expressed in verse the sense of a doomed world, of a fragmentation of spirit. He wrote:

> This is the way the world ends,
> This is the way the world ends,
> This is the way the world ends,
> Not with a bang, but a whimper
> ["The Hollow Men," 1925].

Chekhov's play *Ivanov* is a powerful portrayal of the disillusioned man whose condition is complicated by severe depression: "I do nothing and think about nothing . . . Love is nonsense, caresses are saccharine, work is meaningless, songs and passionate speeches are old and dated. And wherever I go I bring with me misery, a cold boredom, discontent, aversion to live . . . already tired, disenchanted."

Chekhov's depiction of disillusionment is surpassed only by the description of a disillusioned man in one of Thomas Mann's short stories, "Disillusionment." His protagonist asks: "Do you know, my dear sir, what disillusionment is? . . . Not a miscarriage in small unimportant matters, but the great and general disappointment with everything, all that life has in store." In picturing the early years of his antihero as consisting only of words, of shadow rather than substance, form rather than content, an arid environment for affective development, Mann supplies a hint as to the etiology of the condition.

THEORETICAL CONSIDERATIONS

Six months after the outbreak of World War I, Freud (1915e) wrote that the war had brought "disillusionment."

It has brought to light an almost incredible phenomenon: the civilized nations know and understand one
another so little that one can turn against the other with
hate and loathing.... A belligerent state permits itself
every such misdeed, every such act of violence, as
would disgrace the individual.... we are misled into
regarding men as 'better' than they actually are.... we
are certainly misled by our optimism into grossly exaggerating the number of human beings who have been
transformed in a cultural sense.... We may ... derive
one consolation ...: our mortification and our painful
disillusionment on account of the uncivilized behaviour
of our fellow-citizens of the world during this war were
unjustified. They were based on an illusion to which we
had given way. In reality our fellow-citizens have not
sunk so low as we feared, because they had never risen
so high as we believed. The fact that the collective
individuals of mankind, the peoples and states, mutual-
ly abrogated their moral restraints naturally prompted
these individual citizens to withdraw for a while from
the constant pressure of civilization and to grant a
temporary satisfaction to the instincts which they had
been holding in check.... the primitive mind is, in the
fullest meaning of the word, imperishable [pp. 278-286].

Another occurrence which has

shocked us no less than the descent from their ethical
heights which has given us so much pain.... is the want
of insight shown by the best intellects, their obduracy,
their inaccessibility to the most forcible arguments and
their uncritical credulity towards the most disputable
assertions [p. 287].

What can ease our disillusionment? Freud's belief is that
we should "much more easily endure the disappointment" if
our demands were more "modest.... Perhaps they are

recapitulating the course of individual development, and . . . still represent very primitive phases in organization and in the formation of higher unities" (p. 287).

Regarding death, Freud felt illusions about death should be destroyed.

> Should we not confess that in our civilized attitude towards death we are once again living psychologically beyond our means, and should we not rather turn back and recognize the truth? Would it not be better to give death the place in reality and in our thoughts which is its due, and to give a little more prominence to the unconscious attitude towards death which we have hitherto so carefully suppressed? [p. 299].

Although this seems to be a regression, Freud adds:

> But it has the advantage of taking the truth more into account, and of making life more tolerable for us once again. To tolerate life remains, after all, the first duty of all living beings. Illusion becomes valueless if it makes this harder for us [p. 299].

Strictly speaking, we are not justified in feeling so disappointed if an illusion is destroyed. "We welcome illusions because they spare us unpleasurable feelings, and enable us to enjoy satisfactions instead" (p. 280). Therefore, as Freud warns, we must not complain if sometimes we come into collision with some portions of reality. Our illusions have been helpful up to the moment of our intense disappointment, but we must not be "shattered" by our disillusionment. Freud's concern with these themes is reflected in many of his works during the remaining fifteen years of his life (1927b, 1930, 1933b, 1939).

In "The Future of an Illusion" (1927b) Freud made reference to religious beliefs as illusory. "And now you must not be surprised if I plead on behalf of retaining the religious doctrinal system as the basis of education and of man's communal life." One cannot remove this illusion "precisely on account of its wish-fulfilling and consolatory power . . ." (p. 52).

In the last section of "Civilization and Its Discontents" (1930) he wrote: "For a wide variety of reasons, it is very far from my intention to express an opinion upon the value of human civilization. . . . One thing only do I know for certain and that is that man's judgements of value follow directly his wishes for happiness—that, accordingly, they are an attempt to support his illusions with arguments" (pp. 144-145).

Freud's paper "On Transience" (1916b) has direct clinical significance for our understanding of the disillusioned state, although the term "disillusionment" is not used. It deals with the transient nature of beauty which some people complain interferes with their enjoyment of it. "In relation to the length of our lives it can in fact be regarded as eternal. . . . evanescence only lends . . . a fresh charm. . . . since the value of all this beauty and perfection is determined only by its significance for our own emotional lives, it has no need to survive us and is therefore independent of absolute duration" (pp. 305-306). Freud believed that what spoiled some people's enjoyment of beauty, in actuality their enjoyment of life, was the revolt in their minds against mourning.

Freud asks why this detachment of libido from object should be such a painful process. The mystery is resolved when we consider that the libido clings to its objects and will not renounce those that are lost even when a substitute lies ready at hand. Such then is mourning. But mourning, as we know, should come to a spontaneous end no matter how painful it is. "When it has renounced everything that has been lost, then it has consumed itself, and our libido is once more free (in so far as we are still young and active) to replace the lost objects by fresh ones equally or still more precious" (Freud, 1916b, p. 307).

Rycroft (1955) defined the mechanisms involved in the processes of idealization, illusion, and disillusion from the point of view of normal and abnormal events in the human psyche. An individual's life may be strongly influenced by his state of illusion but eventually he may be faced with a "threat of sudden, catastrophic disillusion, the collapse of a 'secondary construction' based on illusion and idealization which was maintained as a defense against a sense of despair and futility" (p. 82).

Elaborating upon the ideas presented by Winnicott (1945) and Milner (1952), Rycroft states:

> The development of a healthy erotic relationship with reality involves that at the moment of consummation of a wish there should be a convergence and merging of this hallucinated imago (and its cathexis) with the imago of the available external object, not a shift of cathexis from one imago to the other. Failure to fuse these imagos leads to a divorce between the imaginative and intellectual functions, that is, in principle, at least unnecessary. Successful fusion, on the other hand, leads to freedom from the belief that the desire and reality are in inevitable opposition to one another ... [p. 85].

The hallucinated imago is formed by a double process of introjection and splitting. This mode of formation explains the compulsion to idealize accompanied by fantasies of internalized bad objects with the subsequent reprojection onto the environment and seeing nature and the environment as actively hostile toward the individual.

One can understand the problem of illusion only if one apprehends that a certain primitive adaptation or response to reality has already taken place in the earliest years of life.

With further reference to the concepts of Winnicott (1945) and Milner (1952), Rycroft describes the process of normal illusion formation and normal disillusionment:

Subjectively, that is, from the infant's point of view, to
the extent that external reality has played into its
unconscious expectations, it will develop the illusion . . .
that it has created its objects, or to put it the other way
round, will be spared for a while the awareness that its
objects are not part of its self, have not been created
omnipotently by its own desires. Though this illusion
will require an eventual disillusion, the disillusionment
will be confined to its belief in its omnipotent control of
reality, not to reality itself. The healthy child's hero
worship of its parents and its belief in their omnipotence
is to be seen as a normal process of idealization which
tides it over this period of disillusion until such time as
it can rely on its own powers and discovers itself as an
individual, potent but not omnipotent [p. 86].

In pathological illusion formation and pathological
disillusionment, there has been a failure of the early environment "to maintain a modicum of the satisfaction, [and]
impulses, to the extent that they have arisen at all in a
frustrating environment, will lack firm attachment to the
imagos of real, external objects and external reality will be
subjectively felt as tantalizing and bad" (p. 86).

Disillusionment is a normal process when it is confined
simply to the child's belief in its own omnipotence and not to
the value of external reality as a whole. Illusions appear,
therefore, to be an essential part of the mental investment in
reality.

Kris (1955) observed that the capacity for appropriate
illusion formation seems to constitute one of the earliest
stages in neutralization. This predominantly and typically
depends on the interaction between mother and child and
prepares the way for identification.

Sperling (1949) felt that the inability to form illusions
reflected an impoverishment of the ego, a symptom which

can be observed in many patients. Often when illusions cannot be sustained it leads to general depression and disillusionment and perhaps even to what he termed a collapse of the whole moral system. He wonders whether rich and colorful experience in life is possible without illusions, and he believes that controlled illusions may be a safe compromise between the reality principle and the pleasure principle.

Jacobson (1964) describes the child as going through

> fleeting, though repeated, experiences of frustration, which are not yet associated with the love object. Only with the establishment of object relations do they turn into experiences of being hurt and disappointed in the parents as human entities . . . . The total effect of his disheartening experiences is a "disillusionment" (*Enttäuschung*, the German term for disappointment) . . . when disillusionment is experienced before the child is ready to fight his hostile devaluation of the parents with the support of idealizations, it may arrest the advance of object relations and interfere with normal ego-ideal and superego formation, which depend on the child's admiration and respect for his parents [pp. 104-105].

She feels this may result in the "cynic," with predominantly selfish infantile ego ideals, or in a defective superego formation.

If the boundaries between self and object are still indistinct, according to Jacobson, and libidinal and aggressive forces are able to move freely back and forth between self and object images, "disappointment and devaluation of objects will impart themselves immediately to the self and cause self devaluation and narcissistic hurt; and, conversely, narcissistic injuries will induce devaluation of the love objects and disappointment in them" (p. 106). In the latter case the devaluation of the love objects and disappointment is the disillusionment, the dissatisfaction with the external world. It would seem that it is the severity of the preoedipal disappointments which result in narcissistic injuries which are of vital importance for the formation of pathological disillusionment.

In effect, the belief in good, gratifying external objects is impaired and when early experiences of severe disappointment and abandonment have prevented the building up of unambivalent object relations and stable identification in childhood and weakened the child's self-esteem and his belief in finding love in the future.

CLINICAL CONSIDERATIONS

Disillusionment is a complex emotional state derived from fear and pain in which there is a disappointment in things, as they are not as one had imagined and hoped. This is coupled with a continuing loss of ability to find value and interest in the external world as it actually is. Succinctly, it can be described as the desire to remain disappointed. Three factors are essential to the definition of disillusionment: (1) the presence of a previously imagined and hoped-for expectation; (2) a loss or disappointment relating to this hope or expectation; (3) a subsequent loss of ability to find value and interest in things as they actually are, i.e., an inability to deal satisfactorily with reality in accordance with the pleasure principle and to make satisfying object cathexes.

The usual responses to experiencing loss and frustration are fear, rage and hate, envy, bitterness, and a host of other emotional states. Depression is an infantile cry in response to loss with the concomitant rage turned against the self and unconsciously designated to regain maternal love, the lost breast, and thereby attain fulfillment.

In demeanor, bearing, gesture, and attitude, the disillusioned person dramatizes his basic philosophy: "So that is what life is all about. This is what one can really expect. I have no further expectations. One can only be deceived, disappointed, and hurt. I know all about it."

Disillusionment must be differentiated from depression. In depression the self is made the target of aggression and feelings of unworthiness while external objects are not denigrated. In disillusionment external objects are bad, while in depression they are not necessarily evil. In disillusionment there is often a self-aggrandizement; in depression the self dwindles with severe loss of self-esteem. In disillusionment the problem is deemed to lie in unsatisfactory external objects, a denial and projection of the intrapsychic conflicts. In depression the self is blamed for both its inadequacies and its failure to gain satisfaction. In the former aggression is externalized; in the latter it is turned against the self. Unlike the depressive, conscious guilt is strikingly absent as a conscious complaint by the disillusioned.

In contrast to the depressed patient, there is often an attempt by the disillusioned to win converts to his feeling of disenchantment with life. Disillusionment may ultimately encase one in hopelessness and despair (quantitative factor). One may go through life without direction, all values missing, hopes gone, pleasures meaningless. A thread of cynicism may be woven into the fabric of life. Resistant to new experiences, one is also aggrieved against others. Not only does he warn others to avoid expectations in general, but he tacitly informs them not to expect anything from him.

The feeling of disappointment experienced in relation to a current frustration should not be confused with disillusionment, the need to *remain* disappointed. A normal reaction of disappointment does not destroy relatedness to external objects or cause one to give up the possibility of gratification. The disillusioned, on the other hand, feel empty and are cut off from libidinal attachments. They are unable to revive their infantile object cathexes which were severely damaged and prematurely destroyed in early childhood instead of having undergone a progressive alteration in significance and meaning for object relatedness and consequent ego fulfillment.

Uncontrolled, unrelieved, and pernicious disillusionment proceeds to misery and cold boredom and repressed aggressive libidinal urges; an overriding discontent; an increasing aversion to life; a decrease in the size of the ego, feelings of rage, both conscious and unconscious, erupting sporadically and alternating with periods of feeling weak; mounting hopelessness giving rise to despair and apathy; a loss of identity—"I don't know who I am"; a loss of purpose and motivation—"I don't know what I want"; a loss of overall meaning in life—"I don't know why I'm living"; ultimately a complete withdrawal of libido.

The numerous overt and covert, conscious and unconscious disappointments in life have varying degrees of significance for the production of pathological disillusionment and its persistence. For example, one may be disillusioned simply because one is mortal. One is disillusioned with the knowledge that under certain circumstances and pushed beyond a certain point men take the law into their own hands and yield to their instinctual aggressive drives or permit others to engage in mass destruction, e.g., on the global level the Nazi extermination of six million Jews; on the community or individual level the denial of help to a victim of criminal acts (the "Bad Samaritan").

A persisting common disillusionment befell us upon the assassination of John F. Kennedy, a symbol for many of their own conscious and unconscious hopes, expectations and wishes for achievement. The realization that love may be unrequited, that evil cannot be magically eradicated by good, are sources of disillusionment. Feelings of love and hate toward the same person are a source of disillusionment for many. That beauty fades, that things do not last forever, that orgastic pleasure is brief, may be disillusioning.

The discovery of the difference between the sexes is a deep disappointment and disillusionment to the little boy and girl, and a double disappointment to the girl in the oedipal period. Her rejection by the mother and the later rejection by the father are often of crucial importance in her total outlook on the future. The knowledge that parents have their own egoistic interests above and beyond those of their child is an unhappy and rueful day for many children. The knowledge of parental intercourse can give rise to disillusionment. The realization that one is not accepted for "oneself" but for material or other gain is a source of pain and embitterment.

Middle age, old age, and senility bring their special disillusionments, particularly to those who have not con-summated their earlier ambitions. Even when childhood wishes have been fulfilled there is often a gnawing feeling on the part of the adult that the price paid in struggle and effort has been far too high and has involved too much sacrifice.

Disillusionment is utilized defensively by those who cannot allow themselves hope because of the inability to bear frustration. It defends against mourning; one remains disillusioned instead of experiencing the more acutely painful affect of depression. Disillusionment maintains a tie to the lost love object; like vengeance (Socarides, 1966), it is a clinging to the old, to the past. There is a clinging to the memory of previous expectations simultaneously with their dethronement.

The following clinical example, in many ways rich in illustrative analytic content, is presented for two reasons:

(1) to enable the reader to share the flavor of the analysis of a profoundly disillusioned man, and (2) to depict the affect of disillusionment as a powerful resistance.

The patient was a thirty-four-year-old businessman, the only child of Jewish parents, who entered analysis because of premature ejaculation. He suffered from moderately severe depression, felt socially inferior, and complained of an engulfing boredom with life. He also presented numerous hypochondriacal symptoms, mostly related to the gastro-intestinal system. For example, he felt he had to completely empty his lower bowel at least five times a day or else felt uncomfortable. This requirement became intensified whenever he was faced with social situations. He had never been able to ejaculate intravaginally.

He recalled that during early childhood his father often humiliated him for failing to compete successfully in sports and compared him unfavorably to other children in the neighborhood. He often teased and derided him with the comment that he was "just like a girl." The mother was completely "browbeaten" by the father and would also turn against her son. The patient felt great bitterness toward both parents, and although employed as an executive in a major business enterprise owned by his father, he worked fitfully and listlessly. He felt sure that his father would never promote him to a higher position. It was his bitter, resentful, and querulous contention that his father, upon retirement, would even block his "right" to assume control of the company. He felt entitled to such rewards as within himself he "knew" that he was the most competent of all his father's employees but he was being "misjudged and overlooked."

During the analysis it was evident that he suffered from an unconscious sense of guilt whenever successful. His dreams were filled with dire punishments, feelings of persecution by others, and by persecutory internal objects, e.g., feces, especially when he asserted himself, attempted to make any satisfactory gains in the competitive areas of life, or expressed his enraged indignation. The analysis was marked by his incessant diatribes against the world, against society, against "ideals" which he proudly and craftily "saw through" and considered "a sham, farce and travesty." Whenever progress was made in therapy and he began to feel more at ease with people, he suddenly developed feelings of intense anxiety.

His carping disillusionment with life was a defense against emotional involvement, a projection of his deepest unconscious feelings of internal persecution, and a displacement of intense self-destructive feelings onto the external world.

He had married an unattractive, somewhat emaciated and physically immature young woman with whom he felt little sexual, emotional, or intellectual affinity. Despite her wish to have a family the marriage was barren, and he was quick to say that he "would never bring children into this rotten world." Although he was endowed with some obvious gifts of good appearance, intelligence, and unmistakable abilities in the business area, he never allowed himself to profit from or experience pleasure through the effective application of these attributes.

He complained that all women were "out to take you," that all men were "ready to abuse you," either socially or in business. Friendship is a "myth," and beneath all virtues lay deceit, falseness, and exploitation. At times his elaboration of this material acquired a paranoidlike quality, although he never experienced formal persecutory delusions or semidelusions. It should be understood that the protean complaints of this patient were delivered for the most part not with depressive affect but in a semijocular tone, at times approaching merriment mixed with superiority, apparent equanimity, and even condescension.

Boastfully and arrogantly he would let the analyst know that already as a young child he "knew the score. Life is rotten and no good. Both my mother and father were bastards and the other kids hated me for being a Jew." Despite his ostensible acceptance of this "reality," these were all extremely painful memories.

His disillusionment with life and with all things constituted a severe block in therapy. He continuously engaged in a denunciation of the world, its values, including the value of analytic interpretation, ethics, morals, people. This was used by him in the service of resistance both in uncovering infantile material and in acquiring insights and applying them in his life.

"What is life? This is what it is, and I speak without bitterness. It is really basically a very boring existence. The average life is only giving and being recompensed by a once-a-week card game or by going to the movies once a week. On a special occasion maybe going to a wedding or to a Bar Mitzvah. Life takes from you. You function, work, accept position and worries and the average person gets inconsequential pleasures. I think I'm right and I'm being objective about it. But the average person, you know, doesn't think about it. I take it that isn't what you think, is it, Doctor? Now you—maybe your life is different because you have different opportunities. You see certain people. You get more out of life. No, no, life comes out on the minus side for everyone. It is pretty bland. There is no purpose to it. My wife, she is stupid, too. She enjoys her mother bringing her a simple dish towel. What are such pleasures?"

His wife, chronically dissatisfied and unhappy in this grim atmosphere, was eventually provoked into leaving him, and within a month after the divorce he decided to terminate the analysis. However, intermittent attacks of severe anxiety forced him to return to the analyst on several occasions.

Significantly, it was during these later visits that he reported he was now suffering from retarded ejaculation, which was interpreted to him as an unwillingness to give anything to anyone, including his sperm—a manifestation of his basic disillusionment with the world. On rare occasions he grudgingly admitted that perhaps his attitudes could be due to his unconscious hate and anger, which would break into consciousness at times, that it was because of "feeling sorry for myself because my mother and father didn't love me or at least that's what I felt. It also may be due to the tendency to hurt myself. It's like cutting off my nose to spite my face. I stop myself from enjoying something special even when I have the chance to."

He would fill the analytic hour with generalizations, empty dialectics, and reduce all activities to a purely mechanistic level. These productions were intended to mitigate an overwhelming fear of discovering his basic conflicts, to give the appearance of communicating, and constituted a covert plea and demand that the analyst love him and compensate him for his infantile deprivation. It was also an accusation against the analyst for not providing total fulfillment.

"What do I do today? I get up at five-thirty, get dressed, shave, come here to see you, go to work, work all day, go home, eat, watch television, go to bed, wake up and repeat the whole thing again. If someone came up to me now and said 'Look, here's a pill. Take it and you'll just disappear as if you never existed and there will be no memory afterwards,' I would gladly do it. Do you think I really want to go through today's activities? I used to hope that things were going to be different and that things would be different for me someday but then day after day they are still the same. This life isn't for me. I just can't get into the swing of things . . . the other people . . . there's a lot of hate involved. I hate them and it's backed up to my eyeballs. I feel physically tired and don't even want to go to work. If you listen to the average person, they bore you. They think they know it all. Most people say a lot of shit . . . all the shit that comes out of their mouths . . . They all know it all. They're right . . . what others say. I always try to look at things objectively, everything is slanted to their way of thinking, though, and it's always prejudiced. They say that they want to believe in others but there are very few people who will speak objectively. It's almost hopeless to speak to people and get the truth out, especially down at the office.

"You're right perhaps when you say that I don't possibly try to get into conversation but it's because people are so biased that they would never say that I was right. I don't think I can expect this. And it's not a matter of patience with them. It's a waste of time. You can't get them to see, the stupid bastards. At a party last night there was some girl talking, something about Europe, and she had only been there once. I have been there twice. It was like she knew it all. I would have deferred if she had been there two times and I only once. But she wouldn't. She was the know-it-all. It doesn't pay to talk to people. Such people only know what they want to know. To 999,000 out of a million life is really pointless. Life is a movie at the end of the week and no person can tell me differently and I'm sure you wouldn't be silly enough to try.

"You get up in the morning and get dressed, you put on your clothes, you go to work, you come home, you eat a meal and you go to sleep. The only thing that might be different is one might have a sex life. But what is sex? Sex is two seconds worth of love. That's all it is. People don't care." He dwelt interminably on the idea that all of us are equally disillusioned but will not admit it, including the analyst, that everyone knew that life was meaningless, pointless, and without value. The patient wanted the analyst to vindicate him, to grant once and for all that there is no basis for hope and that disillusionment is really the only true and proper attitude towards life.

This case material was unusual in the very fact that the patient insistently and relentlessly singled out and tried to destroy all hope for himself as well as for the analyst. With such a patient all experiences were interpreted by him in the context of hopelessness. Consciously he claimed his goal was "to educate the analyst to the facts of life." This served the purpose of justifying his hostile and destructive attitude towards the analyst and himself and to relieve him of guilt. Unconsciously, however, he greatly feared such affirmation and wished the analyst would prove the opposite through devoting himself to him by "loving" him and thereby curing him.

The patient was delighted when he thought he could see any alteration downward in the analyst's mood or any evidence of stress. He would comment in a mildly mocking, semijocular vein: "Things aren't so hot today, are they, Doctor? Not going so well. Perhaps you'll agree with me now that no effort is worth it and nobody appreciates anything."

Despite his adamant protests of being without hope or expectation and the tenacity of this position, he nevertheless persisted in treatment for two years. Hope must not have been entirely extinguished and disillusionment not complete. It must be pointed out that there was hope in early childhood as revealed in the analytic reconstruction. But there were both traumatic precipitating factors and a gradual accretion of disappointing experiences from infancy leading to disillusionment in this patient.

Summary

The affect of disillusionment can be a normal phenomenon, a pathological one, and, in its extreme form, a shattering one. The solution to pathological disillusionment, the desire to remain disappointed, is renunciation and reinvestment or recathexis of objects as suggested by Freud (1916b).

Granted that one of the most painful intrapsychic confrontations any person can face involves the reunification of established interpersonal dependencies, long-term habits, and cherished illusions, renunciation constitutes the voluntary divestment of formerly cathected objects, in this instance of a self-damaging nature.

This is a totally different phenomenon from involuntary deprivation. When rejected in love, denied hoped-for recognition, one can produce many rationalizations, claim inevitability, or reproach fate. But rationally to scrutinize entrenched but unhealthy relationships, prized but unattainable ambitions, heretofore unquestioned and unsatisfactory techniques and solutions, realizing their nonadaptive nature, achieving their renunciation, is a powerful advance in mature integration and acceptance of reality. The choice should be a conscious one, not dependent on external factors. Unless such a choice is made, renunciation achieved, disillusionment avoided, life is faulted and, one after another, all doors to a creative future close, lock, and, in time, disappear.

ON THE AFFECT OF HORROR

James Alexander

(1972)

Along with panic and terror, horror is at the extreme end of those complex feelings derived from anxiety. Perusal of the psychoanalytic literature reveals no article on the affect of terror, and Alexander's paper (with the exception of Bonaparte's [1949] volume on Poe) is a unique contribution to the study of horror.

Experiences of horror are likely to undergo disguise or even transformation into the opposite through dream censorship. Failure of the dream work may then lead to nightmares of horrifying dimensions. The experience of horror implies that the emergency mechanisms of fear and/ or rage, fight and/or flight have been overwhelmed by an external or internal threat to the organism. Thus, automatic processes of phobic avoidances and inhibitory moves and defensive maneuvers are employed to ward off this affect. Exceptions to this general rule (proving the rule) are commonly found in those addicted to "horror movies," where, in accordance with the principle of the repetition compulsion, what cannot be passively endured is actively induced in a substitute form. Acute descents into psychosis may be ushered in by feelings of horror, which are then swiftly converted into psychotic denials of reality and hallucinatory experiences of a restitutive nature.

Much of what is horrifying is subjective and individual. From my own clinical experience I find the following instances.

1. A male homosexual pedophile on the analytic couch jubilantly exults on the loss of dozens of lives in an avalanche which he had read about in the morning newspaper. The childlike gleefulness of the macabre pleasure at death produced a momentary but unmistakable reaction of horror in the analyst. It was not so much the patient's expression of unbridled hate and aggression that produced my response as his accompanying irrational and bizarre eruption of affect.

2. A patient narrates a dream of a figure lying apparently inert on the bed, and then, upon closer inspection, to his astonishment and horror, he discovers that the body is his own. It is filled with feces from his mouth to his anus. The affect of horror, which still lingered as he told the dream, was a reaction on the part of his ego against a social and antisocial ego-syntonic behavior in his external life which he unconsciously abhorred and wished to change, but through which he was continually punishing himself. This horror reaction was worked through, the first step to emancipating himself from self-destructive behavior.

3. It is well known that introjected, hateful objects may become external persecuting objects represented by the feces (Stärcke, 1920; Van Ophuijsen, 1920; Arlow, 1949). A thirty-year-old masochistic business man with paranoid traits reports a dream: "I saw a toilet bowl, and in the bowl was feces and one or two pairs of socks of mine. I tried to get the socks out, and gradually the feces became alive, animal-like, I think snakes, and I got hold of the socks and tried to pull them out. I got afraid and anxious. At one point I felt as if I had only one piece of sock to hang onto and I awoke in a terrible anxiety and horror." In his associations, the patient revealed that the dream had produced a powerful aura of

loathesomeness, frightfulness, horror, and an uncanny feeling of "disgust."

Only recently was he able to clean out the toilet bowl in his apartment; he was usually disgusted by such a procedure. He had actually bought some socks the day before. "I was hurt that these snakes were pulling something on me, taking my property. I caught them doing it. I had to fight for it, and I felt terribly annoyed. I feel sometimes that things are happening against me, that nothing can go smoothly, something very unpleasant. There is a quality of the spooky and something of the irrational about it. There is a big component of hate and fear in these animals, that they are stronger than me. The socks are probably part of myself. The animals are evil spirits, trying to pull me down into their region. And again, these animals are made out of my feces, out of myself, and therefore are a part of me, the bad self, the harmful, dirty part of me."

Horror is an affect closely related to anxiety. It is a particular modulation of anxiety. It is a distinct affect; an affective entity not synonymous with terror, dread, fright, fear, etc., but sharing some of the same qualitative characteristics with them. All these affects belong to the same affect cluster, the anxiety affect cluster. That which is dangerously threatening, but which is also imbued with the awesome, mysterious, ghostly qualities of the weird, the uncanny, the unnatural, the eerie, evokes the affect of horror. Diabolical sadism such as that described in Poe's "The Pit and the Pendulum" and "The Cask of Amontillado" evokes horror because of the complete pitilessness of the sadistic perpetrators of the crimes. Inhuman cruelty, the completely inhumane freedom from compassionate fellow feeling, the total inability to identify sympathetically—these are the characteristic qualities which evoke the affect of horror.

Werewolves, Frankenstein monsters, vampires, and witches are projections into the external world of guilt-producing sadistic fantasies in the form of myths. These mythological creatures are talionic embodiments and always have a substratum of truth. Cannibalism has existed widely, and cannibalistic impulses have existed more or less in the unconscious of everyone. The witch with her polyphallic symbolism is a representation of the horrifying, castrating, phallic mother.

The word "horrify" is a verb which expresses the action or the effect of that which is horrifying to the beholder, and the affect of horror is the emotional reaction in the beholder. Variations exist; different persons find different things horrifying. Repetitions of the same sort of experience tend to reduce the degree of horror. Horror is too painful an affect, generally speaking, to be borne for long periods of time. People tend to become callous if they cannot avoid the horrifying experience, or they resolve it by resorting to some sort of violence: flight, suicide, murder, psychosis. Surprise potentiates the affective response of horror because lack of time to prepare oneself has not permitted the mobilization of sufficient countercathexis. Time allows us to adjust to events. The alien quality lessens with the passage of time. For example, in World War II in Europe one could see children playing apparently rather happily in the ruins of their bombed and burned-out homes.

Real, Mythological, and Other Irrational Causes of Horror

The following event occurred in a state hospital where I was a staff member. An experienced psychiatrist had a male patient known to be severely suicidal. One morning this patient, who was sitting up fully dressed in the ward, greeted the psychiatrist courteously and said: "That is a nice looking metal pencil in your pocket. May I see it?" The psychiatrist handed the patient the pencil, which he at once grasped and thrust with great force into his own eye through the posterior wall of the orbital fossa deep into the frontal lobe. He was dead in a moment.

Another horrifying experience of suicide was related to me by a middle-aged widow who managed an apartment house. The Tuesday of her appointment followed the Fourth of July, which was on Monday. It was very hot weather, and all of her tenants had gone away the preceding Friday. They did not begin to return until early Tuesday morning. One of her tenants was a bachelor in early middle age. The tenants returning home roused her early because of an unbearable stench in the corridor. They soon ascertained that the terrible odor came from the apartment of the bachelor whom she thought had gone away to visit his family in another state. They broke the door down to find that the tenant had hanged himself by stepping off his bed with his belt around his neck and fastened to a ceiling light fixture. His face—and more or less his whole body—was black. His body was swollen to an enormous size, was putrifying in the heat, and was stinking horribly.

Both the psychiatrist and my woman patient were horrified and deeply shaken by the enormity of the brutal self-hatred they had witnessed. Both were sophisticated persons, knowledgeable and observant of themselves and the world around them. Both experienced the evocation of numerous affects such as shock, surprise, disgust, grief, anxiety, and perhaps others. Both, however, stressed that the predominant affect was horror. I stress this to attempt to show that horror, though related to anxiety, fear, and terror, is by no means identical with them. Neither the psychiatrist nor my woman patient were in any danger in the two suicides they were witness to. They had little or nothing to fear. At most, some irrational anxiety may have been aroused. The overwhelmingly predominating affect, however, was horror.

Every age has its own horrors. When the Mongols of Genghis Khan were ravaging Eastern Europe leaving mounds of skulls in every district, horror must have been at its zenith. When, in the Third Punic War, the Carthaginians realized that Rome with ruthless determination meant to annihilate Carthage and its people, their horror and despair must have been complete. The Peloponnesian neighbors and equals of the Spartans must have been constantly horrified by the unwavering intention of the Spartans to reduce them to slavery (to be what the Spartans called "helots"). It may be that the horrors of our own age are no worse than these, but at times it seems so. This may be due to the fact that the horrors of today are closer to us. At the same time, it seems doubtful that any other century has seen so many horrors on so wide a scale: systematic extermination of millions by the Nazis, millions by the Communists, the atom bomb, two World Wars, an increasing drug mania, greater prevalence of cancer, pollution of the water and atmosphere of the planet, etc.

Cannibalism, bestiality, and necrophilia are obscene and sadistic perversions which are real, though rare. These are not mythical, as are the horrifying depredations ascribed to witches, vampires, werewolves, ghouls, trolls, etc. These perversions generally arouse the affect of horror in most people. Horror is very likely to be not the only affect aroused by these perversions. They will also produce such feelings as disgust and outrage.

The feeling of spite often causes horrifying violence ("cut off the nose to spite the face"). Spite is indirect vengeance. The spiteful person injures himself, often severely, in order to hurt those whom he indirectly hates by the indirect means of injuring himself rather than by direct attack upon them. If the spite-filled person injures himself severely, it is done to shock, appall, horrify, and to make the beholder suffer painful affects such as guilt and horror.

Due to modern rapid news transmission, there is a continuous barrage of news, mostly of tragedy and violence, dinned into our ears and flashed before our eyes. Thus, people are continually horrified. Defensively, people harden their hearts and dull their sympathies in order to avoid being overwhelmed by horror. This defensive set impairs their ability to feel tenderness, sympathy, and compassion in circumstances in which these should be felt.

Immense horror is felt by some schizophrenics when they are losing their hold on reality. The ever more rampant scourge of cancer evokes fear in all and horror in many. In an earlier, preantibiotic day, those unfortunate enough to contract syphilis lived in horror of the late sequelae of the disease, such as paresis, tabes, and taboparesis.

Dangers before which we are helpless evoke terror or panic. If the danger possesses qualities of the uncanny, the gruesome, the mysterious, the affect evoked will be horror. We recoil with horror at the pitiless relentlessness of any implementation of destructive hate. The burnings at the stake during the Inquisition evoked such a reaction among the victims and their families. The fear of incest is universal. In many, incest arouses not only fear but horror too.

Thinking in Martin Buber's (1958) "I-Thou" terms, many sensitive people are horrified when they see people being treated not as "Thous" (that is, not as another "I"), but as things. This is horror at the dehumanization of the human. Hanns Sachs (1942) showed that ancient civilizations had the capacity to develop technologically advanced civilizations which they did not because of their horror of automation, because to them it appeared that the inanimate was magically alive. Their civilizations were based on slavery, which was less horrifying to them than humanlike machines, robots, computers, or automation in general. This is horror over the humanization of the nonhuman, actually of the nonliving. Freud (1919) in his paper "The Uncanny" had already foreshadowed the points later elaborated by Sachs. Freud noted that a very good example of what will arouse feelings of the uncanny in us is doubt whether an apparently animate being is really alive, or, conversely, whether a lifeless object might not be in fact animate.

A male patient recently horrified me. He is the father of four children. He had been furious at each pregnancy of his wife. He and his wife attended a party the evening of the day that he learned about her third pregnancy. He was very angry and became intoxicated at the party, where he told everyone present that he hoped the baby would be a girl so that when she was old enough he could sell her into prostitution. This pregnancy did produce his only daughter.

In both clinical and theoretical psychoanalysis, castration fear and castration anxiety (the latter bearing the clear implication of being largely irrational) are referred to frequently; but castration horror is hardly mentioned. Yet it is obvious in many men harboring intense castration anxiety that they react to the penislessness of women and to menstrual blood not merely with anxiety but with horror. Women, who analogously unconsciously interpret their penislessness as the result of castration, are horrified at the thought of vaginal penetration because unconsciously they regard the vagina as a wound. They therefore regard the man as sadistically using their "wound" for his brutal pleasure. Associated with this will be horror of the penis, along with hate and disgust toward it and men in general. The type of men referred to above loathe women and see all women as castrating witches, filled with penis envy. Many of the kind of women just mentioned have a horror of pregnancy and of childbirth. For these women the fantasies of the baby in utero are that it is a parasite devouring their insides, and childbirth stirs up horror of recastration.

A woman patient was horrified by learning that the pregnancy of a woman friend would not be terminated at once by obstetrical intervention when it was learned that after seven months of gestation the baby was dead. The obstetrician advised waiting for spontaneous labor to occur. My patient felt that in her friend's position she would have felt like a living coffin. Another woman patient of mine once described vividly to me the look of horror on the face of a girlfriend whom my patient allowed to use her apartment to have a criminal abortion. It was a pregnancy of three and one half months. Though the pregnant girl had some kind of sedative and she had her legs tied up, the dilation of the cervix and the packing of the uterus with idoform gauze was very painful. She was not only filled with terror but, above all, her face, my patient felt sure, registered horror.

The marked antipathy seen in many to capital punishment is the result of the reaction of horror, not just to death, but to the deliberateness with which the life is taken. The legal ritualism arouses totem feast fears, the sacrificial slaying of not the totem animal, but the human object itself, for which the totem animal stands. Heilbrunn (1955) asserted that the fear of being eaten, that is, cannibalism, is the basic fear. Lewin (1950) saw this fear not merely as reaction to a potentially threatening object but as the result of a wish to be eaten (part of the oral triad).

In totalitarian countries killings occur without due process of law and without publicity. These killings are deliberate, but secret. They do not have the open, public character of the totem feast murder. Intolerance of guilt is greater than the fear of death. To be killed, and be at the same time innocent, is less horrifying than to be killed because one is guilty. The Romans had such a horror of death by crucifixion that capital punishment carried out by that means was forbidden to Roman citizens.

Horror in Literature

I now wish to make a brief excursion into that department of literature known as the horror story. Ambrose Bierce and E. T. A. Hoffmann often use the device of invisibility to produce the effect of horror in their stories, e.g., Bierce's "The Damned Thing" and Hoffmann's "The Entail." These stories exhibit sentient, animate creatures which are destructive malevolence personified but at the same time are invisible, which makes the victims all the more helpless. The effect of the uncanny results, and this changes terror into horror. E. M. Forster, "Saki" (Hector Munro), Isak Dinesen, Charles Williams, and others produce the effect of horror by the device of introducing the reader to scenes of the commonplace. They then introduce into these settings of matter-of-fact reality extraordinary events produced by almost unbelievable yet credible "entities" of pitiless ferocity, bent on wreaking the cruelest destruction upon the unoffending, innocent victims. H. P. Lovecraft, in stories like "The Rats in the Wall," produces the effect of horror by the device of atavistic regression to cannibalism. Robert Louis Stevenson in his story "Dr. Jekyll and Mr. Hyde" produced the effect of horror by the device of the sudden transformation of a decent human being into a bestial humanoid creature. Science-fiction writers sometimes produce the effect of horror by introducing extraterrestrial figures of an inhuman or humanoid kind whose aims are unknown, almost nonunderstandable, whose means are diabolically ruthless, and whose methods are not bound by any sense of compassionate fellow feeling. Marie Bonaparte (1949) shows clearly in her work *Edgar Allen Poe* that in the cases of both Poe and Baudelaire one of the roots of their genius resided in their sublimation of the perversion of necrophilia, certainly one of the most horrifying of the perversions.

HORROR IN DREAMS

Freud (1919) thought that the subject of the uncanny was of sufficient importance to warrant psychoanalytic study. This study involved the investigation of both the feelings of the uncanny and the circumstances evoking these feelings. Horror is a feeling with elements of the uncanny in it. The uncanny and the gruesome occur in dreams. Psychoanalysts as well as patients often fail to identify the affect of horror in dreams. Nightmarish dreams are merely regarded as dreams of severe anxiety to the degree of intensity justly called panic or terror. But many times nightmare dreams are literally horrible because they are infused with the affect of horror. For example, a young man who had recently suffered a schizophrenic breakdown dreamt of being at a banquet as an honored guest. The *pièce de résistance* was a roasted human leg. He realized with suddenness and horror that the leg was his own. The obvious meaning of the dream was masochistic, self-castration. The accompanying affect of horror was the reaction of that part of the ego which remained more or less normally in contact with rational, decent, reality. To comment on the pregenital oral and anal elements in the dream is not sufficiently germane to the theme of this essay.

In the following horror dream the horror was felt less in the dream than in the waking reaction to it. The dream occurred late in the analysis of a middle-aged virgin, the youngest child and only daughter of a very ascetic Roman Catholic family. The patient had come into analysis because of depression, pervasive inhibitions, and rather severe obsessive-compulsive symptoms. She dreamt that she was in a dime store with high-school girlfriends. They were eating cherry pie. She ate a second piece. The other girls seemed satisfied although even as she was demanding it she was not sure that she wanted it. She felt horrified all the following day at her furious demandingness. She said also that she felt less horrified in the dream than after awaking. Her family had made a fetish of eating, especially her mother, and her father ran a delicatessen. She also stated that all her high-school girlfriends were married.

My interpretation of this dream is as follows. The symbolic significance of "cherry" and "piece" are obviously sexual, but expressed in oral-regressive terms. Her girlfriends were all married, and she envied them their easy sexual satisfaction. She was very angry over her own deprivation. It horrified her to realize how rageful, vengeful, spiteful, and demanding she was.

HORROR AND PSYCHOANALYTIC THEORY

What has been said up to this point about horror has had the character of a phenomenological scrutiny without much attempt to articulate it with psychoanalytic psychology. This, it seems to me, is as it should be, that psychoanalysis is an empirical science, and observation of phenomena with description of what is observed should come first. After this should come the attempt to integrate into psychoanalytic psychology the observations of the phenomena described.

What has already been said has some economic, adaptational, dynamic, and genetic implications. Genetically, there have been sketched outlines of circumstances which will evoke the affect of horror. Practically everyone develops the capacity to experience horror. Many experience horror too easily. With them it is a neurotic problem which signifies the existence of horrifying unconscious guilt-producing conflict. The guilt leads to the horrifying expectation of brutal and weirdly perverse punishments. Unconscious fantasies of such punishment makes these individuals very prone to react with horror to anything suggestive of the horrifying. The more rational the individual, the less prone will he be to feel horror except when confronted with actual horrible realities. Many live in horror over their own conscious or unconscious sadistic wishes and fantasies. For them to hear of a gruesome murder, which while not a pleasant thing to hear about, is an experience that fills them with horror. The brutal murder is too near to the actualization of their own unconscious fantasies. To the more normal person the murder is just a grimly unpleasant reality taking place at a distance, only heard about, and being remote from one's personal life.

The foregoing has been genetic, mainly in the sense of activation of the potential or latent feeling of horror. The genesis of the capacity to feel horror in a developmental sense lies in the period of late childhood. Only the precursors of anxiety (Spitz, 1950) can be felt before the eighth month of life. Fully developed anxiety, that is, terror or panic, can occur only after some considerable degree of identity formation has occurred, which is to say that a well-developed sense of self has had to have come to exist before the danger of annihilation of the self can be comprehended and reacted to with terror or panic. To experience horror requires a fairly good grasp of the nature of reality, and hence the capacity to comprehend uncanny departures from usual reality; the realities herein meant are fearsome realities such as evoke terror or panic. In other words, horror is felt when fearsome external realities or destructive fantasies can be judged and known by the individual to be unnatural or weird. The developing capacity to experience horror makes its appearance in the phallic-oedipal period in the boy's castration horror and in the girl's horror at being (as she thinks) already castrated. Prior to this, only anxiety, sometimes to the degree of terror or panic, could be felt. The fully developed capacity to experience horror does not occur before the latency period or perhaps even later in adolescence.

Adaptationally, readiness to react with the affect of horror to many stimuli that rouse conscious or unconscious fantasies of the perversely weird and brutal kind presents the ego with immense defensive problems, such as the attempts to flee phobically from every horror-evoking stimulus. Or else, to combat the phobia counterphobically. Poe's horror at his necrophilia he met counterphobically with the resources of his genius. His horror was not banished or annihilated. It was transmuted by his artistic genius into works of art and made into an aesthetic delight in his short stories. Excessive propensity to feel horror—that is, horror irrationally evoked—imposes great defensive efforts upon the ego. This puts a great burden upon the whole psychic organization. Thus libidinal resources are used up nonproductively, and good adaptation is interfered with by phobic reactions and by energetic attempts to repress horrifying fantasies.

Structurally, horror is an affect which is intersystemic in Peto's (1968) sense. Except in the smallest signal quantities, horror is not just intrasystemic in the system ego, but pervades the whole psychic organization. The ego naturally bears the brunt of this painful emotional experience, but its real seat or its fundamental origin is conjointly in the id and the superego. I wish to call attention at this point to the fact that I am describing an excessive proneness to feel horror and not to reactions to confrontation with shocking and horrifying external horrors. To return to the subject of the part played by id and superego in excessive readiness to feel horror: if there are in the id intense sadistic impulses to torture and torment in revengeful hatred, and the superego condemns equally severely the person harboring these impulses, then such persons live in horror of acting out their baleful impulses or of being punished for them.

FURTHER CONSIDERATIONS OF FREUD'S "THE UNCANNY"

Freud begins his essay on "The Uncanny" as follows: "It is only rarely that a psycho-analyst feels impelled to investigate the subject of aesthetics, even when aesthetics is understood to mean not merely the theory of beauty but the theory of the qualities of feeling" (Freud, 1919, p. 219). I want to single out the last six words of the sentence just quoted. He apparently felt that affects belonged mainly to the discipline of aesthetics. Feelings certainly belong to the aesthetic realm, but, I think, even more to the realm of psychology.

In his essay on the uncanny, Freud examines at great length lexicographically and linguistically the German word for "uncanny," which is *unheimlich*, the literal meaning of which is "unhomely," the German word *heimlich* meaning "homely" or "homelike." He then discusses the importance of the "double" in the evocation of the feeling of the uncanny, and the feeling of the uncanny in connection with blinding in its unconscious castration symbolic significance. Freud discusses the part played by regression also in the experiencing of the uncanny; that is, regression returns the individual to the time when the ego was not sharply differentiated from the external world and from other persons. This leads to impaired reality testing, and superstitions can be taken literally and seriously. Freud also cites as important in the production of the feeling of the uncanny helplessness in the face of the repetition compulsion and the opposite of helplessness, "omnipotence of thoughts" and "animistic thinking." Freud defines an uncanny experience as occurring either when repressed infantile complexes have been revived by some impression, or when the primitive beliefs we have surmounted seem once more to be confirmed. This is his most definitive formulation. Finally, Freud mentions horror several times in "The Uncanny." The gruesome will usually evoke horror but may evoke little or none of the feeling of the uncanny. Conversely, feelings of the uncanny may occur without any feeling of horror. Nonetheless, these two feelings often occur together, that is, both are often aroused by the same event. Freud's findings on the relationship between horror and the uncanny seem to me to be true and definitive.

PSYCHOTHERAPEUTIC IMPLICATIONS OF HORROR

I want now to refer again to the "cherry pie" dream. Psychotherapeutically, the patient's horror had a constructive effect upon her motivation to uncover and work through her disappointment with life, her furious demandingness directed at the world which was caused by unconscious, self-imposed guilt over intense hostile envy. Horror does not always have a constructive effect. Sometimes the person feeling horror will in a self-brutalizing way defiantly refuse to desist from evoking horror.

While frequent and varied references to horror are common experiences shared by everyone, these references are fugitive. Except for horror-story writers, few people ever focus attention upon horror, the horrible, or the horrifying. Few people have ever made the careful study of it which would explicate its qualitative nature and the factors responsible for its evocation. This is true of psychoanalysts too, unfortunately, and unless they recognize the affect of horror when they encounter it in the dreams and other associations of their analysands, its working through will not be accomplished. The analytic aim, of course, is not to eliminate the capacity to experience horror, any more than it would be the aim to abolish the capacity to feel signal anxiety. In regard to anxiety, the aim is to reduce the excessive proneness to experience anxiety, the pathological vulnerability to panic, terror, fright, etc., when realities do not warrant these responses. So too in the case of horror, the analytic aim is to reduce the irrational proneness to it. This will not be accomplished unless the analyst recognizes horror in his analytic material, differentiates it from panic, terror, and other modulations of anxiety. While horror belongs to the anxiety affect cluster, it has qualitative differences from anxiety, and in analysis it cannot be worked through without this recognition on the part of the analyst. Without this recognition the patient will remain excessively subject to this painful and disruptive affect irrationally activated.

Conclusion

To recapitulate, horror is evoked by the pitiless absence of any sense of compassionate fellow feeling. Mystery is an indispensable ingredient in the evocation of horror. Bafflement is felt in the attempt to understand the implacable hate. Impenetrable mystery changes terror into horror, which is a shuddery, dread-filled sense of revulsion. The subject experiencing the affect of horror in response to threats from purposeful intelligence, real but psychotic, or real but sane in pure evil, or from mythical, diabolical "creatures," is reacting to the absolute in unneutralized aggression. Diseases like cancer, dementia paralytica, rabies, etc., produce horror because of their mystery and inexorable destructiveness. On the assumption that affects have functions, what is the function of the affect of horror? Before attempting to answer this question I wish to state that the concept of affect function is based upon Freud's theory that one affect, namely, anxiety, performs a signal or warning function in the ego. Alexander and Isaacs (1964), among others, expanded Freud's (1926) theory of the signal function of anxiety and showed that at least many other, maybe all, affects have functions. Horror is one of the most unpleasant of affects. Its function is to act as the most powerful of deterrents to impulses and acts of the kinds referred to in this paper as horrifying. Horror at horrible people, etc., has the function of initiating the most energetic type of defense against them, to avoid them if possible. In the struggle to adapt, horror initiates the most energetic type of defense against the most repulsive realities, to which no constructive adaptation can be made. Such realities can be dealt with only by flight, by destroying them, or else to succumb to them.

The function of horror within the psychic apparatus is to energize the ego maximally to resist certain ego-dystonic id impulses and/or to resist as energetically as possible external dangers of the most loathesome, gruesome kind threatening the individual from without. This defensive function of horror as a signal or warning against a particular variety of danger does not always work well. Just as anxiety may fail in its signal function through denial of the danger by the ego, or by paralysis of the ego in the face of danger, or by reckless acts of panic, etc., so horror too may fail to produce proper self-preservative actions by the ego. For example, intense reactions of horror may produce such disruption of ego integration as to result in psychosis. Men with reactions of horror to the penislessness of women (castration horror) and women with horror of penetration vaginally by the penis behave phobically and are always in flight. With such persons horror produces failures of adaptation.

In sentient beings the absence of the inhibiting effect of the affects of disgust, guilt, shame, along with the utterly defiant, untamed determination to use unrestricted violence, evokes the affect of horror. This is the same as saying that in such beings the love of evil exists. Evil is no longer on the defensive but has taken the offensive. It is no longer merely a matter of an outbreak of violence but its utter incorrigibility. The wish no longer exists for the undoing of the alienation from the tender love of mankind and of nature in general. All sense of kindredship is lost. Milton understood this very well; witness his having Satan utter the invocation in *Paradise Lost:* "Evil be thou my Good!"

The love of hate horrifies us.

REFERENCES

Abraham, K. (1912), Notes on the Psychoanalytic Investigation and Treatment of Manic-Depressive Insanity and Allied Conditions. *Selected Papers on Psychoanalysis.* New York: Basic Books, 1953, pp. 137-156.

—— (1917), The Spending of Money in Anxiety States. *Selected Papers on Psychoanalysis.* New York: Basic Books, 1953, pp. 299-303.

—— (1920), Manifestations of the Female Castration Complex. *Selected Papers on Psychoanalysis.* New York: Basic Books, 1953, pp. 338-370.

—— (1921), Contributions to the Theory of the Anal Character. *Selected Papers on Psychoanalysis.* New York: Basic Books, 1953, pp. 370-393.

—— (1924a), A Short Study of the Development of the Libido, Viewed in the Light of Mental Disorders. *Selected Papers on Psychoanalysis.* New York: Basic Books, 1953, pp. 418-503.

—— (1924b), Character Formation on the Genital Level of the Libido. *Selected Papers on Psychoanalysis.* New York: Basic Books, 1953, pp. 407-417.

Adatto, C. P. (1957), On Pouting. *J. Amer. Psychoanal. Assn.,* 5:245-249. *Also This Volume,* pp. 251-257.

Alexander, F., French, T., et al. (1941), *Psychogenic Factors in Bronchial Asthma.* Washington: National Research Council.

Alexander, J. (1960), The Psychology of Bitterness. *Internat. J. Psycho-Anal.,* 41:514-520. *Also This Volume,* pp. 295-309.

—— (1968), On Surprise. *Bull. Philadelphia Assn. Psychoanal.,* 18:116-125.

—— (1969), On Courage. *Bull. Philadelphia Assn. Psychoanal.,* 19:16-27.

—— (1971), On Excitement. *Bull. Philadelphia Assn. Psychoanal.,* 21:162-172.

—— (1972), On the Affect of Horror. *Bull. Philadelphia Assn. Psychoanal.,* 22:196-209. *Also This Volume,* pp. 575-593.

—— (1973), On Pathos. *Bull. Philadelphia Assn. Psychoanal.,* 23:115-128.

595

———— & Isaacs, K. S. (1963), Seriousness and Preconscious Affective Attitudes. *Bull. Philadelphia Assn. Psychoanal.*, 44:23-30.

———— ———— (1964), The Function of Affect. *Brit. J. Med. Psychol.*, 37:231-237.

———— ———— (1968), The Psychology of the Fool. *Internat. J. Psycho-Anal.*, 49:420-423.

Altman, L. L. (1977), Some Vicissitudes of Love. *J. Amer. Psychoanal. Assn.*, 25:35-52.

Arlow, J. A. (1949), Anal Sensations and Feelings of Persecution. *Psychoanal. Quart.*, 18:79-84.

———— (1957), On Smugness. *Internat. J. Psycho-Anal.*, 38:1-8. *Also This Volume*, pp. 259-281.

Balint, E. (1963), On Being Empty of Oneself. *Internat. J. Psycho-Anal.*, 44:470-480. *Also This Volume*, pp. 335-354.

Balint, M. (1948), On Genital Love. *Internat. J. Psycho-Anal.*, 29:34-40.

———— (1958), The Three Areas of the Mind. *Internat. J. Psycho-Anal.*, 39:328-340.

Barag, G. (1949), A Case of Pathological Jealousy. *Psychoanal. Quart.*, 18:1-18.

Bellow, S. (1966), Cloister Culture. *New York Times Book Review*, July 10.

Benedek, T. (1938), Adaptation to Reality in Early Infancy. *Psychoanal. Quart.*, 7:200-214.

———— (1977), Ambivalence, Passion, and Love. *J. Amer. Psychoanal. Assn.*, 25:53-79.

Bergler, E. (1933), *The Psychology of the Cynic*. Monterey, Calif.: Edmund & Marianne Bergler Psychiatric Foundation, 1975. (English translation by Hella Freud Bernays as per arrangement by C. W. Socarides.)

———— (1945a), On the Disease Entity Boredom (Alysosis) and Its Psychopathology. *Psychiat. Quart.*, 19:38-57.

———— (1945b), Psychopathology of Ingratitude. *Dis. Nerv. Syst.*, 6:226-229. *Also This Volume*, pp. 135-142.

———— & Eidelberg, L. (1935), Der Mechanismus der Depersonalization. *Internat. Z. Psychoanal.*, 21:258-285.

———— & Jekels, L. (1949), Transference and Love. *Psychoanal. Quart.*, 18:325-350.

Bergmann, M. S. (1963), The Place of Paul Federn's Ego Psychology in Psychoanalytic Metapsychology. *J. Amer. Psychoanal. Assn.*, 11:97-116.

———— (1966), The Intrapsychic and Communicative Aspects of the Dream. *Internat. J. Psycho-Anal.*, 47:356-363.

———— (1971), Psychoanalytic Observations on the Capacity to Love.

In: *Separation-Individuation: Essays in Honor of Margaret S. Mahler*, ed. J. B. McDevitt & C. F. Settlage. New York: International Universities Press, pp. 15-40. *Also This Volume*, pp. 499-531.

Berliner, B. (1958), The Role of Object Relations in Moral Masochism. *Psychoanal. Quart.*, 27:38-56.

Bibring, E. (1953), The Mechanism of Depression. In: *Affective Disorders*, ed. P. Greenacre. New York: International Universities Press, pp. 13-48.

Bion, W. R. (1958), On Arrogance. *Internat. J. Psycho-Anal.*, 39:144-146. *Also This Volume*, pp. 283-293.

Blos, P. (1962), *On Adolescence: A Psychoanalytic Interpretation*. Glencoe, Ill.: Free Press.

Bonaparte, M. (1949), *The Life and Works of Edgar Allan Poe: A Psychoanalytic Interpretation*. London: Imago.

Borquist, A. (1906), Crying. *Amer. J. Psychol.*, 17:149-205.

Bowlby, J. (1960a), Grief and Mourning in Infancy and Early Childhood. *The Psychoanalytic Study of the Child*, 15:9-52. New York: International Universities Press.

—— (1960b), Separation Anxiety. *Internat. J. Psycho-Anal.*, 41:89-113.

—— (1961), Processes of Mourning. *Internat. J. Psycho-Anal.*, 42:317-340.

Bowra, C. M. (1957), *The Greek Experience*. New York: World.

Breuer, J. & Freud, S. (1893-1895), Studies on Hysteria. *Standard Edition*, 2. London: Hogarth Press, 1955.

Brierley, M. (1937), Affects in Theory and Practice. *Internat. J. Psycho-Anal.*, 18:256-268.

—— (1951), *Trends in Psycho-Analysis*. London: Hogarth Press.

Brunswick, R. M. (1929), The Analysis of a Case of Paranoia (Delusions of Jealousy). *J. Nerv. Ment. Dis.*, 70:1-22, 155-178.

Buber, M. (1958), *I and Thou*. New York: Scribner.

Chadwick, M. (1927), The Child's Early Discrimination between Sound and Speech. *Psyche*, 32:58-72, 1928.

Chatterji, N. N. (1948), Paranoid Jealousy. *Yearbook of Psychoanalysis*, ed. S. Lorand, 5:51-60. New York: International Universities Press, 1949.

Darwin, C. (1873), *The Expression of the Emotions in Man and Animals*. New York: AMS Press, 1972.

de Forest, I. (1950), The Self-dedication of the Psychoneurotic Sufferer to Hostile Protests and Revenge. *Psychiat. Quart.*, 24:706-715.

Deutsch, H. (1927), On Contentment, Happiness, and Ecstasy. *Psychoanal. Rev.*, 15:90, 1928.

———— (1933), The Psychology of Manic-Depressive States, with Particular Reference to Chronic Hypomania. In: *Neuroses and Character Types*. New York: International Universities Press, 1965, pp. 203-217.

———— (1937), Absence of Grief. *Psychoanal. Quart.*, 6:12-22. *Also This Volume*, pp. 73-85.

———— (1942), Some Forms of Emotional Disturbance and Their Relationship to Schizophrenia. *Psychoanal. Quart.*, 11:301-321. *Also this Volume*, pp. 109-133.

Diamont, M. (1962), *Jews, God and History*. New York: New American Library.

Dodds, E. R. (1957), *The Greeks and the Irrational*. Boston: Beacon.

Durant, W. (1939), *The Life of Greece*. New York: Simon & Schuster.

Eidelberg, L. (1934), Zur Erniedrigung des Liebesobjekts. *Internat. Z. Psychoanal.*, 20:549-552.

Eissler, K. R. (1951), An Unknown Autobiographical Letter by Freud and a Short Comment. *Internat. J. Psycho-Anal.*, 32:319-324.

———— (1963), *Goethe: A Psychoanalytic Study*, 2 vols. Detroit: Wayne State University Press.

Engel, G. L. (1950), *Fainting; Physiological and Psychological Considerations*. Springfield: Charles C Thomas.

———— (1962), Anxiety and Depression-Withdrawal; The Primary Affects of Unpleasure. *Internat. J. Psycho-Anal.*, 43:89-97.

———— & Reichsman, F. (1956), Spontaneous and Experimentally Induced Depressions in an Infant with a Gastric Fistula. *J. Amer. Psychoanal. Assn.*, 4:428-452.

———— & Segal, H. L. (1956), A Study of an Infant with Gastric Fistula. I. Behavior and the Rate of Total Hydrochloric Acid Secretion. *Psychosomat. Med.*, 18:374-398.

Erikson, E. H. (1950), *Childhood and Society*. New York: Norton.

Federn, P. (1926), Some Variations in Ego Feeling. In: *Ego Psychology and the Psychoses*. New York: Basic Books, 1952, pp. 25-37.

Feldman, S. S. (1941), On Blushing. *Psychiat. Quart.*, 15:249-261.

———— (1956), Crying at the Happy Ending. *J. Amer. Psychoanal. Assn.*, 4:477-485. *Also This Volume*, pp. 239-250.

———— (1959), *Mannerisms of Speech and Gestures in Everyday Life*. New York: International Universities Press.

———— (1962), Blushing, Fear of Blushing, and Shame. *J. Amer. Psychoanal. Assn.*, 10:368-385.

Fenichel, O. (1934a), On the Psychology of Boredom. *Collected Papers*, First Series. New York: Norton, 1953, pp. 292-302.

———— (1934b), Further Light upon the Pre-oedipal Phase in Girls. *Collected Papers*, First Series. New York: Norton, 1953, pp. 241-288.

———— (1935), A Contribution to the Psychology of Jealousy. *Collected Papers*, First Series. New York: Norton, 1953, pp. 349-362.

———— (1939a), The Counter-Phobic Attitude. *Collected Papers*, Second Series. New York: Norton, 1954, pp. 163-173.

———— (1939b), Trophy and Triumph. *Collected Papers*, Second Series. New York: Norton, 1954, pp. 141-163.

———— (1941), The Ego and the Affects. *Collected Papers*, Second Series. New York: Norton, 1954, pp. 215-227.

———— (1945), *The Psychoanalytic Theory of Neurosis*. New York: Norton.

Ferenczi, S. (1911), Obscene Words. *Sex in Psychoanalysis*. New York: Basic Books, 1950, pp. 132-153.

———— (1916), Stages in the Development of the Sense of Reality. *Sex in Psychoanalysis*. New York: Basic Books, 1950, pp. 213-239.

———— (1919), Sunday Neuroses. In: *Further Contributions to the Theory and Technique of Psychoanalysis*. London: Hogarth Press, 1926, pp. 174-177.

Flugel, J. C. (1939), The Examination as Initiation Rite and Anxiety Situation. *Internat. J. Psycho-Anal.*, 20:275-286.

Fodor, N. (1950), Varieties of Nostalgia. *Psychoanal. Rev.*, 37:25-38.

Freedman, A. (1956), The Feeling of Nostalgia and Its Relationship to Phobia. *Bull. Philadelphia Assn. Psychoanal.*, 6:84-92.

French, T. M. (1939), Psychogenic Factors in Asthma. *Amer. J. Psychiat.*, 96:87-101.

———— (1958), *The Integration of Behavior*, Vol. 2. *The Reintegrative Process in a Psychoanalytic Treatment*. Chicago: University of Chicago Press.

Freud, A. (1936), *The Ego and the Mechanisms of Defense. The Writings of Anna Freud*, Vol. 2. New York: International Universities Press, 1966.

———— (1960), Discussion of John Bowlby's Work, Part II. *Research at the Hampstead Child-Therapy Clinic and Other Papers. The Writings of Anna Freud*, Vol. 5. New York: International Universities Press, 1969, pp. 173-186.

———— (1963), The Concept of Developmental Lines. *Normality and Pathology in Childhood. The Writings of Anna Freud*, Vol. 6. New York: International Universities Press, 1965, pp. 62-92.

———— (1965), *Normality and Pathology in Childhood. The Writings of Anna Freud*, Vol. 6. New York: International Universities Press.

Freud, S. (1892-1899), Extracts from the Fliess Papers. *Standard Edition*, 1:175-280. London: Hogarth Press, 1966.

———— (1900), The Interpretation of Dreams. *Standard Edition*, 4 & 5. London: Hogarth Press, 1953.

———— (1905a), Fragment of an Analysis of a Case of Hysteria. *Standard Edition*, 7:3-124. London: Hogarth Press, 1953.

———— (1905b), Jokes and Their Relation to the Unconscious. *Standard Edition*, 8. London: Hogarth Press, 1960.

———— (1905c), Three Essays on the Theory of Sexuality. *Standard Edition*, 7:125-244. London: Hogarth Press, 1953.

———— (1909), Notes upon a Case of Obsessional Neurosis. *Standard Edition*, 10:155-249. London: Hogarth Press, 1955.

———— (1910a), A Special Type of Choice of Object Made by Men. *Standard Edition*, 11:163-175. London: Hogarth Press, 1957.

———— (1910b), The Future Prospect of Psycho-Analytic Therapy. *Standard Edition*, 11:139-151. London: Hogarth Press, 1957.

———— (1911a), Formulations on the Two Principles of Mental Functioning. *Standard Edition*, 12:213-227. London: Hogarth Press, 1958.

———— (1911b), Psycho-Analytic Notes on an Autobiographical Account of a Case of Paranoia (Dementia Paranoides). *Standard Edition*, 12:3-85. London: Hogarth Press, 1958.

———— (1912), On the Universal Tendency to Debasement in the Sphere of Love (Contributions to the Psychology of Love, II). *Standard Edition*, 11:177-191. London: Hogarth Press, 1957.

———— (1914a), On Narcissism: An Introduction. *Standard Edition*, 14:67-102. London: Hogarth Press, 1957.

———— (1914b), Remembering, Repeating and Working Through. *Standard Edition*, 12:145-156. London: Hogarth Press, 1958.

———— (1915a), Instincts and Their Vicissitudes. *Standard Edition*, 14:109-141. London: Hogarth Press, 1957.

———— (1915b), Observations on Transference-Love. *Standard Edition*, 12:157-171. London: Hogarth Press, 1958.

———— (1915c), Repression. *Standard Edition*, 14:141-158. London: Hogarth Press, 1957.

———— (1915d), The Unconscious. *Standard Edition*, 14:159-215. London: Hogarth Press, 1957.

———— (1915e), Thoughts for the Times on War and Death. *Standard Edition*, 14:275-288. London: Hogarth Press, 1957.

———— (1916a), Some Character Types Met with in Psycho-Analytic Work. *Standard Edition*, 14:309-337. London: Hogarth Press, 1957.

———— (1916b), On Transience. *Standard Edition*, 14:305-307. London: Hogarth Press, 1957.

———— (1916-1917), Introductory Lectures on Psycho-Analysis. *Standard Edition*, 15 & 16. London: Hogarth Press, 1963.

———— (1917), Mourning and Melancholia. *Standard Edition*, 14:237-258. London: Hogarth Press, 1957.

———— (1919), The Uncanny. *Standard Edition*, 17:219-256. London: Hogarth Press, 1955.

———— (1920), Beyond the Pleasure Principle. *Standard Edition*, 18:3-67. London: Hogarth Press, 1955.

———— (1921), Group Psychology and the Analysis of the Ego. *Standard Edition*, 18:67-143. London: Hogarth Press, 1955.

———— (1922), Some Neurotic Mechanisms in Jealousy, Paranoia and Homosexuality. *Standard Edition*, 18:221-235. London: Hogarth Press, 1955.

———— (1923), The Ego and the Id. *Standard Edition*, 19:3-69. London: Hogarth Press, 1961.

———— (1924), The Economic Problem of Masochism. *Standard Edition*, 19:157-170. London: Hogarth Press, 1961.

———— (1925), The Resistances to Psycho-Analysis. *Standard Edition*, 19:213-222. London: Hogarth Press, 1961.

———— (1926), Inhibition, Symptoms and Anxiety. *Standard Edition*, 20:87-172. London: Hogarth Press, 1959.

———— (1927a), Humour. *Standard Edition*, 21:159-166. London: Hogarth Press, 1961.

———— (1927b), The Future of an Illusion. *Standard Edition*, 21:3-56. London: Hogarth Press, 1961.

———— (1930), Civilization and Its Discontents. *Standard Edition*, 21:57-145. London: Hogarth Press, 1961.

———— (1931), Female Sexuality. *Standard Edition*, 21:221-243. London: Hogarth Press, 1961.

———— (1933a), Lecture XXX. Dreams and Occultism. *Standard Edition*, 22:31-56. London: Hogarth Press, 1964.

———— (1933b), New Introductory Lectures on Psycho-Analysis. *Standard Edition*, 22:3-182. London: Hogarth Press, 1964.

———— (1937), Analysis Terminable and Interminable. *Standard Edition*, 23:209-253. London: Hogarth Press, 1964.

———— (1939), Moses and Monotheism. *Standard Edition*, 23:3-141. London: Hogarth Press, 1964.

———— (1940), An Outline of Psycho-Analysis. *Standard Edition*, 23:144-207. London: Hogarth Press, 1964.

Fries, M. (1935), Interrelationship of the Physical, Mental and Emotional Life of a Child from Birth to Four Years of Age. *Amer. J. Dis. Child*, 49:1546-1563.

Fromm, E. (1956), *The Art of Loving*. New York: Harper & Row.

Gelb, A. (1964), O'Neill. *New York Times*, December 20.

Gesell, A. & Ilg, F. L. (1943), *Infant and Child in the Culture of Today*. New York: Harper.

Gitelson, M. (1958), On Ego Distortion. *Psychoanalysis: Science and*

Profession. New York: International Universities Press, 1973, pp. 254-290.

Glover, E. (1924), The Significance of the Mouth in Psycho-Analysis. *On the Early Development of Mind.* New York: International Universities Press, 1956, pp. 1-24.

—— (1939), The Psycho-Analysis of Affects. *On the Early Development of Mind.* New York: International Universities Press, 1956, pp. 297-306.

Goldstein, K. (1944), Methodological Approach to the Study of Schizophrenic Thought Disorder. In: *Language and Thought in Schizophrenia,* ed. J. Kasanin. Berkeley: University of California Press, pp. 17-40.

Greenacre, P. (1941), The Predisposition to Anxiety, Part 1 and Part 2. *Trauma, Growth, and Personality.* New York: International Universities Press, 1952, pp. 27-82.

—— (1945a), Pathological Weeping. *Trauma, Growth, and Personality.* New York: International Universities Press, 1952, pp. 120-131.

—— (1945b), Urination and Weeping. *Trauma, Growth, and Personality.* New York: International Universities Press, 1952, pp. 106-119.

—— (1955), *Swift and Carroll: A Psychoanalytic Study of Two Lives.* New York: International Universities Press.

—— (1959), On Focal Symbiosis. *Emotional Growth,* Vol. 1. New York: International Universities Press, 1971, pp. 145-161.

—— (1965), On the Development and Function of Tears. *Emotional Growth,* Vol. 1. New York: International Universities Press, 1971, pp. 249-259.

Greenson, R. R. (1949), The Psychology of Apathy. *Psychoanal. Quart.,* 18:290-302.

—— (1953), On Boredom. *J. Amer. Psychoanal. Assn.,* 1:7-21. *Also This Volume,* pp. 219-237.

—— (1954), On Moods and Introjects. *Bull. Menninger Clin.,* 18:1-11.

—— (1958), Screen Defenses, Screen Hunger, and Screen Identity. *J. Amer. Psychoanal. Assn.,* 6:242-262.

—— (1962), On Enthusiasm. *J. Amer. Psychoanal. Assn.,* 10:3-21. *Also This Volume,* pp. 311-333.

Grinker, R. R. (1953), *Psychosomatic Research.* New York: Norton.

—— (1955), Growth, Inertia and Shame: Their Therapeutic Implications and Dangers. *Internat. J. Psycho-Anal.,* 36:242-253.

—— & Spiegel, J. P. (1945), *Men under Stress.* Philadelphia: Blakiston.

Guthrie, W. K. (1962), *The History of Greek Philosophy*, 2 vols. Cambridge: Cambridge University Press.

Hartocollis, P. (1975), Time and Affect in Psychopathology. *J. Amer. Psychoanal. Assn.*, 23:383-395.

Hartmann, H. (1939), *Ego Psychology and the Problem of Adaptation.* New York: International Universities Press, 1958.

—— (1950), Comments on the Psychoanalytic Theory of the Ego. *Essays on Ego Psychology.* New York: International Universities Press, 1964, pp. 113-141.

—— (1955), Notes on the Theory of Sublimation. *Essays on Ego Psychology.* New York: International Universities Press, 1964, pp. 215-240.

Hazo, R. G. (1967), *The Idea of Love.* New York: Praeger.

Heilbrunn, G. (1955), On Weeping. *Psychoanal. Quart.*, 24:245-255.

Hendrick, I. (1951), Early Development of the Ego: Identification in Infancy. *Psychoanal. Quart.*, 20:44-61.

Hertz, J. H., ed. (1938), *The Pentateuch: Hebrew Text, English Translation and Commentary.* London: Soncino.

Hesselbach, C. (1962), Superego Regression in Paranoia. *Psychoanal. Quart.*, 31:341-350.

Hitschmann, E. (1952), Freud's Conception of Love. *Internat. J. Psycho-Anal.*, 33:421-428.

Hobbes, T. (1651), *Leviathan.* Chicago: Regnery, 1956.

Hoffer, E. (1954), *The Passionate State of Mind.* New York: Harper.

Horney, K. (1948), The Value of Vindictiveness. *Amer. J. Psychiat.*, 8:3-13.

Huizinga, J. (1954), *The Waning of the Middle Ages.* New York: Anchor Books.

Isaacs, K. S. (1956), *Relatability; A Proposed Construct and an Approach to Its Validation.* Unpublished doctoral dissertation, University of Chicago.

—— Alexander, J., & Haggard, E. A. (1963), Faith, Trust and Gullibility. *Internat. J. Psycho-Anal.*, 44:461-469. *Also This Volume*, pp. 355-375.

Isaacs, S. (1948), The Nature and Function of Phantasy. *Internat. J. Psycho-Anal.*, 29:73-97.

—— (1949), *Childhood and After.* New York: International Universities Press.

Jackson, E. N. (1957), *Understanding Grief.* Nashville, Tenn.: Abingdon Press.

Jacobson, E. (1953a), Contribution to the Metapsychology of Cyclothymic Depression. In: *Affective Disorders*, ed. P. Greenacre. New York: International Universities Press, pp. 49-83.

———— (1953b), The Affects and Their Pleasure-Unpleasure Qualities, in Relation to the Psychic Discharge Processes. In: *Drives, Affects, Behavior* [Vol. 1], ed. R. M. Loewenstein. New York: International Universities Press, pp. 38-66.

———— (1957a), Denial and Repression. *J. Amer. Psychoanal. Assn.*, 5:61-92.

———— (1957b), Normal and Pathological Moods: Their Nature and Functions. *The Psychoanalytic Study of the Child*, 12:73-114. New York: International Universities Press.

———— (1964), *The Self and the Object World*. New York: International Universities Press.

———— (1967), *Psychotic Conflict and Reality*. New York: International Universities Press.

———— (1971), *Depression: Comparative Studies of Normal, Neurotic, and Psychotic Conditions*. New York: International Universities Press.

Jobes, G. (1961), *Dictionary of Mythology, Folklore, and Symbols*. New York: Scarecrow.

Jones, E. (1911), The Pathology of Morbid Anxiety. *Papers on Psycho-Analysis*, 4th ed. London: Balliere, Tindall & Cox, 1938, pp. 407-432.

———— (1913), The God-Complex. *Essays in Applied Psycho-Analysis.* London: Hogarth Press, 1923.

———— (1929a), Fear, Guilt, and Hate. *Papers on Psycho-Analysis*, 4th ed. London: Balliere, Tindall & Cox, 1938, pp. 444-459.

———— (1929b), Jealousy. *Papers on Psycho-Analysis*, 5th ed. London: Balliere, Tindall & Cox, 1948, pp. 325-340.

———— (1929c), The Psychopathology of Anxiety. *Papers on Psycho-Analysis*, 5th ed. London: Balliere, Tindall & Cox, 1948, pp. 294-303.

———— (1936), Psychoanalysis and the Instincts. *Papers on Psycho-Analysis*, 5th ed. London: Balliere, Tindall & Cox, 1948, pp. 153-169.

Kaplan, S. M. & Whitman, R. M. (1965), The Negative Ego-Ideal. *Internat. J. Psycho-Anal.*, 46:183-187.

Katan, A. (1934), Einige Bemerkungen über den Optimismus. *Internat. Z. Psychoanal.*, 20:191-199.

Katan, M. (1953), Mania and the Pleasure Principle. In: *Affective Disorders*, ed. P. Greenacre. New York: International Universities Press, pp. 140-209.

———— (1959), Schreber's Hereafter: Its Building Up and Its Downfall. *The Psychoanalytic Study of the Child*, 14:314-382. New York: International Universities Press.

Kepecs, J. G., et al. (1951a), Relationship between Certain Emotional States and Exudation into the Skin. *Psychosom. Med.*, 13:10.

———— et al. (1951b), Atopic Dermatitis. *Psychosom. Med.*, 13:1-9.

Kernberg, O. F. (1974a), Barriers to Falling and Remaining in Love. *J. Amer. Psychoanal. Assn.*, 22:486-512.

———— (1974b), Mature Love: Prerequisites and Characteristics. *J. Amer. Psychoanal. Assn.*, 22:743-769.

———— (1975), *Borderline Conditions and Pathological Narcissism.* New York: Jason Aronson.

———— (1977), Boundaries and Structure in Love Relations. *J. Amer. Psychoanal. Assn.*, 25:81-114.

Khan, M. M. R. (1963), The Concept of Cumulative Trauma. In: *The Privacy of the Self.* New York: International Universities Press, 1974, pp. 42-58.

Klein, M. (1927), Criminal Tendencies in Normal Children. *Contributions to Psycho-Analysis, 1921-1945.* London: Hogarth Press, 1948, pp. 185-201.

———— (1932), *The Psycho-Analysis of Children.* London: Hogarth Press and the Institute of Psycho-Analysis.

———— (1935), A Contribution to the Psychogenesis of Manic-Depressive States. *Contributions to Psycho-Analysis, 1921-1945.* London: Hogarth Press, 1948, pp. 282-310.

———— (1940), Mourning and Its Relation to Manic-Depressive States. *Contributions to Psycho-Analysis, 1921-1945.* London: Hogarth Press, 1948, pp. 311-338.

———— (1945), The Oedipus Complex in the Light of Early Anxieties. *Contributions to Psycho-Analysis, 1921-1945.* London: Hogarth Press, 1948, pp. 339-390.

———— (1946), Notes on Some Schizoid Mechanisms. *Internat. J. Psycho-Anal.*, 27:99-110.

———— (1948), *Contributions to Psychoanalysis, 1921-1945.* London: Hogarth Press.

———— (1957), *Envy and Gratitude: A Study of Unconscious Sources.* New York: Basic Books.

———— & Riviere, J. (1937), *Love, Hate and Repression.* London: Hogarth Press.

Kleiner, J. (1970), On Nostalgia. *Bull. Philadelphia Assn. Psychoanal.*, 20:11-30. *Also This Volume*, pp. 471-498.

Kris, E. (1940), Laughter as an Expressive Process: Contributions to the Psycho-Analysis of Expressive Behavior. *Internat. J. Psycho-Anal.*, 21:314-341. *Also This Volume*, pp. 87-107.

———— (1950), On Preconscious Mental Processes. *Psychoanal. Quart.*, 19:540-560.

———— (1952a), Ego Development and the Comic. *Psychoanalytic Explorations in Art.* New York: International Universities Press, pp. 204-216.

———— (1952b), *Psychoanalytic Explorations in Art.* New York: International Universities Press.

———— (1955), Neutralization and Sublimation: Observations on Young Children. *The Psychoanalytic Study of the Child,* 10:30-47. New York: International Universities Press.

Lagache, D. (1950), Homosexuality and Jealousy. *Internat. J. Psycho-Anal.,* 31:24-31.

Laing, R. D. (1960), *The Divided Self.* New York: Pantheon, 1969.

Landauer, K. (1938), Affects, Passions and Temperament. *Internat. J. Psycho-Anal.,* 19:388-415.

Lanzkron, J. (1963), Murder and Insanity: A Survey. *Amer. J. Psychiat.,* 119:754-759.

Levin, S. (1964), Mastery of Fear in Psychoanalysis. *Psychoanal. Quart.,* 33:375-387.

———— (1965), Some Suggestions for Treating the Depressed Patient. *Psychoanal. Quart.,* 34:37-65.

———— (1967a), Some Metapsychological Considerations on the Differentiation between Shame and Guilt. *Internat. J. Psycho-Anal.,* 48:267-276.

———— (1967b), Some Group Observations on Reactions to Separation from Home in First-Year College Students. *J. Amer. Acad. Child Psychiat.,* 6:644-654.

———— (1969), Further Comments on a Common Type of Marital Incompatibility. *J. Amer. Psychoanal. Assn.,* 17:1097-1113.

———— (1971), The Psychoanalysis of Shame. *Internat. J. Psycho-Anal.,* 52:355-362. *Also This Volume,* pp. 533-551.

Lewin, B. (1933), The Body as Phallus. *Selected Writings.* New York: Psychoanalytic Quarterly, 1973, pp. 28-47.

———— (1946), Sleep, the Mouth, and the Dream Screen. *Selected Writings.* New York: Psychoanalytic Quarterly, 1973, pp. 87-100.

———— (1950), *The Psychoanalysis of Elation.* New York: Norton.

Lewinsky, H. (1951), Pathological Generosity. *Internat. J. Psycho-Anal.,* 32:185-189. *Also This Volume,* pp. 205-217.

Loewenstein, R. M. (1940), The Vital or Somatic Instincts. *Internat. J. Psycho-Anal.,* 21:377-400.

———— (1951), *Christians and Jews.* New York: International Universities Press.

———— (1957), A Contribution to the Psychoanalytic Theory of Masochism. *J. Amer. Psychoanal. Assn.,* 5:197-234.

Lorenz, K. (1966), *On Aggression.* New York: Harcourt Brace.

Mahler, M. S. (1966), Notes on the Development of Basic Moods: The Depressive Affect. In: *Psychoanalysis—A General Psychology: Essays in Honor of Heinz Hartmann*, ed. R. M. Loewenstein et al. New York: International Universities Press, pp. 152-168.

—— (1967), On Human Symbiosis and the Vicissitudes of Individuation. *J. Amer. Psychoanal. Assn.*, 15:740-763.

Martin, A. (1954), Nostalgia. *Amer. J. Psychoanal.*, 14:93-104.

Masserman, J. H. (1954), The Conceptual Dynamics of Person, Religion, and Self. *Psychoanal. Rev.*, 41:303-329.

McCann, W. H. (1941), Nostalgia; A Review of the Literature. *Psychol. Bull.*, 38:165-182.

Menninger, K. A. (1959), *A Psychiatrist's World*. New York: Viking.

Miller, M. (1956), *Nostalgia: A Psychoanalytic Study of Marcel Proust.* Boston: Houghton Mifflin.

Milner, M. (1952), Aspects of Symbolism in Comprehension of the Not-Self. *Internat. J. Psycho-Anal.*, 33:181-195.

Money-Kyrle, R. (1939), *Superstition and Society*. London: Hogarth Press.

Nietzsche, F. (1920), Die Geburt der Tragödie aus dem Geiste der Musik. *Gesammelte Werke III*. Munich: Musarion Verlag.

Oates, W. J. & O'Neil, E., Jr., eds. (1938), *The Complete Greek Drama.* New York: Random House.

Oberndorf, C. P. (1934), Depersonalization in Relation to Erotization of Thought. *Internat. J. Psycho-Anal.*, 15:271-295.

—— (1935), The Genesis of the Feeling of Unreality. *Internat. J. Psycho-Anal.*, 16:296-306.

Oxford Universal Dictionary on Historical Principles (1955), 3rd ed. London: Oxford University Press.

Panel (1966), Clinical and Theoretical Aspects of the "As If" Characters. J. Weiss, reporter. *J. Amer. Psychoanal. Assn.*, 14:569-590.

—— (1968), Psychoanalytic Theory of Affects. L. B. Lofgren, reporter. *J. Amer. Psychoanal. Assn.*, 16:638-651.

—— (1969), The Theory of Genital Primacy in the Light of Ego Psychology. M. A. Berezin, reporter. *J. Amer. Psychoanal. Assn.*, 17:968-987.

—— (1974), Toward a Theory of Affects. P. Castelnuovo-Tedesco, reporter. *J. Amer. Psychoanal. Assn.*, 22:612-626.

Panofsky, E. (1939), Blind Cupid. *Studies in Iconology*. New York: Harper Torchbooks, 1962.

Pao, P.-N. (1969), Pathological Jealousy. *Psychoanal. Quart.*, 38:616-638. *Also This Volume*, pp. 445-470.

Peck, R. F. & Havighurst, R. J. (1960), *The Psychology of Character Development*. New York: Wiley.

Peto, A. (1946), Weeping and Laughing. *Internat. J. Psycho-Anal.*, 27:129-133.

―――― (1968), On Affect Control. *Internat. J. Psycho-Anal.*, 49:471-476.

Piers, G. & Singer, M. B. (1953), *Shame and Guilt: A Psychoanalytic and Cultural Study.* Springfield, Ill.: Charles C Thomas.

Pulver, S. E. (1971), Can Affects Be Unconscious? *Internat. J. Psycho-Anal.*, 52:347-354.

Rado, S. (1926), The Psychic Effects of Intoxication. *Internat. J. Psycho-Anal.*, 9:301-317, 1928.

―――― (1927a), An Anxious Mother. *Internat. J. Psycho-Anal.*, 9:219-226, 1928.

―――― (1927b), The Problem of Melancholia. *Internat. J. Psycho-Anal.*, 9:420-438, 1928. *Also This Volume*, pp. 9-27.

―――― (1933), The Psychoanalysis of Pharmacothymia (Drug Addiction). *Psychoanal. Quart.*, 2:1-23.

Rangell, L. (1954), The Psychology of Poise. With a Special Elaboration of the Psychic Significance of the Snout or Perioral Region. *Internat. J. Psycho-Anal.*, 35:313-332.

Rapaport, D. (1942), *Emotions and Memory*, 5th ed. New York: International Universities Press, 1971.

―――― (1950), On the Psychoanalytic Theory of Thinking. *Collected Papers*. New York: Basic Books, 1967, pp. 313-328.

―――― (1953), On the Psychoanalytic Theory of Affects. *Collected Papers*. New York: Basic Books, 1967, pp. 476-512.

―――― (1961), Some Metapsychological Considerations concerning Activity and Passivity. *Collected Papers*. New York: Basic Books, 1967, pp. 530-568.

Reich, A. (1953), Narcissistic Object Choice in Women. In: *Psychoanalytic Contributions*. New York: International Universities Press, 1973, pp. 179-208.

Reich, W. (1927), *Die Funktion des Orgasmus. Zur Psychopathologie und zur Soziologie des Geschlechtslebens*. Internationale Psychoanalytischer Verlag.

Reik, T. (1941), Aggression from Anxiety. *Internat. J. Psycho-Anal.*, 22:7-16.

―――― (1944), *A Psychologist Looks at Love*. New York: Farrar & Rinehart.

Ritvo, S. (1966), Correlation of a Childhood and Adult Neurosis. *Internat. J. Psycho-Anal.*, 47:130-131.

Riviere, J. (1932), Jealousy as a Mechanism of Defence. *Internat. J. Psycho-Anal.*, 13:414-424.

Rochlin, G. (1959), The Loss Complex. *J. Amer. Psychoanal. Assn.*, 7:299-316.

Ross, N. (1967), The "As If" Concept. *J. Amer. Psychoanal. Assn.*, 15:59-82.

Russell, B. (1930), *The Conquest of Happiness*. London: Allen & Unwin.

—— (1951), *The Autobiography of Bertrand Russell*, Vol. 1. Boston: Little, Brown.

Rycroft, C. (1955), Two Notes on Idealization, Illusion and Disillusion as Normal and Abnormal Psychological Processes. *Internat. J. Psycho-Anal.*, 36:81-87.

Sachs, H. (1942), *The Creative Unconscious*. Cambridge, Mass.: Sci-Art.

Sadoff, R. L. (1966), On the Nature of Crying and Weeping. *Psychiat. Quart.*, 40:490-503. *Also This Volume*, pp. 377-389.

Sandler, J., Holder, A., & Meers, D. (1963), The Ego Ideal and the Ideal Self. *The Psychoanalytic Study of the Child*, 18:139-158. New York: International Universities Press.

Saul, L. J. (1938), Psychogenic Factors in the Etiology of the Common Cold and Related Symptoms. *Internat. J. Psycho-Anal.*, 19:451-470.

—— & Bernstein, C., Jr. (1941), The Emotional Settings of Some Attacks of Urticaria. *Psychosom. Med.*, 3:349-369.

Schafer, R. (1964), The Clinical Analysis of Affects. *J. Amer. Psychoanal. Assn.*, 12:275-299.

Schilder, P. (1923), *Das Korperschema*. Berlin: Springer.

—— (1939), Treatment of Depersonalization. *Bull. N. Y. Acad. Med.*, 15:258-272.

—— (1950), *The Image and Appearance of the Human Body*. New York: International Universities Press.

Schlesinger, H. J. (1961), A Contribution to a Theory of Promising: 1. Primary and Secondary Promising. Paper read at the meeting of the American Psychoanalytic Association, May.

Schmideberg, M. (1946), On Querulance. *Psychoanal. Quart.*, 15:472-501. *Also This Volume*, pp. 143-172.

Scott, W. C. M. (1948), Some Embryological, Neurological, Psychiatric and Psychoanalytic Implications of the Body Schema. *Internat. J. Psycho-Anal.*, 29:141-155.

Searl, M. N. (1933), The Psychology of Screaming. *Internat. J. Psycho-Anal.*, 14:193-205. *Also This Volume*, pp. 29-43.

Searles, H. F. (1956), The Psychodynamics of Vengefulness. *Psychiatry*, 19:31-41.

—— (1960), *The Nonhuman Environment in Normal Development and in Schizophrenia*. New York: International Universities Press.

Sechehaye, M. A. (1951), *Symbolic Realization*. New York: International Universities Press.

Seidenberg, R. (1952), Jealousy: The Wish. *Psychoanal. Rev.*, 39:345-352.

Sharpe, E. F. (1940), Psycho-physical Problems Revealed in Language: An Examination of Metaphor. In: *The Psychoanalytic Reader*, ed. R. Fliess. New York: International Universities Press, 1948, pp. 306-319.

Siegman, A. (1954), Emotionality: A Hysterical Character Defense. *Psychoanal. Quart.*, 23:339-354.

Slap, J. W. (1966), On Sarcasm. *Psychoanal. Quart.*, 35:98-107. *Also This Volume*, pp. 391-402.

Socarides, C. W. (1966), On Vengeance: The Desire to "Get Even." *J. Amer. Psychoanal. Assn.*, 14:356-375. *Also This Volume*, pp. 403-425.

———— (1971), On Disillusionment: The Desire to Remain Disappointed. *Brit. J. Med. Psychol.*, 44:35-44. *Also This Volume*, pp. 553-574.

Sperling, O. (1948), On the Mechanisms of Spacing and Crowding Emotions. *The Yearbook of Psychoanalysis*, 6:234-240. New York: International Universities Press, 1950. *Also This Volume*, pp. 173-181.

———— (1949), Illusions, Naïve or Controlled. *Internat. J. Psycho-Anal.*, 30:206.

Spitz, R. A. (1937), Wiederholung, Rhythmus, Langeweile. *Imago*, 23:171-196.

———— (1945-1946), Hospitalism. *The Psychoanalytic Study of the Child*, 1:53-74; 2:113-117. New York: International Universities Press.

———— (1946), Anaclitic Depression. *The Psychoanalytic Study of the Child*, 2:313-342. New York: International Universities Press.

———— (1950), Anxiety in Infancy: A Study of Its Manifestations in the First Year of Life. *Internat. J. Psycho-Anal.*, 31:138-143.

———— (1959), *A Genetic Field Theory of Ego Formation*. New York: International Universities Press.

———— (1965), *The First Year of Life: A Psychoanalytic Study of Normal and Deviant Development of Object Relations*. In collaboration with W. G. Cobliner. New York: International Universities Press.

———— & Wolf, K. M. (1946), The Smiling Response: A Contribution to the Ontogenesis of Social Relations. *Genet. Psychol. Monogr.*, 34:57-125.

Spurgeon, C. (1958), *Shakespeare's Imagery*. Boston: Beacon.

Stärcke, A. (1919), The Reversal of the Libido-Sign in Delusions of Persecution. *Internat. J. Psycho-Anal.*, 1:231-239, 1920.

Sterba, E. (1940), Homesickness and the Mother's Breast. *Psychiat. Quart.*, 14:701-707.

Tartakoff, H. H. (1966), The Normal Personality in Our Culture and the Nobel Prize Complex. In: *Psychoanalysis—A General Psychology*, ed. R. M. Loewenstein et al. New York: International Universities Press, pp. 222-252.

Uniform Crime Reports (1962), Crime in the United States. Washington: Federal Bureau of Investigation, U.S. Department of Justice.

Valenstein, A. F. (1961), Appendix B, Glossary of Defenses. In: G. L. Bibring et al., A Study of the Psychological Processes in Pregnancy and of the Earliest Mother-Child Relationship. *The Psychoanalytic Study of the Child*, 16:9-72. New York: International Universities Press.

Van der Heide, C. (1941), A Case of Pollakiuria Nervosa. *Psychoanal. Quart.*, 10:267-283.

Van Ophuijsen, J. H. W. (1920), On the Origin of the Feeling of Persecution. *Internat. J. Psycho-Anal.*, 1:235-239.

Weill, J. R. (1948), *Yellow Kid Weill: The Autobiography of America's Master Swindler*. Chicago: Ziff Davis.

Weiss, Joseph (1952), Crying at the Happy Ending. *Psychoanal. Rev.*, 39:338.

——— (1959), Intensity as a Character Trait. *Psychoanal. Quart.*, 28:64-72.

Werman, D. S. (1977), Normal and Pathological Nostalgia. *J. Amer. Psychoanal. Assn.*, 25, in press.

Whitman, R. & Alexander, J. (1968), On Gloating. *Internat. J. Psycho-Anal.*, 49:732-738. *Also This Volume*, pp. 427-443.

Winnicott, D. W. (1945), Primitive Emotional Development. *Internat. J. Psycho-Anal.*, 26:137-143.

——— (1958a), Aggression in Relation to Emotional Development. In: *Collected Papers: Through Pediatrics to Psychoanalysis*. New York: Basic Books, pp. 204-219.

——— (1958b), *Collected Papers: Through Pediatrics to Psychoanalysis*. New York: Basic Books.

——— (1958c), The Capacity to Be Alone. *Internat. J. Psycho-Anal.*, 39:416-420.

Winterstein, A. (1930), Angst vor dem Neuen, Neugier und Langeweile. *Psychoanal. Bewegung*, 2:540-554.

——— & Bergler, E. (1935), The Psychology of Pathos. *Internat. J. Psycho-Anal.*, 16:414-424. *Also This Volume*, pp. 63-72.

Wolff, H. (1953), *Stress and Distress*. Springfield, Ill.: Charles C Thomas.

Wulff, M. (1932), Über einen interessanten oralen Symptomenkomplex und seine Beziehungen zur Sucht. *Internat. Z. Psychoanal.*, 18:281-302.

Zetzel, E. R. (1949), Anxiety and the Capacity to Bear It. *Internat. J. Psycho-Anal.*, 20:1-12. *Also This Volume*, pp. 183-204.

——— (1965), Depression and the Incapacity to Bear It. In: *Drives, Affects, Behavior*, Vol. 2, ed. M. Schur. New York: International Universities Press, pp. 243-277.

Zilboorg, G. (1933), Anxiety without Affect. *Psychoanal. Quart.*, 2:48-67. *Also This Volume*, pp. 45-61.

NAME INDEX

SUBJECT INDEX

Adolescence, 175, 209, 299, 315, 321, 538, 549

Affect, 1-7, 359
  and anxiety, 45-61, 183-204, 533, 570, 577, 579-580, 585, 591
  and "as if" personality, 110-133
  and defense, 1, 5-6, 19, 45, 73-85, 146, 147, 172-181, 251-252, 366.
  and depression, 12-27
  and ego, 103, 297-309, 553-555, 592
  expression of, 239-257, 259-281, 377-389, 427-443
  and mood, 311-333, 406-408
  and psychoanalytic therapy, 5-6, 12, 89, 283-293, 371-372
  time sense and, 221
  see also specific affects

Aggression, 1, 6, 11, 14, 18-19, 22-25, 31-34, 36, 41-42, 64, 87, 91, 103-105, 111, 116, 120, 122, 129, 138-139, 156, 158, 172, 234, 239, 242, 252, 296, 299, 306-308, 323, 331, 350, 352, 354, 400, 408, 414-423, 425, 441-443, 464, 467, 493, 496-497, 513, 566, 591
  and anxiety, 187-189

and guilt, 67-69, 72, 74, 143, 145, 153, 155, 536, 565
and sexuality, 177-178, 199, 415, 519, 534
see also Death instinct; Instinctual drives; Libido; Psychic energy

Alcoholism, 274, 306, 369-370

Ambivalence, 11, 23-25, 32, 40, 69, 74-75, 266, 407-408, 454, 478-479, 501, 519-521, 528

Anality, 25, 70, 89, 125, 150, 155-157, 170, 206, 209-210, 216-217, 321, 408-409, 435-436, 438, 461, 464

Anorexia, 175-176, 339

Anxiety, 5-6, 31, 37, 39, 42, 127, 149, 151-154, 169, 183-204, 289, 290, 299, 304, 309, 343, 353, 366, 377-379, 417, 455, 459-460, 480-481, 587-588
  and affect, 45-61, 69, 75-76, 183-204, 533, 570, 577, 579-580, 585, 591
  and defense, 46, 88, 104-105, 114, 126, 128-129, 159-160, 174, 186-187, 192, 194-197, 200-202, 204, 455-456, 554, 592-593